THE BATTLE WAS THE LORD'S:
A History of the Free Methodist Church in Canada

BY
JOHN WILKINS SIGSWORTH

First Fruits Press
Wilmore, Kentucky
c2016

The battle was the Lord's: a history of the Free Methodist Church in Canada.
By John Wilkins Sigsworth.

First Fruits Press, ©2016

Previously published by Sage Publishers, ©1960.

ISBN: 9781621715078 (print) 9781621715085 (digital) 9781621715092 (kindle)

Digital version at http://place.asburyseminary.edu/freemethodistbooks/16/

First Fruits Press is a digital imprint of the Asbury Theological Seminary, B.L. Fisher Library. Asbury Theological Seminary is the legal owner of the material previously published by the Pentecostal Publishing Co. and reserves the right to release new editions of this material as well as new material produced by Asbury Theological Seminary. Its publications are available for noncommercial and educational uses, such as research, teaching and private study. First Fruits Press has licensed the digital version of this work under the Creative Commons Attribution Noncommercial 3.0 United States License. To view a copy of this license, visit http://creativecommons.org/licenses/by-nc/3.0/us/.

For all other uses, contact:

First Fruits Press
B.L. Fisher Library
Asbury Theological Seminary
204 N. Lexington Ave.
Wilmore, KY 40390
http://place.asburyseminary.edu/firstfruits

Sigsworth, John Wilkins.

The battle was the Lord's : a history of the Free Methodist Church in Canada / by John Wilkins Sigsworth.
Wilmore, Kentucky : First Fruits Press, ©2016.
301 pages : illustrations, portrait ; 21 cm.
Includes bibliographical references and index.

Reprint. Previously published: Oshawa, Ont. : Sage Publishers, ©1960.
ISBN: 9781621715078 (paperback)

1. Free Methodist Church in Canada--History. I. Title

BX8251.S5 2016   987.9

Cover design by Jonathan Ramsay

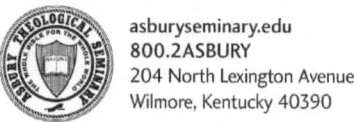

asburyseminary.edu
800.2ASBURY
204 North Lexington Avenue
Wilmore, Kentucky 40390

First Fruits Press
The Academic Open Press of Asbury Theological Seminary
204 N. Lexington Ave., Wilmore, KY 40390
859-858-2236
first.fruits@asburyseminary.edu
asbury.to/firstfruits

The Battle Was the Lord's

THE AUTHOR

A fourth generation Free Methodist on his mother's side and a third on his father's, the writer of this book was born on a farm in Frontenac County near Harrowsmith, Ontario, educated at Slack's Public School, Sydenham High School, Lorne Park College, Queen's University, and the Ontario College of Education. He has taught at Lorne Park College for eight years, and in various provincial secondary schools, at present being employed in Oshawa's Donevan Collegiate where, besides teaching mathematics, he has charge of the guidance program. He is a past president of the Christian Writers' Association of Canada and a former editor (the first) of its quarterly bulletin, *Canadian Christian Writer*. He has compiled career books for Moody Press and Zondervan's, and has written for many periodicals, especially on biography. He is a Canadian correspondent for *Christian Life* and *United Evangelical Action*. Either in his boyhood, school, or teaching days he has had association with the Free Methodist Church in each of the following East Ontario centres: Petworth, Harrowsmith, Verona, Kingston, Toronto (Broadview), Castleton, Frankford, Gananoque, Enterprise, Lorne Park, and Oshawa. While teaching at Frankford he was assistant for one year to the pastor. For another year, while teaching at Gananoque, he was in full charge of the small church there. He holds a local preacher's license and and is the Public Relations Committee for the East Ontario Conference. His wife, the former Doris Grant of Odessa, is a sister of Lois Snider (missionary in Japan) and a niece-by-marriage of Bishop C. V. Fairbairn.

The Battle Was the Lord's

A HISTORY

of

THE FREE METHODIST CHURCH IN CANADA

by

JOHN WILKINS SIGSWORTH

SAGE PUBLISHERS
300 Humber Ave.
Oshawa, Ont.

Book Division
of
Canadian Executive Board,
Free Methodist Church in Canada

Copyright, 1960
by
Canadian Executive Board
FREE METHODIST CHURCH IN CANADA

Printed and bound by
LIGHT AND LIFE PRESS,
Winona Lake, Indiana

INTRODUCTION

Mr. Sigsworth has done a very worthwhile work, not only for Free Methodists but for all who are interested in the advance of the Kingdom of God. He has brought out valuable lessons for us all. His compiling and editing of *Careers for Christian Youth* for Moody Press and *How I Found God's Will for My Life* for Zondervan's and his writing of many articles for the secular and religious press have provided him a good training.

This volume is no mere recitation of events. It is an interpretation of the past and present and a forecast of the future. His sensitivity to the significance of events and his evaluation of the influence of individuals are almost uncanny. It is an interesting story told in a thrilling manner.

R. Barclay Warren

Preface

Because it is so long since the material for this book began to be assembled and because so many have had a part in its production, it seems right to first give the reader a record of its making—a history of the history. The story, as it was recoverable, runs something like this:

Back in 1920, the Provisional Canadian Executive Board, newly elected at the Sarnia All-Canada Convention, decided it was time to start a historical collection and accordingly appointed A. Sims a custodian of records and photos for a history that might some day be written. That was the first action for the country as a whole, and taken on the first occasion anything of that sort could have been looked after. Though Mr. Sims advertised his office, it does not appear that he accumulated any material.

Even before this, however, the Albertans had been busy. At their third annual conference, which was held at Edmonton in March of 1917, a Conference Historical Committee was named. The members—R. H. Shoup, R. R. Haight, and F. B. Lewis—went quickly to work and in a few years had ready a detailed history of their early years from 1905 on.

Prodded by the West Ontario Conference of 1926, the Canadian Executive Board shortly requested each conference to appoint a collector of materials for use in publishing a Canadian history. Alice E. Walls was named West Ontario's committee in 1929. Like the Westerners, she too was soon active. In 1948 R. H. Hamilton and G. A. Lees were listed also. From 1949 to 1952 various East Ontario committees were named. Not all members seem to have made submissions.

In 1952 the Canadian Executive Board asked its president, R. H. Hamilton, to be responsible for the history's publication, but at his suggestion a Consultation Committee was named. It included Alice Walls and L. A. Freeman of West Ontario, Sara Gregory and R. L. Casement of East Ontario and M. C. Miller of Saskatchewan. It appears Alice Walls was soon given special authority to head up the project. Mr. Hamilton personally collected and edited much material, especially from Saskatchewan. Sara Gregory was likewise busy in East Ontario.

R. H. Hamilton died in 1954. In 1956, R. B. Warren was appointed to assist Alice Walls. A year later because of Miss Walls' serious illness, Sara Gregory and myself were added to the Board's editorial committee. I had been on the East Ontario slate of 1952.

A few months before Miss Walls' passing in early 1959, R. L. Casement, Secretary of the Board, and myself met with her and discussed pictures, possible organization, format and choice of publisher. I had several other meetings with her about this time and know how close to her heart this effort of thirty years was. She was especially concerned that certain earlier-published inaccuracies about the Canadian work should be corrected. All lovers of church history will be forever in her debt.

Miss Walls left in typing (done largely by Mildred Stewart of the Oshawa Church) or handwritten copy a richly detailed account of the period up to 1895—roughly the story of the first twenty years replete with numerous lengthy quotations. (It was more she knew than could be used.) There were also on file hundreds of handwritten articles largely copied by herself from old issues of *The Free Methodist*. Many of these proved most useful in continuing with the later years and in checking against other versions of the same incidents. There had been scores of manuscripts gathered in, some done in the 1800's, others in recent years by local scribes here and there. There were booklets on historic occasions and of course dozens of pictures—some very ancient. These materials I inherited in late June, 1959, because of an earlier suggestion from R. B. Warren that I had better be the one of the committee to finish the work. (He was already tied down with the pastoring of Kingston Church, editing the *Canadian Free Methodist Herald*, and writing a weekly column for 150 newspapers; and Sara Gregory's health would not permit her tackling such an enterprise.) Although Methodists have always used laymen widely in other ministries, this could be the first time that a layman has been selected to write a Methodist history.

As I have intimated, we have been a long time getting this story out of the boxes and into a book. It will doubtless be a long time before another of its nature appears. Much effort has been expended to make it good. If the history should prove to be something more than a dry-as-dust chronicle, that will be because it was intended to be different. The matter for the making of a vibrant volume packed with sparkle, chuckle and challenge was on hand. It is hoped the reader will rate the result thus. Deciding what to include or omit, or which version of several conflicting ones to use was not easy. Some readers will surely discount the book's detail; others will berate its brevity; still more will detect the inevitable error. (Only God knows how many errors were caught in time.) Certain personalities and places may have been given little prominence because the impressive information had not been sent in or been made to seem important.

PREFACE

Though the history contains the names of hundreds of people and places, and a multitude of footnotes, I am very conscious of remaining wide gaps. The reader's indulgence where I have erred or omitted. From where I stood, this is about the way things looked. As for dates, many in late-written reports did not agree with early records. The book includes many more words and pictures than earlier sanctioned. Yet only a fraction of the available pictures were used. Conference balance here, as in other places, had to be reasonably retained.

Let no one think I write easily. I feel much kinship with Dr. Orville S. Walters of our American church who in medical metaphor describes himself as "one of those bleeders—every word a drop of blood." The military motif forced itself but took tedious hours with *Roget's Thesaurus* to develop—both as to skeleton and to body.

Neither was the work leisurely done. Despite Miss Walls' earlier research and preliminary writing, it demanded a summer of digesting, distilling, reorganizing, writing, revising, and corresponding, plus a fall and partial winter of early-and-late continued concentration on the side from teaching high school—the kind that one can take once in a lifetime—to ensure the book's readiness for the Centenary General Conference. Wide correspondence to fill some of the discovered gaps proved especially time-consuming.

But if this has been a demanding task, it has also been an enlightening and moving experience. Again and again my discoveries stirred me to the depths as I caught the quality of someone's character or saw how God worked his Supernatural among an earnest people. There is need that the secrets of those early successes be unearthed and labelled. I hope the contents of this book will be as disturbing to others as they have been to me, as disturbing as were the previously lost books of the Law when brought to King Josiah.

Except for the change of tense, the history's main title is borrowed from I Samuel 17:47. A certain God-trusting Hebrew shepherd boy spoke the words to a certain self-sufficient Philistine giant who stood confronting him. What happened to that enemy of the Lord a moment later is common knowledge. As used here, the title-words openly acknowledge that those who humanly made this history were activated by motives of divine conquest. They also testify that this generation of Canadian Free Methodists gives to the Lord of Hosts the glory for all successes. Changing the tense again for the last section, afforded excellent opportunity to point our responsibility and opportunity today.

I have suggested that the military metaphor was pursued because it best seemed suited to wrap the record in. A further defense of its use appears in the chapter, "They Thought a War Was On." It is hoped that the reader will smell the smoke on many a page and even feel the flame. May one result of its study be the enlisting of lengthy lines of glad recruits for the continuation of the Holy War today and tomorrow. The organization and general treatment were in part designed for the non-Free Methodist reader. We have a big public relations job yet to do.

The comments of the other members of the current committee, along with those of Zella Nixon on the Saskatchewan chapter and Rev. E. H. Childerhose on the Holiness Movement Merger chapter, have been most helpful. Mrs. Jennie Hamilton (a sister of Alice Walls and now retired in Oshawa) contributed immensely through her lending of old histories, *Heralds*, and photos, her identification of faces and dates, her supplying of anecdotal material, her help on Saskatchewan and West Ontario, and her criticism of certain manuscripts. Lorne Park College library supplied many Methodist histories and an almost complete list of Combined Minutes. These latter books must have been consulted several thousand times. My own library and envelope and photo collections also proved invaluable.

A fairly complete list of acknowledgements appears in the back of the book, but one other name must be mentioned here—Elmira Webb Freeman, for the beautiful and appropriate cover design.

And I could never have completed the task in time had not my 16-year-old son Grant (despite his studies and an appendix operation) been able to convert, with patience and despatch, my shockingly imperfect handwriting into readable typed copy; and my wife Doris to assist in processing the pictures, compiling the lists, completing the proofreading, and preparing the index. The organization of the book is such that the reader will want to use this index constantly.

Early in the effort, as the magnitude of our family task was becoming more apparent, we came upon Job's outcry: "Oh that my words were now written! oh that they were printed in a book!" As a family we rejoice that our 100,000 words *are* finally written and soon to be printed. The prayers of many have made the near-impossible come to pass.

Oshawa, Ontario
February, 1960   John W. Sigsworth

Table of Contents

SECTION 1: *Back of the Attack*

1. Methodism, a Movement of God 13
2. Free Methodism, a Necessity in New York 15
3. Canada When It Came 16

SECTION 2: *Some Methods of Free Methodists*

1. They Thought a War Was On 19
2. They Stood Upon the Impregnable Rock of Holy Writ . . 21
3. They Depended on the Dynamic of the Holy Spirit . . 21
4. They Inducted an Itinerant Ministry 24
5. They Catered to the Common People 26
6. They Reverted to Revivals 26
7. They Requested a Testimony 28
8. They Kept the Class Meeting 29
9. They Copied the Camp Meeting 30
10. They Continued the Quarterly Meeting 32
11. They Developed the District Meeting 32
12. They Practised Prayer and Fasting 34
13. They Cultivated Congregational Music 36
14. They Employed Visitation Evangelism 37
15. They Overcame the Obstacle of Inadequacy . . . 39
16. They Went to College at Home 40
17. They Enlisted Lay Leadership 41
18. They Allowed Ladies to Carry Arms 42
19. They Demanded the Discipline of a Separated Life . . . 45
20. They Worked With the Young 46
21. They Sanctioned Salvation Schools 49
22. They Let Literature Help Them 50

9

23. They Remembered the Regions Beyond 52
24. They Financed by Free-Will Offerings 54
25. They Denied Themselves for the Welfare of the Work . . 54
26. They Endured Hardness as Good Soldiers 56
27. They Suffered Persecution for Righteousness 57
28. They Handed Us a Heritage 60

SECTION 3: *Ontario Opens for Occupation*
1. How It Happened 61
2. Canada, C. H. Sage 63
3. Winning a Footing 65
4. Local War Council—The First Canada Conference, 1880 . 76
5. Further Fighting of the First Two Decades 77
6. Fission: The Division Divides, 1895 104

SECTION 4: *Continuing the Conquest*
1. Onward in East Ontario 107
2. Forward in West Ontario 136

SECTION 5: *Warfare in Western Canada*
1. The Sword of the Lord in Saskatchewan 153
2. The Attack in Alberta 167
3. The Battle in British Columbia 175

SECTION 6: *Giants . . . In Those Days*
1. Some Militant Men of the Ministry 179
2. Some Worthy Women Also 191
3. Some Local Laymen Who Could Lift 196
4. Some Canadian Fighters on Foreign Soils 201
5. Burnishing a Bishop—Some Bishop! 210

SECTION 7: *Strategic Twentieth-Century Instruments of War*
1. A Canadian High Command 216

2. A National Line of Communication 221
  3. A Dominion Government Charter 222
  4. Regional Training Centres 224
  5. Permanent Camps 235
  6. Welcome Reinforcements 238

Section 8: *Meaningful Twentieth-Century Milestones*
  1. Canada Conference's Semi-Centennial, 1930 242
  2. Armadale's Sixtieth Anniversary, 1940 243
  3. Eastern Conferences' Golden Anniversary, 1945 . . . 243
  4. Western Canada's Semi-Centennial, 1948 244
  5. Church-Wide Centenary (Canadian Version), 1960 . . 244

Section 9: *Recent Review*
  1. Progress Across the Provinces 246
  2. Impact Beyond Our Borders 258
  3. Has Free Methodism Changed Too? 261

Section 10: *The Battle Is the Lord's*
  1. Reconnaissance—Canada, 1960 265
  2. The Present Issue 268
  3. The Engagement Must Intensify 270
  4. "Ye Christian Soldiers, Rise" 273
  5. "Lead On, O King Eternal" 275

Section 11: Appendices
  1. *Summary of Historical Highlights* 276
  2. *Lists of Labourers* 277
  3. *Acknowledgements* 283
  4. *Index* 285

Section 1: Back of The Attack

Every church history needs some background. The question is how far back to begin. John Wesley and the English Methodists seem a logical starting point here. But Canadian Free Methodism was a child of American Free Methodism so the latter's origins become necessary too. That the reader may the better understand Canada (actually the former Upper Canada) politically, educationally, and religiously (especially Methodistically), we also include "Canada When It Came."

1.
METHODISM, A MOVEMENT OF GOD

Social life and morality had sunk to disgraceful depths. Religion was cold and formal. Such was early eighteenth century England when the "Holy Club" at Oxford began its methodical program of fasting and prayer, piety and study, charity and jail-visiting. But out of the club grew the great Methodist movement which God has used in the centuries since to transform sinners into saints the world over. And the term Methodist which began as a nickname grew to be an epithet of great dignity.

Like their father, the Wesley brothers John and Charles, who were leaders in the club, became Anglican clergymen. They remained such all their lives. Their early mission attempt in Georgia was a flat failure. Not till his historic Aldersgate heart-warming at age thirty-five did John receive personal assurance of salvation.[1] From then almost until his death at age eighty-eight he was tireless in promoting the necessity and certainty of conversion. He discovered, too, from a careful study of the Bible and the writings of à Kempis, Taylor, and Law that a deeper experience of heart cleansing which he called Christian Perfection was in God's plan. In fact, he made this the cardinal doctrine of Methodism maintaining that God had raised it up to "spread scriptural holiness throughout these lands."

For fifty years he rose at five in the morning. It is estimated that he rode on horseback more than 250,000 miles over England and Ireland and preached more than 40,000 sermons—once to 32,000 people. He wrote prolifically too.

Those who accepted his teachings on "the witness of the Spirit," Wesley formed into Methodist societies or classes conducted by "class-leaders" many of whom with training became themselves powerful preachers and writers. John Fletcher and Adam Clarke were two. Workers spread out to

THE BATTLE WAS THE LORD'S

every part of the British Isles and soon some, as Asbury and Coke, to the American colonies. Charles Wesley was a capable preacher, but is best known for his gifts of singing and song-composing. He could hear hymns in his horse's hoof-beats and is credited with 6,500 of them. At John's death in 1781, Methodists numbered into the thousands on both sides of the Atlantic.

For the early years of his ministry, John Wesley was opposed by Anglican churchmen, but he still considered himself a loyal church member and Methodism a voluntary society within the church. It was really his followers in Britain who formed a separate church after his death.

The eighteenth century spiritual awakening, which under God he precipitated, has come to be known as The Evangelical Revival. Because of its purifying influence on social and religious life, the religious organizations it eventually begot, and the political and social reforms it precipitated, there are good grounds for considering him, as historian John Wesley Bready did, "the greatest character in modern history." [2]

Early Methodism stressed two "works of grace"; separation from the world; and attendance on the "means of grace," this phrase meaning the preaching services and the prayer and class meetings. Probably no movement since New Testament days has had more of God in it. Too bad it was that such an enterprise seemed destined so soon to lose its vigour.

---

1. Charles received his "witness" only a few days previous.
2. See *Wesley and Democracy*, Thorn Press, Toronto.

John Wesley

B. T. Roberts

2.
FREE METHODISM, A NECESSITY IN NEW YORK

The Free Methodist Church sprang from the Methodist Episcopal Church in New York not because of secession but because of expulsion, not of choice but of necessity.

Early American Methodism had a wholesome effect on the national life. Soon it attracted many people who became prosperous and influential and whose wealth helped to build costly churches. Worldliness in dress, amusements and friendships became especially pronounced in the churches of the Genesee Conference of western New York State. Ministers who were also Freemasons or Odd Fellows seemed to dominate the conference.[1] Revivals and Wesleyan doctrine were being neglected. But not all ministers were partners to the trend. In the 1850's a distinct cleavage came, with one, Benjamin Titus Roberts by name, assuming leadership of the contenders for original Methodism. In 1858, because of a piece of writing decrying New School Methodism, as he called it, this college-trained spiritual giant was expelled from the conference on a charge of so-called "unchristian and immoral conduct."[2] Another man named McCreery was expelled at the same time. After many others, both ministers and laymen were also expelled,[3] and appeals for reinstatement to the General Conference failed, fifteen ministers and eighty sympathetic laymen held a convention in the summer of 1860 on the farm of I. M. Chesbrough at Pekin, N.Y. The necessity of organizing a *new* Methodist church was apparent. The designation "Free," adopted as part of the name, could indicate, said Rev. C. D. Brooks who proposed it, (1) freedom from the domination of secret societies, (2) freedom from slavery (an issue in the old church then), (3) free seats (many churches sold or rented seats then), (4) freedom of the Spirit in the services. B. T. Roberts was named General Superintendent (title changed to Bishop in 1907) and a democratic government granting laymen equal representation with the ministers was set up.[4]

According to Bishop Wilson T. Hogue, in his *History of the Free Methodist Church*. "It was the first distinctively Holiness Church organized in the United States." And it might be added that, among the denominations of the modern holiness movement, Free Methodism was the first in Canada. Even the Salvation Army did not arrive until 1882.

---

1. According to Bishop Marston in the *Free Methodist* of Jan. 12, 1960, it was clearly pointed out by a report of the 1866 General Conference "that but for the secret society evil there would have been no necessity for the Free Methodist Church."

2. The final expulsion came after the article had been republished by another man who did it without consulting Mr. Roberts and admitted that he did it. Mr. Roberts' surrendered credentials were restored to his son many years later at the Methodist conference of 1910, accompanied with an admission of former wrong.

3. According to Bishop A. D. Zahniser in one of his published sermons, they turned out 200 at one time. (See *Servant of God*, p. 108.)

4. The date of organization was Aug. 23, 1860.

3.
CANADA WHEN IT CAME

After its 1860 beginning, Free Methodism spread fast to widely separated parts of the United States. At the end of two decades, it was even entrenched in a conference in this country.

When shall we date its arrival here? With the coming of the first layman? With the entry of the first Free Methodist-edited magazine? With the first Free Methodist preaching? With the first Free Methodist members made? With the first "appointed" minister? With the first society? With the first conference? Some case might be made for each. Perhaps in the first "appointment" we have the official coming. That was in 1876. It is an easy date to recall as a beginning, for it also marks the beginning of the fourth quarter of the nineteenth century. A quick look at Canada then —especially Ontario (formerly Upper Canada), the foothold province— should prove helpful.

Following the successful American Revolution nearly a century earlier, people by the thousands were driven from their homes. As refugee Loyalists, many by boat or oxcart streamed into Canada for a new homeland. Here, they gained by 1791 a separation of Quebec into Upper and Lower Canada. With the separation came something unfamiliar to the resident French—an elected assembly. On invitation, Americans continued coming in the next century. It was land that lured them. Besides, almost a million settlers from the British Isles surged in during the notable 1815-1850 migrations. (Many came to escape the depression that followed the Napoleanic Wars.) Building log cabins and crude furniture, clearing forests, and plowing among the stumps to grow enough food to live on— these made pioneer life a grim struggle.

Confederation—the union of the first four provinces, Nova Scotia, New Brunswick, and the two Canadas—was achieved in 1867. MacDonald shaped it mainly, but Brown and Tilley (both God-fearing men) and a host of other Fathers cannot be forgotten. One legend has it that Tilley proposed the descriptive word *Dominion* after reading Psalm 72:8, "He shall have dominion also from sea to sea." [1] The name *Canada* had originated with Cartier, probably a corruption of an Indian word meaning a collection of huts.

By 1876 much of southern Ontario had been cleared. Rural people were prospering. The appearance of a second crop of homes—of lumber, stone or brick—testified to that. Perhaps a dozen Ontario cities existed. Toronto, which in 1791 had contained two families of Mississauga Indians, now boasted nearly 100,00 people. Villages and towns by the score had sprung up with their mills, blacksmith shops, general stores, inns, and even schools and churches. That brings us to the education and religion of the day.

Upper Canada's earliest schools had been maintained by subscriptions and fees, and were taught in numerous cases by untrained cripples or discharged soldiers. Bibles and spellers were sometimes the only books. By

1876 (thanks in part to Governor Simcoe's work in the early 1800's but mostly to Methodist minister Egerton Ryerson's brilliant leadership as Superintendent of Education from 1844 on), a model school system was in operation. Education was free and compulsory, practical as well as intellectual, and above all, founded on religion. The curriculum included Bible history, basic doctrine and morality. Inspected elementary schools staffed with licensed teachers trained in Ryerson-sponsored normal schools dotted the province. Even secondary schools were getting fairly common.

The religious picture by 1876 will concern the reader most and again the story is given for Ontario where Free Methodism first came and where the majority of its membership have always lived.

Although Jesuits had brought Roman Catholicism during the French Regime, the Church of England soon established itself with the coming of the British in 1763. And Methodism was not far behind. Indeed, so rapidly did it grow that Walsh in his *Christian Church in Canada* (Ryerson Press, Toronto) was able to say, "Methodism has long been recognized as one of the determining influences in shaping the national character of English-speaking Canada."

The first Methodist preacher in Canada was a local preacher army officer named Tuffey and stationed at Quebec. The first Methodist foothold in Upper Canada was gained by former Americans (originally from Ireland) who came north as Loyalists. These included the widow and son of a local preacher, Philip Embury, who had come to this continent in 1760 (before even Asbury and Coke) as well as Paul Heck and Barbara Heck (she was called the mother of American Methodism) and their family. This party settled near Prescott and formed a Methodist Episcopal class in 1778. Other Methodist classes were organized by a Wm. Losee in the Hay Bay area (west of Kingston) where he built the first Methodist chapel in Upper Canada.[2] That organizing and building took place in 1792, only one year after the first Parliament in Upper Canada met. Losee, the first appointed pastor here, had 165 members to report to his New York Conference in a matter of months.[3]

Upper Canada Methodists became independent from New York in 1828, constituting the Methodist Episcopal Church in Canada. Shortly, Primitive Methodism, direct from England, organized in York (later Toronto). Then came (also from the Old Country) the Bible Christian Church, a Methodist branch. The Wesleyan Methodist Church was organized here a little later. This Wesleyan Methodist group joined the Methodist New Connexion in 1874 creating the Methodist Church of Canada, but, as we have seen, there were still three other Methodist bodies carrying on.[4] Clearly in 1876 Canada did not need another Methodist member, unless such a member offered something very distinctive. Free Methodism did.

The situation was this: Canadian Methodism had her divisions, but her greater problems were her declensions.[5] Perhaps the Primitive Methodist group, which had been raised up to conserve the vitality of English Methodism and which had been especially active in Upper Canada in the Toronto-Markham-Scarboro area had kept its burning zeal longest. Yet one who knew it well lamented that from 1860 on, it began to depart from its earlier simplicity.[6] After travelling widely for over a year, the first Free Methodist minister assigned to Canada bluntly concluded that "real Methodism has nearly all run out in Canada." This was doubtless an overstatement, but it seems to have contained too much truth to be dismissed lightly. Numerous Methodist class leaders were numbered among the Free Methodist converts. Free Methodism was to bring a new flame of the old fire, for as Rev. C. V. Fairbairn so aptly defined it in 1925, it was essentially "Old-Fashioned Methodism revived."

The elderly Methodists remembered better days and sometimes said so nostalgically. A saintly soul from Caledonia, greeting the heat of a Free Methodist quarterly meeting at Hannon in 1879, exclaimed: "What will I tell the people where I live? . . . I will tell them the old kind of religion is coming through the land." When the Hagle-Thomas team of ladies held services in a schoolhouse in 1883 near Iona, some residents were decidedly opposed. Not so, numbers of the older set. They attended and said: "This is nothing new you are hearing and seeing; it is just the old-time salvation." Or take this confession from an aged lady who was joyfully converted at Port Credit about 1889: "I know this is pure religion for I saw this among the Methodists, but we do not see it any more."

Free Methodists were soon to make this "pure religion" more common in dozens of Ontario centres and other communities in the West.

---

1. When Free Methodism officially got to Western Canada in 1898, Alberta and Saskatchewan were still in the Northwest Territories but Manitoba had been a province since 1870. It was 1905 before Alberta and Saskatchewan were named provinces. Something of their state of development when Free Methodism arrived is in later chapters.

2. The Hay Bay chapel still stands, Mecca for a United Church late-August pilgrimage each year. (See *United Church Observer*, Aug. '59.)

3. Of Mr. Losee it was said: "He was a son of thunder, he feared no man, but warned every careless soul he met on the Bay of Quinte to be reconciled to God (See *History of the Meth. Episcopal Church in Canada*—Webster.)

4. These 4 Methodist groups—Methodist Episcopal, Primitive Methodist, Bible Christian, and Methodist Church of Canada amalgamated 10 years later in 1884 to form the Methodist Church. The Methodist Church of Canada in 1874 had 560,000 adherents. The new Methodist Church of 1884 boasted at least 800,000 members, making it the largest Protestant body in Canada then.

5. One would not suspect the declensions from reading the Wesleyan orthodoxy, beautifully built into the 1884 Catechism, or the new General Superintendent Carman's Union-time address on "Holiness, Our Hope." They show up from other sources.

6. An interesting survey of Primitive Methodism up to the 1884 union was written by a Mrs. Hopper whose father James Agar joined a Primitive Methodist class in York (Toronto) in 1830 and was a close friend of Robert Walker, a local preacher there who later became Conference President. It would be helpful at this point to turn ahead to the chapter "They Demanded the Discipline of a Separated Life" and read a quotation from Walker's conference address of 1875 deploring the current "conformity to the world" as he saw it.

Section 2: Some Methods of Free Methodists

The name Methodist, we have seen, was first given to a handful of methodical Oxford students. Canadian Free Methodists continued many of the unique methods that Wesley devised for his early "Societies." Others they borrowed from American Methodism or developed themselves. A lengthy list is furnished here, with clarification and limited illustration. If Free Methodism through the years may be said to have had any genius, that genius is likely to be discovered in the elements of this list.

1.
THEY THOUGHT A WAR WAS ON

In studying the story of their exploits, and especially in searching for the explanation of their successes, one is driven to the realization that those early church fathers thought and acted in terms of war. The war was between the cohorts of King Jesus, whose soldiers they were, and the hosts of Prince Beelzebub. In true Pauline fashion their own written reports bristled with vivid martial metaphor. Let us look at some:

In 1874, a J. Ireland wrote of a sally into Canada: "The enemy fled in utter dismay and left us in full possession of the field, with all the dead (that is, dead to sin) and the severely wounded in our hands. The slightly wounded got away for the present."

In 1878 T. P. Jarnagan wrote of West Ontario Jericho meetings: "We had some hot and close contacts with the enemy, but our God always got to himself the victory."

Rev. C. H. Sage, after some successful services in Bracebridge in 1879, wrote: "Canada needs some saved young men and women who will . . . care more for souls than for money, a good name or partners in life, can take a pony and travel, take soldiers' fare, trusting God for support, as the early Methodists did, . . . and take their pay in stock in glory. . . . If anyone can afford to accept the terms, write me soon. . . . Yours in the war, anywhere on the line."

It was said of the services held by two early lady pastors, "The war has been raging all winter."

The Committee on the State of the Work at the early conference of 1881 declared, "We are not looking for storms but for victory," then added, "We shall have it."

Rev. A. H. Norrington reported on a successful camp meeting at Crown

THE BATTLE WAS THE LORD'S

Hill in 1891 and spoke of the evangelist Rev. B. Winget approvingly thus: "Canada needs a cohort of such men to carry the banner before us."

General Superintendent B. R. Jones came late to a Bracebridge camp meeting in 1895 and "found the battle in progress with good prospects."

The classic item with the military metaphor sustained was a 13-inch column of fine print in a late spring *Free Methodist* of 1889 by a superintendent named James Craig. It is a progress report for Muskoka and Toronto Districts, then under him. We give you snatches: "The ministerial force has been doing some hard fighting. . . . They have so effectively blown the war-bugle that many who have been resting on rusty arms have taken the field with burnished weapons and actually begun to look like men of war. Bro. Allguire (Huntsville) . . . has been reconnoitering on the northern frontier and has succeeded in making some inroads. . . . Bro. Burnham and his loyal band (near Bracebridge) have routed the powers of darkness. . . . Bro. Hector Gibbs (Severn Bridge) . . . has been throwing from his sling some smooth stones from the brook of truth. . . . Bro. J. A. Prosser (Crown Hill) has been endeavoring to storm the citadels of sin. . . . Sister Nancy Schantz (Belhaven) rallied the hosts of Israel . . . and captured some souls. . . . Sister Kate Booth (Uxbridge) has, with her army, been waging a successful warfare. . . . Sister Sipprell (near Stouffville) has been feeling the enemy's position. . . . Bro. Walls (Armadale) is holding the fort . . . and doing a little skirmishing on the outposts. . . . Sister Diller and Sister Page (Healey's Falls) have been wielding the sword of the Spirit. . . . Bro. B. P. Clark and Bro. and Sister Norrington . . . planted their batteries first at Petworth, and then at Verona. . . . The cries of the wounded and the groans of the dying could be heard from afar." These warriors of the Lord must indeed have been "terrible as an army with banners."

But the battle hadn't always gone so briskly. Rev. Craig's 1883 report of London reveals that an occasional "down" was mingled with the "up's": "I have seen the house full," he wrote, "but there have been Achans in the camp and Babylonish garments and wedges of gold have been taken and secreted. The Spirit of God has been grieved, the battle has turned against us until the field has had to be abandoned." [1]

Sometimes the picture got changed to a ripe harvest, as here, by the same man Craig on an 1887 tour through his territory: "Oh, for a host of Spirit-baptized love-constrained laborers to enter into these fields white already for the harvest." Or here, in A. H. Norrington's 1891 verdict, after the Verona dedication: "This land is one vast field of waiting harvest. . . . We are praying God to send us some earnest laborers to reap this vast field of human souls."

But battling or harvesting, there was that same awful urgency—a job to be done, daringly, speedily, for the Lord. The gains, which we shall see that they made in those early years, demonstrate well their deep devotion. Like Paul, in II Corinthians 10:4, they did not believe in carnal weapons.

The spiritual weapons they did use were "mighty through God to the pulling down of strongholds." The remaining chapters of this section try to highlight and illustrate those weapons or methods.

---

1. The report concluded: "There is no trace of a society there now and Bro. Showers has an empty building and is about $500 out of pocket."

2.
THEY STOOD UPON THE IMPREGNABLE ROCK OF HOLY WRIT

Even though Mr. Roberts and others of his colleagues among the first ministers were college-trained, they were fundamental to the core when it came to believing the Bible to be the inspired unerring Oracles. Not that it merely *contained* the Word of God but that it *was*. Naturally their spiritual sons followed them.

The classic evangelical doctrines—the Trinity, original sin, atonement, repentance, full salvation, the resurrection, ascension, and second coming, eternal happiness and eternal punishment—all these and many more were built into their Articles of Religion which were largely borrowed from the parent church. One of their secrets of success was the certitude with which they expounded them—not a matter of defending, but rather of proclaiming.

Of Jerusha Hagle and Martha Thomas at Florence in 1880—81 Mr. Sage wrote: "They act just as though they believed the people were going to the judgment and if not saved would drop into hell, and then their blood would be required at their hands." This was surely Biblical.

And speaking of rocks, they had a thoroughly Reformed view on what the "Rock" meant in Christ's famous declaration to Peter. One of founder Roberts' greatest sermons—one which he preached repeatedly—was based on that passage as a text.

3.
THEY DEPENDED ON THE DYNAMIC OF THE HOLY SPIRIT

They said full salvation customarily came by two crises. By the first, one was "saved," forgiven of his sins, "born again" of the Spirit, adopted into the family of God. But they said that the sins of the disposition, the Biblical "carnal mind," still remained and, on provocation, easily produced downfall. They said deliverance from this "remains of sin" was possible and even obligatory and was obtained as at conversion by confession of need, obedience, and exercise of faith. This deliverance didn't make one incapable of further sinning, or even free from temptation, for Christ had had a holy heart yet was tempted. It was not freedom from infirmity or ignorance either. John Wesley who had clarified this doctrine in his day called the superior state when attained, "Christian Perfection" and wrote a book about it.[1] It was a purification of the motives, a perfection of love[2] —he maintained—a love towards God and one's fellow men that filled the soul to the exclusion of sinful and selfish inclinations.[3] This crisis went by the name of "entire sanctification" or being "sanctified wholly," a completion of the sanctifying work begun in conversion or regeneration. Wesley insisted that such Bible passages as these pointed unmistakably to the validity of the doctrine:

1) And the very God of peace sanctify you wholly. I Thes. 5:23 (this written to a church of believers.)
2) Be ye perfect, as your Father who is in heaven is perfect. Matt. 5:48.
3) Having these promises, let us cleanse ourselves from all filthiness of the flesh and spirit, perfecting holiness in the fear of God. II Cor. 7:1.
4) If we confess our sins, he is faithful and just to forgive us our sins and to cleanse us from all unrighteousness. I John 1:9.
5) If we walk in the light, as he is in the light, we have fellowship one with another, and the blood of Jesus Christ his Son cleanseth us from all sin. I John 1:7.
6) Thou shalt love the Lord thy God with all thy heart. Matt. 22:37.

Charles Wesley wrote dozens of hymns proclaiming belief in heart holiness. This stanza of one is a fair example:

> "Let others hug their chains,
> For sin and Satan plead,
> And say from sin's remains
> They never can be freed;
> Rejoice in hope, rejoice with me;
> We shall from all our sins be free."

Numerous Methodists in their day testified to it. The saintly John Fletcher of Madeley was one who confessed: "I am free from sin." He was Wesley's model and even Voltaire admitted his blamelessness.

Canadian Methodism's Nathan Bangs wrote a tremendously clear description of his reception of this experience which had taken place at Niagara Falls several years before the Hay Bay camp described later.

This two-fold nature of salvation had been grasped by some outside Methodism. Baptist Spurgeon, according to his Baptist biographer, Dr. Richard Ellsworth Day, in *Shadow of the Broad Brim* (Judson Press), had a second transforming experience. (Day called the two crises Revision and Invasion, and said the two were usually separated in time.) Congregationalist Moody before his great preaching successes was led into this second experience by two Chicago Free Methodist ladies who sensed his lack. Ailing Presbyterians had sought and found it as "dying grace," and then recovered. Savonarola and numerous other mediaeval saints had seemed to know it. Kempis and Law and Taylor had caught glimpses of it.[4] This heart holiness that Wesley had caught from the Scriptures and from the writings of these latter three men while at Oxford, the Free Methodists taught, their converts sought, and, as among Wesley's followers, many insisted that the work had been wrought in their own hearts. And their conviction was that, like early Methodists, they had been raised up to spread this kind of scriptural holiness over the land.

Charles Sage, Canada's first appointed pastor, found this experience of heart purity after seeking for two weeks and consecrating to leave the popular Methodist Church for a place among the despised Free Methodists. Wesley Walls had his Pentecost and received his power for service kneeling beside a huge Muskoka rock shortly after being summoned to Huntsville to preach. Rev. A. Sims, a Primitive Methodist minister who went to a Free Methodist Tonawanda camp meeting to seek this experience found it after first discovering himself "back-slidden" and repenting of that condition. Miss Matilda Sipprell of Baptist background made a complete consecration at a Hannon Free Methodist camp meeting and experienced "the cleansing blood." Thereafter she spent many years as an evangelist.

John Wesley was an inexcitable Anglican. Not all his spiritual descendants have been so constrained. The congregational kind of services that Methodism modelled and the deep kind of assurance that she has majored in have combined to produce a tradition not easily understood. Sometimes the great joy that attended the sense of divine favour or deliverance made Methodists behave in ways that seemed "strange" to people who yet saw nothing out of place in near-hysterics at a ball game. Dignified David had done a holy dance before the Lord and all the hosts of Israel had shouted with him when the ark was returning to Jerusalem. The once-lame temple-gate beggar after his healing, had entered the temple with Peter and John "walking and leaping and praising God." Mediaeval St. Francis had had his "ecstacies." Matilda Sipprell, who was to become one of Canadian Free Methodism's most effective lady evangelists, "danced before the Lord" after her Canaan entry. Nehemiah had said, "The joy of the Lord is your strength." True Free Methodists had that joy and gave evidence in many ways.

Weeping was another frequent expression, weeping tears of joy. (Charles Wesley was quite guilty of this.) Shouting, the shouting of the saints, was common in any camp meeting zone. Or it could be laughing. A minister from the Christian Church, who had heard much about Free Methodist noise visited a Toronto District camp near Belhaven. He was convinced the laughing was supernatural and stated he would never find any fault with their laughing as they had done it there. Even leaping occurred. At a Verona District Meeting in 1891 one man testified how he had been converted from Romanism alone in the woods after hearing two Protestant sermons. Although he had never seen anyone shout, he "leaped and shouted for joy."

One Mrs. Henry from Sombra who had been deprived of the "love feasts" for about three years was so happy at a Craig-held quarterly meeting in the Ousley chapel on the Florence and Shetland circuit she "testified three or four times."

Sometimes in service a person might begin singing spontaneously. M. S. Benn tells of a girl at Kingston church who felt constrained to start a solo. The preacher sensing it was of the Lord invited the congregation to stand and join her. Sixteen people found the Lord in that service and it precipitated an eight-week revival.

These behaviour patterns Free Methodists called exercising "the freedom of the Spirit," one of the four freedoms behind the "Free" in the church name. The preachers who brought Free Methodism to Canada were not showmen. But they did often speak in the Pauline way—"in demonstration of the Spirit and of power"—and saw no reason for suppressing a holy hilarity in their converts so long as it was buttressed by a holy walk before God and man.

Many were the scoffers in those early days who went to church to get entertainment but ended up by getting salvation. As in Goldsmith's *Deserted Village*, these "fools who came to mock remained to pray."

Rev. A. Sims prophesied in a report in 1884, "Canada has hardly begun to see the power that will shake the Dominion." It would seem that it was because they depended on His Spirit and honoured His Spirit that God poured out His Spirit then in such tides of blessing and waves of salvation.

---

1. This book, now a classic in its field, is entitled *Plain Account of Christian Perfection*.
2. He did not call it "sinless perfection"—that was a "straw man" of the critics.
3. Telford in *Popular History of Methodism* says: "His teaching was greatly misunderstood but when he explained it to the Bishop of London, Dr. Gibson replied: 'Mr. Wesley, if this be all you mean, publish it to all the world.'"
4. For more testimony on this topic read *Deeper Experiences of Famous Christians* by Lawson (Warner Press).

4.
THEY INDUCTED AN ITINERANT MINISTRY

A strong feature of British Methodism brought to America was the itinerant ministry of the circuit system. Wesley had worked it out to look after his scattered societies in the British Isles, but it fitted frontier North America well, too.[1]

Methodist ministers in those days did not choose their field of labour but as one historian put it: "With saddle bags packed and horses tied to the fence, they awaited God's will as revealed to the Stationing Committee."

Daniel in his *History of Methodism* described in some detail the way Bishop Asbury of America regarded the itineracy, concluding his description with these words: "The system killed off the feeble ones and drove off the lazy ones but those who remained were the giants of those days, and indeed, of all days; for, taking the world over and the centuries through, no class of God's servants have ever given a better account of themselves, or left behind them more abundant proofs of faithfulness and power."

Free Methodists borrowed the system from the parent American Methodist Episcopal body. The Stationing Committee would consist of the General Superintendent or Bishop, the District Chairmen and several laymen. You went where you were appointed and stayed never more than three years. Often it was only one or two.[2] It took consecration to resign to that regime, decade after decade. But the system seemed to get results, all the while reminding the itinerant and his wife and family that "here we have no continuing city." Who will blame the parsonage lady for shedding a quiet tear when the relevant song "That Will Be the Last Move for Me" appeared?

The circuit could be any size. Young Nathan Bangs of the early Methodists shared one—Oswegotchie—that comprised seven St. Lawrence townships. It didn't seem to hurt him for he pops up later as an illustrious editor and historian. He even appears as Dr. Nathan Bangs, President of Wesleyan University at Middleton, Conn.—the college that doctored Egerton Ryerson and from which B. T. Roberts took his Bachelor's and Master's Degrees.[3]

But the first Canadian Free Methodist circuit was bigger than Bangs'. There is a short chapter on the appointment later on. We read of one buggy drive that took the appointee, C. H. Sage, when he later became District Chairman, from Galt to Gananoque. It was fitting that another early Chairman, James Craig, should write of his scattered ministrations under the title "Itinerating"—travelling from place to place as a minister.

---

1. Wesley himself was the itinerant supreme. Telford in his *Popular History of Methodism* says that Wesley sometimes rode on horseback as many as ninety miles a day to keep appointments and that he paid more turnpike toll than any man who ever lived.

2. Emerson Snyder moved twenty-five times to put in his nearly forty years in the East Ontario ministry.

3. It appears likely that Bangs was president when Roberts attended. Who knows what echoes Roberts heard there of pioneer Canadian Methodism, he who was destined to assist so encouragingly in pioneer Canadian Free Methodism.

5.
THEY CATERED TO THE COMMON PEOPLE

Mark wrote of Christ that "the common people heard him gladly." Years later scholarly Paul observed to the Corinthians "not many wise . . . , not many mighty, not many noble are called."

Wesley, though a former Oxford don himself, found that his best response came from the poorer classes—miners, sailors, and the like. And Free Methodist B. T. Roberts with his Master's degree did not waste much time on the "upper crust." Free Methodism's ministry in both the United States and Canada has been largely to the lower middle class.

C. H. Sage, the first Canadian missionary and himself not a lettered man, found the people who welcomed him and followed him were pretty much common folk. After three years of working here he wrote in the *Free Methodist*: "It is over 1,100 miles across the Canada District with a membership of 190, all told, and mostly poor people." By the next summer when he was trying to get a Canada Conference formed he wrote again: "We do hope the chairman will find a place nearer than Coopersville for it will be nearly impossible for us to get there from Canada, the distance is so great and means so scarce." (Coopersville was in Michigan where they would normally be expected to go.)

Mr. Sage was blamed for not training the people to give systematically. His defense was that had he begun to talk money at the time, the work would likely have been greatly retarded. He was thinking of the general poverty among them.

You will read references to early Free Methodist activities among the Indians. And the story of negro Charlie Fisher's response to a little love before his early death is a touching one.

There were some townspeople who were "comfortable" and farmers who were "doing well." No doubt many became prosperous from the frugal living that Free Methodism enjoined. But, in general, it may be stated that the prospect of "treasures in heaven" appealed most to those who had few treasures on this earth.

6.
THEY REVERTED TO REVIVALS

A vital ingredient in the genius of early Methodism, both in the United States and Canada, was the revival. "The old-time revival service," wrote an old-timer, "was as regularly expected as the winter and everything had to bend to it." Some persisted even beyond the coming of Free Methodism. But many of those remaining, in Ontario at least, must have been much less virile than the Free Methodist brand. It caused such a commotion in many a community because it seemed so new.

SOME METHODS OF FREE METHODISTS

The Bible had spoken about times of reviving, and Free Methodism, using the proven Methodist methods, multiplied itself substantially by the periodic revival or "protracted meeting." Again and again one reads of them with their dozens—even scores—of restorations, new conversions and deeper cleansings, followed by gains in church membership. The preacher might be an imported evangelist, male or female. Often he was the district chairman or only the pastor. Sometimes the meetings ran on and on. Rev. A. Sims held a rural one for twelve weeks near Woodstock in 1879.

The services would often begin with much prayer for conviction of sin on the community and then continue till men and women surrendered to God. W. H. Gregory and congregation held on once at Belhaven for six weeks without any response. Then revival broke and services lasted eight more weeks harvesting the results of their prayers. J. A. Fletcher had a similar experience at Ormiston in Saskatchewan.

A few outstanding ones will be described in some detail as we come to them. These will include ones at Hannon in 1878, at Armadale in 1879-80, at Thedford in 1881, at Verona-Oak Flats in 1889-90, at Keith (Charlemont) in 1889-90, at Vennachar in 1893, at Bracebridge in 1894, at Westview in 1900, at North Marmora in 1901, at Petworth in 1902, and at Kelvin in 1920. Many others will be mentioned.

A fellow named Fairbairn, who features prominently in this book later and who was quite a revivalist even before he joined the Free Methodists, has furnished us in his autobiography, *I Call to Remembrance*, an account of a typical rural revival in the Desert Lake (north of Kingston) area during his early evangelistic days. Recaptured vividly are the solemnity of the occasion, the preliminary singing and praying, the simple preaching with its earnest appeal for an immediate decision, the "altar call" with its songs of invitation interspersed by words of exhortation, the response, the "altar service" with its united praying, the interjections of song, the testimonies of victory or determination, the additional testimonies precipitated from the pilgrims, the shouts of praise, the final exhortation to keep praying, and, at almost midnight, the benediction.

Contrary to popular opinion, a surprising percentage of the converts of many revivals survived. At a Saskatchewan Weyburn Camp in the early 1900's, about 25 converts of a previous Estevan circuit revival were on hand. A Fairbairn-Shelhamer meeting at Verona was forced to close in mid-December, 1918, because of the "flu" rage. When services could be resumed in the spring, pastor Gregory there "opened the doors of the church" and took in 50 members at one time.

One common result of a great revival was noteworthy: the moving into the ministry of numbers of the converts. Thus we have the appearance of what Sara Gregory calls "feeder churches"—individual churches which, themselves revived and reinforced, have enriched the whole Canadian church through the sending of their best sons and daughters to war.

Verona was such a church, and Kingston, and Gunter, and Uxbridge, and Charlemont, and Riverview in Saskatchewan. You will read more about these, and come to appreciate them as you have not before.

7.
THEY REQUESTED A TESTIMONY

Most early Free Methodist services featured a phase called the testimony meeting. Those who "professed religion" were expected to periodically tell about it. Actually this was often such a popular part of the worship service that one or more people might be standing, waiting a turn to witness to God's Grace. On occasion some spoke twice. If the service was to be "evangelistic," testimonies would normally precede preaching; otherwise they came after. Then too, following the "altar service" each "seeker" would have opportunity to report his spiritual progress. Occasionally the reports, or those of former converts that they induced, produced such hunger in other "sinners" that these would come to the front in second or even third waves of seeking after God.

It seemed that at times the testimony could do what the sermon could not. Once a Mr. Burkholder at Bracebridge boldly declared, "I'm saved and sanctified and ready for heaven." W. H. Gregory's specially slanted sermon had fizzled on influential, yet twelve years backslidden, Uriah MacDonald—but not those words. As he chopped wood at home they echoed and re-echoed in his mind till they brought this future local preacher to the midweek prayer meeting and the altar.

The person who could not produce a testimony was suspect to the congregation and the preacher. He was a candidate for the altar as were some others who talked in generalities instead of telling "what great things the Lord had done."

Of course it was expected that a testimony existed when one first presented himself for church membership. It had been enough in the American Methodist Episcopal Church to profess "a desire to flee from the wrath to come." But this loose method had brought in swarms of members whose desire did not seem to last long. Free Methodists tightened down probationary membership with this pointed question: "Have you the assurance of sins forgiven?" At the time one later presented himself for full membership, besides affirming one had the witness of the Spirit to being a child of God, an additional statement was required: that one had obtained the second crisis of "perfect love" or, if not, would seek diligently until he obtained it.

Free Methodists were obviously people who declared themselves. And they did it again and again.

8.
THEY KEPT THE CLASS MEETING

To help conserve the gains of the Evangelical Revival, Wesley organized his followers into small companies of about twelve each, called classes. Each class had a leader, one of whose main duties was to meet his people weekly to check on their spiritual growth and give advice when needed.[1] Church historians today are generally agreed that this "class meeting" was, as Walsh puts it, "the secret strength of Methodism." [2]

Gradually in both American and Canadian Methodism the class meeting became unpopular. Robert Walker, a conference president of the Primitive Methodists in Ontario in 1875 deplored the "loose views and skeptical notions" that had developed towards it. It was his observation that the members who attended most faithfully were the brightest Christians and he feared that repeated absence indicated a fading witness of acceptance with God.

The Free Methodist Church, when organized, kept the class meeting, and Bishop Wilson T. Hogue even wrote a book on its virtues: *The Class Meeting as a Means of Grace.* In the sessions, each member or adherent gave a testimony which was often more personal than that given in the public service.[3] Sometimes the leader, who was elected to this office, would, because of his maturity, ask quite personal questions—questions about habits of secret prayer and Bible reading and attendance at church and growth in grace and patience at home and love for the other members and faithfulness in cross-bearing. A skilled leader might purposely ask questions of the successful member to get statements helpful to the needy one.

There was great therapeutic value in this sharing of experiences by young and old in small groups but the value did not end there. Many whose assurance had grown dim were helped to find it again. Many were encouraged to press on to their own Pentecost (as others told of their experiences), and did it there. All were encouraged. Attendance by the new convert proved an excellent preparation for church membership before the days of preparatory classes. A member's failure to attend might draw a visit from the leader.

Adolphus Freeman was the first class leader in the Hannon church. He had held the same office in the old Bartonville M. E. Church before he got new victory and threw away his tobacco. Mrs. Emma Richardson, a charter member at Warkworth, was cited by Sara Gregory as a very effective leader in a later day. She held the local office for nearly thirty years. Mrs. Annie Teal of Ridgeway made an even more impressive record—forty years of good leading.

A strong church would have several classes with a leader for each. The young in those cases might have their separate meetings after school or on a Sunday afternoon.

Those who object to the class meeting technique must remember that true Methodists have always been people "in earnest to get to heaven." It is evident that the class meeting must have been a decided help to such people.

---

1. Actually the leaders first visited the people in their homes to collect their gifts and a little later to enquire into their conduct as well. The plan began in Bristol. When visiting became impractical, the group all met together under the leader and the class meeting was born.
2. See *The Christian Church in Canada,* by H. H. Walsh and published by Ryerson Press, Toronto. Permission to quote granted.
3. In no sense, however, are these meetings to be equated with those of secret orders. Anyone of good will could attend and no pledges or secrecy were demanded.

9.
THEY COPIED THE CAMP MEETING

The camp meeting was essentially an American institution. Primitive Methodists in England held one-day camps in some places but the longer meet came into its own on this continent with pioneer life. Webster, in his *History of the Methodist Episcopal Church in Canada,* says the first one was a joint Presbyterian and Methodist project in Kentucky in 1800.

The first one—Methodist—ever known in Canada was held at Adolphustown (west of Kingston) in 1805 on the Peter Huff farm near that first Upper Canada Methodist chapel mentioned before. Nathan Bangs attended this camp as a young minister and left us a vivid account. Here is a condensation:

Whole families made a pilgrimage. Processions of wagons and pedestrians trekked over the roads. Bangs himself came through the forest from his remote circuit of Oswegotchie in the present Brockville—Cornwall area. The meeting started with about 250 present. The first day, a Friday, saw singing, sermons, exhortations, special prayers and the power of God. Services continued till midnight with six converts the first day. A Saturday morning prayer meeting began at five. By preaching time some 2,500 were there. At the sermon's height, young Bangs, followed by the other ministers, began moving among the people. Christians were filled with joy and sinners were weeping. The moving ministers exhorted the impenitent and comforted the distressed. A dozen praying circles developed. Parents wept over children and neighbours exhorted unconverted neighbours to repent. With more preaching, that service continued all night. About forty persons received grace.

On Sunday morning with an increased crowd two sermons were offered at once, one from the regular stand and one from a wagon. The Lord's Supper was administered at noon. A despairing backslider who had become a maniac was brought in and held while prayers were offered. He found hope and joy and peace.

On the last night (it lasted a week), prayer and praise were everywhere. Before the meeting broke up people wept, sang, shouted, and hung on each other's necks. And afterwards, general revival spread around the circuits especially in that Bay of Quinte district.

That was Methodism. It is understandable that Free Methodists would continue anything so evangelistically effective. They held camp meetings in the United States before coming to Canada. As early as 1878 the Buffalo District (Genesee Conference) people, who had crossed the Niagara River and started holding services at Chippawa, were invited to have a camp in Canada but declined for some reason.

The first one came a year later in Andrew Freeman's woods at Hannon, near Hamilton. Equipment was simple—a preacher's platform of boards facing an open-air seated area. Campers lived mostly in board tents. There were no canvas tents at all. Wood fires, on raised pole platforms covered with earth, gave needed night light. Some campers came over one hundred miles. For evangelists, a Coleman-Matthews team of American ministers was invited. Nearly fifty people were converted.

Camp meetings became a regular feature of each district program. They normally lasted ten days. It was claimed that some ten thousand attended one about 1896 at Teeterville near Kelvin. Even as recently as 1935, the crowd on the last Sunday of Harrowsmith camp was estimated at five thousand.

The 1899 Charlemont area camp had one all-day meeting that Bishop Sellew said was the closest to Pentecost he had ever seen.

There were also the "tent" meetings which any minister might have on his circuit. As well, early "bush" and "grove" meetings are spoken of. These latter kinds were distinctly without a tent.

Early campers, who could not afford to rent a tent to live in, sometimes strung fastened-together sheets over a framework of poles to form a shelter.

We shall see that the Free Methodist foothold in Western Canada was achieved by tent campaigns. For years these tent and camp meeting pitchings dotted the treeless prairies and featured prominently in getting an early human harvest garnered for God.

That was the precise aim of any tent effort—evangelism. Lest the people forget, the advertising sometimes bluntly said so. Leslie Freeman, whose father Rev. G. W. Freeman was connected with the Canadian church for more than sixty years, still has a bill of a 1913 Sarnia District camp that reads: "This is not a picnic nor camp of rest, but a meeting solely for the salvation of sinners and sanctification of believers."

10.
THEY CONTINUED THE QUARTERLY MEETING

Early Methodism had these quarterly gatherings when the people from the several societies of a circuit came together for a week-end rally presided over by a district chairman. It was customary to issue beforehand quarterly tickets to all members in good standing entitling them to the Lord's Supper which would be observed at the close of the Sunday morning service. The first one ever held in Canada was conducted by ordained Darius Dunham and unordained Wm. Losee in Sept., 1792, in a Parrot barn in Ernesttown township near Kingston.

Free Methodist quarterly meetings were times of great blessing. The Friday night service would conclude with a meeting of the "Official Board" to review the quarter's business, recommend probationers and local preachers, appoint exhorters, etc. The Sunday morning service always began with the "Love Feast," an occasion when the "pilgrims" first shook hands all around as they shared a square of bread with each other (this was called "breaking bread"), and then testified for an hour or so, the testimonies interspersed with congregational songs started spontaneously and sung from memory. It was a "dry" Love Feast if God's blessing did not fall at some one or more points during this phase of the service. The evening services were evangelistic. Often new members would be admitted at quarterly meeting time and sometimes in warm weather a baptismal service would be held at a nearby lake or river. The district chairman spent his time holding revivals here and there and conducting these week-end services around his area. Galt probably had the first Free Methodist one in Canada on the occasion of Mr. Sage's first visit and class-forming in the fall of 1876.

There is a record of a Brother and Sister Carter from Galt driving sixty-five miles by horse and cutter to get to an 1879 London quarterly meeting. It was written of a quarterly meeting at Walsingham Centre in the summer of 1891 that "long before the hour for the love feast Sunday morning the church was filled. One load drove sixteen miles and was on hand at eight o'clock."

We read of three men walking twenty miles to get to an early spring one held by James Craig in a log schoolhouse near Muskoka's Severn Bridge, in 1882. Two of them "joined the pilgrim band." Mr. Craig left several detailed accounts of travelling his districts for quarterly meetings. These will be referred to later.

11.
THEY DEVELOPED THE DISTRICT MEETING

Methodism on this continent seems to have had its district meetings but they hardly assumed the significance that the later Free Methodist ones did. Among early Canadian Methodists there was a custom of having two a year, a fall one largely concerned with finances and a May one serving as a sort of annual business meeting.

Free Methodists had four a year—District Quarterly Meetings they were called—and what meetings they were! On these occasions the people from many or all the circuits on a district would converge at some previously arranged church for a super Thursday-night-to-Sunday-night area muster. Democrat loads drove as many as eighty miles.

People had to come by horse so planned to stay for the entire period. Hospitality, however, was handsome, with free billets for everybody. The local parsonage could usually be expected to house more than its share of guests. Rev. W. H. Gregory confides that by making beds on the floor, his wife would entertain up to seventeen week-enders. The Gregory children would get sent to the hay loft to sleep.[1]

An even sterner story relates to a January district meeting on northern St. Joseph Island in the early 1900's. A heavy snow fall on Saturday made it necessary for many of the guests to stay that night at the nearby Kirk home. A feather tick in the middle of the dining room floor made a pillow for twenty-one men who covered themselves with their fur robes. Six women slept crosswise on a large bed with their feet on a board supported by chairs. Everyone floundered in the snow the next morning when one church-bound sleigh upset. But God's Spirit was outpoured, and that was all that seemed to matter.

A district meeting's business session (often held on Saturday) was called its Quarterly Conference, with all key officers from the local churches eligible to vote. They were the bodies that licensed local preachers on the recommendations of the local Official Boards, but there was other district business too—making camp meeting plans, for instance, and giving circuit reports. Sunday services were much like those at a local quarterly meeting but on a grander scale. They made great occasions for holding the dedication of a host church and if the money hadn't all been provided to pay for it, the "outsiders" could be expected to help pay off the debt. Frequently a district meeting would be a time when many people found the Lord or experienced heart cleansing.

Ministers of the district would customarily leave their home services in the care of local help and be on hand for these rallies. It was an impressive sight to see these brethren all seated on the platform for the Sunday morning service. And it may be assumed that they often returned to their charges refilled with needed courage.

---

1. Speaking of entertaining, Mrs. Gregory is said to have looked after twenty-five or more in the parsonage in the days when annual conferences were cared for by individual circuits.

12.
THEY PRACTISED PRAYER AND FASTING

Early Canadian Free Methodists took seriously Christ's words that certain victories were only possible by the media of prayer and fasting.

There were plenty of circumstances to discourage those early pioneers unless they dwelt deep in God. Mr. Sage tells that on one occasion, after he had spent some years in Canada, he was on the verge of giving up. Some had stepped aside from the rugged road; others had turned out to be imposters and had disgraced the church; one minister even had brought serious reproach. Then it was he took his Bible to Dr. Brown's Woodstock garret and prayed, "Lord, if you desire me to go on with this work you will have to encourage me." He reported that he opened his Bible at just the right words to give him the needed lift.

Afternoon prayer meetings seemed to be a common practice during the early days when a protracted meeting was on. We read of them being held from house to house in connection with a Jericho (near Thedford) campaign conducted by a Brother Shorter in 1878. The report continues, "Quite a number of people were clearly saved and several were sanctified." And at early Hannon, Mr. Sage "held services in the evenings and prayer meetings in the afternoons."

Kneeling was the customary prayer posture in service. Kneeling for a silent prayer upon entering the place of service was common too.

Camp meetings were times of much extra prayer. Of a Tillsonburg camp in 1887 it was said, "Morning, noon and night, the sound of prayer rose from the tents until time for the service." Of a district camp held in Toronto in 1894, someone noted that a distinctive feature was "the lack of social visiting and constant stream of prayer both private and public."

A. H. Norrington wrote of a Crown Hill camp in 1891: "I am glad to find that the pilgrims here think more of family worship on the camp than they do of fat tables and social chitchat." Mr. Sims told of a Thorncliffe camp in the same year at which "the Lord came in power while the saints were engaged in evening devotions and six or seven were saved in one tent." He added that the spirit of prayer was so great that night, they dispensed with preaching. Yet the meeting ran late. And the altar was again filled at an early meeting the next morning.

One factor in the live spiritual births of those days was the volume of altar prayer. Wrote Bishop Pearce of a 1906 Canboro camp: "Like a well-drilled regiment the pilgrims surrounded the altar . . . and poured out their hearts to God."

Some remarkable stories are available about the effectiveness of family worship carried on at normal times. Take the instance of Mrs. Adeline Rush, the only convert of a schoolhouse revival in the Bracebridge area in the winter of 1886-87. Her family prayers proved so powerful that the schoolteacher who came to board in her home broke down after a few sessions, asked for prayer, was converted, joined the church, and became the Canadian church's first missionary to China. His name: C. Floyd Appleton.

Or take young Richard Burnham's contest with his Uxbridge father at threshing time after he returned from his Armadale conversion. "Richard," his father said, "we have no time for so much religion. We can't have a group of men here wasting their time."

Richard's reply was kindly but insistent: "Father, we must honour the Lord first, even if we pray all the forenoon and thresh this afternoon."

Father Burnham reluctantly agreed and afterwards admitted his son had done the right thing, for even the machinery seemed to work better when the day was started with prayer. And Richard's faithfulness to his conviction doubtless proved a stepping-stone towards the ministry for him. For he entered it and his son Fletcher after him.

Big David Allan was converted while working in a Bracebridge lumber camp in January, 1889. He asked the other men to remain after meals for Bible reading and prayer. The result, in his own words, was this: "Thank God, for about two months every man remained for prayer and before the camp broke up in the spring there were eight of us prayed three times a day." The reader will not be surprised to learn that Mr. Allan became a powerful worker for the Lord and his daughters Elizabeth and Margaret as well.

Little Georgia Wilkins was converted as a young girl at a Verona Camp in the 1890's. So great was her joy on the way home that it seemed the very trees were clapping their hands. But a heavy cross awaited her. Neither her father, mother, nor any of her ten brothers and sisters knew the Lord and there was a "family altar" to erect. To make the matter harder, frequent commercial travellers stayed at the home overnight, for the father was in other business along with his farming.

But for years Georgia read the Bible and carried on family prayers. And her devotion paid off. She lived to see her parents and several brothers and sisters saved and her three children in the church. At her death—the result of a car accident—people turned out to give her the biggest funeral the local undertaker had ever known. Her younger brother Harry, that she nurtured, has been a delegate to General Conference and a Lorne Park trustee. Her son has taught eight years at Lorne Park and has the present responsibility of completing this history.

Ready evidence for early fasting is understandably not as abundant as for praying. But pastors and people in good numbers frequently showed their concern for the work of the Lord by denying themselves thus and using the extra time for earnest prayer. This was especially practised at times of revival services when it was not uncommon for burden-bearers to fast a meal a day for definite people.

The *Free Methodist Discipline* in its "General Rules" (borrowed from Wesley) declares that those who desire to continue in the societies should attend upon all the ordinances of God and lists several including fasting and abstinence as well as family and private praying. Ministers to be received into full membership in an annual conference were to "recommend fasting or abstinence both by precept and example." Any minister was "to see that a fast be held in every society in his circuit on the Friday preceding every quarterly meeting."

In his own personal life the minister was advised to rise at five in the morning and spend the five-to-six hour in prayer, meditation, and the reading of the Scriptures and the writings of Mr. Wesley. Rev. H. B. Luck who laboured with more than average success in both eastern and western Canada went one better. According to his daughter, Mae Luck Gleddie, he rose between four and five A.M. to spend the morning hours in prayer. She goes on: "To stay abed any later, he felt for him would be grieving the Spirit. Beside this, on Tuesday and Friday, Dad fasted for breakfast and lunch using this extra time for prayer and study."

There could be some connection between that kind of religious discipline and a revival her letter spoke of. It was a fourteen-week Holt campaign her father conducted without the aid of an evangelist. In it some eighty people were converted and several dozen joined the church.

13.
THEY CULTIVATED CONGREGATIONAL MUSIC

The matter was never a moral issue. Yet those who founded the Free Methodist Church observing certain abuses in the parent body decided it would make for greater simplicity in worship to refrain from the use of choirs and musical instruments and concentrate instead on congregational music as Wesley had evidently done.

Small congregations doubtless suffered, but music composed of nothing but the human voice often produced some highly effective results. General Superintendent Jones after a Brantford camp meeting in 1895 wrote: "Large audiences were frequently held spell-bound by the harmonies and affecting melodies of the saints." So lusty was the singing at camp meetings in general that the singing on a calm evening could often be heard several miles away.

Between testimonies, there was a freedom in starting up songs suited to the sentiments expressed; anyone started them and the rest followed from memory for a verse or two. The same thing occurred during an "altar service." Many a time the earnest singing of a hymn of consecration around the altar was the inspiration that brought the seeker through to a desired assurance. Often those who gathered early for a service would improve the waiting minutes by this same kind of spontaneous singing. With such a beginning, the spirit of worship had well set in before the minister rose to announce the opening hymn. Of course, the "altar call" itself consisted of invitation singing punctuated with exhortations. As many as three or four songs might be used at one of these occasions.

The jazzy frothy chorus gaining a degree of popularity in evangelical circles in recent years is alien to the tone of early Free Methodism. In the main, the songs they sang were solid Bible-based ones that ran the whole range of human experience. What a wealth there was for every theme! Songs of warning as "Say, Where Is Thy Refuge, Poor Sinner?"; of invitation as "O Do Not Let the Word Depart"; of repentance as "I've Wandered Far Away From God"; of assurance as "How Firm a Foundation"; of recollection as "O Happy Day"; of consecration as "Jesus, I My Cross Have Taken"; of yearning for holiness as "O For a Faith That Will Not Shrink," or "O For That Flame of Living Fire," or "O For a Heart That Is Whiter Than Snow," or "O Glorious Hope of Perfect Love"; of holiness attained as "All Glory to Jesus Be Given," or "The Comforter Has Come," or "I Am Dwelling on the Mountain"; of trust as "He Leadeth Me"; of devotion as "Take Time to Be Holy," or "My Heart Is Fixed, Eternal God; of warfare as "I Storm the Gates of Strife"; of celestial bliss as "There's a Land Far Away."

Pity the poor person who has not participated in the congregational singing of songs such as these![1]

---

1. Hogue, in *History of the Free Methodist Church*, vividly recalls how the spontaneous singing of "Come on My Partners in Distress" by Rev. Wm. C. Kendall at the 1856 Genesee Conference, wonderfully encouraged some persecuted preachers who had just been read off for poor circuits because of their adherence to Basic Methodism.

14.
THEY EMPLOYED VISITATION EVANGELISM

Visitation evangelism is the modern name. The old timers called it pastoral calling, but, as we shall see, more than the pastors practised it.

And how they visited in those days—not just chatty social calls, but occasions for discussion of spiritual needs and pointed prayers. A common pattern for revival meetings was to spend the afternoons visiting in the homes with prayer meetings there. It seemed an effective way of getting the people out to evening service as well as softening their hearts for the invitation to the altar. Better still, they might get converted during the prayer meeting. W. H. Gregory tells of one such meeting with fourteen attendants and seven conversions.

At one early Hannon afternoon meeting, Mr. Sage told the host, a wicked old man, "It is now or never." When the sleigh loads started to leave, the old man murmured, "They have gone and left me to be damned," then fell on the floor crying for mercy. By the time the people had returned he was happy in the Lord. And the old fellow very soon was out telling his relatives and friends, "I am born again. Glory to God!"

At Sheffield Mr. Sage was warned not to stop at a certain house where a backslidden local preacher, now a drunkard, lived. It was feared the old man would give nothing but abuse. Mr. Sage did go, however, and won a convert instead. When the old man confided that he used to be a preacher but was "gone now," Mr. Sage told him to finish lighting his pipe and then sit down while he himself would sing. The song was "How Lost Was My Condition Till Jesus Made Me Whole." It made the old man cry like a child. A few nights after, he found God again.

M. S. Benn tells of an old man who rediscovered the Free Methodists through visiting, after knowing them eighteen years earlier. He came to church and sat at the back at first but night after night worked his way forward, until he began seeking the Lord. He had been steeped in tobacco for fifty years but finally got the victory over it and went about the village telling of his deliverance. The man was in heaven eleven months later.

At Brantford Mrs. Grace Cowherd, mother of India missionaries Effie Cowherd and Harriet McCready, found the Lord because a Mrs. Taylor visited over the line fence and invited her out to prayer meeting. You will read how a David Allan convert in Muskoka sparked a revival by visiting and persuading his hosts to read the Bible when he couldn't read himself.

Rev. R. Burnham while at Verona in 1895 was commended by his superintendent for his activity in visiting. The report added: "No man is a true pastor who for any excuse fails to visit his people in their homes." It is not strange that this man was "well liked on the circuit," and that God was "coming in power to Verona."

Tommy Clark, a layman who says he was probably the first Free Methodist in Canada, and who features again and again in the early story, shows in his Free Tract Society autobiography "Happy Tom" just what was possible through visiting. He wrote: "I believe the Lord called me, soon after I was converted, to visit homes, read and pray with people and try to get them saved.[1] The Lord has rewarded my labours, for I have seen many converted in their homes. One place I visited where two families lived in the same house, I invited them all into one room to have prayer meeting. If I remember right, all the grown people sought the Lord and professed to be saved, except one old man, and he said he would seek until he found the Lord.

"Another time I visited the home of a young woman. I asked her if she was a Christian. She said she was a Church member. I talked to her about salvation, then we knelt down and she began to seek the Lord, and when her husband came in she jumped up and put her arms around his neck and said, 'I've got it; I've got it.'"

---

1. He reported 515 visits one year while living in Toronto.

15.
THEY OVERCAME THE OBSTACLE OF INADEQUACY

The desirable situation was, of course, a church at each preaching point, a parsonage for each circuit, and to man the work, a male educated parson who had offered himself to the conference. But in an expansion program of the sort they ran, a community might frequently be devoid of all these desirables and yet get Free Methodized. They used the technique called improvising.

Quite often the "meeting house" was simply somebody's home or the town hall; the parsonage, some donated or rented quarters anywhere; and the parson a pair of girls who had offered themselves, or a conscripted layman who preached while studying at home on the curriculum for travelling preachers. He might even be only a resident "local preacher" who held things together while earning his living in the usual local way. The women workers, the local leaders and the home study program will be developed separately in later chapters but a bit more on the improvised churches and parsonages will be noted here.

The first meetings reported in Galt were being held in a Rhodes home before the first Canadian pastor even arrived. The first Sombra services were in a Haley home. In May 1881, the Gananoque pastor, Austin Allguire, rowed Mr. Sage a dozen miles or more down the St. Lawrence to hold a quarterly meeting in the David home on Wells Island (one of the famous Thousand Islands). About thirty-five took the Lord's Supper and twelve were baptized. In the same year James Craig preached to "a good congregation in Sister Scott's kitchen" ten miles out of Huntsville.

These homes were often regarded as "hitching posts" in new communities. Such a one too was that of a "Sister Stockwell" converted in some Marston meetings at Sheffield. A negro attended these services and invited Mr. Sage to his home. Some feared a decline in interest but in the end that negro and his wife were born into the family that knows no skin barriers.

A Brantford society formed about 1885, grew to thirty members and still met in private homes.

Living quarters, we have noted, posed a real problem when a new minister was sent to an undeveloped circuit. In 1892 we read of "Brother Angus Harnden" of Harnden's Mills north of Cobourg having set aside two rooms for the pastor and his wife and another for preaching. The pastor at this time was Emerson Snyder.

In 1895, W. H. Gregory took his bride of about a year to a newly created Westport-Fermoy circuit where there was no parsonage, no church, no membership, and no calling list—a perfect "paper circuit." Mrs. Gregory used her hope chest for a cupboard and what they used for a cover from the weather is not recorded, but it was in the predominantly Roman Catholic community of Fermoy.

The important thing, however, for which they went was achieved—they raised up a circuit. When they left in 1898 regular services were being held not only at the two specified points but in two other communities near Westport as well as at Maberly some distance away. And societies had been organized at Maberly and Fermoy. There were still no churches but a town hall, an upstairs hall, a union church or private home sufficed.

16.
THEY WENT TO COLLEGE AT HOME

The classic definition of a college is Mark Hopkins, a famous American teacher, on one end of a log and a boy on the other. The quaint picture illustrates the teacher-pupil relation, so essential in any learning process. But if the pupil can't go to the teacher, it is often possible for the pupil to get the teacher's book and study that—with very helpful results.

Opportunities for advanced study in college, Bible school, or even high school were often most limited in Free Methodism's early days. For those men who were pressed into the ministry with little formal education, more study was imperative and a home study course was the answer.

Free Methodism did not pioneer this program for its ministers. Wesley had a study schedule for his preachers and, following it, some of them became very cultured men. The great Egerton Ryerson of Canadian Methodism was not university-bred, though he became president of Methodism's Victoria College and then Superintendent of Ontario's educational system. The Methodist ministers' course of study cannot be overlooked in the making of this mighty man. By a special Carleton University lecture (now published), Prof. Robin Harris of Toronto University has recently made sure that it isn't.[1]

The 1875 study program laid down for Free Methodist ministers had a "Preliminary Course For Those Who Wished to Join the Travelling Connection on Trial." It included Composition, Grammar, Spelling, Geography, Arithmetic, and Free Methodist Discipline.

This was followed by a four-year schedule that prepared candidates academically for both ordinations—deacon and elder. Some of the solid books to be mastered for examination were Watson's *Institutes*, Binney's *Compend*, Wesley's *Plain Account* and *Sermons*, Arthur's *Tongue of Fire*, Roberts' *Fishers of Men*, Wood's *Perfect Love*, Bangs' *History of Methodism*, Bowen's *Origin of the Free Methodist Church*, Angus' *Hand-Book of the Bible*, True's *Logic*, Butler's *Analogy*, and Mosheim's *Church History*.

From time to time some of the texts and course content changed. For instance, Ralston's *Divinity* replaced Watson's *Institutes*; Hogue's *Homiletics and Pastoral Theology*, Reed's *Rules of Order* and Hurlbut's *Biblical Geography* all came later. Sim's *Helps to Bible Study* served its time too.

It was a program that took application to complete, and study habits developed were not likely to be suddenly dropped. Lest they should be, the report of the Committee on Education in 1883 reminded preachers that the duty to study "by no means ceases when our examinations on the courses of study are over." [2] Without formal high schooling, F. A. Daw left the plow for the pulpit in 1920, yet with the foundation of the home-study program he became such a keen scholar, prolific writer and preacher of the Word that he served with distinction as editor of the *Canadian Free Methodist Herald* for several years before his early death and in 1939 received an impressive number of votes at General Conference for the bishopric.

---

1. See *Our Living Tradition* (University of Toronto Press), a collection of special lectures on great Canadians given at Carleton University.
2. Wesley expected his preachers to spend at least five hours daily in reading useful books. For those who had no taste he directed: "Contract a taste . . . , or return to your former employment." The *Free Methodist Discipline* incorporated all of this Methodist matter.

17.
THEY ENLISTED LAY LEADERSHIP

A shortage of workers is not just a modern condition; it has existed from the beginning. The echo of the need seems particularly strong in the records of the early 1890's. One reads in James Craig's "Itinerating" of 1891, at the point where he describes his quarterly meeting visit to Harwood, a busy saw-milling village on Rice Lake, "People are calling for Free Methodist preaching and it seems there might soon be a circuit worked up if some good labourer could give some time to the field." Or in A. Sims' "Notes by the Way" of 1892: "I pray God to send us some more fire-baptized men and women . . . the labourers are few." The near despair of A. H. Norrington about this time comes out pathetically in his written prayer: "O Lord, can they not be found?"

With such a scarcity it is understandable that the leaders did not always wait for volunteers. If a young man showed some promise in his prayers and exhortations he was in a fair way to get asked. B. P. Clark, staying in the home of young Miles Benn at Petworth, sought the privilege of sleeping with Miles. The reason: so he could ask "Miley" about the ministry. "Have you ever felt called to be a preacher?" he began. "I have consulted all the spiritual people in the community, and all agree you should be." Young Miles couldn't answer "No" to the question, so in due time he was "read off." [1]

But often they relied heavily on strong laymen to help out on the home circuit. These might be granted first an "Exhorter's License" and later, as their gifts grew, a "Local Preacher's License." One such would probably be a class leader and help with the prayer meetings and preaching on some of the out-points, especially if the pastor were busy elsewhere or attending district meeting. And if no pastor could be found at conference time, he might "supply" as a pastor locally if the conference didn't read him off for a circuit somewhere else. It was not wise in those days to take on the name of being a disciple, if you were unwilling to assume the responsibilities of discipleship. Some of these men were decidedly used of God in exhortation at revivals, in preaching, and in prayer. If they had a gift of song too, as Will Goodberry at Verona had, they were doubly a blessing.

The custom actually goes back to English Methodism days. Mabel Richmond Brailsford in her biography, *A Tale of Two Brothers* (Rupert Hart-Davis) tells us that John Wesley's decision to let men preach without ordination was based on urgings from his mother Susanna. (Charles, in particular, was very adverse to the idea.) They would work at a trade or in business, prepare sermons in their spare time and deliver these free of charge at some neighbouring chapel on Sunday. While the custom has its obvious dangers, God has nevertheless used it through the years since, in Methodist meetings around the world.[2] He certainly used it in Free Methodist meetings in Canada.

You will read about a few individual titans in the later chapter, "Some Local Laymen Who Could Lift."

---

1. Mr. Benn declares that before this he had heard—almost audibly—"Go preach my gospel." Evidently he had not yet made it public.

2. Both John Wesley and B. T. Roberts were themselves led to conversion by lay churchmen.

18.
THEY ALLOWED LADIES TO CARRY ARMS

Sketching the course of events in 1898 (twenty-two years after the Free Methodist foothold had been gained) James Craig, a District Elder then, wrote: "One of the most prominent facts in connection with this work is that much of it has been raised up by the labours of female preachers. These female preachers do not have a very conspicuous place in the records of the church, but their record is on high and their work of faith and labour of love is alike creditable to themselves and the church."

Mr. Craig's wife, Mary, herself an able preacher, did a 1700-word tribute to the ladies for the *Free Methodist* of May 3, 1898. An elegant piece of writing, it was called "Woman's Work in Canadian Free Methodism," and is included here only in part:

"... most of those employed have been women of very moderate native ability and with few educational advantages. Their labours as preachers of the gospel have been signally successful, notwithstanding a great deal of aversion to and prejudice against them as labourers in this capacity. . . . They have served the church as stewards, class leaders, Sabbath school teachers and superintendents, delegates to the annual conferences and preachers of the gospel. . . . They have gone alike to the homes of the rich and the poor. Indeed, this visiting from house to house has been one of the marked features of their work, and has no doubt been productive of much of the good which has been accomplished. Sometimes they have found comfortable lodgings, and sometimes very uncomfortable; but, realizing they were following in the footsteps of the One who came 'not to be ministered unto, but to minister,' they have cheerfully pressed forward to rescue the perishing and bring them as trophies to the cross of Christ. They have sung the sweet songs of Zion; they have offered the fervent, effectual prayer, which availeth much; with their own skilful hands they have lifted burdens from other over-laden shoulders; they have cheered the weary pilgrim, lifted up the down-trodden, have spoken the word in season to the discouraged one, and faithfully admonished those who have needed reproof. They have also stood before large assemblies of attentive listeners, and, with lips that had felt the touch of the 'live coal' from off God's altar, have been enabled to 'preach the word' with the Holy Ghost sent down from heaven; thus proving the declaration of Scripture true, that the hand-maidens, as well as the servants, shall in these last days prophesy.

"Some of the most extensive and lasting revivals which have been connected with the Free Methodist church in Canada have been conducted by women. Some of our best preachers have been converted in these revivals. Some of our largest and best circuits have been raised up under their labours. Also through their management church property has been acquired and church buildings have been erected.

"The work of women has not been altogether as evangelists, but they have also been very successful as pastors. It can easily be perceived that the Free Methodist Church in Canada could not well afford to be depleted by eliminating from their work that which has been accomplished through the agency of women. . . .[1]

"We think no country can boast of better wives, better mothers, or better daughters, than this fair Dominion of Canada. Get them saved and they are a host for God. They have proven themselves trustworthy. Put them in the home, if God wills, and let them fill the honoured place of wife and mother. Put them in the kitchen, if there they can shine to the greatest advantage. Let them go forth as so-called deaconesses to minister to the sick, alleviate the sufferings of the poor, and carry the sunshine of Christian sympathy and kindness into the dark attics and damp cellars of squalor and misery. This is a good work, 'a noble work,' and they can do it well. Or, if divinely called and qualified to carry the message of reconciliation and salvation to the perishing millions of the earth, as freely accord to them that privilege also, and give them the liberty of the pulpit and platform; that so the Scripture prophecy may speedily be fulfilled, which declares, 'The women that published the tidings are a great host.' "

Hogue's *History of the Free Methodist Church* states that the employment of women in the ministry had been done "by no other Conference so extensively as the Canada." (The single conference till 1895 was called the Canada Conference.) The conference of 1882 sent at least ten of them out—"all neatly and plainly dressed," wrote B. T. Roberts. He added, "Bro. Sage says that the young men whom God has called to the work generally refuse to go, and so he has to send out the young women."

Mr. Sage said further in his *Autobiography*: "When I persuaded the sisters to enter the work, I told them particularly that they need not try to preach. I told them to take their Bibles and read a chapter and explain it as best they could, and then call on the people to pray with them and thus in a simple way carry them the gospel message. If I had set them to preaching the first thing, they would have made a failure. . . . They went out into the streets and lanes and prayed with the people and urged them to come to Christ. They went forth weeping, bearing precious seed and souls were saved through these means."

Mr. Roberts was strongly behind the use of women too. In 1891 he published a book called *Ordaining Women* which he said was written from a strong conviction of duty. It was customary at first to license the Canadian women simply as "Evangelists." [2] Yet armed with little else but Bibles and hymnbooks, some of these evangelists cut swaths incredibly wide and clean into Satan's Kingdom.

And lest it be suspected that the unmarried ones reduced their chances of matrimony by this practice, let it be stated here that dozens of them eventually married (often preachers), and one even became a bishop's wife.

---

1. Mr. Craig in 1894 wrote a pamphlet stating that the last session of conference had given appointments to one elder, three deacons, three evangelists, and four preachers not yet ordained, that had been converted under the labours of women. It noted also that the following circuits were "raised up principally by the labours of female preachers": Armadale, Belhaven, Severn Bridge and Barkway, Lansdowne, Port Credit, Ebenezer, Middlemiss, Walsingham, Brantford, Keith and Thorncliffe.

2. Free Methodists were later among the first to ordain women in Canada. This was after the General Conference of 1911 made provision for Women Deacons on an equal basis with men. Alice Walls of West Ontario was the first Free Methodist woman ordained in Canada (in 1918) and probably the second of any denomination. Sara Gregory and Bessie Reid in 1934 were East Ontario's first.

19.
THEY DEMANDED THE DISCIPLINE OF A SEPARATED LIFE

Wesley, according to Dr. George Turner in *The More Excellent Way* (Light and Life Press) pioneered an "emphasis on religion as purity of life as well as purity of faith." But Canadian Methodism, about the time Free Methodism was arriving, seemed to be getting plagued with something called worldliness. Of course, not all accepted it silently.

Robert Walker, a Primitive Methodist conference president, in his annual address of 1875 grieved over conditions as he saw them. What courage it must have taken to speak so frankly:

"Dress like the world; talk like the world; dissemble like the world; mix with the world; dance with the world; play with the world; join with the world in foolish amusements; go to the theatre and opera with the world; marry with the world; and the great majority of professors who do this are in great danger of finally going to hell with the world."

But he was apparently unable to halt the trend much. Free Methodists did "draw the line" on these and a lot of other "popular sins." As well as holding an orthodox body of doctrine, they insisted solidly on standards of conduct. Some activities winked at by other communions were just not for their members. The list included many things: taking the Lord's name in vain; profaning the Lord's day; buying, selling or imbibing spirituous liquors; buying, selling or using tobacco; buying or selling smuggled goods; belonging to secret orders; indulging in uncharitable conversation; wearing gold, pearls or other superfluous adornments, also costly clothes; living beyond one's income level; singing and reading what did not tend to the knowledge or love of God; taking diversions as could not be used in the name of the Lord Jesus. (This latter restriction was commonly considered to refer to such practices as dancing, card-playing, and theatre or movie-house attending.)

Again and again one reads of revivals that produced radical wardrobe revisions, changes in habits, associations and the like.[1] Perhaps at times some externals were over emphasized, but the stress was a constant reminder that evangelical conversion was a thorough thing and must reach to every area of one's living.

It is admitted that such standards would be irksome or even impossible for the "natural man," but let it be remembered that they were made for people who by the grace of God had already become "new creatures" and were now "in earnest to get to heaven." To defend, one by one, these disciplines is not the purpose of this chapter, although it should be noted that stronger cases can be made for them than many people suppose.

Actually when one had undergone deep conviction for sin, many of the old habits often had a way of dropping off quite naturally. As Wesley put it of his General Rules, "All these we know the Spirit writes on truly awakened hearts." Take Mrs. Kile of Battram, Sask., who came to church dressed like a haughty movie star. She sought the Lord the first night. The next night she was back "dressed like a saint," yet no one had mentioned clothes to her. Or Hannon's Adolphus Freeman (church member and class leader) who threw away his tobacco once convinced that it was not for Christians.[2]

Discipline, properly understood, is actually a means of making people free. It frees them from the things that are either harmful or trivial, so time, money, energy and health may be conserved for the things that are significant and eternal. Wise old Wesley probably realized these ends of discipline as few people in history. He considered, for instance, that ornamentation or extravagance in dress was unworthy of Christians because it engendered pride, tended to increase vanity or love of admiration, and left less money with which to help the needy. The argument of being able to "afford" fine things impressed him not at all. "O lay aside forever that idle nonsensical word! No Christian can afford to waste any part of the substance which God has entrusted him with," he preached.

Among Free Methodists, jewellry, along with many other things, went. A Mrs. Robert Elsom of Moose Jaw understood the spirit of I Peter 3:3-4 well, when asked by a friend, "Why do you never wear jewellry?" Her answer: "I think God is more pleased with us if we wear it on the inside."

We have pointed out that discipline's negatives can help people be more positive. Free Methodists were expected to be super positive, separated *from* some things so they could the better be separated *unto* more important things. They were to be busy in deeds of mercy such as feeding the hungry, clothing the naked, visiting the sick, as well as attending the various church services, giving sacrificially of their money for the church's program, and sharing responsibility generally. Keeping their personal faith bright by Bible study and prayer was a part of the discipline too.

All of this broadly interpreted program of separation went to make up what was commonly called "practical godliness."

---

1. Martha Thomas, Kelvin's fashionable dressmaker, did not take long after her conversion to decide that making fashionable clothes was as questionable as wearing them.

2. Long before the days when medical science began pointing towards a relation between tobacco using and certain diseases, Free Methodists had decided the habit was costly, useless and even filthy—quite unworthy of one who regarded his body as "the temple of the Holy Ghost."

20.
THEY WORKED WITH THE YOUNG

Sunday Schools seem to have begun among the Free Methodists almost as early as preaching services. One year after the church was planted in

Canada, it was recorded that two of the four existing societies had Sunday Schools employing between them ten officers and teachers and enrolling forty scholars altogether.

There is a record of a Sunday School with an attendance of about fifty at Merrill's Mills near Norwich as early as 1880. This came on the heels of a Sims-held revival that had produced a new society.

It was the feeling of a "Sabbath School Committee" at the conference of 1883 that both the laity and the preachers weren't getting behind the movement as they should and the report they wrote roasted the offenders properly. It read in part:

"As a people we are entirely too negligent about Sabbath-schools. The reports from our circuits are quite often all a blank on this subject. My brethren, these things ought not so to be. We have talents for this work that are buried, and God will hold us to an account for them at the judgment. There are many fathers and mothers and young people that can occupy plenty of time in our meetings; they can pray loud and strong, and talk loud; but when they come to the important work of gathering in, and teaching the dear little ones, they have no heart, talent nor tact, neither money to be used in this direction. Why this lack of interest? Simply because it is not begun and pushed forward by our preachers. They are the generals and captains of this salvation army. And unless a persistent effort is made in this direction, and backed up by our people, the matter will remain a dead letter; and our children will go uninstructed on the Sabbath day. We have plenty of latent power available; all we lack is action—yes, continued, energetic effort on our part as a people. Shall we have it? We are resolved that we will."

This blast must have infused new fervour into the phlegmatic, for the next year despite a lull in church membership gains, there were more Sunday Schools, more workers, and at least 25 per cent more attendants.

Any mention of Sunday Schools would be incomplete without reference to the work of David Kirk in Western Canada. Mr. Kirk, who directed the first one there near Belmont, Manitoba, used to pick up both children and adults in his old lumber wagon. As he moved in Abrahamic fashion across the West, it became a habit not to build an altar but to start a new Sunday School wherever he stopped.

Sunday School reports for each of the three existing conferences were published in the *Free Methodist* as part of a church-wide semi-centennial stock-taking in 1910. East and West Ontario boasted thirty-three and thirty-nine schools respectively, but East Ontario had the bigger membership: 1,425 against 1,037. Western Canada, though not yet four years old as a conference, had twelve schools and 486 scholars enrolled. West Ontario had begun Teacher Training classes in some places (as Sarnia in 1908) and had held two Sunday School conventions during the previous year.

Special evangelistic children's meetings were often held at the camp meetings, with conversions as clear as those of the adults. Long before the days of formal child and youth organizations, Mrs. W. H. Gregory was a very effective worker among the young wherever her pastor-husband was sent. At Bracebridge, for instance, she held daily after-school meetings for the high school group. Numbers got established in the Christian way at those meetings and from them came stalwart preachers and preachers' wives. When her husband was a district elder, she would organize children's services at the weekend quarterly meetings. At these many children were converted. All this was not at the expense of Sunday School emphasis. Mrs. Gregory herself was responsible for the organization of twelve new Sunday Schools in East Ontario. In the 1930's she was that conference's Sunday School Secretary. (Miss Kate Clark, while holding the same office earlier, made 1917 a special promotional year by seeing that the various circuits got a personal visit—the first time it had happened—to urge more interest in the Sunday School department.)

Eventually a distinct youth organization appeared across the church—the Young People's Missionary Society in 1919. Actually it was more than a missionary society for it functioned under four departments—evangelism, education, service, and missions. For eight early years, Dr. B. H. Pearson, who has since become widely known outside the church as a missionary, educator, and author, was General Superintendent of the Y.P.M.S., as it was called, and made frequent trips to Canada. Mostly, Canada has been looked after through a Regional Director who on several occasions has been a Canadian. Rev. E. A. Cooper of West Ontario and Rev. D. H. Russell of Alberta have both held this office for the region that included the Canadian conferences. Through this organization with its conference, district and local executives, young people have gained practice in preparing programs, conducting meetings, holding offices, raising money, giving money, and taking responsibility generally. Sometimes they sponsored meetings of evangelism. One stated aim was to seek and maintain among its members the highest type of Christian experience . . . and to prepare them for efficient membership in the Free Methodist Church. Each local society had an adult superintendent responsible for its organization and promotion. Even before the Y.P.M.S. was functioning, there was an active J.M.S. on many circuits training the children in missionary matters.

More recently—in the 1930's—a C.Y.C. or Christian Youth Crusaders organization has appeared. Designed for both boys and girls of the intermediate age, it is organized to some extent on scouting principles but with a strong salvation emphasis. It is filling a gap that existed for a long time and with its program of summer camps holds promise of winning and holding for God and the Church many who otherwise would have been lost.

21.
THEY SANCTIONED SALVATION SCHOOLS

The term is not used now but it was a live one forty to seventy years ago in the Canadian church. Free Methodism's founder Roberts and some of his colleagues were college-trained. (Roberts like Wesley, had the M.A. degree.) They knew they must have a school to train ministers, missionaries, and even sound laymen. Six years after the American church was formed, Roberts, assuming a $10,000 mortgage himself,[1] bought a farm at North Chili, near Rochester, and started a school which still continues. (It is degree-granting Roberts Wesleyan College today.) Michigan had its Spring Arbor Seminary by 1873. Others followed in later decades.

Few of the leaders of early Canadian Free Methodism were educated men in the formal sense. But they had a healthy regard for schools and learning. It is interesting to trace the growth of this sentiment through the early records.

As early as 1883, it appears. The conference report of the three-man Committee On Education extolls the virtues of education, stresses its special importance for the minister and concludes:

"We have great pleasure in recommending our seminaries at Spring Arbor, Mich., and North Chili, N.Y., to our people in Canada. And we earnestly advise them to send their children to these schools. These institutions are conducted on sound principles and are in an eminent sense, salvation schools. We are profoundly convinced of the immense advantages, both mentally and morally, to be derived from a training in these seminaries, and we pledge to patronize them."

The 1884 report was in similar vein but spoke of four seminaries, especially the two nearer ones. It is said that in the animated discussion that followed the reading of it many were "melted to tears."

By early 1887, Rev. A. Sims was emboldened to urge lengthily in *The Free Methodist*, "A Salvation School for Canada." It would give birth to more labourers, provide an alternative for the unsatisfactory atmosphere of the common schools, and encourage many to get an education who wouldn't go across the border. "In a Dominion that boasts of more square miles than there are in the whole United States, we know of not a single school conducted on salvation principles," he wrote. Mr. Sims reviewed the resources—waiting centrally-located land, sufficient money, trained teachers—and suggested the matter be "ventilated a little" through the church paper.

How much it got ventilated we did not investigate, but at conference time in October (the article had appeared in February) a fresh five-man Committee On Establishing a School in Canada chaired by J. Craig hustled together a get-going report. In particular, it recommended another commitee of five to secure a site and solicit subscriptions. Such a committee (mostly themselves) was straightway named.

But the committee must have been dormant or just over-cautious. By

1891 there was still only a committee, although the personnel was partly changed.

It was the daring Westerners twenty years later who first experimented. Their project was a short-term Bible School opened in the chapel at Weyburn, Saskatchewan, the same fall its board was appointed.[2] It ran for a three-month period through the winter of 1911-1912 with twenty students and seemed a success but was not continued.[3] R. H. Hamilton, the Weyburn pastor, had been the drive behind it. He failed to find sufficient leadership to justify opening again the next year at quarters partly arranged for in Estevan.

Not till 1924 did something permanent get started—Lorne Park Seminary (now College) at Port Credit, Ont., Saskatchewan followed with Moose Jaw Bible School (now College) in 1940. Their stories will be told later.

One feels that a major reason for the Free Methodist delay in starting "salvation schools" must have been the shortage of men in their ranks who themselves had much formal education. Such a handicap would make it difficult to display real leadership. But although they did not start salvation schools for a long time, the fathers kept the vision and, as we have said, sanctioned such institutions.

And while they tarried, numbers of ministerial candidates did attend denominational salvation schools in the United States. Those who didn't were required to work off the church's home-study course in preparation for ordination. Another reference later to this.

---

1. Mr. Roberts carried the school property mortgage personally for twenty years.
2. The Board was composed of F. M. Wees (President), R. H. Hamilton (Secretary-Treasurer), E. Steer, Robert Stephenson, and David Kirk.
3. Midford Kirk, son of David Kirk, and Midford's wife were among the students. They were also among the early students at Moose Jaw more than a dozen years later.

22.
THEY LET LITERATURE HELP THEM

Literature has always been a Methodist emphasis. John Wesley, besides preaching more than 40,000 sermons, published over 200 books and pamphlets and pioneered tract evangelism. He considered literature promotion a serious religious obligation. Editor Egerton Ryerson made the Methodist *Christian Guardian* the most widely circulated newspaper in Upper Canada about 1834. B. T. Roberts founded his own *Earnest Christian* magazine before he founded Free Methodism and continued to publish it for many years afterwards. He wrote books too on a variety of subjects ranging from evangelism to economics.

The *Free Methodist* magazine was first started by Rev. T. B. Arnold as a personal project to promote Free Methodism. It was bought by the church in 1886.¹ Long before Canadian Free Methodists had their own periodical this deeply devotional weekly came into many of their homes keeping them informed on policies of the church, as well as its progress both below and above the border. A great deal was written on Canada—some by American leaders who visited Canada, but much by Canadians themselves. Indeed, those early writings were a prominent source of facts for this history. Some of these scribes, as may be seen from excerpts used, were penmen and penwomen of ability. Arnold on his Chicago press early published a series of Sunday School papers which were widely used. The Canada Conference of 1883 commended them.

The *Missionary Tidings* appeared in 1897 and helped Canadians keep in touch with denominational activity around the world, including that of their own missionaries. Two early Canadian women, Mrs. Mary Craig and Mrs. Agnes Benn served periods as associate editors.

Rev. A. Sims for some years around 1900 operated his own publishing business in Toronto and seems to have been quite a promoter of his products and others.² His included over one hundred tracts and a monthly magazine that carried various names at various times. (*The Holiness Berean*, and *The Lamp of Life* were two.) His magazine helped people hear of Free Methodism. He made Trent Bridge (near Norwood), a preaching point because a lady had run across his magazine in the early eighties and wrote in for services. Mr. Sims wrote and published over fifty books and booklets too. His *Helps to Bible Study* was for years on the church-wide ministerial curriculum and his literature in general seemed well received.

An official monthly called *Western Tidings* was published in Alberta for a time beginning in December, 1910, and covered the prairie provinces.³ Later (in the fall of 1921) the Saskatchewan people began their short-lived *Saskatchewan Tidings*.

Gradually the notion of a distinctly all-Canadian magazine caught on. The story of its beginning, growth, and ministry will be reserved for later treatment.

---

1. It was through reading one or the other of *Earnest Christian* or *Free Methodist* that Canadians Robert Loveless and George Bunce first learned of Free Methodism.

2. A note at the bottom of an advertising page in the back of one of his books reads: "Agents wanted in every town, city and country to sell our Publications. Liberal terms for cash. Write for particulars. Catalogue free." He even on occasion would send an unsolicited bundle to a brother minister in the hope of increasing circulation.

3. Before Alberta's first preacher, Rev. O. L. King, had been in the Edmonton area for a year we read his "district" purchased a secondhand printing press for $50.

23.
THEY REMEMBERED THE REGIONS BEYOND

Methodism came to America because Asbury and others had missionary hearts and offered themselves. Free Methodism came to Canada because C. H. Sage who officially brought it had what Mr. Roberts called "the missionary fire" and did not falter when appointed.

Mrs. Mary Craig, wife of a pioneer Canadian superintendent, developed a burden for missions as early as 1891 and shared it with General Superintendent Hart at Brantford conference time.[1] Accordingly, she and Mrs. Elizabeth Sims, wife of the eastern superintendent, were given conference authority to organize Women's Foreign Missionary Societies across Canada Conference.[2] (An offering and subscription of $129.62 were taken at that conference—probably the first Free Methodist mission money raised in Canada.) The pair must have taken the assignment seriously, for they came back in a year and reported 18 societies with 176 active members and 64 honorary ones and $65 gathered. Promotion must have been stronger in the western end of the province where Mrs. Craig was, for she had organized thirteen of the societies and had all the money. Her husband was cited as having strong mission interest too.

The conference executive of 1893 included Mrs. Craig as president, Miss Josie Rusk (later Mrs. F. M. Wees) as secretary and Mrs. Martha (wife of Rev. W. H.) Wilson as treasurer. Givings for that 1892-93 year and for the next two showed a healthy upward swing. The figures read $174.20, $186.98 and $327.02.

The 1895 year was the last for the Canada Conference. From 1896 on, we read of East Ontario and West Ontario instead. By the end of that first year on a divided basis, East Ontario had taken the lead in giving—$250.91 against $243.25, a total of $494.16.

Western Canada was soon to have the status of a mission field with some of our ladies named above there themselves. We shall see that the Wilsons and the Wees went, also Mrs. Wilson's sister, Jennie Robinson, and a young man named J. W. Haley.

Mr. Haley had a W.F.M.S. society moving on his new Westview, Sask., circuit in 1900. By 1903 the women of the new Manitoba and Northwest District of the West Ontario Conference had organized at Moose Jaw at the district level and in 1907 the Alberta sisters at a Hurry District Meeting made Mrs. Lizzie King their first district president.

1920 turns out to be a historic year in Canadian Free Methodism. By then, four Canadian conferences functioned. In them over sixty W.F.M.S. societies flourished. Total givings for missions in Canada, in that 1919-20 year was over $12,700. About $100,000 had been raised since the mission emphasis began.

But Canadian Free Methodists were not content with gifts of money and workers to the West. As would be expected, some began hearing the more distant call and offered themselves for foreign service. It started with J. W. Haley. Two years after going to Western Canada he was on his way in 1902 to a distinguished 43-year career in Africa—first in the south, later pioneering in the Belgian Congo. His wife, Esther Jane, followed in 1905 and his brother Albert and future wife Matilda in 1905 and 1906, they also to Africa and for almost as long.

Others kept going. C. Floyd Appleton to China in 1904, Lucy Tittemore (later Perkins) to the same country in 1907, Effie G. Cowherd to India in 1914, J. W. Winans to the Dominican Republic in 1907, I. S. W. Ryding to China in 1916 (this followed by service in Hong Kong), Ethel Davey (later Ryff) to South Africa in 1918, Bessie Reid (later Kresge) to China in 1925 (this followed by South Africa service), Lawrence and Ruth (Secord) Arksey to Portuguese East Africa in 1927 (this followed by a period in Southern Rhodesia), Pearl Reid to China in 1934 (this followed by more recent service in Japan), Ronald and Margaret (Henwood) Collett to the Belgian Congo in 1937, Wesley and Lela (Swayze) DeMille to Portuguese East Africa in the same year (more recently in Transvaal), Dr. Lois Kent to India in 1938, Marjorie Peach to Congo-Nile in 1938 (since 1948 in South Africa as wife of Dr. Lowell Rice), Burton and Dorothy (Haley) McCready to the Belgian Congo in 1940, Peace (Haley) Berg to the Belgian Congo in 1940. Fuller stories on most of these people will appear in the biography part.

Other missionaries who have gone out from 1950 on will be mentioned in a later section. Home Missions in Northern Ontario will be dealt with later, also.

While missions should be everybody's business and men have naturally done much of the actual giving as well as attending meetings and participating in programs as honorary members, the fact remains that in the Free Methodist Church the ladies through their W.F.M.S. (or since 1925, W.M.S.), have been the mainspring of the missionary emphasis. As Rev. Carl Howland puts it in *The Story of Our Church*, they have "furnished the larger part of the enthusiasm and raised the larger part of the money."

It was this ladies' organization, too, that sponsored both the J.M.S. for the children and the Y.P.M.S. for youth when there seemed a need for missionary societies geared to these different age groups.

---

1. According to Mrs. Craig, this burden developed before she knew there was any such organization in the church. She had, however, been earlier connected with a Home Missions Society in the U. S. before coming to Canada.

2. The first foreign mission organization among any American F. M. ladies had occurred only two years before, although a General Missionary Board had been in existence from 1874. The General W. F. M. S. did not begin till 1894, so Mrs. Craig had the distinction of drafting a "Constitution and By-Laws" a year before the general church had one.

24.
THEY FINANCED BY FREE-WILL OFFERINGS

Free Methodists could find no scriptural basis for raising needed church money by entertainment or supper sales and consequently did not employ these methods. In fact, the increasing tendency among Ontario Methodist congregations to resort to church socials made not a few members more ready than ever to welcome a different brand of Methodism. The George Teals of Ridgeway, for instance, were a couple who sought out a Free Methodist preacher across the border in Buffalo after they had decided that tea meetings were not for them and had started prayer meetings in their homes.

It was amazing how money really needed came in by the voluntary approach. J. A. Robb recalls a camp meeting near Fort William in 1918—the first in the area—where Elder Allan, with embarrassment told the congregation of scarcely fifty people that $250 was needed for camp expenses. A few minutes later, with tears running down his face, he was exclaiming, "Stop, brethren, we have more than we asked for." Mr. Robb continued, "Never have I witnessed more joyous giving nor more of the blessing of the Lord descend upon a congregation in the act of giving."

The method meant, of course, that individual members had to assume larger chunks of debt when a church or parsonage was built or bought. But they did it cheerfully and kept costs to the minimum by donating many hours of labour. (See, for example, Hymers and Kingston stories.) Before a church was dedicated, it was customary to have it paid for, or at least have the remaining debt covered by subscriptions. The pledging portion of one of those services was an expectant occasion as members, adherents and visiting friends, "promised to pay." The Doxology often got sung more than once in the holy hilarity that followed the announcement of a reached objective. You will read such a story in the Oak Flats report.

Voluntary giving provided surprising sums for foreign missions too. It seemed the Alberta saints were constantly giving to one cause or another outside their borders.

Yet there were at least a few laymen, even in those days, who were branded as "stingy."

25.
THEY DENIED THEMSELVES FOR THE WELFARE OF THE WORK

Closely related to the theme of the last chapter was the practice of self-denial so common among people and preacher alike.

Members gave sacrificially for regular expenses and especially for expansion programs. Hiram Gilroy of St. Joseph Island in 1897 pledged ten dollars on the new church and earned it by picking stone from sunrise to sunset at 75 cents a day. Those acquainted with the Gananoque-Lansdowne circuit in the decades around 1900 cannot forget the big hearts of the William McNeils. Annie Slack (later Ball) wrote: "Very few sacrifice like they did that they might support the work." W. H. Gregory claims that the Gananoque church and parsonage were built largely through the generosity of those saintly farm folk.

Denying oneself to assist the Lord's work or worker was considered to bring its own blessing. M. S. Benn protested once that a poor sister could not "afford" the butter and eggs she wanted to give him. Her reply: "Are you going to rob me of my blessing?"

But the parsonage folk generally knew the meaning of self-denial best. Pastors' receipts in 1895, a key year, were all under $400 but numerous preachers received less than $200. And beginners sometimes got "next to nothing." Mr. Sage, during his second year here (1877-78) received $40 for support. He was district chairman then too. Seven years after coming to Canada he mentioned that he had never received any missionary appropriations or asked a committee to say what he should receive. "I just did the best I could . . . and took what they gave me, and my wife helped bring up the rear without any complaint."

Henry Mellor, an early pastor in Toronto, received "$53 and some cents" for his first year. He added philosophically, "I suppose it was as much as we were worth." Then noting that "our (house) rent was $84," he explained, "I was an expert financier or we would have been in the hole." Actually both Mr. and Mrs. Mellor were experienced tailors and necessarily made part of their living on the side.

Many factors may account for the small offerings—general poverty, small memberships, hall rents, building and buying programs, mission givings, absence of budgets or conference funds for evangelism, and perhaps hesitation on the part of the preachers to point out congregational responsibility.

Ministers who gave from their limited stores or pledged in faith sometimes saw the near-miracle follow. M. S. Benn at Kelvin went to visit a sick old man and though "hard up" himself, asked his wife to prepare half their roll of butter, half a dozen cookies and some syrups for him to take along. While returning, he stopped and had prayer with a woman sympathetic to his church. She asked the privilege of giving him a basket. Its contents proved to be these: two quarts of maple syrup, two dozen cookies and twice as much butter as he had taken. Mr. Benn also tells about pledging $10 for missions and then at each of his next two quarterly meetings (he was district elder then) receiving $5 beyond expectations.

Sometimes ministers had to seek secular employment to supplement their meagre offerings. That so many didn't, yet were able to buy clothes and furniture, maintain a horse, buggy and cutter, feed and educate their families, pay doctor bills, give a tithe and beyond—this is a mystery to our prodigal generation. Like Mr. Mellor, many of them must have been expert financiers. And God's blessing must have rested on their pittances in multiplying grace.

26.
THEY ENDURED HARDNESS AS GOOD SOLDIERS

This hardness was partly due to a lack of money and partly to primitive facilities in general at that early time. It was endured because the ends desired were felt worthy enough to make the sacrifices involved.

Mr. Sage was fifty years old when he came to Canada. He left his family back in Michigan. "I used to go home about once in three months," he wrote, "and would work myself nearly sick helping my wife and Frankie get the home affairs in shape so they could get along during my absence. ... Sometimes I would work so hard while at home that I would bring on the erysipelas and would go back to my work with my face swollen and my eyes red."

An 1878 report by Mrs. Ellen Smith of Galt speaks of this condition: "We could hardly discover that it was Bro. Sage," she wrote. One winter he got a cold and cough which, aggravated by trimming his orchard at home, led to lung bleeding on his way back to Canada.

Mr. Sims has left us two lively accounts of tough quarterly meeting trips into Muskoka in the early months of 1884 and 1886. The first included a seventeen-mile sleigh ride with only a thin knee covering. The horses walked because their driver "ignorantly supposed it was a sin to let his horses trot." One house where Mr. Sims stayed was so cold that his whiskers were white with hoar-frost when he arose in the morning. Once he had to walk some distance with his valise on a road covered with about two feet of snow. Starting his return, he missed the stage for Bracebridge and had to run with his valise "the most of four miles" to overtake it at its next stopping place. Once he awoke with his neck stiff and swollen because of a hole directly above in the roof. Yet the report ended with a hearty "Glory to God for His blessing on my soul!" and a three-stanza poem about the delights ahead, should he prove faithful.

The other winter trip had its share of slow rides too. Once he froze his nose and numbed his whole body crossing a wind-swept lake. One horse was sick and got worse as they proceeded on the trip. There were constant stops with the journey extending on into the late night. "I feel thankful I came through without freezing," Mr. Sims wrote, adding, "Oh, what a privilege to have any part in helping to save souls!"

Mrs. Gregory's grim days at Westport-Fermoy were mentioned earlier. Mr. Gregory didn't have any pie at home for a twelve-month period because they couldn't afford it. Fifty cents worth of sugar was all they had for one year. The five preaching points on the Gregory circuit made a round trip of fifty bad-road miles by summer buggy or winter cutter.

Buggy riding was dangerous as well as arduous. A Miss Jerusha Hagle was once thrown from a buggy when the horse made a quick turn. She was laid aside for a year because of a thigh bone broken in the accident.

If you didn't have a horse to drive, you could still walk. Mr. Craig in his "Itinerating" report for the summer of 1891 told of visiting Huntsville where "the two sisters travelling this circuit have walked about eight hundred miles (as many as twenty in one day) this conference year and expect to make it one thousand." He recalled walking twelve miles with them one icy night in the previous winter and finding them more efficient than himself.[1]

Misses Emma Snider and Mary Milliken preached in the Clarendon area when it meant wading snow to their waists sometimes.

There was often hardship for the congregation getting to service. The Petworth Henry Wattams and others from their direction used to attend Sunday evening services at Verona seven miles away. The road, lying through a deep swamp, used to flood in spots during the fall and spring. Sometimes the water was deep enough to enter the buggy box. If thin ice covered it, they might leave their horses in an old barn en route and walk the ice to the railroad track, following that with their lanterns to Verona and church. Once when the ladies were returning in bachelor John's buggy (he had dared to put his through), the harnesss broke mid-swamp and the ladies had to wait stranded till their husbands, walking behind, arrived to guide them to safe walking ice. But those people could still sing lustily at church, "It Is Good to Be Here." In Western Canada, distance was the big factor in getting to general gatherings. Some people came four hundred miles to an Estevan camp in 1913.

You will read of Rev. O. L. King and family spending a bitter Alberta winter in a sidehill dugout after a fire fouled their home-building plans.

Fulton Oursler in *Why I Know There Is a God* (Permabooks) has labelled Communists as people having "zeal without ethics" and, in contrast, the present Western world as made up of folks having "ethics without zeal." Who would deny that those early Free Methodists had a big bundle of both?

---

1. The two sisters in question were Josie Rusk and Mary Milliken.

27.
THEY SUFFERED PERSECUTION FOR RIGHTEOUSNESS

The dynamic of the Holy Spirit mentioned previously helped them to "keep encouraged" under the most discouraging of circumstances. Persecutions, for example, seemed almost their constant lot. We read such reports as this of 1880: "Bitter opposition developed and it seemed the devil made a most desperate effort to divide the little flock" (re services near Norwich). Or this of 1881: "Fierce opposition, slander and reproach have met us at every turn from hireling priests and backslidden churches" (from the conference report on the State of the Work). This again in 1895: "Our people at most points in Canada, as well as elsewhere, are bitterly opposed and persecuted" (from a report by General Superintendent B. R. Jones after a tour).

At Southwold, about 1878, Mr. Sage was accused of being "an old Mormon with nine wives, and two of them at Iona." He called the charge "the devil ringing the bell" for service next day. Surely enough, the place of worship was filled.

James Craig in 1891 wrote of "a fictitious and scandalous story about the Free Methodists which has lately been going the rounds of the public press throughout Canada and the United States." He too took it as Satan's reply to their effective "batteries of truth."

At a Northfield "grove" meeting in 1880, plans were made one night to catch Mr. Sims as he left, and tar and feather him. But "God . . . put it in the heart of one of his children" that night to invite Mr. Sims to his home and the party left in a different direction. It was years afterwards when Mr. Sims heard of the plot. He wrote of that place that preachers from the pulpit labelled them a dangerous sect and went around begging their members to keep aloof.

The persecution at an early Bracebridge tent meeting took the form of cutting the ropes and letting the tent down. This technique was, in fact, a fairly common one. Once a mob threatened to hang A. H. Norrington, eight men coming to the front of the hall with a rope.

On occasion, the abuse came to church. A Toronto preacher came to a Scarboro camp in 1882, shared its hospitality for a time, and then, after asking permission to speak, exploded. Another preacher came to a Thorncliffe camp in 1891 and, in his "testimony" following the sermon, twice called Rev. W. J. Campbell, the evangelist, a liar. At Westport about 1900 it almost came to church, as husbands followed wives to the church door unsuccessfully forbidding them to go. Be sure to notice in the 1879-80 story what happened when bitter Ephraim Bowman of Kelvin barred his house door against his disobedient wife.

Methodists shutting their doors in Miss Sipprell's face has already been mentioned in the "Visitation" chapter. But once—at Houghton—this evangelist got far more disgraceful treatment from a householder. She was calling at homes in connection with local tent meetings being held by Alma Smith and herself. One gruff man named West would not allow her in to pray but grudgingly consented to her praying on his step. Then, while she knelt, he spat tobacco juice down her white dress. However, you will find Mr. West listed among the first converts in the Houghton story. The burning of their tent and its sequel are related there also. Perhaps it should be noted how that a young man who broke up a tent meeting service here wearing a false face, later fell from a windmill and died suddenly.

Annie Slack Ball relates that once a winter quarterly meeting was scheduled for a school just east of Gananoque, but when the Elder and people arrived, they found the stove pipes taken down. Of course, they put the pipes up and proceeded with their meeting.

Persecutions at both Kingston and Harrowsmith in their birth-pang days took the form of vegetable throwing. George Fuller Jr. remembers flying tomatoes in the vicinity of the Harrowsmith town hall, when he and James F. Gregory were helping in some Fairbairn-sponsored meetings there.

Part of the early unpopularity seemed to be associated with members of secret orders. It was a special victory then when a member got converted. An 1893 report from East Toronto told of a man who belonged to three secret orders and engaged in horse-racing taking the Way. The report said: "He has left all his secret societies, sold his fast horse and has a shining face."

Mrs. Charles Goodrich of Vennachar got saved in W. H. Gregory's great revival of 1893. She with others went back to her home church to testify. For saying "Praise the Lord" aloud (disturbing a religious service) she was fined. When her husband refused to pay the third fine, the sheriff, intent on getting his commission, seized the "offended" pastor's horse and buggy to be sold at auction. The congregation at that turn of events raised the money and paid the fine of the woman they had prosecuted.[1]

Something similar but even more interesting happened to her brother Simon Ball. He too had been a nominal church member without heartwarming or heart-changing grace. Being anxious that his former friends should know his joy after the big transformation, he also went back to worship. For saying "Amen" aloud at a point of approval, he got clapped into Napanee jail for twenty-two days. But the jailer soon sensed he had a safe man and let Mr. Ball go loose in the town by day to return at night. Mr. Ball even got invited to eat at the jailer's table where he, the "prisoner," gave thanks for the food.

But most of the persecution contained little humor. It took granite men and women, spirit-filled, to stand.

There was nothing like a sermon by founder Roberts to keep the grit in their souls. Especially when he took a text as this one used at the 1887 Uxbridge conference: "For I reckon that the sufferings of this present time are not worthy to be compared with the glory which shall be revealed in us."

---

1. Mr. Goodrich, a church official who had not been too sympathetic to his wife's new religion, a little later got converted himself. But it was not until Mr. Gregory had told him, "You haven't one spark of salvation," when he first wanted to join the Free Methodist Church. He eventually became a preacher also.

28.
THEY HANDED US A HERITAGE

Some may argue that this is not a "method." But to have something valuable, to demonstrate openly that it works, and then when promoted to pass it on in good condition to a younger generation certainly constitutes handing over a heritage. And the action provides such a perfect precedent for us that it amounts to a technique worthy of inclusion in this list. The thought here is that their effective labours must spur today's Free Methodists to match their achievement.

A student asked his university professor why history must be studied. The professor answered with another question, "What happens to a man who loses his memory?" Obviously a man who had completely lost his memory would have to learn even elemental things all over again. History may truly be regarded as civilization's memory conserving the record of successes and failures of the past, hoping their knowledge will make for better building in the present. Thus the man who persistently ignores history has already demonstrated himself something of a fool.

After the study of the detailed story in the next seven sections, the reader will be the better readied for the challenge of his heritage. An attempt is made to point it in the closing section.

Section 3: Ontario Opens for Occupation

The previous section mentioned some broad methods of basic Free Methodism and briefly illustrated most of them. This procedure necessitated giving away snatches of the history itself. We come now to the connected story telling how Free Methodism got invited, came, saw, and began to conquer Ontario. It is a tale of faith, adventure, struggle and God—intoxicated heroism. Read it prayerfully. It will challenge you to new twentieth-century dedications and exploits.

1.
HOW IT HAPPENED

Of course nothing happens without some cause. But the cause may be a God-directed chain of events. Free Methodism's coming seems that kind.

Actually it came into Canada unofficially before 1876. This chapter tells the story of how God providentially brought this new Methodist communion into the Dominion. It was before the days of almost all the evangelistic churches now common here. It begins with a Primitive Methodist layman named Loveless who had grown spiritually hungry and a born-again builder named Tommy Clark who subscribed to a magazine that communicated the Bread of Life.

Robert Loveless was of English stock, a class leader of the Zion Primitive Methodist Church at Wexford in Scarboro Township, York County, just northeast of Toronto. He had been converted as a moral young man in 1848, after conviction over cheating in some young people's game had constrained him to make an altar between his plow handles. He had married—in 1860—Jane Wallace Thomson of Presbyterian ancestry, after praying for her and seeing her converted in a Methodist revival. To better serve his home community of Ellesmere (east of Wexford), he had built a small "Meeting House" on the corner of his farm at the village crossroads and held an afternoon Union Sunday School there. But the Lovelesses grew increasingly distressed over formality and worldliness in their Zion home church.

One day Robert's sister Mrs. Alice Milne, the local postmistress, showed him a copy of the *Earnest Christian*, a magazine coming to a Free Methodist, Tommy Clark, who had lately moved from Buffalo to work as a stone mason in the area. Robert liked the magazine, went to the church where Tommy attended, invited him home after service for Sunday din-

THE BATTLE WAS THE LORD'S

"Tommy" Clark

Mr. and Mrs. Robert Loveless

Old Loveless Home on Kennedy Road just off 401 Highway.

Loveless "Meeting House"

62

ner and soon became a subscriber. The Rev. B. T. Roberts of North Chili, New York, was its editor. He was also, as we have seen, General Superintendent of the newly founded Free Methodist Church.

The magazine proved so satisfying that editor-superintendent Roberts received an invitation to come to Canada and preach. And so it was that the first Free Methodist preaching in Canada was a Sunday-to-Sunday series in 1873 in Mr. Loveless' "Meeting House" at Ellesmere on the Kennedy Road, a few miles northeast of Toronto and only a short distance south of the present 401 highway. That preaching was so accepted by the congregation that when Mr. Roberts asked how many would support such preaching, a line formed across the front of the "house."

He came again, on invitation, in February of the next year and stayed more than a week preaching several times at each of Ellesmere and Stouffville. Stouffville was a town fourteen miles north of Ellesmere. Tommy Clark, having moved there to practise his trade, was doubtless responsible for its meetings.

Mr. Roberts seems to have sent a man named J. Ireland of Rochester back to Canada to follow up his preaching, for in the *Free Methodist* of April 9, 1874, Mr. Ireland had a report telling of a personal short-term expedition into Canada. When he arrived some brother (likely Robert Loveless) went out, until eleven o'clock at night, to spread the news of his arrival. Mr. Ireland preached twenty-three times (recall his vivid military language quoted earlier) and organized two Free Methodist societies—at Stouffville, five members; at Ellesmere, ten members. The report concludes with the words: "We think this is the first introduction of Free Methodist in Canada." [1]

Later the same year, Mr. Roberts came for a short time to Paris (near Brantford), invited by a Gilbert Showers. Unable to stay, he suggested inviting Rev. W. A. Sellew (later Bishop Sellew), the pastor at Tonawanda, New York. Mr. Sellew with his wife came in December for some services. As a result, Gilbert Showers joined his Tonawanda society.

---

1. Mr. Ireland apparently returned to Canada for two later campaigns. In late 1874 he wrote from the Ellesmere area and in the following spring from Galt. Both times he was full of courage.

2.
CANADA, C. H. SAGE

All this rates "unofficial." But official action followed soon. People from Michigan and New York kept moving into Canada, some already touched by Free Methodism and ready to welcome it in their new homeland. Many others too, besides Robert Loveless, among Canada's Methodists had grown more and more dissatisfied with the lessening spiritual vitality

THE BATTLE WAS THE LORD'S

Rev. C. H. Sage

in their local churches. Prayers to God and invitations to the Free Methodists preceded the appointment described here.

Let us go back to that auspicious moment. It is the fall of 1876. The final session of the first North Michigan Conference at St. Johns, Sept. 27 to Oct. 2, is almost over. Rev. Roberts is reading the circuits before the closing presidential prayer. He is now at the last one—an appointment that proves the presence of true mission vision among those beginning Michiganders. He reads: "Canada, C. H. Sage."

Mr. Sage already had to his credit some successes in opening new churches in America. With his wife in poor health, he had just built and paid for a home for her and "little Frankie" near Port Huron before conference. Preparations completed at home, this ex-blacksmith, ex-farmer, ex-carpenter buggied across the border to his new battlefield. He was the first preacher of the so-called modern holiness movement to be stationed in this country.

You will want to read carefully the outline of his whole life in the "Giants" section.[1] Better still, borrow his fast-moving *Autobiography of Charles H. Sage* and see what "manner of man" he really was. Perhaps this portion, taken from his account of the conference will offer some insight:

"I went to conference free as a bird and told the Lord I was ready for any field of labour. When the appointments were read, the last one was, 'Canada, C. H. Sage.' When I received the blessing of holiness I just signed the blank, and asked God to fill it out. I had turned my life over into the hands of God and asked him to do with me as seemed good to him, and I was to say yes, to God's will, but it seemed to me that this would crush me. As soon as I could I said to Brother Roberts, the president of our conference, 'You have educated and talented men in the east, why did you not send one of them instead of such an ignorant man as I am?' He looked at me so fatherly, and said, 'Brother Sage, we have got the educated and talented men, but they have not got the missionary fire. You will have to go.'"

Few preachers have ever been given a bigger assignment than he was.

Few have entered into their tasks with more consecration. Few will have richer rewards in heaven.

---

1. Some readers will find the running account most satisfactory if these biographical portions are read at the first mention of the person concerned.

3.
WINNING A FOOTING
1876-77

On his way east, Mr. Sage paused in Galt long enough to enlarge an existing society for the records speak of nine charter members and four probationers at this time. It appears a Mrs. George Smith from Tonawanda, N.Y. had held some services and won some converts in the home of an Edward Rhodes of 56 Brock St. Because of their significance, the names of the nine originals that Mrs. Smith must have previously enrolled are included: William Carter, Isabel Carter, Albert Showers, Eliza Shaver, Clarissa Moore, James Pink, Emma Pink, Edward Rhodes, Mary Ann Rhodes. The four new ones: T. P. Jarnagan from Buffalo;[1] J. W. Banta, a local preacher from New York; Ellen Smith from Tonawanda, and Phoebe Richardson of Sheffield, Ontario.

Mr. Sage continued to Ellesmere to the Loveless home. Mr. Loveless he described as "just a humble, quiet, God-fearing man, but his home, his property, his soul and body were a living sacrifice to God and His cause." His companion he called "a humble quiet godly woman caring for all of the saints as they came as she would have cared for the Master." The first services there proved quite unsuccessful. He had advertised himself as a "live Yankee" and the title seemed to arouse prejudice for some Americans had recently discredited themselves in those parts. "I could not have done a worse thing," he later wrote. But before the year's end a small society was organized at Ellesmere.

At Stouffville, Mr. Loveless had purchased and fitted up a church capable of seating 250 people. Christians there had been praying for a revival. The church was dedicated by Mr. Sage on Oct. 29 and services were held for a week or more with increasing attention, a few conversions, and bright prospects for more.[2] Then difficulties arose concerning Seventh Day Adventists and little of permanence was accomplished afterwards.

But invitations came from other centres. Unsuccessful services in the school house at Widder Station (now Thedford and about thirty miles east of Sarnia)[3] were followed by house services in London where an afterwards-unstable class was formed. Another preaching point, a rural one, seems to have been Jericho near Thedford. By then it was March of 1877.

Because, in general, successes were so meager and hindrances so great, Mr. Sage shortly wrote his district chairman for permission to return to

Michigan for the rest of the year. He received it and supplied a Michigan circuit, Goodland, for a few months.

But little groups at the places he had been, and at others as Oakville, Woodstock, and Port Credit, continued to pray. At Galt they even built a small church on land donated by Edward Rhodes and pushed their membership up to twenty. J. W. Banta advertised in the *Free Methodist* a second Galt-Paris quarterly meeting in late May. In late June George Bunce from London reported a first London quarterly meeting with conversions and great blessing even among the children.[4]

Some time during this decade there appears to have been some Free Methodist tent meetings held at Ivy Lea, just east of Gananoque on the St. Lawrence. A Rev. Thomas Whiffen, whose daughters later became missionaries in the Dominican Republic, conducted them. He was from the Susquehanna Conference of New York State. Whether the early classes in Gananoque and Lansdowne attracted any converts of these meetings could not be ascertained.[5]

But back to Mr. Sage again. The people urged his return and advertised several September quarterly meetings where he was to be present.[6] He came in the late summer of 1877. He visited Jericho (near Thedford) again where he held meetings in a John Toole's house, and organized a small class that included one or more Tooles, the Hagle sisters (one Maggie Jerusha later became a preacher and eventually the second Mrs. Sage), besides George Shorter and John Hilbourn—men who show up again later. He visited Galt and London too, at both of which he held their quarterly meetings. The Galt society by now had a church nearly paid for and God's blessing was on the people. Encouraged again, Mr. Sage wrote: "There is a sound of abundance of rain in that direction." At London too, with its membership increased to twenty his hopes heightened. The report on that meeting concluded with a rugged appeal: "The Macedonian cry comes from many parts. Experienced labourers are needed; those who can sacrifice for God's cause and who enjoy the Holy Ghost. None need come expecting a large support, for nearly all are poor. . . . We are praying for help.[7]

1877-78

The October North Michigan conference of 1877 sent Mr. Sage packing back, but not as pastor. A new Canada District of the Michigan Conference had been created and he now was chairman. The report made on Canada had shown four societies, forty-nine members (including the probationers), three local preachers, two Sunday Schools, and church property worth $350 (probably the Stouffville church). The new Canada slate showed five appointments. Three were assigned to Ontario men—Warwick (later Thedford) to George E. Shorter; Ellesmere to Gilbert Showers; Gananoque (a new point) to J. W. Banta; Galt went to another Michigander, young D. D. Marston (uncle of our present Bishop L. R. Marston).[8] London was left "To be supplied," this phrase soon to become a familiar one in stationing committee decisions. A year before, Mr. Sage had rated a "paper circuit." Now he had earned a "paper district."

Together the two Michigan men, each with his own horse and buggy, drove into the Dominion. After a pause at London, Mr. Marston went on to his Galt circuit and Mr. Sage answered an invitation to begin a work in Woodstock. He preached successfully in a private house and himself stayed in the house of a dentist Brown who with his loyal Free Methodist wife and daughter had moved from Michigan. A German Mennonite girl named Nancy Schantz had invited him to preach. She exhorted effectively.

George Bunce meanwhile continued to hold meetings in his own house at London. In October he wrote courageously outlining their weekly four-meeting schedule and typical simple "order of service":

"In our meetings we generally sing some good old hymns, two or three engage in prayer, some one reads a chapter and speaks a few words; then we have another season of prayer, after which we give an opportunity to anyone that has a word of exhortation and invite poor sinners to come forward and give their hearts to God. Then we go in for a live prayer meeting, asking and expecting that God will save souls and bless His people. We hold our meetings Sunday morning and night, Tuesday and Friday nights. We expect to see souls converted every time we meet together." God must have honoured that faith for he was able to say their number had increased from eight to "about twenty-three."

Chairman Sage lost little time in getting started with his new district duties. By November he had a schedule of fall and early winter quarterly meetings published. At the first, the Warwick one, the Hagle sisters who had been converted in a Primitive Methodist meeting, found the experience of entire sanctification along with John Toole.[9] The London one proved something of a district rally with God's blessing throughout and fifteen Sunday-night "seekers." Galt got the real District Meeting, a glad time of outpouring and a time also of fresh salvation with "the altar . . . filled." "It was the best quarterly meeting we have attended in Canada," wrote our Mrs. Smith. Mr. Marston seemed doing well. Mr. Sage headed his horse towards Ellesmere (and possibly Gananoque) next.[10]

Some time during that same year of 1877-78 preachers from the Buffalo District of the Genesee Conference began crossing the Niagara River and starting services in Canada. A layman named William Fell reported from Chippawa in early '78 that his pastor and his wife, Rev. and Mrs. W. F. Requa, were holding successful meetings "in Bro. George Huff's house" and that they hoped for a camp meeting in a McClive grove.[11] The camp did not materialize however, probably vetoed by the Buffalo District "quarterly conference."

George Shorter, the local man who had been assigned the Warwick (Thedford) post, held a seven-week Jericho revival with Banta help. It was followed by the enrolling of a baker's dozen of new members at the January '78 quarterly meeting[12] and the converting of the old Thedford cooper shop into a church and upstairs parsonage. This was the first Free Methodist property in Canada beyond the Loveless-purchased Stouffville church. Jerusha Hagle after a revival at Thedford helped get a class of twenty-five going there. Early members included Stephensons, Brooks, Dillers, Hoovers and Baileys.

In February Mr. Sage was joined by two Michigan girls, Mary Crittenden and Frankie Davis, the first women to join the itinerant ranks. They helped also at London, then Warwick, Jericho and Thedford. A Wm. McKearnin came from somewhere to take charge of the London planting. A Templar Hall there was rented, then later bought and whitewashed for worship. Mr. Sage continued a circuit of quarterly meetings through May and June—London, Ellesmere, Gananoque, Galt, Musselman's Lake (north of Stouffville). Mr. Banta must not have gone to "Gan" as appointed, or must not have stayed, if he did go, for a Lutz-Pattison family newly moved in were calling for help. Mr. Sage found theirs a "blessed home" when he got there.[13] He formed classes at both Gananoque and Musselman's Lake.

A little later he was at Southwold in the west, invited by a McKay family originally from Michigan. It was here the "Mormon" charge brought the people out, only to have their prejudice dissolved. Mr. McKay held a successful revival himself there directly after this, so that Mr. Sage was able to begin a July class in the place with Mary Crittenden as leader.

Back on the Galt circuit, Mr. Sage held a September quarterly meeting at Sheffield, six miles out of town. The United Brethren people there, many of whom had been earlier converted under the labours of a reformed drunkard, John Barnell, said it seemed like "old times."

1878-79

And this brings us, after an encouraging year, up to North Michigan Conference time in 1878. Showers, Shorter, McKearnin and a James Winter were there as Canadian delegates. Sage and Shorter were on the Stationing Committee. Mr. Sage was able to report increasing calls or interest (as at Toronto) despite opposition. Besides keeping a regular quarterly schedule, he had pushed revivals extensively in both established and new centres. He was returned as Chairman and under him, as circuit appointees, appear the names Winter to Thedford, Shorter to London, McKay to Iona, Marston to Galt,[14] Showers to Ellesmere, and McKearnin to Gananoque.

The first big news of the new year was the organizing of a twenty-member Free Methodist society at Hannon just south of Hamilton in February. The background is most interesting. A fearless Watertown Baptist minister named Brown held a "protracted meeting" in the Bartonville Methodist Episcopal Church. Among the "converts" were backslidden Adolphus and Barbara Freeman, he the tobacco-using class leader. Adolphus' brother Andrew and his wife, of another M. E. Church, "came through" too.

Adolphus Freeman   Maggie Jerusha Hagle   Valtina Brown

When opposition got unbearable in the Bartonville Church (the pastor evidently joined it), Adolphus wrote the evangelist for advice. Along with his encouragement, Brown suggested corresponding with Mr. Sage, then in meetings at Sheffield near Galt.[15]

Mr. Sage soon went, hunted up some old unconverted Michigan friends nearby—the Fletchers and Wests—visited and prayed with the people, and started services in homes and swept barns. Many a life was swept clean too in that revival. A Sunday School was started in Andrew's home, and a hall in nearby Clinesville (now Elfrida) was obtained for Sunday church. That new class formed included seven Freemans and two Wrights. Adolphus Freeman was selected for class leader and served many years. By conference, the membership had swollen to thirty. Miss Valtina Brown and T. P. Jarnagan took turns in holding services till conference.

At Hannon's March '79 quarterly meeting it was decided to have a June camp meeting on Andrew Freeman's farm.[16] This one did materialize, as we have seen, the first Free Methodist camp in Canada. The hospitality shown visitors broke down much prejudice, and the powerful preaching and exhortations resulted in the nearly fifty conversions mentioned in an earlier chapter. Sixty-year-old Daniel Fletcher, who shortly served two years as supply pastor for Bracebridge, was one convert.[17]

Earlier that conference year, W. R. Pattison, reporting from Gananoque, told that among recent converts had been a 94-year-old woman who found again the faith she had known eighty years before. "The few saints here are alive to God, and Jesus meets with us in power," he wrote, adding, "Some have entered perfect love."

In March a class was organized at Ancaster. Charter members included a Brother and Sister Wedge. In early April, Mr. Sage began services in a schoolhouse near Bracebridge. The Hannon Fletchers had moved to Muskoka directly after their conversion and invited him to make the long trip north. Despite deep snow still, the settlers thronged to service. When Mr.

Sage returned south, he left behind a new 34-member class, the first in Muskoka. He described the country, with its granite rocks, pine stumps and summer frosts, as the worst he had ever seen for making a living.[18] But the people—he had never seen any so ready to embrace the gospel.[19] Here "over the rocks and crossways and corduroy bridges" he first met the Hiram Haley family whose sons feature conspicuously in this history. Mrs. Haley, a few months later, went down to the June Hannon camp and found peace.

Mr. Sage had prayed earlier for a Bracebridge worker and received two letters. Valtina Brown (of Woodstock) and Jerusha Hagle (from London) were feeling the tug towards service. So he invited them both—the first Canadian women evangelists sent out.[20] With a three-appointment circuit eight miles long, the ladies, often walking, kept busy. But they soon had several additional classes in the area. Mr. Sage returned in July for more revivals and grove meetings. It was his report on these services that ended with the earlier quoted battle call which prescribed a truly rugged discipline for those needed in Canada.

The Niagara area pilgrims had the desired outdoor meeting at Chippawa in June of that year, a quarterly meeting of the Tonawanda circuit in a 300-capacity two-tent setup. Chairman Coleman from Buffalo way was there and numerous other Americans came across the river. The meeting was rated a "spiritual tornado." There were members on the Canadian side now.

The report of an August quarterly meeting at Ellesmere revealed that its class had recently been disintegrating. Local church member misdemeanours and Free Methodist tramps ("floodwood from the United States") had blighted it. But a more recent Hagle—Brown revival had brought new life.[21]

Many Chippawans attended a sweeping Tonawanda camp in August. Up to forty would seek the Lord in a single service. Up to ten would rise simultaneously to testify on the last Sunday.

An August grove meeting on a Williams' farm near Thedford (the first in the area) finished the conference year's "specials."

1879-80

The Canada District had ten societies to report at the 1879 North Michigan conference with a total of 180 members. And three interesting new men were posted in the Canada District that year—James Craig to Galt, Albert Sims to Woodstock, and C. M. Smith to Hannon. The first two were to give conspicuous leadership as district chairmen; the last one to be known as a pastor, a church builder and an evangelist.[22]

Continuing as Chairman, Mr. Sage went to Muskoka that fall and found their appointed pastor, G. D. Marks, absent. But lay leadership had been so aggressive that a new neighbourhood was getting evangelized with ten people ready for baptism and twenty-seven for full membership. The

Rev. and Mrs. Albert Sims and Family

Rev. James Craig

total class then numbered forty-eight. "They are truly alive and several feel the call to preach," wrote the chairman. This was about the time that the David Kirks were converted. Apparently a small church was built near Bracebridge directly after the visit for the next year's Minutes show a $100 property there.

That fall and winter Valtina Brown of Woodstock and a Miss Arlette Eddy from Michigan held lengthy services in the Ellesmere area where Thomas Carveth was pastor. These began in the spacious farm home of Silas Phoenix near Armadale, then continued two months in an old Evangelical Church nearby.[23] About eighty people sought the Lord and the society's report showed forty-five probationers alone at next conference. Among the converts were these: William Stonehouse, Martha Stonehouse, Marion Stewart, Tom McAuley, Mary Loveless and James, William, John, and Alex Macklin. Richard Burnham (from Uxbridge, but working in the district) was another. Both he and Martha Stonehouse will feature prominently in the later story.

Armadale soon had a church too. Francis Underwood offered an acre of land. With much labour donated, the 20' x 40' frame building cost less than $400. Work began in May and it was finished by conference time.[24]

Shortly after the Armadale revival, i.e., in early 1880, Miss Brown assisted by another young lady, Matilda Sipprell, began a new work and class in Uxbridge some forty miles northeast of Toronto. The effort began with cottage prayer meetings, then continued in a hall over a Main Street store.

We go back a bit now to Mr. Sims and his new

Armadale Church

Woodstock charge. When he arrived after the '79 conference he found three members but no church. A Schantz family eight miles out let him hold eight weeks of services in their home where some conversions occurred.

When he read the General Rules the last night of the calendar year no one would accept the invitation to join. There was later regret for this failure on the part of some, and, as for Mr. Sims, he was both embarrassed and discouraged at the time.

Mr. Sage shortly asked him to go to the Norwich area not far away, after a former Michigander there, Mrs. Maria Beckham, had started services in her home community, gained some converts and called for assistance. At Merrill's Mills near Norwich in early 1880 he visited and prayed with the people; sanctified Mrs. Beckham testified and prayed powerfully—and a revival followed that produced a new twelve-member class[25] and a Sunday School of fifty. (Early congregations met in the homes of James Carter and William Cooper.) But these fruits were not won without resisting the customary "bitter opposition."

We detect even at this early stage in Mr. Sims' ministry his interest in literature promotion. We read that tracts and copies of the *Free Methodist* and the *Earnest Christian* were distributed, and these helped greatly.

At Northfield, three miles away, the upper storey of a wagon shop became chapel for the next Sims services. Everyone here, it seemed, professed religion and belonged to a church, "but it was impossible to distinguish them from the world except by their dead prayers and hollow testimonies." [26] As the preaching exposed ungodliness and worldliness, people vowed they would not return, but found they couldn't stay away. A number repented and found the Lord. Matilda Sipprell there was a young woman of twenty-four. She had been converted in early youth, had drifted away, and then had recently repented. Raised from a sick bed a short time before, she attended the services, sought and found cleansing, and was soon in the armour herself at Uxbridge (as we have seen) beginning what proved to be a thirty-year battle-bout for the Lord.[27] That second camp—in the same Freeman bush as before—had "modern" facilities: kerosene torches, and sleeping tents made of factory cotton which were erected with steep sides to shed possible rain.

In connection with the camp, they tell a touching story of how little George Freeman, Adolphus' eight-year-old son, got converted while the members' children were holding church. They had been left at Uncle Andrew's house during the camp preparations, many of them already saved. Little George knelt at his kitchen chair and prayed till the joy filled his heart. He joined the church soon afterwards and later was to serve many years as an effective pastor. His sons, Leslie, Stanley and James are active West Ontario laymen today.

A Jones and Manley pair of preachers served as evangelists at the camp that year. One couple of noteworthy converts were a Mr. and Mrs. J. W.

ONTARIO OPENS FOR OCCUPATION

Stuart from Northfield, he the class leader of the Methodist church there. They were given some pretty uncomplimentary names when they went home afterwards, but continued to hold fast to their life in Christ Jesus. Nancy Schantz received the blessing of holiness at this camp.

Mr. Sims conducted a good grove meeting in their Northfield community right after the official camp. It was there that the previously mentioned attempt to tar and feather him was divinely aborted. Four Hutchinson sisters were numbered among the converts. Elizabeth, a year later, became Albert Sims' bride. Jemima, Teresa, and Mary were pastors later.

Kelvin had a campaign next. Services began Sunday afternoons. Grist mill steps made a pulpit. Planks below made the seats. Eventually a carpenter shop was fitted for a meeting house. Interest quickened till farmers drove long miles in busy harvest time to attend. This was the revival in which fashionable Martha Thomas found herself and her God. A class of about a dozen was organized at each of Northfield and Kelvin after these blitzes.

Rev. George Freeman

Martha Thomas

The story is on record that Mrs. Ephraim Bowman, a charter member at Kelvin, disobeyed her husband and attended prayer meeting one night. Mr. Bowman drove two nails over the latch to keep her outside. Returning home on the bitterly cold night, she found the door fastened. Kneeling there outside, she reminded the Lord of prison doors that He had opened and told Him she believed He was willing and able to do something similar for her. Then she arose and found the door responsive. Her husband, convinced that this was a supernatural opening, was soon converted himself.[28]

Free Methodism became established in the Florence-Shetland-Ousley area in the summer of 1880 and in an interesting fashion. George Coates, in early 1879, after reading the life of Peter Cartwright, grew stirred over the deadness of the churches in his area. Through an American Baptist evangelist named Brown who had been sanctified at a Free Methodist camp and later came to the district for union revival, he heard of the Free Methodists. Discovering Thedford had some, he wrote local preacher John Hilbourn who brought his pastor J. H. Winter over for schoolhouse meetings. Mr. Hilbourn's shouting and laughing amused the Coates boys but displeased some of the local church members. Mr. Sage visited later and soon both the Coates parents were sanctified.

In June of 1880 Mr. Sage sent the Hagle-Eddy team to the district and a successful June grove meeting followed. Seven-year-old R. A. Coates was one convert. Thomas Moorhouse, Benjamin DeMille, Henry Stevens and their wives were others.[29] Societies were shortly formed at all three centres and several churches built.

In August, a second official camp meeting was held, this one near Markham. A host of preachers were on hand, and an abundance of money was raised for those days ($62.36 for camp expenses and $192 for a tabernacle). The salvation success of the camp is not mentioned.

During this year sometime, the Misses Hagle and Davis were reported doing a good work at Grimsby. Miss Hagle had started this work previously while at Hannon.

A July Warwick quarterly meeting attracted about 400 to "Father" Williams' grove. A riverside baptismal service was an interesting feature on Saturday afternoon.

And this brings us to the coming-of-age that fell that fall.

---

1. The detailed account of Jarnagan's conversion in Dec., 1875, appeared in Roberts' *Earnest Christian* of June, 1876. He wrote numerous sermonic articles for it afterwards, as well as Canadian news articles for the *Free Methodist*.

2. Tommy Clark's autobiography says Mr. Sage organized a class here of "about fourteen members," but the 1874 Ireland article in the *Free Methodist* says Mr. Roberts organized one on his visit there that year and also one at Ellesmere. It could be that, with no pastor, the 1874 societies had evaporated.

3. Yankee mischief had centered here too—preaching, starting a class, marrying a woman, getting her property, then migrating to Michigan.

4. George Bunce had been led among the Free Methodists by somehow getting a copy of the *Free Methodist*.

5. We shall see that there were Free Methodists in Gananoque by late 1877. Mr. Whiffen was not assigned specifically to the Watertown area (where he was also stationed elder) till late 1878.

6. The one in London was to be in the home of George Bunce, 577 Oxford St.

7. Some earlier content of this London report is interesting too: "The London Quarterly Meeting was glorious to me. I had formed a class of eight last winter, but they had not counted the cost sufficiently, and when the trying time came, six out of the eight left. I don't know but they thought we read over our discipline and then laid it on the shelf, like last year's almanac, but we are doing business for God and eternity. We had rather have three persons saved of God than a ten acre lot full of limber-backed limsey-wolsey that run when they smell powder."

8. The Sage autobiography places Stouffville and Widder Station incidents in the next year and indicates Mr. Sage stayed in Michigan till conference. It also gives the year of Mr. Marston's first coming as 1877. Other records disagree. The autobiography appeared in 1903. We judge Mr. Sage's memory had failed him here and at some later points of chronology. Young Marston cried like a child after the appointments were read. "The idea of sending a boy to Canada!" he sobbed. He was to say it again later when he found what he was getting into.

9. At Jericho the previous summer, Mr. Sage had preached what came to be called his "pattern sermon" which had shed much light on the experience of holiness and prepared these people for it.

10. Ellesmere only was mentioned in the published schedule, but Mrs. Smith's Galt report spoke of Mr. Sage leaving there for Gananoque. It is likely that he paid Gananoque an unofficial first visit after the Ellesmere quarterly meeting in early Jan. 1878.

11. T. P. Jarnagan said it was Fell's witnessing and praying that first brought conviction to him. He was calling in the Fell home on business.

12. James Clink, who was to help introduce Free Methodism to Sarnia and who later became a minister, probably joined at this time. His Methodist class leader had called him pharisaical when he reported his private conversion, but he found the new Free Methodists preached what he had.

13. Pattison was the son-in-law of a Mrs. Lutz and later became a minister.

14. Mr. Marston appears not to have gone, for at next conference he reported from a Michigan circuit.

15. Mr. Sage's handwritten reply to the Freeman invitation is still preserved. He promised to come when free, and asked six questions about local matters, one being "How many are there that sympathize with the real deep work of God?" The letter reveals him a man of organization and discernment.

16. It was here the elderly Caledonia pilgrim made her joyful exclamation quoted in "Canada When It Came." Sage, Brown and Jarnagan all participated.

17. Mrs. James F. (Fredrea) Gregory, Leila Fletcher, and Dan Fletcher are his great grandchildren.

18. The government, he said, had stripped the valuable timber and then had advertised 200 acres of free land to settlers. Apparently there was a lot of free rock also.

19. Mr. Sage wrote: "When I would give an invitation the rostrum that ran across the schoolroom would be full before I could sing one verse."

20. Miss Brown had arrived while he was there; Miss Hagle came soon afterwards.

21. When the ladies arrived, their wardrobes were reduced from giving away clothes. Mr. Loveless gave each $5 and put a horse and buggy at their disposal. "Visit, hold meetings, and get souls saved," he instructed; "I will care for you temporally."

22. Mr. Smith was the grandfather of W L., Albert and Hart Smith of the Toronto area now. He had previously been an ordained minister in the United Brethren Church.

23. According to a Sept. 3, 1927 *Globe* clipping reporting the death of his oldest son William John, Silas Phoenix came from the Old Land where his education had been neglected, so he attended S. S. #2 Scarboro with his four children to get more schooling. He became a class leader after his conversion, sharing that local responsibility with Robert Loveless.

24. These two churches vie for the distinction of being the first built within the bounds of the present East Ontario Conference. Only the Armadale one remains.

25. Mr. and Mrs. Francis Lees, who were to help get Free Methodism planted in Norwich later, were probably in this class for they formerly lived at Merrill's Mills and were converted about 1880.

26. See Mr. Sims' autobiography, *Yet Not I*.

27. Still available is an Evangelist's License of Miss Sipprell signed by Mr. Sage and dated Feb. 4, 1882, at Kelvin.

28. Mr. Bowman had gone to the first Kelvin meetings and reported to his wife that, "about two services from that man, and your religion would be preached all away." Although angered at first, Mrs. Bowman later attended at Northfield where, gaudily and haughtily dressed, she sat on the front seat. Soon "down she came with a crash" and gained the restored favour of God.

29. Three Coates sons and a son-in-law were to become ordained ministers. Thomas Moorehouse was to become active in local, district and conference activities. The Benjamin DeMilles feature prominently in this history a little later.

4.
LOCAL WAR COUNCIL—THE FIRST CANADA CONFERENCE, 1880

By the year 1880, continuing growth pointed towards the need of a Canadian conference. Mr. Sage had announced in early summer it might be organized at the Markham camp meeting but Mr. Roberts had informed him the matter would have to wait for committee study after completion of the American conferences. This meant the Canadian ministers and delegates would be expected to make the long trek back to Michigan in the fall again, an excursion that was getting irksome. Some at least did go (James Craig was ordained an elder there), but the proposal was ratified in due time so they didn't have to go again.

In late October Mr. Roberts came up to the Galt chapel and the "blessed event" took place, with Albert Sims the chronicler. Eleven circuits containing thirteen points gave reports. Already four churches and one parsonage were owned. The total membership of 324 indicated encouraging progress since that day—only four years earlier—when Mr. Sage, with saving grace, had first sallied into Ontario.

That progress was to continue—through the next forty years especially—as we shall see in the first chapter of Section VI.

Here are the thirteen appointments as drawn up for that new two-district one-chairman conference:[1]

London District—C. H. Sage, Chairman

Grimsby	C. M. Smith[2]
Hannon	A. C. Leonard, supply
Galt	J. H. Winter
Woodstock	A. Sims
London	M. Harrison, supply
Iona	J. Wright, supply
Florence	Jerusha Hagle and Martha Thomas, supplies
Thedford	J. Craig

Toronto District—C. H. Sage, Chairman

Ellesmere	J. A. Adams, supply
Stouffville	T. Carveth
Keswick	W. McKearnin
Muskoka	D. Fletcher, supply
Gananoque	A. Allguire, supply

The Hagle-Thomas team's being sent to Florence marked the first time women received a conference appointment in Canada. But whether men or women, all appointees knew what was expected of them, for the report of the Committee on the State of the Work that year had been quite explicit.[3] It read in part: "We expect to be aggressive by the help of God; we expect to sustain the present work and push out into new territory. Our conference embraces the Dominion, and the work already spreads over an area of eleven hundred miles. We have no place for lounging, whining preachers, nor for travelling chairmen who need a nice comfortable place fitted up for them to retire into, and a study to fit them up for their arduous labours, but we have need for men baptized with the Holy Ghost and fire, with the love of souls at heart to such an extent that their constant prayer is 'Give me souls or I die'—men that know just enough to obey and follow God, and have never learned a retreat, and don't know when they are whipped. With such preachers and members, and no others, we expect to succeed."

---

1. The earlier North Michigan Conference had stationed eight men and left five circuits to be supplied. The new Canada Conference ratified most of the earlier appointments and filled the remaining gaps.
2. At least one person who attended that distant conference is still alive; A. E. Smith of Pickering (son of C. M. Smith) was there as a child of two years.
3. The committee was composed of C. H. Sage, C. M. Smith, and James Carter, a Kelvin layman.

5.
FURTHER FIGHTING OF THE FIRST TWO DECADES

It was four years from the first coming of C. H. Sage to the formation of a Canada Conference. It was fifteen more years to the splitting of that conference into eastern and western units. This chapter will briefly outline events and progress across those years from 1880 to 1895.

1880-81

On October 31 of that year, 1880, Superintendent Roberts dedicated the new Armadale Church to God free of debt, giving on the occasion his famous sermon based on Matthew 16:18—"Upon this rock I will build my church, and the gates of hell shall not prevail against it." Mr. Roberts came over from Galt for this occasion after completing, the Sunday before, the first session of the Canada Conference described in the last chapter.

Albert Sims from his Woodstock base carried revival fire to at least eight other places scattered widely.

Grimsby, under C. M. Smith, had a new society by December.

A lady convert of the early 1880 Uxbridge services, a Mrs. Ferrier, had moved promptly to Belhaven in North Gwillimbury township, another twenty-five miles northwest. She started June prayer meetings in her home, then called for help after increasing crowds made it necessary to take the meetings first to the drive-shed and then the barn. Mr. Sage sent up the German girl, Nancy Schantz. With her first sermon, the man of the house where she was billeted became unwilling for her to stay longer. But Nancy had felt the call to preach and she was not to be driven away. Another home soon opened and she continued a converting work all winter in that and a nearby neighbourhood. A September, 1881, tent meeting with Mr. Sage in this area drew 1,500 people and produced twenty-two baptisms in Lake Simcoe. Thomas Glover was one of the first Belhaven members.

Florence's new lady pastors, the Misses Hagle and Thomas, stirred the whole countryside that winter and soon had regular services at six points. The Ousley society, at least, was formed under them, as well as the Florence church built. In the spring Miss Hagle had the accident that laid her aside for a year.

A new society was raised up at Sombra by Miss Thomas after the Muskoka Haleys moved there and opened their home.

James Craig at Thedford ran a revival that netted nineteen new members.

Newly converted Daniel Fletcher, living now at Bracebridge, was giving strong leadership as a supply preacher when Chairman Sage made his February visit.[1] This "Muskoka Mission" held its services in a schoolhouse at one point.

After some meetings at Huntsville farther north, Mr. Sage sent for young Wesley Walls of Scarboro, a former Primitive Methodist Ellesmere-Union-Sunday-School superintendent, now recently revived and enrolled as a Free Methodist. Shortly after beginning his labours northeast of Huntsville, he had his Pentecost and received his power for service kneeling beside a huge Muskoka rock. By next conference, he reported thirty-two probationers and a little log church built.

A Hoffman and Bretz pair of lady evangelists at Severn Bridge raised up a class of fourteen during the year.

At a Keswick quarterly meeting Mr. Sage baptized thirty-five and enrolled twelve new members, besides receiving twenty-six in full.

It was in May of that year that he held his Thousand Island quarterly meeting already described. After his twelve-mile row-boat ride down the river to Wells Island and back, he seemed justified in suggesting: "Work on this island could be cared for more easily by the Susquehanna Conference." Mr. Allguire had previously conducted an island revival and enrolled a class of twenty-three.

A Tillsonburg grove meeting held in June by Mr. Sims provided the nucleus of a later class in that town.[2]

Another Rev. Requa from New York State after visiting the Armadale camp that year dedicated a new church at Scarboro during a quarterly meeting. Nineteen lakeside baptisms were also a part of that meeting. Mrs. Requa stayed longer and conducted some house-to-house meetings in Toronto. At that time only one Free Methodist lived there—a Mrs. Hall newly come from Galt. Several Methodist class leaders came to her meetings. She stayed in the home of one, a Mr. Duncan of Queen Street Wesleyan Church.

Hannon built a fine church that year and newly raised Kelvin another. James Fletcher gave the land for the former and Jacob Miller the logs for the lumber of the latter. Layman James Carter built this Kelvin one. Kelvin became the area headquarters after that.

1881-82

Confernce at Hannon under General Superintendent E.P. Hart, a Roberts colleague, showed a 50 per cent swell in membership over the previous year and the number of appointments jumped from thirteen to eighteen. As proof of solid growth Free Methodists could point to six new churches owned. Superintendent Hart dedicated the new Hannon church while there. Ellesmere, Thedford, Galt, Hannon, Kelvin and Belhaven were the six strong circuits. Something progressive was done at that conference in the appointment of a Sage-Craig-Loveless Committee on Conference Missions and the ordering of a Conference-wide fall offering to help support preachers on new fields.

James Craig, then of Ellesmere, has left us a detailed account of a Muskoka quarterly meeting trip he took in the spring of 1882 for Mr. Sage. The northerners were jubilant. Bracebridge was still under Daniel Fletcher. The chapel was said to be on a granite ridge two miles from Bracebridge. Three men walked twenty miles to reach a service at Severn Bridge. This point was now served by Miss Hoffman and a Mrs. Laura Warren whose deceased American husband had once served in the Chippawa area of the Genesee Conference.[3]

Tommy Clark enters the history again at this point. Some Naish relatives at Port Credit found his religion so appealing when he visited them that they grew curious about his church and asked for some workers. Mr. Sage sent Matilda Sipprell and Mary Hutchinson who held services in an Orange Hall. Converts included some Sharps, Naishs, Johnsons, and Shavers.[4] One Mr. Shaver owned the farm and home later bought for Lorne Park College, and Mr. Craig once held a quarterly meeting in the parlour that later became Lorne Park College's reception room. Mr. Johnson later moved to Niagara Falls and continued active in the church; Mr. Sharp likewise to Galt and later Hamilton.

The June camp meeting was held near Sutton on Lake Simcoe close to some Indian islands. Indians came and some sought the Lord, after the chief had attended and given permission. One Indian girl desired prompt baptism and it was administered by lamp light after a late service. Scarboro had an August camp that same year. It was here the Toronto preacher exploded with abuse.

Uxbridge's Free Methodism extended to Victoria Corners that year.

During 1880-81, an A. C. Leonard stationed at Hannon had raised up a Clifton and Chippawa circuit. During 1881-82, this circuit's name became Niagara Falls and Chippawa.

1882-83

Waterloo Township was the location chosen for the annual conference, although it seems to have had no class or pastor yet. Continuing conference growth called for a second travelling chairman and James Craig received the honours. D. D. Marston who had been back in Michigan for two years returned as Stationed Chairman of the newly created Muskoka

Mission District. St. Catherines was annexed to Niagara Falls. This was the conference that sent out the ten loyal ladies to which Mr. Roberts referred so favourably. James Craig and Robert Loveless were named delegates to General Conference in Iowa the next month.

Carpenter-preacher C. M. Smith was read off for Waterloo where he was to build a church.

W. C. Walls was sent to Belhaven circuit to consolidate the phenomenal gains of Nancy Schantz during the previous two years. The membership had climbed to ninety-eight (almost double that of any other circuit in the conference) and two churches—one at Dry Town and the other north of Belhaven—now were built.[5]

While at Sheffield that fall Mr. Sage had an interesting experience with a Negro, Charlie Fisher. Fisher got an apple and an invitation to the Stockwell-home meeting from Mr. Sage who stopped while the former was ploughing near the road. Fisher hesitated to attend because of expected prejudice, but with his wife went, then asked for a meeting in his shanty. Both husband and wife were converted as a result. Charlie became the new society's "sweet singer" until killed a little later during church-building operations.

It was on this Sheffield visit that Mr. Sage's own sweet singing broke the hard heart of the one-time local preacher.

The Muskoka school community near Iona had its first Free Methodist preaching in March with Martha Thomas and Jerusha Hagle.[6] Joseph Milton, long since from Michigan, said he had been waiting to hear that kind of preaching for twenty years. He eventually "got the victory" over his tobacco and became a sturdy member; in fact, across nearly thirty-five years till his death he was late for church only once, and that lateness occurred because of an accident. His son James was to become a conference delegate repeatedly, his daughter Jennie (Agar) a class leader continuously, and his daughter Amy (McCallum) a preacher's wife in Ontario and Saskatchewan. This revival produced nineteen probationers for the Middlemiss society.

The London District camp of 1883 was held on the Thomas Moorehouse farm, up Bear Creek from Dresden. Ten Michigan visitors travelled partly by boat. For the last sixteen miles willing teamsters transported them.

Sunderland area saw a grove meeting that summer in a Michael Baker woods. Mr. Baker, from Ireland, had heard the famous Gideon Ousley preach and had been in Philip Embury's old-country home. Mrs. Baker was a Heck, relative of Barbara.

1883-84

Albert Sims was appointed a District Chairman at Kelvin conference that fall. He replaced C. H. Sage who by this time was feeling he had done all he could for Canada and left for pioneer work in Tennessee. There were twenty circuits then and 587 members. D. D. Marston went to Ellesmere (Armadale) but apparently during the year just past had built several more churches on his Muskoka Mission and shaped it up for an extra circuit. This was the conference whose Sabbath School Committee gave the big blast to the indifferent.

At Norwood during the conference year the new preacher J. Ruttan raised up a new class. One of his converts was Samuel Rogers who became an effective pioneer preacher in the Harwood-Warkworth zone and elsewhere.

Ridgeway experienced its first Free Methodist assault that year too. It came through Methodist George and Annie Teal's feeling out of place in tea meetings and reading a sermon on separation by Wilson T. Hogue. George's brother, Robert, found Mr. Hogue in Buffalo and invited him across the river.[7] By conference, Ridgeway had thirty-four members. About 1888 the class purchased the large local brick M. E. Church made vacant by the union of 1884, after earlier use of a hall south of the tracks.

This was the year of Mr. Sims' first bleak Muskoka winter trip described in the "Hardness" chapter. But the chairman was not daunted. During his second round of quarterly meetings in the Port Credit to Gananoque belt he discovered so many encouraging signs that he concluded his report with the previously quoted words: "Canada has hardly begun to see the power that will shake the Dominion."

Farther west, Walsingham was given its first taste of Free Methodism by means of a Warren-Stonehouse bush meeting. (At the next conference, the Port Royal-Marston circuit assigned to the lady evangelists included this new centre where the ladies soon built two churches.

C. M. Smith, now at Tillsonburg, built another new church during the year. It was outside the town and called Ebenezer Chapel. The land was donated by Edward Barnim.[8]

The London District camp was at Kelvin with B. T. Roberts and the power of God both on hand. The people gave $130 for a new district tabernacle.

1884-85

At Armadale conference—the first in what is now East Ontario—D. D. Marston transferred to Michigan and Wesley C. Walls received deacon's ordination. Mr. Walls' Belhaven membership had swollen to 112. The conference circuit count now stood at twenty-three, the Sunday School at nineteen. A new Hamilton district was carved from the London one, still under the same chairman, James Craig. Ridgeway now became a circuit. Mr. Hogue, Buffalo pastor in the Genesee Conference, was also named Ridgeway's supply pastor by the Canada conference—a unique arrangement.

It was during that conference year that Trent Bridge became a preaching point (annexed to Norwood) and the Uxbridge society bought their village's old M. E. Church.

Port Credit provided the locale for the 1885 Toronto District camp with Rev. C. B. Barrett of Oil City, Pa., a prominent visitor. He was so constantly victorious he had been nicknamed "The Happy Alleganian." [9] Mr. Barrett raised his Hallelujahs at the London-Thedford camp that summer, too. Rev. M. Devoist, the Thedford evangelist, was impressed with the way cold-hearted people were wooed back to God. "It surely must be an uncomfortable place for a formal professor among the Canada pilgrims," he commented.

That same summer Free Methodism moved into prosperous Brantford, a city of 12,000. Mr. Craig arrived to hold some tent meetings on the same day the London-converted George and Mary Taylor moved in.[10] For the new congregation that resulted, Mr. Taylor was made class leader and Mrs. Taylor supply preacher. The couple held one class meeting and three prayer meetings a week, besides Sunday services. These gatherings were in homes of the various city sections (including Whiskey Hollow), except the summer Sunday services went to the Market Square. Irish-born Mrs. Taylor remained in charge at Brantford for about five years, preaching at practically every service and visiting extensively from house to house to invite the people to prayer meeting. A student of the Bible and an effective speaker with commanding appearance, she carried the work forward, "fish being caught one at a time."

Mrs. Frederick Sutch, one of the local members, invited a Mrs. Henry Mellor to a prayer meeting, then to an annual conference. She became converted and later her husband also, a man who was to spend a period in the ministry and leave us reminiscences both numerous and humorous. The fish phrase above is his.

During the conference year, Olive Diller and Kate Booth, who had been sent to Iona (Middlemiss), fearing they would be excluded from the area schoolhouse, built a $700 church that still stands. B. T. Roberts dedicated it the next year.

1885-86

Crawford Baird

The conference met at Galt under General Superintendent Hart. The local delegate was Crawford Baird, a young man who was to represent his circuit periodically into the next century and to become known as a faithful local preacher and class leader. (Rev. Crawford Cowherd, present Superintendent of the West Ontario Conference is Mr. Baird's grandson. It is significant that he is also a grandson of Mrs. Thomas Cowherd who was one of Brantford's earliest members—probably another one of the "fish" referred to above.)

It was decided at that session to invite the General Conference evangelists to labour in Canada. This could have been because the membership at this and the previous conference had not only levelled off—it had slumped. Whether they came is not clear, but by next conference the total membrship had strangely dropped even more.

An interesting event in August of 1886 was a tent meeting among the Indians of Kettle Point on Lake Huron. They had asked the Thedford pastor, Rev. W. H. Burkholder, for it, and responded by seeking the Lord in altar fulls. Their own chief was converted and in one service an Indian himself, called Brother Moses Wolf, preached.

A Muskoka-Toronto union camp that summer centred in Thomas Luck's grove at Crown Hill (near Barrie) and was reported excellent. It probably provided the basis for the new class there listed at conference time. Thomas Luck, a former Methodist, became one of the charter members. He was to become a local preacher for thirty years, and hold many other local offices besides being a delegate to both annual and general conferences. H. B. Luck, whose name appears again and again among the ministers, was his son.

W. C. Walls served the Walsingham Centre-Tillsonburg circuit this year and the next. He was aided by G. A. Prior, then James Clink. Up to eight preaching points were cared for. During the second year the Walsingham church was built. B. T. Roberts came for the dedication.

1886-87

The fall conference at Hannon saw the return of Mr. Sage. He had decided his Tennessee "leadings" were a mistake and was assigned Ellesmere.[11] Matilda Sipprell and Mary Hutchinson who were at Iona and Southwold had the new little church at Middlemiss (begun the year before) ready for its dedication by December. B. T. Roberts came up for that and another at Thedford.[12]

Crown Hill, where the summer camp had been held, saw an encouraging late fall protracted meeting led by A. Sims. W. H. Burkholder, now at Bracebridge, held a six-week winter schoolhouse revival in his area. Only one convert resulted, a Mrs. James (Adeline) Rush. But she found "old-time religion" in good measure and herself soon had another convert, C. Floyd Appleton, as reported before.

Some time after Christmas Mr. Sims made his second grim Muskoka trip mentioned earlier.

A Tillsonburg camp the next summer brought a deluge of salvation. The evangelist, Rev. J. S. McGeary from Pittsbury remarked: "Some differences of manners and customs were apparent after we entered the Queen's Dominion, but we could feel and see no difference in salvation. The Canada pilgrims speak the language of Canaan just as do the pilgrims in the States." Thedford and Crown Hill had the camps that summer for their districts. At the latter, a tremendous altar response began one evening while the evangelist, a man named Manley, was still preaching. Ryde and Huntsville had bush meetings, and Stoney Creek (in the fruit belt) a tent meeting before conference.

THE BATTLE WAS THE LORD'S

One interesting record of this conference year is James Craig's 4,500-word account of his last quarterly and camp meeting buggy tour with his old horse Turk over the Hamilton and London Districts. He called it "Jottings By the Way." It reveals a lot of geography of southwestern Ontario as well as church activity.

Pausing near the brow of Niagara Escarpment "mountain" he viewed "a beautiful commingling of ripe wheat, green crops, apple and peach orchards laden with fruit and clumps of woodland adorned with green foliage. . . . The aspect of the whole scene indicated peace and plenty." Grimsby was "a quiet little village." Its park was called "the Chautauqua of Canada." St. Catherines was "a city of about 12,000 inhabitants." Turk got another rest while his owner "looked down on the great cataract" from above the Michigan Central Railway at Niagara. Of another view, this time above the falls, he wrote:

"The scene inspired my soul with awe and caused me to think of the great masses of humanity that are hurrying on to the bottomless pit and plunging into the fiery gulf from whence a wail shall arise with the smoke of their torment forever and ever."

At Ridgeway he "waited a few days to attend to a little circuit business and to give Bro. George Teal time to repair my buggy which he did gratis." Fonthill had its large nurseries even in those days. Hamilton's Jolley Cut was there then too. The city itself had 42,000 people. Galt had a population of 7,000. At both it and Stoney Creek, Mr. Craig held street meetings besides quarterly meetings. Brantford had 12,000 to 14,000 at the time. The class of five organized there two years before had now become twenty-one, but it still had no church. The account appealed for help to raise $2,000 for an available brick one. Glenshea, near Northfield, where a chapel had been donated, now had a new class organized. Walshingham's sixty-mile circuit of six societies had seen five of these formed in the last four years.

After a pause at home (Northfield), Mr. Craig pushed on to the nearby Kelvin camp where a blind Pittsburg preacher named Gaines helped out, and some of the goodly attendance of campers had to stay in the homes nearby.

Back westward through Norwich, Tillsonburg, and St. Thomas, Mr. Craig drove, heading for Middlemiss. Log cabins and delapidated frame houses were disappearing in favour of fine brick dwellings. Thedford (400-500 people) came next, then Ousley to the south where the aforesaid lady, long absent from church, kept testifying again and again.

The last meeting over, Mr. Craig hustled eastward towards Uxbridge for the coming conference, stopping by night here and there with the saints. At an unofficial Stoney Creek street meeting en route, one feeble old lady, long since from Massachusetts and probably new to Free Methodism, sat in her chair on the street, and listened with tears to the testimonies before giving her own. Mr. Craig wrote of her:

"Referring to the pilgrims, she said she would like to live with such a good people. The Lord grant that she may live with them forever. Amen!"

The account is repeatedly punctuated with Praise the Lord, Hallelujah or Amen. Mr. Craig felt things looked well. He had concrete reasons, for the membership was mounting as he went from place to place.

Toronto, he said, has "about 120,000 inhabitants" and "bids fair to be the principal city in Canada." A night at the Loveless Ellesmere home, a train ride from Agincourt —and he was at Uxbridge conference.

1887-88

This was the conference which appointed the first committee to work towards establishing a school. The two district chairmen exchanged districts that fall. Rev. Wesley Walls received his ordination as elder and his appointment to Armadale.

At the Toronto-Armadale camp the next year we first meet Rev. and Mrs. A. H. Norrington who were to play active parts in the conference soon. They came as visitors and seem to have been invited to stay and labour in the eastern part of the province.[13]

The Norringtons

1888-89

Richard Burnham went to the Kelvin fall conference as the Uxbridge delegate but left as the Bracebridge-Baysville pastor. During that first year—in January—his Bracebridge revival netted a big fish, Barkway's lumber-jack, David Allan. Both men find their places among the "Giants" of this history.

The Report on the State of the Work at that session was a particularly long one. Read by James Craig, the Committee Chairman, and presumably largely written by him, it attempted to point out some of the conference's weaknesses and causes of stagnation. There was, for instance, a fear that some people had "more regard for an outward compliance to certain stringent regulations than for an inward conformity to the divine image." Some were evidently riding "anti" hobbies to the extent that they created unnecessary prejudice and made it difficult to reach the unsaved.

Then there were the failures in some cases to follow the discipline closely, to care for finances systematically, to support workers adequately, to indoctrinate new converts properly, to even bring about true evangelical repentance in seekers.

Preachers received a generous share of censure. Some had a disposition to "take things altogether too easy." They did not visit enough and deal faithfully and personally with their people. Some did not pay enough attention to the rules for conduct, nor seem to preach much "under the divine anointing." People in general were probably failing to manifest much of "the fervour of Christian love" in their contacts.

The report lashed out at "the evil abroad which is making encroachments upon the church leading them to set up little institutions where they may be the head of some puny thing of their own creation." "There is," it went on, "plenty of room and opportunity to exercise our magnificent abilities and capacious powers in the authorized departments and channels of the church." What this strong language was aimed at, one can only guess.

The report wasn't all negative, however. Such wholesome suggestions as these came out: having a teachable spirit to learn from past failures, observing the relation between cause and effect, studying the methods of those succeeding, preaching a class of truth suited to the people "with hearts of love and tongues of fire," studying human nature as well as books, maintaining peace and unity among themselves. Clearly Mr. Craig was a keen analyst and a first-rate counsellor.

That fall we find the Norringtons launching a fruitful ministry in the East that began at a new point, Petworth, northeast of Napanee. Some Friends ladies preaching there did not quite suit Isaac Benn who was very dissatisfied with his local Methodist Church. They recommended the Norringtons (then working in the Belleville area) and evidently contacted them and a B. P. Clark.[14] At any rate in a few days Mr. Clark arrived and when young Miles had helped secure the Orange Hall, the services began. The Norringtons arrived shortly afterwards. Miles Benn and Alfred Wattam were two converts who shortly were to join the ministry.[15] Eventually the Orangemen closed the hall but services continued in a house. Mr. Clark was a dynamic preacher. The Norringtons themselves had attractive personalities and both could preach. Mrs. Norrington was a beautiful singer. A new society was organized at the close and a church built in 1891.

From Petworth the Clark-Norrington trio moved on to Verona (a few miles northeast) and during the winter, using an Orange Hall again, planted a work and started a class that has remained strong to this day.[16] The next summer an excellent camp meeting at Verona boosted the beginning.

Sometime during 1889 the David Kirks moved from Bracebridge to Toronto where God was to use them in the first of a whole sequence of Free Methodist plantings.

1889-90

At Ridgeway conference the reported membership total of 632 revealed the slump ended and a new upswing underway. A memorial service was held for Martha Stonehouse, a gifted lady evangelist who had served about six years and died during the year. Her will included two significant bequests —$1,000 for future school purposes and $400 to establish a mission in

Africa.[17] It was reported that the Toronto and Muskoka Districts had purchased a parsonage at Uxbridge for their chairman James Craig. This was big news for here was the first parsonage to be "bought" in the conference.

A. H. Norrington was appointed to Verona and Petworth and before year's end a new church was opened at Verona and a powerful revival was on again. This outpouring of the Holy Spirit spread to the Oak Flats schoolhouse. Sometimes conviction would grip people even after the sleigh loads had started home and the horses would have to be stopped while seekers knelt in the snow banks to make contact with God. This revival and the one of the previous winter garnered in a host of people, many of whose names were to become synonymous with spirituality. Some were Abraham, Caleb, Almiron, D. C., Miles, Lydia, W. P., and Sperry Snyder, (or Snider—both names belong), William and Eliza Hamilton, William and Esther Goodberry, and Stewart Walker. (Mrs. D. C. Snyder and W. H. Reynolds had recently been converted in some Quaker services there and W. H. Gregory was converted at home about this time.) It is said that at least twelve of that year's new converts eventually became preachers.

Among them were J. M. Eagle to West Ontario, Emerson Snyder and J. Commodore to Gunter, Emma Snider and Minnie Bauder[18] to Clarendon, Charles Babcock to Fermoy, and Ethel Davey (later Ryff) to Gananoque and eventually to Africa. Their efforts marked the beginnings of Free Methodism in a number of these places.

"Will" Goodberry

But the revival did not stop at Verona and Oak Flats. Deyo's Corners, Holleford, Fifth Lake, Wagarville and Enterprise all felt it. People were especially busy squaring up accounts with their fellow men. One future class leader rode horseback through a raging blizzard to confess the burning of a neighbour's barn.

That same 1889-90 winter saw a great awakening at Keith (later to be called Charlemont). It really began the year before and a woman was behind it. Keith was a store-post office centre in the extreme west of West Ontario between Dresden and Wallaceburg, some four hundred miles from Verona. To this community the Benjamin DeMille's had recently moved from Florence or Shetland where, as noted earlier, they had become Free Methodists in some Coates-sponsored meetings in 1880. Mr. DeMille was a faithful Christian but his wife was a talented and very devout woman who got a burden for her neighbours and started calling on them and inviting them to a prayer meeting at her house.[19] The first night they filled her house and part of the yard. Everybody raised his hand for more meetings; those outside pushed hands in through the open windows.

Mrs. Benjamin DeMille

In the services that followed, Mrs. DeMille was soon setting out chairs for an altar and having converts, and almost every night was becoming prayer meeting night. (The nightly service actually continued till the next fall.)

Mr. Sims, the District Chairman in the area, soon received an appeal for help and sent Laura Warren and Annie Green whose Middlemiss community sixty miles away was closed to services because of small-pox. The DeMille home housed them through the winter, even though dad and mother had to make for themselves a bed on the floor.

Point Edward (no stationed pastor here yet, but probably a society) had a camp meeting the next summer, that is, in 1889. Mrs. Robert Hamilton (mother of R. H.), and sister-in-law, Mrs. Annie Robinson, of that community were among five women who went with Mrs. Warren—and were converted. They were on hand for prayer power when services began in the fall again, this time at the Coon Climb schoolhouse. The same two lady preachers (now stationed at Dresden nearby) were on hand. When Mrs. Warren, fearful of a flock of superficial converts, began insisting that the people get down to business in their seeking, results followed. Mr. Sims came for a quarterly meeting in that open clay-mud winter and asked how he should preach. He was advised that the class of truth the people needed was "Hell fire and damnation; give it strong."

Over one hundred people were converted in that revival and some conversions were remarkable. Rough men, proud women, and formal professors of religion confessed their sins, found victory and arose to live transformed lives. Card-playing Jonah Jarvis was among the first. His ex-bartender partner, Josephus Harris, followed after and became a local preacher and class leader. Big wicked Neil McGugan repented and was soon in schoolhouses nearby winning souls himself for God. (He later entered the ministry in Western Canada and won many more.) The Orange Lodge closed down after the Grand Master was saved and few members were left to carry on. Some services continued until nearly morning. Three or four rows of penitents sometimes knelt at once around the school platform praying earnestly and loudly. Seeking and experiencing holiness was prevalent—sometimes within a few days of conversion.

Like the Verona revival, the Keith one was a producer of preachers. Besides Neil McGugan, there was W. H. Wilson, Orangeman, Methodist member and schoolteacher, who was destined to become the Canada Conference's first missionary in the Northwest; also his sister Mrs. Jennie Robinson who was to join him there.[20] On the preacher list too, were the brothers Jacob and Robert Hamilton; the former becoming the father of Mrs. J. W. Haley and Mrs. John Fletcher, the latter to have a son, R. H., whose contributions and leadership in the Canadian church would be enormous.[21] Miss Anna Botting was another. Mrs. Clara Deyo, converted at the camp already mentioned, was to become a great prayer warrior and burden bearer and, like Jacob Hamilton, give a daughter to Africa as the wife of the other Haley brother, A. E.[22]

Keith had a new 28' x 40' church built during the early months of 1890. It was dedicated at the August quarterly meeting by A. Sims. Membership additions pushed the nearby Dresden-Shetland circuit up to over sixty (seventy-two by conference) and baptisms numbered eighteen. Some other new "joiners," besides people already named, were the following: Henry and Eliza Wilson, Philip and Hannah Robinson, Henry and Beulah Robinson, James Robinson, Sarah Long, Mrs. Neil McGugan, a Mrs. Walker, and a Mrs. Peters. Numbers of these people had for some reason migrated from the Kingston—Verona area earlier. Other communities around Keith such as Thorncliffe were soon to feel the impact of that revival too. It would appear that, during this same winter, the lady evangelists had a fifty-convert revival at their home base of Dresden.

The Hamilton District camp in the summer of 1890 was held at Otterville. Tents numbered twenty-four, a big pitching for those days. A. D. Gaines who was there from Pennsylvania called it "the best of six camps I have attended in Canada." He also mentioned the arrival of a Genesee man, L. A. Sager, who was going to stay in Ontario and who did, in fact, receive appointment to Uxbridge and Mount Albert that fall.

1890-91

They had a great conference that fall—at Uxbridge. It was considered "the most spiritual and harmonious session . . . yet held in Canada." We can understand this for with at least three tremendous revivals, at least two fruitful camp meetings, three new churches, three new societies and the total conference membership up to 723, things looked very encouraging. W. H. Wilson who had already been active in his home community was read off for Walsingham. Richard Burnham was ordained deacon.

And the year which followed that conference was another good one. Tupperville's new church was dedicated and eighteen people there were baptized on the same day. Thorncliffe (on the Dresden-Keith circuit) with its own campaign by the ladies plus a camp meeting in June of 1891 was shaped up as an appointment (with Keith) for the next year. One man was said to have been entirely sanctified on the same day as his conversion. Another man and his wife rode sixty miles to get to a March district meeting at Keith.

Verona's church was dedicated at the April District Meeting. Mr. Roberts crossed Lake Ontario on an iceboat to be present but was delayed in arriving. Mr. Craig, thinking the General Superintendent would not be getting there, proceeded to preach at the appointed afternoon hour. A midsermon telegram from Kingston raised a volley of shouts, and when Mr.

Roberts finally reached there in the evening, he gave them another sermon, his famous Petros-Petra one. Nearly seventy years afterward, Minnie Bauder Crimmins wrote of that occasion: "His preaching was wonderful. So much of the Spirit I felt like shouting all the time he preached." Giving had been hilarious that day—$350 counting pledges. Blind Hattie Steele put $5 into the cause and her friends, touched by her generosity, returned to her over $50. A new Lansdowne circuit, raised up without outside help, was represented at this district gathering for the first time. That was the time that pastor Norrington spoke of the land as "one vast field of waiting harvest."

Otterville's summer camp meeting had four altar services per day on all but two days, and one of those was a Sunday when morning and afternoon crowds made altar services impossible. The main evangelist was J. S. McGeary of Pittsburg, but W. A. Sellew was there too and wrote the report. A Crown Hill camp with evangelist Winget was referred to earlier. Said A. H. Norrington of a young Methodist minister who came 150 miles to get to it: "He was invited to preach which he did with a good degree of liberty, but in a succeeding service he went forward for holiness and after a long struggle he fell prostrate in the straw and groaned it out. Oh, hallelujah! I love to hear the death rattle and be present on such funeral occasions."

At Walsingham quarterly meeting that summer one load drove sixteen miles and arrived at eight o'clock on Sunday morning. When Mr. Sims preached on "Take ye away the stone" it was said that "sandy foundations were shaken, decayed timbers crumbled, dead religion was put under foot and the Bible standard raised high." At Keith, Mr. Sims found that "the greater number" of the over one hundred converts were remaining steadfast.

Some time during this conference year, David Burkholder, supply pastor at Hannon, formed a class in Hamilton city. About April a church on Herkimer Street in the southwest was bought. Mr. Sims held an August quarterly meeting in it and participated also in a successful Bretz-Warren-Green tabernacle meeting that summer in Hamilton.

This was the year Mr. Craig, evidently an inveterate diarist, wrote another long travelogue, this one under the title "Itinerating." Again, this is helpfully geographical as well as historical. Entraining at Uxbridge in mid-June, 1891, he stopped at Orillia, "a stirring business and manufacturing town of 4,000 inhabitants," for the night, then pushed on through Barrie to Crown Hill camp meeting where the young Methodist minister "died." After helping Uxbridge's L. A. Sager put up the district tabernacle nearby and preaching a few times in the campaign (Mr. Sager had raised a thirty-member class at Glen Major near there the year before), Mr. Craig and wife headed for Huntsville and the log chapel six miles out. We have already mentioned the walking-women pastors there. Back at Bracebridge with their little rural church burned down[23] and their pastor seeming "to

ONTARIO OPENS FOR OCCUPATION

care more for the fleece than the flock," there had been temptations to discouragement. But the Lord blessed his people and a singing march into town gathered "a large congregation" for a circle street meeting at the post office. James Rusk lent his horse and buckboard for a twelve-mile drive over "the roughest road I ever travelled" to Bro. Thos. Holliday's for a visit and meeting.

The next week-end Mr. Craig held a Barkway-Housey's Rapids quarterly meeting. It featured six new memberships and thirteen baptisms. Barkway's church had been built during the previous conference year under Austin Allguire. This is almost our first mention of Barkway, but in 1882-83 when D. D. Marston had been serving Severn Bridge as pastor and the Muskoka Mission District as Stationed Chairman, he held some meetings in the area in "Bushes' School" and in the home of Ira Davey. As early as 1886 John Benzinger, a Marston convert who was known affectionately to many for years before his recent death as "Grandpa" Benzinger, had served as a class leader at Housey's Rapids.[24]

From Uxbridge home base, pastor Sager drove chairman Craig to Belhaven for a meeting. The fast horse, good roads, pleasant weather, beautiful farms and bumper crops combined to elevate Mr. Craig's spirits. He wrote: "In many respects this is a fine world to live in, when at the same time we live in God and God in us." Five hundred people attended an afternoon baptismal service in Lake Simcoe. It cared for converts of W. C. Walls' previous winter revival.

"Grandpa" Benzinger and family connections

The next two weekends took him to Port Credit and to Toronto—with Saturday night street meetings at each place. The Toronto quarterly meeting was in Caledonia Hall at Queen and York and the street meeting at Yonge and Shuter. Toronto as yet had no conference-appointed pastor, but since April at Mr. Craig's request, J. M. Eagle and Alfred Wattam had been holding services in the city, and a class now existed.[25] The population of Toronto then stood at about 200,000. Mr. Craig described Toronto as "perhaps the most religious and orderly city on the American continent. No street cars run and no hawking of papers on Sunday."

A boat trip across Lake Ontario to Lewiston took the writer and his wife to a Buffalo district camp for a few days. Another boat ride, skirting the south of the lake, stopping at intervals en route, brought them to Clayton and the Thousand Islands. At the Union Church five miles east of Lansdowne, Mr. Craig held a quarterly meeting.

The couple travelled on—by train this time—to a camp meeting at Verona. The circuit now had four societies and another ready to organize at Clarendon. The Verona church was described as "one of the best and most comfortable... that we own in Canada." Mr. Craig took in seventeen new members at the end of the camp, besides receiving ten in full. Stewart Walker drove him to Sydenham to attend a tabernacle meeting sponsored by Rev. R. C. Horner who was still in the Montreal Conference of the Methodist Church, but already quite unpopular.

Another train ride—ninety-four miles north and west—and the Craigs were in Havelock, near the next quarterly meeting stop of Trent Bridge. A recess at home was followed by a visit to Harwood via the steamer *Daisy*, sailing from Peterborough down the Otonabee River and across Rice Lake. A huge five-gate saw mill at Harwood could turn out up to 115,000 feet of lumber a day. There was no preacher yet available for this place, but a society had been started.

An Armadale quarterly meeting and an Uxbridge district meeting[26] completed the three and one-half-month cycle and a four-year attachment to the two eastern districts. This was to be the end of Mr. Craig's labours in the east, for at the coming conference he and Mr. Sims exchanged areas again. He had seen 10 new societies, two churches and one parsonage appear, and felt that "the prospects for the future of our work are quite encouraging."

1891-92

Brantford entertained the fall conference with Superintendent Hart as chairman. Her local preacher delegate, Henry Mellor, was assigned that year to supply Toronto—Port Credit, while the Eagle-Wattam team from that circuit was split and sent to Hannon and Hamilton.[27] This action makes Mr. Wattam, Hamilton's first appointed pastor. These two latter men along with W. H. Wilson and L. A. Sager, joined the conference. W. C. Walls went to Keith and Thorncliffe to consolidate the Warren-Green gains as he had earlier done at Belhaven with Miss Schantz's revival fruitage. (He was a sound teacher well suited for this necessary work.) R. H. Hamilton and David Allan received their first charges. Actually they were assigned the same circuit—Severn Bridge, Barkway, and Housey's Rapids—the home zone for Mr. Allan. Mr. Norrington was given Elginburg as a new point attached to Petworth. His wife was to supply Lansdowne, 35 or more miles away. Brantford was about to have a church at last, for it received a $417.84 boost in the Saturday evening offering towards the $1200-purchase-price of the Primitive Methodist Church on Market Street. As we have previously noted, that conference marked the beginning of foreign mission society organizing and giving. It also saw the Kingston District carved out of the area's eastern flank, but including only four circuits—Lansdowne, Petworth and Elginburg, Verona and Oak Flats, and Clarendon.

David Allan, who before this time had been an exhorter, class leader and a delegate to conference twice, won a convert at his first Sunday afternoon service in Brookes' schoolhouse. That convert took his Bible from house to house, asked his hosts to read it (because he couldn't), and followed the reading with prayer. The action immediately precipitated a revival with forty converts. A man fourteen miles away at Cooper's Falls wrote a letter asking for the kind of salvation that the schoolhouse people had, and offering a free hall. When a little later the two preachers were ordered out of the hall, the local tavern keeper, hating to see the services close, offered to seat his large room. Consquently, meeting next night was announced for McNab's Bar Room. The reader can easily predict the sequel—McNab and wife and son were among the converts as a fresh surge of salvation rolled through the community.[28]

At Armadale, where W. H. Wilson had gone, several of the Loveless children found the Lord in the yearly revival. Thomas was to become a local preacher and a repeated delegate to annual and general conference; Elijah, a capable pastor in West Ontario for about thirty years; and Hannah, the wife of J. M. Eagle.[29] One judges that Robert Loveless was well repaid personally for exerting himself to keep "the narrow way."

E. Slingerland of Crown Hill accompanied chairman Sims into Muskoka for a Barkway district meeting and a look around. The former reported that at the first table of the Lord's Supper "the saints were so blessed it was some time before they could be dismissed." He mentions also a service with "a large congregation" and "some seekers" in Orillia. Later that year they returned to Orillia and formed a class.

Some Norrington meetings at Wilmur, a "suburb" of the Elginburg preaching point, were going well as the people renounced "popular sins" and corrected their lives. Despite roads made near impassable by mud, Verona church was very inadequate to hold its district meeting crowd. This was the occasion that the new Protestant had "leaped and shouted" without precedent.

Gunter, that pocket of preacher potential in rugged northern Hastings county, now enters the story. In early months of the previous year, 1891, "Abey" Gunter of Gunter had received an impressive letter from friends in Alamonda, Michigan. In it they said that in meetings held by a queer class of people called Free Methodists, they had been converted by faith in the blood of Jesus Christ—and they knew it. Mr. Gunter was a Methodist local preacher but didn't have that knowledge. So great was his hunger to have it, however, that he sold his only cow and with his wife took the train for Michigan. There, his friends instructed him and he received "the Witness." [30]

Back at home, he was not allowed to tell his experience in the local church, so Grandfather Potter (father of Rev. John) said he could use his large dining room. Interest developed till regular services became the order, even though the Gunters (without a horse) had to walk and carry a baby five miles each way. Conversions followed and some people somehow found cleansing. This was one stage beyond Mr. Gunter himself, so he sent an S. O. S. to Mr. Sims to "come yourself or send us a man, for Jesus' sake." [31] Some of the partitions in Dexter Trumble's large house were removed and the house was packed an hour before Mr. Sims' train reached Gilmour Station on a late December afternoon.

Just at the moment in the first sermon when the foolish virgins were knocking to get in to the wedding feast, the local persecuting pastor and eight of his members rapped on the front door. The scribe cut us off on that story but young Emerson Snyder was shortly asked to serve as Gunter pastor. He went in April, 1892.

Because he spoke a couple of times without a text, the community decided he couldn't preach and the house was full for the third service when he did announce a text: "Tekel" (Dan. 5:25). At the finish of the sermon, he commanded, "Everybody that wants to get saved from falling into hell and get to heaven, drop on your knees and pray." It was said the people fell on their knees "like leaves from autumn trees." The meeting lasted till four in the morning but three future ministers—Charles Cunningham, John Potter and Sam Gunter—and their wives were among the good grain from that harvesting. Mr. Snyder organized a class of fourteen shortly.

Elginburg, on the Norrington charge, had a visitation of God that winter with numerous happy deliverances.[32]

When James Craig reminded the people in February of their Brantford pledges he added, "It seems to me we should put forth greater and more united efforts in planting an earnest Christianity in all the centres of population in the Dominion of Canada." Then mentioning that the poor and hard-working classes were mainly the ones to take the Way, he concluded: "If we succeed . . . , we shall need to . . . make up our minds to cheerfully sacrifice of our means."

In April, W. J. Campbell of Belhaven reviewed the Toronto picture: the main business centre in the province, a struggle for years to raise up a work, the David Kirk's bringing "Jerusalem fire" from Muskoka three years earlier and seeing at last a small harvest from their prayers and tears, the previous year's Eagle-Wattam efforts, and now some successful Mellor-sponsored Sager meetings.[33] One notes a similarity between an earlier statement by Mr. Sage on Canada and Mr. Campbell's conclusion on Toronto: "This city is full of churches and religion but there is little salvation."

The Mellors[34] have also left us an interesting account of the state of the work. There was no parsonage or church yet. They rented a house (on DeGrassi St. just east of Broadview Ave.) for $7.00 a month and rented a vacant store (on Queen St. near DeGrassi) for services at $10 a month. Besides Kirks, the congregation contained some Bassetts, a Mrs. Ferrier, Clara Luck, Charles Graham, William Dulmage and John Montgomery.[35] (Mr. Craig says there were sixteen members at the time.) There were always some "religious tramps" dropping in, who "could quote Scripture by the yard" and "had all the texts on Perfection right at their fingers' ends." The Mellors went to Port Credit every other Sunday. When summer came, they held a six-week tent meeting in a vacant lot near the store with Clarence Wright, a North Chili student, as helper.

Henry Mellor nearly drowned when with "Sager, Campbell, Rogers, Wright, and Wilson" he went swimming at Hanlan's Point on the Monday after a Toronto District meeting that summer. Unable to swim, he got out beyond his depth but, wrote Mr. Mellor, "Clarence Wright took in the situation and rescued me."

That same year Walsingham circuit had a great revival with nearly one hundred seeking salvation. (The evangelist was Rev. A. G. Matthewson.) Fort Erie organized a W. F. M. S. Verona camp meeting, with a Rev. M. S. Babcock as evangelist, saw its altars doubled to hold the seekers.[36] And Crown Hill built a church, on land donated by Thomas Luck.

1892-93

Yes, 1891-92 had been a good year—almost better even than the one before—with widespread revival, one new parsonage, eight new churches, thirteen new societies and total membership zooming to nearly one thousand (over 250 above the figure of two years previous.)[37]

The Uxbridge Conference that year with Rev. W. A. Sellew presiding, is significant to us because it is the only Canada Conference for which a photograph is still available. Of those people present, this writer could ascertain for certain that only two still remain: Annie Robertson (later Walls, later Campbell)[38] who received her first charge—Huntsville—a year earlier, and M. S. Benn who attended as a Petworth delegate and received his first appointment—Bracebridge and Baysville—that year. (Minnie Bauder may be in group.) Another new Petworth person (Almira Hogle) went to Orillia. Verona's Emma Snider was named to help supply Verona.[39] Mr. Norrington was listed as conference evangelist.

Robert Hamilton, alone this year on the Severn Bridge circuit, built or completed a new church before winter at the Housey's Rapids point.

Verona's Emerson Snyder received his first conference appointment—to Harwood and Harnden's Mills—leaving Gunter to an Isaac Lake.[40] Isaac, it seems, married Angus Harnden's daughter that December when Mr. Sims came to the Mills for a quarterly meeting. Mr. Sims reported in "Notes By the Way" that the blessing of God fell, even at the wedding. Pastor Emerson's two-room apartment in layman Angus' home has been mentioned already. The pastor seems to have had a new bride that fall too, the former Mary Milliken who had helped supply the Clarendon circuit the year before.

Although they did not remain for the whole year, the two girls, Josie Rusk and Annie Robertson, became that year for Point Edward (later Sarnia circuit) its first appointed supply pastors. Actually a Mrs. Eliza Wees had been the first to hold meetings in the area. After getting converted alone in her home, this woman began witnessing to her neighbours

Canada Conference at Uxbridge, 1892. Right to left: IMMEDIATE FRONT: Walter A. Sellew (President), Mrs. Walter A. Sellew. FIRST ROW: Robert Hamilton, Mrs. Geo. Overpaugh, Geo. Overpaugh, L. A. Sager, Mrs. L. A. Sager, A. Sims, Mrs. A. Sims, A. H. Norrington, Mrs. A. H. Norrington, C. H. Reed. Mrs. C. H. Reed, Mrs. W. C. Walls, W. C. Walls. SECOND ROW: Mrs. Robert Hamilton, Geo. Prior, Mrs. George Prior, W. J. Campbell, Mrs. W. J. Campbell, Mrs. Henry Mellor, Nellie Fulton, Mrs. Edward Slingerland, Edward Slingerland, Armcey Wiancko, Unrecognized, Unrecognized. THIRD ROW: Emerson Snyder, Edward Walker, Henry Mellor, Thomas Loveless, J. M. Eagle, Alfred Wattam, Elijah Loveless, William Wees, Richard Burnham, Unrecognized, Joseph Bretz. FOURTH ROW: Robert Garbutt, Minnie Bauder, Unrecognized, Agnes Norris, Jemima Macklin, Hannah Loveless, W. H. Reynolds, W. R. Pattison, W. H. Wilson, Mrs. Thomas Clark, David Burkholder. FIFTH ROW: Loretta Breckin, Mrs. Thomas Glover, Almira Hoyle, Mary Milliken, Mrs. Jennie Robinson, Mrs. Laura J. Warren, Lydia Bortz, Mrs. Stanton, Mrs. Gilbert Showers, Mrs. Ferrier, Mrs. Eliza Free, Mrs. Thomas Luck. SIXTH ROW: Mrs. Robert Loveless, Annie L. Green, Nancy Schantz, Mrs. Geo. Taylor, Geo. Taylor, Jane Hill. SEVENTH ROW: Robert Loveless, Josie Rusk, Annie Robertson, S. Rogers, Jemima Hutchinson. EIGHTH ROW: John Norris, Mr. Harmer, Geo. Cook, Unrecognized, Stewart Walker, Mary Hutchinson, Geo. Teal. NINTH ROW: Unrecognized, Thomas Luck, Thomas Glover, Gilbert Showers, Thomas Clark, Unrecognized, Josephus Harris. Not Shown: James Craig, Mary C. Craig, Miles Benn.

and conducting services in their homes. After crowds increased, the services were taken to a room above a store, then to a hall. About this time, James Clink, a Thedford Free Methodist, came to Point Edward to fish and helped Mrs. Wees in special meetings. All of Mrs. Wees' family were saved (F. M. Wees was one son), as well as a son-in-law Jim Rose who became known for his singing ability. Mrs. James Wilson and Mrs. Teeter were probably converted at this time too. Shortly a class was organized and now several years after Mrs. Wees' initiative began, this conference appointment followed.

Wm. Wees at Galt had seven weeks of "special meetings" with help from George Overpaugh and nearly fifty came forward. Mr. Sims dedicated the Petworth church on December 11 then moved to Verona for a quarterly meeting that precipitated a revival under the pastor L. A. Sager.

Henry Mellor stayed on at Toronto because a Susquehanna American, F. J. Dunham, never came after being appointed. A Rev. J. D. Christie came from Chicago and had a good revival with him during the year. The horse-racing lodge member mentioned before was one convert of this campaign. Mr. Mellor did some tailoring, and finding his evangelist in serious need of a suit, bought some wholesale cloth and made one. Jennie Robinson helped some at Toronto towards the end of that year.

Little Lansdowne pastored by Mrs. Norrington had a May district meeting, but distance and busy season kept most visitors away.

Mr. Craig reported a Kelvin camp with blind evangelist Gaines. "Nancy Schantz, the irrepressible pastor . . . had things on the move" when Mr. Craig arrived. Another camp took him to Chatham, a new point where Matilda Sipprell had been serving. Mr. Sellew came for part of this. Toronto, in the eastern half of the conference, had a June camp meeting. Rev. Albert Bean was one of several Americans attending.

During this year a church was built under the pastorate of C. H. Reed on the Trent Bridge circuit. It was likely at Victoria, for that point boasts of having the oldest church on the Peterborough District.

1893-94

Brantford was the location and W. T. Hogue the chairman of the 1893 conference. The Warren-Green team of ladies were joint pastors there and supervised the entertaining of over 130 guests. Promising Alfred Wattam's sad memorial service was held that year. Mr. Wattam, a probationer, was the first preacher of the conference to cross over.[41] While in his second year at Hamilton, he had developed fatal consumption from a cold. A third middle administrative unit in the western part of the conference was formed—the Brantford District; and in the east, Toronto District divided again with the creation of a three-circuit Peterborough District.[42] Both it and the Kingston District were placed under A. H. Norrington. Wilton and Violet appear as a new circuit under Austin Allguire. Clarendon under Mary Diller was separated from Verona. Port Credit was separated from Toronto and given to Emma Snider.

THE BATTLE WAS THE LORD'S

New Wilton had a blessed November quarterly meeting with ten members received and plans announced to build a church. Gunter had been given no pastor, but young J. W. Commodore was sent soon after conference, found it alive, and, with the help of local Charles Cunningham, built a church. It was dedicated in August, 1894, by G. W. Overpaugh.[43] Huntsville, under David Allan, was in good spiritual shape when the January Sims-held district meeting came. (Huntsville then was the home of the Henwoods who later pioneered in the Northwest and gave a long-term missionary to the Belgian Congo—Margaret, wife of Rev. Ronald Collett.) The Muskoka Cooper's Falls church was built about this time.

Robert Hamilton at Bracebridge had that area's greatest revival during the conference year. It lasted all winter, saw conversions by the scores, and made the Free Methodist Church the most popular one in the town. One convert was the wife of J. D. Shier, a prosperous lumberman and the town's mayor. Mrs. Shier came to church in her "rustling silks" but under the Holy Spirit's movings found herself at the altar pleading for mercy. Mr. Sims felt that M. S. Benn's district tent meetings of the year previous had prepared the people for this revival. Robert Hamilton attributed some of the success to Mrs. Benn's prayers at the time of those meetings. Mrs. Shier had attended them several times.

The next summer Mr. Shier who had at one time been critical, offered his grove for a camp meeting. Chairman Sims and General Superintendent Jones did the preaching. The "big" convert was J. D. Shier himself who with his wife was soon baptized and enrolled as a church member.[44] His indirect but large part in opening Western Canada is a later story.

When E. Slingerland went to Walsingham that year he plunged into revivals there and a little later at Glenshea, and saw both those places truly revived. At the latter, the congregation had not exceeded eight for four years, but soon attendance soared till the church would not hold the people.

Burnley, east of Rice Lake, appears as a new society at this time, opened up by Isaac Lake and his father-in-law, Angus Harnden. Mr. Harnden had a sawmill there. Up to twenty-two went forward at once in services they held, and seven joined the church on a quarterly meeting Sunday. A Clarendon quarterly meeting in May received honourable mention too that year. A Bro. Shay was referred to as pastor.

During this year W. H. Gregory from Verona began to get active at Vennachar in northern Frontenac county. Even the year previous, he and singer Thos. Flake had won some converts in a ten-day Orange Hall meeting at nearby Denbigh. Then this year, appointed by his district elder sometime after conference, he and a Verona singing colleague, Lyford Snider,[45] walked twenty-four miles from Clarendon along a bush road to be greeted by a packed Vennachar schoolhouse. They planned to sleep in the school but a settler, Jacob Drader, who had been converted at Verona, invited them home.[46]

ONTARIO OPENS FOR OCCUPATION

On the third night when the first altar call came, the front of the school filled with Balls, Cowans, Hughes, Jacksons, Connors, and Wilsons crying for mercy. During this year or the next, Mr. Gregory carried the good news of "sins forgiven and hell subdued" to the people of wild Matawachan and Miller Townships, with meetings in a drive-house, schoolhouse or home. He persuaded a "charming young woman" of ability named Caroline Brisco to become a Christian and shortly after to become his wife.

A Hannon camp meeting in the summer of 1894 was large and successful, but saw so much cold rainy weather that the children wore their grey flannel night caps.[47] The evangelists were Rev. and Mrs. J. Barnhart. Rev. C. B. Barrett, the "Happy Alleganian," was also at the camp—his twenty-seventh in Canada.

1894 Union Camp of Hamilton and Brantford Districts at Hannon under James Craig.

Toronto District camp was in Toronto again with a Ronpe and Clarke team as evangelists and repeatedly filled altars as the fruitage. A report of this latter meeting mentions Toronto as a city of churches with religious sentiment very strong. Electric cars were banned from Sunday-running by a large majority vote and omnibus lines, while running, could not collect Sunday fares. Apparently Robert Ingersoll, the famous American infidel, had recently requested the privilege of lecturing in Toronto but was refused with the mayor's rebuff, "We have a God over here in Canada."

There was considerable curiosity at the London District Tupperville camp but much of it turned to sympathy as the people decided this was essentially the forty-year-ago brand of Methodism. A Moraviantown Indian named W. R. Snake contributed much with his illustration-laden testimonies. R. Burnham, the Tupperville area pastor at the time, continued two weeks longer in a tent meeting.

Cataraqui appeared in the records for the first time during this year— and annexed to Elingburg. H. L. Miner (father of B. N.), as pastor, seems to have built a church in this Kingston suburb right away.

1894-95

Minnie Bauder

By now Toronto, with some Armadale assistance, was strong enough to "entertain" conference even though that conference area comprised thirty-four circuits with thirty churches and 1,111 members. W. J. Campbell had been the pastor there for a year and was returned. Mr. Gregory was officially sent to Clarendon and Vennachar as already seen, but joined by J. W. Commodore who was moved from Gunter. Gunter was left to Emma Snider and Minnie Bauder—both Verona girls. Verona's Lyford Snider plus a J. E. Foreman were slated for a new circuit northeast of Kingston called Perth Road and Zion. It had thirteen members already under the care of a Jonathan Sexsmith assigned some time since the previous conference.

R. Burnham was sent to Verona. Even in December its church could not accommodate the quarterly meeting crowd. Writing of the gathering, Chairman Norrington said, "Verona is the Jerusalem of the Kingston District and thither do the tribes go up."

Dawn Mills in the London District acquired a church that year, an old English Chapel renovated to become "the best church building our people have" on that district. This class was an offshoot from Shetland. Forest people, farther west, bought an old Roman Catholic church and moved it (with remodelling) into a centrally located lot. Unfortunately this work, begun by C. H. Reed, later declined and the church was sold.

Pastor H. L. Miner at Cataraqui during that year reported "continual revival" without revivalist or extra meetings. "Every week someone is saved or sanctified," his note read, and fourteen people had joined on probation. These Cataraqui converts were soon participating in prayer meetings in Kingston.

Petworth, pastored by L. A. Sager, had a winter revival with Mr. Burnham from Verona and Mr. Coates. This was probably the revival in which Maggie Venus (later Mrs. Henry Wattam) experienced conversion.

The Gunter ladies reported a spring revival that produced about twenty converts. One girl who had made fun of the pilgrims, found herself acting just like several she had despised. One young man who had almost grieved away the Spirit of God was wondrously saved after a prolonged prayer concentration.

Superintendent Craig, in the western half of the conference, had an April item in the *Free Methodist* that spoke of advance at Sheffield, Kelvin, Ebenezer, Walsingham and Brantford. Brantford, then of population 15,000, saw a district camp meeting in Mohawk Park. Over four thousand attended on Sunday. It was the biggest Free Methodist meeting in Canada up to that time and necessitated two large overflow services in different parts of the park. (Brantford street cars took Sunday holidays too.) General Superintendent Jones was special evangelist there. Before the conference of 1896 (probably late in 1895) Brantford was to replace its old church with a new one on the same spot.

Mr. Jones went on to Verona for the following Sunday where he says that "the meetings moved off in good old Methodist style." An immense curious crowd was on hand in the afternoon for a baptismal service "in the clear waters of Rock Lake." He had another interesting name for Verona: "The Mecca of Free Methodism in East Ontario." How like Mr. Norrington's "Jerusalem" one it was! A few days at Havelock (Peterborough District) Camp and a few more at Bracebridge (Muskoka District) Camp preceded his return to the United States. Of the people and Rev. Robert Hamilton at Bracebridge he wrote: "They were very much attached to their pastor." By way of a general Canadian impression he wrote: "The type of Free Methodism in Canada compares favourably with the work as it will average throughout the connection."

Ravenshoe on the Belhaven circuit accommodated the Toronto District camp that summer. It was there that the visiting preacher was so impressed with the "supernatural" laughing. An interesting note on the Havelock gathering mentions an Indian colony within the encampment. One Indian, Bro. Smoke, declared he would carry fire home with him. His wife was so touched by a message on giving, that she wished she had saved the price of her hat and had come bare-headed. As proof of her sincerity she promptly contributed some money given to her by a testing friend.

Lake Ontario Park was the setting for another Kingston District camp. One of the three evangelists was Rev. Thomas Whiffen of Oswego, N.Y., the man who had held the Ivy Lea (St. Lawrence) tent meetings about the time Mr. Sage first came to Canada.

Rev. G. W. Coleman participated in the dedication of a new church at Perth Road that June, so presumably the boy pastors had been busy. The Gregory-Commodore team at Vennachar circuit now had a new church built (probably erected the previous fall) and a society of twenty-eight members enrolled. Numbers of these were former Methodists who did not find a satisfactory spiritual life in their own church. The accounts of two who got into trouble when they went back were told earlier.

The conference of 1895 was a very special one. The whole next chapter deals with it. As in 1880, the Galt church, although recently enlarged under pastor J. M. Eagle, provided the meeting place.

---

1. Mr. Sims was so encouraged after this visit that he concluded his report with another challenge: "God is wonderfully raising up labourers, natural-born Canadians, for this work, who can't be bought by money, nor won by flattering words, nor frightened by threats, nor daunted by sneers, nor hindered by poorhouse devils. God give us this stamp, filled with the Holy Ghost, and we will take Canada for God. Yours in Jesus, enlisted to die on the battle field."

THE BATTLE WAS THE LORD'S

2. Some time earlier, Mr. Sage, driving through the town, had enquired for a Christian home in which to spend the night and ended up with a Mr. and Mrs. Wills who were Methodists. A prayer offered by Mr. Sage before the family retired so impressed his hosts that they enquired about his power the next morning and found the experience of sanctification themselves at the family altar.

3. These ladies introduced Free Methodism to Housey's Rapids that year using "Brookes' School."

4. T. A. Shaver who supplied the details of this story in 1933 wrote of the lady evangelists: "To tell the truth I did not have to be told they were Christians as their countenance shone with glory. This kind of salvation I heard my dead father talk about, although up to that time I had not seen such a thing in my church."

5. A dozen years later Belhaven membership was still largest in the conference.

6. This Muskoka—in western Ontario—must not be confused with the Muskoka District of East Ontario.

7. In 1892 Mr. Hogue was elected a bishop.

8. Mr. Smith's cash salary that year was a record low—$29. He apparently had some other income and the people knew it.

9. Mr. Gregory recalls one hitherto unfruitful camp at Wilton where this man was called on to pray. He said: "Lord, we thank Thee for what Thou hast done, for what Thou art doing and what Thou art going to do. Amen. Hallelujah!" During the singing of the hymn that followed, everyone in the tent rushed to the altar.

10. With carpenter work becoming scarce, this couple had traded their London property for 200 acres of Parry Sound rocks, hills, woods and swamp. After a prayerful two weeks there, they left for Brantford where they were to contribute so much. A Sister Teresa Botwright earlier converted at Kelvin, became one of Brantford's first members. Another was Amos Bridge who later moved to Odessa. Of a Sunday afternoon service, Henry Mellor quoted the Expositor as saying that Mr. Craig, preaching on the town hall steps "made more noise that the Salvation Army and the big drum combined."

11. Mr. Sage had found the Southerners quite indifferent to Northerners and Bible salvation. They liked to visit and eat at church after Sunday morning service and "most of the people would pay much more to support a dog and a gun than they would to support the gospel." His stay in Canada this second time lasted only a year but his autobiography is strangely silent of any reference to it. He transferred in 1887 to Dakota.

12. Here, the Primitive Methodist Church, left empty by the union of 1884, had recently been purchased to provide something better than the old converted cooper shop.

13. Mr. Norrington was listed in the 1887 Minutes as a Conference Evangelist in the West Kansas Conference but he had laboured in about a dozen American conferences. He is said to have walked from Kentucky to Spring Arbor Seminary in Michigan to get an education.

14. Mr. Clark was a member of the Illinois Conference but had been left free that year. The Norringtons had earlier laboured in his conference. Their West Kansas Conference listed Mr. Norrington that year as "Missionary to Canada" and the Canada Conference paid moving expenses up from Nebraska where he had lived last. Mrs. Norrington had been born in Ontario.

15. Miles Benn was actually saved in his father's barn about this time, but may be counted a convert.

16. Among the 10 charter members were this writer's great grandparents on his mother's side—Lorenzo and Hester Goodberry. Actually Mr. Craig was on hand for the organizing which took place on March 24, 1889.

17. The school money was evidently to help needy ministerial students.

18. Minnie Bauder (Later Crimmins) is still alive at Sanborn, N. Y. She received

her first appointment—by Elder Sims, with Emma Snider—in early 1893.

19. As might be expected, Mrs. DeMille was a happy radiant Christian. Although she lived long, she remained youthful in spirit. She desired to enter the church triumphant on the Lord's day. God granted this desire after 47 years of church membership. A son, E. A., became a minister, and a daughter, Mary, became the wife of Rev. J. H. Roberts. (Her daughter, Marion Roberts Bright, taught several years at Lorne Park.) A grandson, Wesley, and great-grandson, Clark, are now missionaries in Africa.

20. It is said that Mrs. Robinson died the day King George V visited Moose Jaw. On her way to see the temporal king, she took a weak spell and went instead to see the King, Immortal, Eternal, whom she loved and served.

21. When Robert Hamilton's class leader confessed that early Methodist meetings were like these Free Methodist ones and that Mrs. DeMille probably had more religion than them all, he became angry at his class leader's unfaithfulness and said, "I'm throwing my religion in the ditch right here." It wasn't long till he did find real salvation though.

22. The Haley family, met earlier in Muskoka, had moved to Thornyhurst in that district.

23. It burned during November, 1890.

24. Before his death Mr. Benzinger saw twenty-eight of his family connection attending church and nearly all were members. His story under the caption, "My Unforgettable Christian," was written for *Light and Life Evangel* by Rev. L. C. Ball, when a pastor on the circuit.

25. From detailed articles by Mrs. Kirk and Mr. Eagle in the *Heralds* of January and March, 1923, we learn that (1) the Kirks had held services in at least three places—a Yonge St. room, a hard-to-heat Baptist church and this Caledonia Hall; (2) both Mr. and Mrs. Craig had helped them in services some; (3) Mr. Craig had organized a class of thirteen that included Kirks, Bassets, Fulton sisters, Thompson sisters, and other ladies with surnames Hough, Ferrier, Macklin; (4) Mr. Sims gave the new preacher boys a quantity of tracts to distribute; (5) the boys called on the Geo. Fullers at the suggestion of Mrs. Fuller's father, a Bro. Thompson of Oak Flats.

26. The Uxbridge services included four on the street. Mr. Craig's partiality for street meetings has been demonstrated to the reader again and again. After Uxbridge he wrote: "We are more and more convinced that our preachers and people ought to engage much more than they do in the street work."

27. Mr. Eagle was to give forty years of leadership in Ontario, but Mr. Wattam, though very promising, was cut off by death in his second year at Hamilton.

28. David Allan has left us a most readable autobiography called *From Lumber Camp to the Pulpit*.

29. Elijah, the youngest, was converted beforehand—shortly after Mr. Wilson arrived, in fact. A distress had seized him. The doctor was powerless to give relief, for it was conviction. Mr. Wilson attributed it to the prayers of an older sister Mary, already married to W. C. Walls. Besides the hospitality of the Loveless family during his two-year stay, Mr. Wilson recalled that of Mr. and Mrs. John Beare and Mr. and Mrs. Alexander Macklin, as well as the inspiration of a Sister Harmer, whose brother, John Timbers, was converted and later became a minister in both Canada and the United States. (He is still alive.) Some Phoenix girls (by then, Beares) were probably converted that year.

30. There is another part of this cow story that is too good to leave out. Mr. Gunter customarily rose before dawn to pray in his empty cow stall. One morning in the darkness he stumbled against something that felt very bovine. Striking a match, he found a cow indeed, a cow with a tag on its tail. The tag read, "According to your faith, be it unto you." He believed God had inspired the gift but never learned where it came from. After his death, the family found out neighbors had purchased the cow in appreciation of his bringing the good news of "sins forgiven" to their community.

THE BATTLE WAS THE LORD'S

31. Mr. Sims' book, *Bible Salvation and Popular Religion Contrasted*, had found its way into the community even before the Michigan trip but Mr. Gunter didn't know Mr. Sims was a Free Methodist or that there were any of this denomination in Canada.

32. Mr. Norrington that year had Petworth and Elginburg while his wife looked after Gananoque.

33. The Kirks left Toronto for Manitoba shortly after this. Mr. Kirk's health demanded a change of climate. He had been a policeman in Toronto.

34. Rev. Lloyd Knox, present Light and Life Press Publisher, is a grandson of the Mellors.

35. John Montgomery was one who came to the conclusion he was not converted but "got cleared up after some time." Clara Luck got converted earlier and as a singer and preacher was "a great help in the meetings."

36. Mr. Norrington wrote of blessings at the time: "A cry of wild fire and fanaticism has gone out about this work, but it is spiritual bone and sinew."

37. The net gain that year was 127.

38. Mrs. Campbell now lives in Brantford.

39. Emma Snider later married Wilmott Harnden.

40. Judging from a later report by the next pastor, J. W. Commodore, and from the Minutes, it would appear Mr. Lake did not go.

41. He had joined the conference on trial a year before.

42. Seven new societies had sprung up and membership gain stood at 92.

43. We shall see that building churches became something of a habit with Mr. Commodore.

44. According to Josie Wees' version of this conversion, when Proud Mr. Shier (her uncle) prayed through, "He held pastor Hamilton's hand and, with his face shining, he jumped straight up and down and shouted, 'I know now what makes them jump!'"

45. Lyford Snider was the grandfather of Rev. K. Lavern Snider, now superintendent of the Free Methodist Mission in Japan.

46. Charles Babcock, working in the lumber camps in the winter of 1892-93, had held some Free Methodist services in a local schoolhouse, the first at Vennachar.

47. At the last afternoon service about 40 seekers came to the altar. Numbers of children were saved at the camp. Eighteen people were said to have been sanctified.

6.
FISSION: THE DIVISION DIVIDES, 1895

With the splitting of the atom, *fission* became almost a household word. Specifically, it is the technical name for a process: "The spontaneous division of a cell or organism into new cells or organisms, especially as a mode of reproduction," says Funk and Wagnalls' dictionary. It is the way the lowly amoeba multiplies himself. It is also the way Canadian Free Methodism, a division of the larger church of North America, chose to gird itself for growth beyond 1895. In that year the old Canada Conference in its sixteenth session split into two—East Ontario and West Ontario. The events leading to the division run this way:

Because of the large territory embraced in the Canada Conference by 1894, many were thinking of the wisdom of becoming two conferences and a committee was appointed that year to consider the matter. Its

ONTARIO OPENS FOR OCCUPATION

members were James Craig, Albert Sims, A. H. Norrington, J. H. Winter and Amos Bridge. The latter two were laymen. At the 1895 conference (G. W. Coleman, W. H. Wilson, and W. C. Walls were president, secretary, and treasurer respectively), the committee reported favourably and the conference voted without dissenters to petition the General Superintendents to divide them into East and West Ontario Conferences.[1] Telegrams were sent to the absent General Superintendents and to headquarters to ask approval. That gained, the partitioning proceeded.

The selected boundary line lay west of Peel and Simcoe counties and the Nipissing District. Of the total membership of 1,232,[2] over 60 per cent turned out to be in the eastern conference. It had twenty circuits also (one a new one) to the western's sixteen, but fared more poorly with parsonages—two to three. Preachers were asked to state their preference for a conference to serve in, and the stationing committee was advised to respect each preference as able.

Because this was a significant moment in the Church's history we include the appointments of that last Canada Conference of 1895 when it divided itself.

East Ontario Conference

Kingston District—A. Sims, D. E.

Lansdowne	Nancy Schantz, supply
Cataraqui & Elginburg	George Overpaugh
Verona & Petworth	H. L. Miner
Wilton & Violet	L. A. Sager
Clarendon & Vennachar	J. W. Commodore, Charles Cunningham, supply
Perth Road & Inverary	To be supplied
Westport & Fermoy	W. H. Gregory

Peterborough District—A. Sims, D. E.

Gunter	To be supplied
Trent Bridge & Healey's Falls	R. Burnham
Burnley & Eddystone	Samuel Rogers
Beaver Creek	Jennie Robinson

Toronto District—J. Craig, D. E.

Toronto	W. H. Wilson
Port Credit & Cooksville	Lottie Babcock and Jemima Macklin, supplies
Armadale & Unionville	J. Clink
Uxbridge & Mt. Pleasant	A. Allguire

Edward Walker left without appointment, member Tor. Dist., Ont. Conf.

Muskoka District—J. Craig, D. E.

Crown Hill & Barrie	Emerson Snyder

105

THE BATTLE WAS THE LORD'S

Orillia ..... To be supplied
Barkway & Severn Bridge ..... Wm. Miller & Bernard Boone, supplies
Bracebridge ..... Stewart Walker
Huntsville ..... Jonathan Sexsmith

West Ontario Conference
Hamilton District—W. C. Walls, D. E.

Niagara Falls ..... Josie Rusk
Ridgeway & Fort Erie ..... Miles S. Benn
Kimbo & Attercliffe ..... Charles H. Reed
Hannon ..... Marcus O. Coates
Hamilton ..... To be supplied

Brantford District—W. C. Walls, D. E.

Brantford ..... William J. Campbell
Galt & Sheffield ..... R. Hamilton
Kelvin ..... J. M. Eagle
Ebenezer & Otterville ..... Matilda Sipprell[3]
Walsingham ..... David Allan

Joseph Bretz left without an appointment at his own request.

Sarnia District—A. H. Norrington, D. E.

Middlemiss ..... To be supplied
Shetland ..... Christopher Schantz
Dawn Mills & Dresden ..... Emma Snider & Mary Botting, sup.
Keith ..... Laura J. Warren & Annie L. Green, supplies
Point Edward ..... To be supplied
Thedford & Forest ..... Edward Slingerland

There was deeper feeling than usual that year in the final singing of "God Be With You Till We Meet Again." The singers knew well that many of them would not meet again till they met around the Throne in the Heavenly City. Only two of the appointees of this conference are known by this writer to be still living: Miles Benn of Tampa, Florida, and W. H. Gregory of Verona.

The first session of each separate Ontario conference dates from the next year, 1896.[4] Armadale and Brantford churches entertained.

---

1. It was also at Galt fifteen years earlier that the Canada Conference had been first organized.
2. The net gain that year had been 121.
3. Alma Smith was named as an assistant to Matilda Sipprell some time after conference.
4. First W. M. S. officers in each conference were the following: East Ontario—Mary Craig, Pres.; Eva Breeze, Sec.; Martha Wilson, Treas. West Ontario—Mary Walls, Pres.; Josie Rusk, Sec.; Hannah Eagle, Treas.

Section 4: Continuing the Conquest

With the Canada Conference divided in 1895, the story of how the two newly formed Ontario conferences gained more ground for God must be pursued separately. In the two following chapters, the Ontario narrative will be carried ahead to about 1950 leaving latest developments for the section "Recent Review" and the treatment will change from a detailed year-by-year conference-wide diary to a swift circuit-by-circuit narrative in a district-by-district arrangement. Obviously the history, collected or collectable, is far more complete for some churches than for others. Besides, certain places have much more to tell.

1.
ONWARD IN EAST ONTARIO
A. Toronto District

Armadale—By 1895, this "mother church," though small, could boast having sent out three preachers and three evangelists and to have seen five camp meetings held nearby. Elijah Loveless was superintendent of the thirty-five-scholar Sunday school. Preachers' salaries were set at $300.

It was fitting that in 1896 the first session of the East Ontario Conference should be invited to this community where the founder of Free Methodism had first been invited in 1873. General Superintendent Jones was the chairman, and W. H. Wilson the secretary, J. Clink being local pastor.

There was still no parsonage when W. H. Gregory served the society 1899-1901 and the Gregory family had to move twice. But that handicap did not prevent their being used of God in a general quickening of the church.

By 1912, however, the membership, which had been nearly fifty in the early 1880's, had dwindled to nine with most of them too far away to get to church regularly or at all. Mrs. Maude Bovee, daughter of Thomas Loveless, recalls vividly those low years that followed when the circuit was frequently left "to be supplied" and her father had to do the preaching. Sometimes in winter her father would drive the six shivering miles, light the fire, read the Sunday-school lesson, have prayer and go home. No one but his family might come, yet he couldn't afford to let the neighbourhood children think he wasn't interested any longer. His faithfulness was later rewarded when some of the local children, such as the

Jarvis boys, found the Lord. His faith continues today in his grandson, Leon Bovee, a minister in East Michigan.

John Tidball who moved into the community some time around 1920 became a staunch supporter of the church for years before his passing.

The Armadale church impressively celebrated its sixtieth anniversary in 1940 during J. T. King's pastorate. Because of the general historic significance of the occasion, it will be described separately in the "Milestones" chapter. Mr. King built the parsonage while at Armadale.

We shall see that this church, which would surely have closed except for Mr. Loveless' concern, has now come into better days and that it will feature in the centenary observance of 1960.

Belhaven and Baldwin—The Nancy Schantz beginnings and early sustained strength have been noted. Dry Town, Ravenshoe and Baldwin were all early appointments of this circuit. In 1896-97 Stewart Walker had about sixty seekers in a winter revival. W. H. Gregory, there for 1901-02, conducted extended and fruitful campaigns at three points including formerly-abandoned Baldwin. Among the seekers were Arkseys, Kays, Crowders, Arnolds and Smallwoods. It appears the parsonage was built about 1907 and that the village church was moved to its present location beside the parsonage from an original north-of-town spot in the late winter of 1928. Considerable remodelling was done after the moving. J. W. Corey was in charge then. Roy Sedore had been converted in this earlier "North Star" church under B. E. Stevenson about 1914.

Holt and Brown Hill—In 1909, L. Slingerland (previously at nearby Belhaven) was assigned the new circuit of Holt and Newmarket. He seems to have lived at Holt and inherited or shortly organized a class of five. A "most excellent district camp meeting" was held in the summer of 1910 at Mount Albert not far from Holt. At the end of Mr. Slingerland's two-year pastorate we find thirty-two members at that point. Kings and Couches were among early Holt converts.

The circuit was divided in 1916 with H. B. Luck, who had been pastoring both places since 1914, continuing at Holt till 1918. His fourteen-week eighty-convert campaign mentioned earlier was about 1915. Roy Sedore, a new convert from Belhaven, attended. He recalls Hopkins, Coates, Rye, Wrightman, Norris, Thompson, Crowder and Sedore families among the saved. Part of the prolonged seige was at Brown Hill.

Brown Hill became listed as a new point under Mr. Luck in 1917. In early 1924 when John King was here serving his first circuit, a revival at Brown Hill produced some forty seekers. N. F. Perry, Uxbridge pastor, and John Potter, conference evangelist, assisted. Sleigh loads sometimes had to drive away for lack of room in the church.

Lorne Park College—A small society has existed here for many years but composed mainly of staff members and a few students. The principal has usually served as pastor. Some success has been achieved in gathering children from the community for Sunday School and C.Y.C. But the program's summer irregularity, the pressure of school duties, the early auditorium handicap, and the lack even yet of a separate chapel have militated against the gathering in of any appreciable local adult congregation.

Conference at Newmarket, 1923

Newmarket—This town, as we have seen, first appeared in conference minutes in 1909 when L. Slingerland was sent to Holt and Newmarket. The Newmarket class was organized about 1911 either by Mr. Slingerland or Sperry Snyder who followed him that year.

The Snyders stayed till 1914 concentrating on Newmarket. By then, services had moved out of the "uncomfortable old Temperance Hall" into a newly-built generous-sized church which Bishop Sellew dedicated in April, 1914. Mr. Snyder had supervised the erection in 1913.

With the appointment of M. S. Benn in 1916, Newmarket alone became a full-time circuit. Mr. Benn had been preceded by H. B. Luck who had pushed the total Newmarket-Holt membership up to seventy-three. Mr. Benn purchased the parsonage during his three-year pastorate.

W. H. Linstead reported a late 1923 revival at Newmarket when most of the "about sixty seekers" found peace. The 1923 conference had been held here.

This society has continued as one of the strong ones in the conference. For years it and its pastors have been closely associated with the district camp meetings—earlier at Holland Landing and now at Pine Orchard.

Oshawa—This fast-growing General Motors city first appeared in the conference records of 1929. Then, R. L. Casement was transferred from Gravenhurst to Uxbridge, with Oshawa (thirty miles away) as a new preaching point. Just previous to the 1929 conference, pastor-evangelist E. R. Orser of Armadale, assisted by singer Neil Stonness of Westport, had conducted a several-week tent campaign in Oshawa and had organized a nine-member society. This new class met for a time both before and after conference in a classroom rented from the local business college. Joe Taite of the present congregation was a member of that first class.

THE BATTLE WAS THE LORD'S

During the first three years that Mr. Casement came for services, it proved difficult to find a suitable place of worship, especially for holding revival meetings. Moving became an annual affair. Finally in the fall of 1932, God answered the earnest prayers of the congregation and made possible the purchase of a 36' x 50' "Sons of Temperance" hall in the south end of the city. The hall cost only $150.

Those were days of depression and relief. And the building needed a new roof, a new floor, new wiring, new decorating, and, of course, chairs. But district preachers and local men supplied labour and an Uxbridge member offered a loan. The building was ready for use in weeks and a district meeting the next spring more than looked after the local debts.

The 1933 conference sent Rev. T. L. Fletcher to the Uxbridge—Oshawa circuit. A year later, at his suggestion, Mr. Fletcher was assigned Oshawa as his sole charge. After another year under Rev. Eldon Linstead, Oshawa was left "to be supplied," for the people could not support a pastor. Different people gave a hand in the supplying of those several grim years. Aden Halliday worked and preached—and then died. Youthful farmworkers, Earl Bull and Austin Thaxter (now both ministers) came long distances at different times to fill in. Superannuate W. Zurbrigg of Toronto helped. For a time, interest so dwindled that some felt the purchase had been a mistake. Then in 1942 Roy Goodrich came.

For part of his period, Roy was also attending Lorne Park College; part of the time he worked in the local Motors plant. But he brought in the children and rallied a congregation, numbers of whom are still attending. Jim Aldous worked beside the preacher boy in "The Motors." He liked him, went to hear him preach, gathered enough money from colleagues to buy a piano, found the Lord himself and became a zealous Sunday School worker. The A. E. and W. L. Smith families of Pickering (formerly from Toronto) began attending and helping in the Oshawa Church program in the early 1940's. By 1944 the Sunday School was up to fifty.

That fall, Layman Fletcher, son of T. L. Fletcher, was appointed to the Oshawa charge and early the next year a parsonage was bought. (Roy Goodrich had lived in a room in the church.) With more and more children coming to Sunday School, expansion became necessary. How the basement hole was dug, the walls built, the necessary equipment installed, and the bills paid is a multi-miracle story. And the expansion has continued through the last decade.

Uxbridge—We have traced at some length the Uxbridge beginning in an earlier section. Not much history was available for the years since 1895. But it can be disclosed that this society has unleashed a healthy number of her sons into the Free Methodist ministry. Besides R. Burnham from the early days, one could mention A. F. Ball, R. Slingerland, F. L. Jones, and A. J. Thaxter. And Uxbridge people like to recall that Fletcher Burnham, Francis and Lorne Casement, Arthur Perry, Layman Fletcher and William Daw were boys in their Sunday school when their ministerial fathers lived there. Herbert and Eldon Linstead and Arthur Cresswell were Uxbridge Sunday-school boys who became United Church ministers.[1]

The Uxbridge parsonage was bought in 1904, Sperry Snyder being stationed there. At that time and for some years later, another point called Mount Pleasant formed part of the circuit.

Mrs. Alberta Sims Webb remembers Charles Prior as a widely respected and saintly local preacher at Uxbridge when her father and family lived in the chairman's parsonage there in the early 1890's.

Right: Toronto Broadview Church. Courtesy of the "Toronto Telegram."

Below: Union Youth Rally for East and West Ontario at Toronto, Broadview, October 1939.

Toronto, Broadview—The Toronto beginnings have also been given in some detail. In the summer of 1895 Chairman Sims wrote: "The work in Toronto is slowly yet surely gaining." Under W. J. Campbell as pastor the membership stood at twenty-seven. After W. H. Wilson's one-year pastorate, the work was left in 1897 "To be supplied." Layman John Montgomery looked after it then and in certain later years when no preacher was sent. (Port Credit faded out entirely shortly after 1900.)

About 1900 the Toronto society bought or built a small brick church at 222 Broadview Ave., but to save money to speed payments on it, they held the services themselves till 1902. Then another pastor was sent.

M. S. Benn came in 1911 and found thirty members. When he left in 1914 after one or two excellent revivals, the membership was doubled. And the people had purchased a needed parsonage.

The Gregorys in 1926-27 conducted a deep revival that pushed the membership to 75.

In 1929, pastor B. E. Stevenson was instrumental in the purchase of the present church at Broadview and Mount Stephen. It had been occupied by the Congregational people before the union of 1925.

Broadview should be considered the "mother church" for Toronto, with the Eglinton and West Toronto units as being to some extent her children. She has been host to many conferences. And numerous other special gatherings have gravitated there too. In October, 1939, for example, General Y.P.M.S. Superintendent B. H. Pearson and Spring Arbor's President L. M. Lowell were present for an All-Ontario Youth Rally—the first of its kind—in this provincially central church. And here also in November, 1943, the Canadian Holiness Federation was born.

Toronto, Eglinton—About 1919 a Mrs. Allen started visiting and inviting children to a Mission Sunday School held in a vacant store on North Yonge Street near Eglinton Ave. It prospered. In the spring of that year, before or after the Sunday School's beginning, Rev. C. V. Fairbairn held four weeks of services in that same store and gathered the nucleus of a class. The Broadview people and their pastor, Rev. Emerson Snyder, participated. In 1920 the conference annexed this North Toronto to the Broadview circuit and appointed Gordon Bray as pastor. By 1921 a cement block basement was built on Eglinton Ave., the project superintended by the pastor who himself also worked considerably. At the conference of 1922, this North Toronto Mission was changed in name to Eglinton Ave. Free Methodist Church with its own pastor, Rev. M. S. Benn. By that time the Sunday School was looking after about seventy people in six classes under J. C. Swart as superintendent.

From 1926 to 1944, Mrs. Annie M. Cooper gave remarkable leadership in this office. Altar services were frequent and testimony periods were regular among the children in the open session of the school. Attendance increased till up to ten classes carried on at once in the one-room sanctuary. Mrs. Cooper's burden for and gift with children found expression also in seven years of wonderful work among the boys of the district camp. In her own special tent through picture and story she often led a score or more to the Lord in one camp. Many of her boys are now active across the conference, more than one in the ministry. During the depression years of 1930 to 1935, Mrs. Cooper systematically visited in numerous North York Township homes. From her basket she distributed food and clothes and from her Bible she dispensed the Living Bread. Then she prayed. A 1932 revival that produced twenty-seven converts and some new Eglinton members grew out of cottage prayer meetings that followed.

West Toronto—Free Methodism was established in West Toronto in 1939 after the East Ontario Conference was invited by the West Toronto Holiness Mission to take over its work at 2747 Dundas St. W. Mr. and Mrs. Ronald McCallum, students at Lorne Park College, first supplied the mission, services being held in a former store. Across nine years the following part-time pastors took turns in serving: Mr. and Mrs. Bert Gunter, Ross Crowder and Lavern Snider. In 1948 a parsonage was bought and Mr. and Mrs. Norman Hart came full-time. Services were held in Lakeview Hall until 1950 when a new church at 2611 Dundas St. W. had been sufficiently finished to accommodate a congregation. Backbone of the West Toronto program in its earliest years was Miss Olive Hicks, a Toronto schoolteacher who had formerly served at Lorne Park College.

B. Kingston District

Kingston—George Overpaugh, who was at Cataraqui and Elginburg in 1895-96, began services in the city itself and despite "expense and other difficulties" had a measure of success.[2] Beginning the next year, services were held in an old stone schoolhouse on Queen St. J. W. Commodore reported on a district meeting in August, 1897 with four hundred people present, some having to look through the windows. Writing of the way the Spirit of God was poured out, he said: "Many members of popular churches of the city stole away from their cushioned pews and came to our humble cottage to get a meal."

The conference of 1900 met at Cataraqui, the first east of Trent Bridge. Charles Cunningham was pastor. He was followed by S. Rogers, then C. A. Fox. For 1904-05, the circuit received no pastor, but laymen such an Angus Harnden along with supernumeraries Frank Bradley and W. H. Reynolds gave leadership.

In 1905 the Gregorys moved from Bracebridge to Kingston—a three hundred-mile horse-and-buggy drive for father William and son James F. Services were held in a Sydenham St. building in a second-floor room reached by a rear entrance. This was the place of persecution mentioned earlier. In two years' time the Gregorys had added twenty-seven members and built a church. The membership climb came because God gave them in that unpretentious hall a bounteous revival that brought in the people and reconciled them to Himself. The church, on the present Colborne St. lot, was made by dismantling the stonework of the old city reservoir previously standing there and rebuilding the stones. Only some new ones for the front were needed.

They tell that more than one night after the experienced tradesmen had gone home, the church men and their wives came and took over. With babies laid on the floor beams, the women held lanterns while the men did what they could. That church was free of debt and dedicated by B. R. Jones as the Gregorys left at conference time in 1907. Dan Zurbrigg has been at Kingston church ever since those Gregory days.

Interior of remodelled Kingston church.

Of a camp meeting at Kingston in 1907, R. A. Zahniser, the evangelist, wrote: "So many were cleared up in earlier services, fear was expressed that we would run out of material, but attendance increased. . . ."

Kingston church was to see later revivals of note. Evangelist Leonard Slingerland assisted pastor Emerson Snyder in early 1912 when "about forty seekers" came forward. M. S. Benn as pastor during 1920-22 had one of his best revivals, doing his own preaching for eight weeks.

The double-house beside the church, to serve as both circuit and district parsonages, was built in 1912 or shortly afterwards by either Emerson or Sperry Snyder.

Kingston has had its share of conferences. The one of 1934, when Sunday congregations met in the "Limestone City's" beautiful county courthouse, was perhaps most memorable. Bishop Pearce presided, but B. H. Pearson from our Mexican Mission and Ethel Ryff and Bessie Reid from Africa and China, respectively, all participated. Sara Gregory and Bessie Reid received ordination, the first East Ontario women to win this honour. Bessie was about to return to China taking sister Pearl with her. Among those swept into the kingdom, in the victorious altar service that climaxed the gathering, knelt brother Bruce—another Reid destined to become well known across the church.

During F. A. Daw's Kingston pastorate in the late 1930's, it was frequently necessary to use chairs in the church aisles to accommodate the congregations. It was then that a fund was begun for church enlargement, a project that was completed around 1950 under C. W. Kay.

Gananoque and Lansdowne—Until the recent taking over of an American planting in Clarenceville, Quebec, followed by the Holiness Movement Merger, this circuit, while small, has represented the most easterly Free Methodist work not only in Ontario but in Canada.

Though both places have been mentioned earlier, it might be noted that for a time around 1895, Gananoque disappeared entirely from the annual stationings, and, despite a year with energetic Nancy Schantz, even Lansdowne remained pastorless most of the time till 1902 when Emerson Snyder began a term serving both places. By 1905 he had built up the circuit considerably and seen a new Gananoque church dedicated free of debt. William Zurbrigg who followed for one year built the parsonage on a lot donated by a Brother and Sister Kettle, and held a tent meeting east of Gananoque in a grove beside the St. Lawrence.

Then to the circuit came the Gregorys. Five Gregory children plus two adults to support was "terrifying to some of the members, but God was sufficient." Annie Slack was a convert of one revival held at Gananoque. She was to become the very effective wife of Rev. A. F. Ball.

The saintly McNeils and their extreme generosity have been mentioned. They gave to the church in both life and death.

At various times in recent decades, the Kingston pastors, as F. A. Daw, B. E. Stevenson and C. W. Kay, were responsible for Gananoque also. For the year 1946-47, this writer, while teaching in the local high school, was in charge of the small work. Not infrequently during cold weather he built the fire, collected a congregation, taught the adult Sunday School class, gave a "sermon," and took the people home. Gananoque has since seen better days.

Verona, Oak Flats and Deyo's Corners—As early as 1895 it was written that on this circuit twenty-three letters of membership had been given to those called of God to the ministry (including wives). Yet the circuit was even then the strongest in Canada. Mr. Sims wrote in early 1896: "There are enough forces on this circuit, if properly disciplined and marshalled, to storm a whole country."

In late 1898, Elder Norrington reported a quarterly meeting at Verona whose Sunday program ran thus: "Love Feast" from 9:00 to 11:15; reception of new members (twelve in full and five on probation); altar service

Camp at Verona, 1908.

till one o'clock, "Love Feast" resumed at 2:30, communion service at 4:00. A well-attended and fruitful evening service followed.

A year later as conference evangelist, Mr. Norrington returned for a revival. He had one, but lamented the reading habits of the members. Only one subscription to the church paper had been reported at the previous conference, he confessed "with shame," and called for a revival in that area too.

Verona circuit frequently was host to the district camp meeting. Mr. Norrington reported one in 1905 with "fifteen to twenty seekers about every time." American evangelist D. C. Stanton said of his 1908 camp visit: "The Kingston district is blest with some of the best preachers and lay members that live outside of heaven. They are plain in dress, holy in life and mighty in prayer. . . . It was the greatest degree of old school Methodism that I have ever been in."

Barnet Babcock of that circuit (he later became a minister) wrote of a remarkable personal healing in 1910. He fell in his barn and was given "little hope of recovery" by his doctor. But as a result of prayers and faith he was plowing in three days.

In early 1918 Verona had an impressive farewell service for Ethel Davey leaving for Africa. Pastor A. F. Ball wrote exultantly: "We believe Verona has the honour of producing more preachers than any other East Ontario

Front Row—Fletcher Burnham, Myrtle Snider Walroth, Cecil Goodberry, Una Snider Truscotte, Wesley Revell; Middle Row—Fleta Embury McLeod, Wilhemina Goodberry Chatson, Rev. and Mrs. Alfred Ball, Betty Reynolds Westervelt, Iva Snider. Back Row—Orval Snider, Luella Martin Reynolds, Edith Dixon, Florence Vanluven, Nellie Snider Revell, Dollie Smith, Mary Scales Snider, Ezra Snider.

circuit, and now a missionary." As the photo shows, the Balls had an unusually fine group of young people at that time.³ Wrote Mrs. Ball: "How we thank the Lord for the privilege of going to Heaven by way of Verona and of helping to get some of the precious young people into the Kingdom."

As a result of evangelistic concentration in the Verona area by C. V. Fairbairn (partly as a Methodist) from 1916 to 1920, numerous additions to the Free Methodist church resulted. (Fifty people alone joined when services resumed after the 1918-19 flu interruption.) Those in the Desert Lake community, under W. H. Gregory of Verona, built a church at Deyo's Corners in 1920. (One great tent meeting had been in the grove of Sylvenus "Big Vene" Deyo.) Looking back, Mr. Gregory declares "There were spiritual giants in that era." He kept three horses, for Mrs. Gregory and their son James did preaching too, besides local layman "Will" Goodberry. They were all needed, for the 1919-20 circuit included Verona, Holleford, Desert Lake, Cole Lake, Wagarville and Oak Flats.

Oak Flats after some thirty years of ordinary services experienced an unusual awakening in the winter of 1924-25. Rev. Frank Loft was pastor then. Over fifty were said converted and many sanctified wholly. For years, services had been in the local schoolhouse but now the congregation got busy and built a 28' x 40' cement block church. C. V. Fairbairn, elder at the time, dedicated it in April, 1926. Describing the last of the dedicatory service's $1,100 money-raising phase, he wrote: " 'Put me down for five dollars,' said a young sister; and over the top we went, ten cents past our objective. Down came fire and glory and the crowd rose and sang twice over 'Praise God from whom all blessings flow.' " This writer was there and remembers Irish Arthur Buckley rising and offering to donate some little pigs if anyone would raise them and give the proceeds.

In the late winter and spring of 1931 Verona enjoyed an extended visitation of the Spirit that resulted in over one hundred seekers before the meetings were transferred to Deyo's Corners. Harry Wilkins was one of the converts. Zealous Rev. Walter Brown, as pastor, did a great deal of the preaching, though in failing health. Still young, he passed away the next year.

When Sara Gregory was pastor at Verona over seventy sought the Lord in an early 1933 revival. Again in 1935 Rev. E. R. Orser assisted in an effort that resulted in membership additions. Miss Gregory and Verona entertained the 1933 conference which was presided over by Bishop Zahniser. This writer's family were members at Verona at that time.

F. A. Daw gave strong leadership in his Verona pastorate about 1940.

Newburgh and Odessa—Odessa seems to have first encountered Free Methodism in the early months of 1896 when fiery "Lew" Sager of Wilton and Violet campaigned there. One convert was described as one of the most wicked men in the community. He had formerly sold liquor at a camp meeting.

THE BATTLE WAS THE LORD'S

In 1898 the Gregorys were sent to Wilton, Violet and Odessa. They lived at Odessa but no class, church or parsonage existed at that point. Services were held in the town hall and a class organized before their departure in 1900.

The Odessa church appears to have been built by Sperry Snyder and during the year 1906-07.

Richard Babcock as pastor, assisted by Richard Burnham the district elder, conducted a notable revival of at least nine weeks' duration in early 1911.

The Gregorys returned to Odessa (and Petworth) in 1915. Once while Mr. Gregory was away at Warkworth helping in meetings, and Mrs. Gregory and Eugene Smith were conducting services at home, a revival of such intensity developed that Mr. Gregory was called home by phone. Converts of that outpouring are now doing the Lord's work as far away as Oklahoma and Illinois.

The Newburgh work had an interesting beginning. In the spring of 1918 godly but hungry Mrs. George Wartman was surprised to read in the Methodist *Christian Guardian* that C. V. Fairbairn had held a holiness convention in connection with a revival in the Verona Methodist Church. "If there is a man preaching holiness in the Methodist Church, I would like to hear him," she said, and soon with her daughter-in-law boarded a train for Verona. (They arrived the night that Montreal Conference men came also to see what was going on. See later Fairbairn story.) Mrs. Wartman invited Mr. Fairbairn to her needy community and prayed earnestly he would come. He soon did, with tent and worker band that included Marion and Mother Whitney and Bessie Reid (later Kresge). Mother Wartman denied herself an earlier planned trip to the Pacific Coast to be present, but was rewarded with the conversion of not only her neighbours but her two sons and a daughter-in-law. (We shall see that D. S. Wartman soon became Harrowsmith's first pastor.) Mr. Fairbairn pitched a tent again in 1919 and 1920. Mrs. Fairbairn lived at Newburgh and held services.

Young S. B. Griffith came to Odessa in 1920 for his first circuit and during the year that followed became Newburgh's first pastor, Mr. Fairbairn having organized a class in the fall of 1920. An excellent revival with Fairbairn aid was held that first winter, services being in a hall. As usual, there was opposition. During that same winter, Mr. and Mrs. Griffith were injured and narrowly escaped death when, en route to a Verona district meeting, their horse and buggy were struck by a fast nonblowing train near Harrowsmith.[4] Rev. W. H. Linstead built the Newburgh church in 1928, and N. F. Perry built the circuit parsonage (at Odessa) in the middle forties. Odessa nurtured K. Bauder, B. Dawson & Lois Grant Snider.

Harrowsmith, Holleford and Petworth—We have seen Petworth as the second earliest foothold on the Kingston district. An extended revival there, in early 1902 with an evangelist named Blanchard is remembered for its sixty seekers. Among converts that time were Charles and Dexter Sigsworth whose mother, a Hartington Methodist, had not discouraged her boys from attending Free Methodist meetings, because she had been open-minded enough to recognize that here was more spiritual life than her own church provided. Lay orator Henry Wattam (brother of Alfred), was also saved at that time. "Mr. Wattam," wrote Sara Gregory, "farmed for a living but lived with the great literary masters. His testimonies were eloquent with quotations from "Paradise Lost.' . . ." Until 1910 or later, Petworth was often part of the Verona circuit. For a time it was joined to Odessa. Then after Harrowsmith opened up, it became part of that circuit. This writer attended at Petworth as a young boy, heard John Amos and Grace Wattam teach Sunday School, Henry Wattam deliver soaring testimonies, and Grace German sing "Why would you do without Him?" He joined the church there in 1930 when G. H. Bache was serving. In 1935 C. W. Reynolds as pastor, assisted by I. M. Loucks, saw a considerable awakening at Petworth.

Holleford church was built and dedicated about 1904 under S. T. Gunter of the Verona circuit.

C. V. Fairbairn planted Free Methodism in Harrowsmith with sieges in the fall of 1918 and the spring of 1919. Opposition was intense—"the greatest organized resistance we ever encountered," wrote Mr. Fairbairn later. But the township hall was secured after 250 taxpayers signed a petition requesting its use. Evangelist E. E. Shelhamer helped and Newburgh's young D. S. Wartman who had felt the call to preach was left in charge.[5] In the renewed Fairbairn campaign of the spring, James Gregory, George Fuller, Jr., and George Wilson played a part also. A class of eighteen was organized then. Shortly, a large stone church and adjacent eleven-room brick parsonage were bought from the Presbyterians. The church was dedicated in 1924 at a conference there. To accommodate the crowds, the district tabernacle was pitched on the church lot.

Ebenezer Campground near Harrowsmith drew record crowds in the 20's and 30's. The 1933 gathering with evangelist Paul Wheelock produced over one hundred seeking the Lord.

Cole Lake, Parham and Wagarville—Balls, Shellingtons, Freemans, Lees, Kennedys, and others from the Cole Lake community were converted in C. V. Fairbairn's first Godfrey (Bethel Methodist) revival of 1916. These people soon looked back to the Free Methodists of the nearby sprawling Verona circuit for leadership. To serve Cole Lake and other points, James Gregory was appointed assistant to his father in 1919. By then a Cole Lake Class had been organized and services were held in farm homes. Mrs. Gregory or "Will" Goodberry had often conducted the services during the previous year.

In 1927 G. H. Bache was appointed to Tichborne, Cole Lake, and Crowe Lake. Before the next conference a 26'x36' church had been built at Cole Lake and dedicated by District Elder E. J. Lee. In 1930 Mr. Bache held a successful tent meeting on the old Godfrey campground. Seekers numbered forty-four. Clarence Chatson, on the circuit during 1930-33, opened a work in the Echo Lake area. The Parham church was built by Gordon Babcock in 1938. For a time, about then, Echo Lake and other neighbouring communities including Wagarville constituted a circuit.[6] Also, Mountain Grove to the northwest was the hub of another.

Yarker and Enterprise—Yarker appears in the records as early as 1897, a new point on the Verona-Petworth circuit. George Overpaugh was made pastor. A year later Enterprise was added and David Gunter became an assistant supply pastor. In 1905, Enterprise, Fifth Lake and Wagarville were constituted a circuit under Miles Babcock. S. T. Gunter of Verona had already built or started a church at Fifth Lake. (Later this church burned.)

For several years from 1935 on, Enterprise was joined with Odessa and Newburgh under G. H. Bache. Then beginning in 1939 Gerald Sedore served Enterprise and Petworth and a two-storey stone building (formerly a bank) was purchased for a chapel and parsonage. B. E. Stevenson preached the dedicatory message. The Cummings and Wagar families have been members at Enterprise for many years.

Yarker, after a lengthy period of dormancy, was revived about 1938 by B. E. Stevenson while on the Verona circuit. Mr. Stevenson held services in homes, then purchased a two-storey former hotel, remodelling it for a church and upstairs parsonage.

In 1939 he was moved to Yarker to be pastor of a new Odessa-Newburgh-Yarker combination.

Since the late 1940's, Yarker and Enterprise have been one circuit, with the pastor, in most recent years, living at Yarker.

Napanee—For one early year, 1905-06, Napanee was listed as a point on the Odessa circuit and nine members were enrolled. Not again till the late 1920's was a mission revived. Eugene Smith of Odessa took earliest responsibility and held services over a store. Mrs. Edna Wright and Mrs. Dora Barnes were among the earliest members of that era.

The present church was built in the early 1940's. Young people of the Kingston congregation raised the money to purchase a rural Presbyterian church which was dismantled, moved and rebuilt in the town. District Elder Daw dedicated it in May, 1943, at the opening service.

Westport and Bolingbroke—We have seen elsewhere that W. H. Gregory in 1895 was Westport-Fermoy's first appointed minister, and that at the end of two years, despite hardships innumerable for him and his bride, services were being conducted at five points including also Zion, The Mountain, and distant Maberly. Mr. Sims seems to have visited the circuit just after the Gregorys arrived and enrolled at Fermoy a small class of ex-Methodists from Burridge. Charles Babcock of Verona had previously been holding prayer meetings in nearby Burridge homes with conversion successes.

The Gregorys used Fermoy's township hall for worship and often had Roman Catholics attending. Services at Westport were in homes. The next minister, J. W. Commodore in 1897-98, built the Westport church.

Westport became host to a Kingston District camp meeting as early as 1897 and again in 1900. F. I. Labrum, an American visitor at the first one, wrote of twenty at the altar seeking God in every service for the four days he was there.

From 1914 to 1918 the Westport work was very low and had no regular pastor; in fact, for part of this time the church was closed. Yet a remnant remained. Through the dark days, R. J. Whaley, a Westport druggist, who had become a member about 1900 under Lottie Babcock, served the church in love and loyalty as local preacher and superintendent. He was responsible for having the church re-opened in the white-heat of a 1918 revival. At conference time, A. F. Ball was sent. C. V. Fairbairn assisted in revivals once or twice during Mr. Ball's three-year stay and then came himself for another three years of glorious advance. (See details in Fairbairn story.) Bolingbroke class was organized during those years. While Mr. Fairbairn worked at many points, the "Westport pilgrims . . . without a murmur" carried on locally and at the same time continued his salary.

In 1932 under J. W. Corey, Westport had a notable awakening with the Chases as evangelists.

Although only a village, Westport has for years had at least six Protestant churches besides a strong Roman Catholic element. This situation has tended to make it a difficult community.

For many years before his passing, Neil Stoness was Westport's most widely known member. This trained tenor singer refused offers from the operatic stage, choosing rather to serve as a singing evangelist in the Free Methodist Church. As a song leader, a soloist, and altar worker, he contributed immeasurably to many a camp meeting and revival.

Perth Road—We have seen a new church dedicated here just before the 1895 conference. Ira Brown supplied for the latter part of the next year and then Jonathan Sexsmith returned again. Both he and Mr. Sims wrote

Mr. and Mrs. Neil Stoness   Lottie Babcock, Emma Snider

of a good revival in early 1897. It lasted eleven weeks and saw over twenty clear conversions. At least eight joined the church as a result of it.

In early 1901 Mr. Sims told of an "old-fashioned revival" that produced shining faces, ringing testimonies and shouts of joy—also twenty-one probationers. Emma Snider was pastor then, but George Alton and Lottie Babcock participated also in this movement of God. When N. P. Hoover served the circuit in the early summer of 1932, E. R. Orser assisted in a revival that resulted in "twenty-five claiming victory."

Clarenceville—This English-speaking community of Quebec is about thirty-five miles south of Montreal and just north of the New York-Vermont border. As early as 1900, Free Methodist societies were organized here and at nearby St. Armand Center. A Rev. C. J. Hessler of the Burlington District of the Susquehanna Conference was the first Clarenceville pastor. Very early a church was built. Clarenceville had a camp meeting in 1916. For about thirty years Clarence Hawley and his wife carried on a Sunday School, some of the time in their home. Only in the past decade has it been joined to this conference. See the later story.

Bracebridge young people during Gregory pastorate

C. Muskoka District

Bracebridge—With seventy-three members, Bracebridge in 1895 ranked as one of the strongest societies in the conference. It was still strong in 1899 during the first pastorate of beloved F. D. Bradley when an excellent revival meeting and a victorious camp meeting were conducted there. Mr. Norrington, the conference evangelist, came the following winter for another revival that resulted in some seventy seekers, thirty-three on one night.

Bracebridge entertained in its Town Hall the annual conference of 1901 (Muskoka's first). Superintendent G. W. Coleman presided, accompanied by his one-time Canada-evangelist wife, the former Laura Warren. W. H. Gregory was ordained deacon at that conference. He succeeded S. Rogers as pastor in 1902 and stayed for three fruitful years. J. D. Shier was still mayor of the town, but he found time to be superintendent of the Free Methodist Sunday School as well. Sara Gregory describes the Bracebridge Church of that period as "pulsating with divine life." Children and young people were especially responsive to the ministry of the Gregorys, with a large number of them seeking their fathers' God. These included Shiers, Rusks, Priors, Harndens, Sharps, Gibsons, Scotts, Dicksons, Harps, Nobles, Rousehorns and others. Few societies have held more of their young people to the church than Bracebridge of that time. C. Floyd Appleton, the Canadian church's first missionary to China left during that pastorate.

The annual conference of 1906 met at Bracebridge and is memorable for a marriage contracted there. Just at the end of the Saturday business session while the congregation anxiously awaited the reading of the appointments, the song "Am I a Soldier of the Cross" was announced and two workers walked forward for wedlock. They were freshly resigned District Elder Norrington from West Ontario and evangelist Amanda Hughes who with Gertrude Pratt had been supplying Warkworth. (The first Mrs. Norrington had died about two years before.) The whole three workers were sent to Warkworth for the next year, but Campbellford was added as a new point. Mr. Norrington had to be listed as a supply, since he had come without credentials.

Conference came again in 1909 to a new four hundred-capacity brick church (with basement) just built by F. D. Bradley, there now a second time. Rev. B. Winget who presided that year dedicated the new building. Mr. Bradley conducted a campaign in the spring of 1911 that produced at least twenty probationers.

James Rusk, father of evangelist Josie Rusk, was one of Bracebridge's most dependable members about the time the new church was built.

Huntsville—Mrs. Margaret Bray (married by A. Sims in 1895 but still alive) has called this circuit "a training ground for young preachers." She recalls that at least the following men of the earlier days were fairly inexperienced when there: David Allan, Tobias Fletcher, Jonathan Sexsmith,

Bernard Boone, Charles Cunningham. To this list could be added some later "beginners" such as C. W. Kay and E. S. Bull.

The first Walls-built log church was several miles from town, as noted before. Later a church was built in the town.

At intervals one finds linked with Huntsville different nearby locations as Lake Vernon, Swindon or Silverdale.

Housey's Rapids, Barkway and Cooper's Falls—There is a record of a rewarding Barkway revival in the winter of 1897-98 when H. L. Miner was pastor here. Superintendent W. H. Reynolds assisted. The circuit parsonage was built in the fall of 1900 just after Emerson Snyder and wife arrived. He did the carpentering, she did the collecting (and even some of the sawing), while the local members assisted in clearing the land, getting the logs sawed and digging the basement. The house was inhabited a week before Christmas. Preachers in those days were usually very itinerant. Though the first lady evangelists as we have been, came to the area in 1881, not till 1903-06 was any preacher left as long as three years. That was L. Slingerland. In late 1911 Mr. Slingerland was back as an evangelist and reported for Barkway "the deepest move this point has had for twenty years." The revival was needed, for earlier that same year one scribe had cited the membership there as "four ladies whose husbands are unsaved."

The circuit has been host to district camps at various times. In 1932 over thirty people were baptized by immersion in Kahshe Lake when the camp was at Housey's Rapids.

In October, 1942, while L. C. Ball served the circuit and R. L. Casement was district superintendent, Housey's Rapids celebrated its Semi-Centennial. The anniversary was observed in an impressive program linked with a district meeting. Highlights of the occasion were historical addresses by the pastor and superintendent, reminiscences by "Grandpa" Benzinger (member since 1886), and reading of communications from scattered former associates. These included R. H. Hamilton who had been an eight-year-old boy when his father was first appointed to the circuit with David Allan in 1891, Mrs. Charles Dierks, William Zurbrigg, Emerson Snyder and others.

This circuit has produced at least the following Christian workers: David Allan, Mabel Robinson, Charles Dierks and wife, and Elmer Goheen.

Gravenhurst and Pine Lake—Free Methodism first invaded this rough lumbering Muskoka town in early 1900 when A. H. Norrington as conference evangelist conducted a several-months-long campaign. He was assisted by saints from Bracebridge and Ryde who drove fourteen to sixteen miles to get there. Mr. Norrington did extensive calling—130 visits by April's end—and circulated thousands of tracts, besides church papers. At least eighteen people professed conversion and thirteen joined a class organized after the meetings.

CONTINUING THE CONQUEST

A camp meeting was held in the early summer of the same year, with Rev. J. O'Regan of Buffalo and Rev. David Allan of Charlemont as evangelists. It was said that more of the numerous converts of this camp found the Lord in private prayer in the bush than at the altar. Rev. W. H. Reynolds, the district elder at the time, was described as "greatly beloved." Both he and Mr. O'Regan had been Roman Catholics earlier.

Some lady workers (in lighter mood) at Gravenhurst Camp, 1907. Included are Eliza Free, Louise (Hicks) Findlay, Frances Botting, Lotta Babcock, Kate Clark, Alberta Sims, Esther (Goodberry) Brown, Olive Butcher

The conference that year sent S. Rogers to Bracebridge but he seems to have supplied both Baysville and Gravenhurst as well. The following year, 1901, Charles Dierks, a beginning preacher, came specifically to Gravenhurst. He was followed in a year by Emma Snider, she to be succeeded for several years by Eliza Free and Louise Hicks. These ladies stayed till 1907 and built the membership up to forty-three. They also built a cement block church which General Superintendent Jones dedicated in October, 1906. The district camp meeting in 1907 was held in the town park where twenty tents were pitched. Most of the ladies in the accompanying picture (some married) were under appointment on the district at the time.

F. A. Daw served his first pastorate at Gravenhurst. During this 1920-23 stay he walked to a community called Pine Lake outside the town and built a little white frame church. Fiction-writer L. M. Montgomery attended some services during the building of the church and was much impressed by the sincerity and the singing ability of the Free Methodists. With modifications she used the setting for her book *Blue Castle*.

Orillia and Severn Bridge—Supply pastors (mostly women) were sent to this town after A. Sims formed a class in early 1892, but the work soon faded out. It came to life again in early 1932 when R. Sedore, the Graven-

125

hurst pastor, after an effective prayer meeting in the William Elder home, turned evangelist and campaigned for seven weeks using not only that home but those of Henry Pilger and P. K. Grant. Although encouraging crowds came, not till the last night of the last week was there any response. Then during the delayed altar call, the Holy Spirit descended with the suddenness and power of Pentecost and the revival was on.[7] Among the converts that night was aged William Hoover, his long white beard stained brown by the smoking of many years. God gave him complete deliverance from his habit and made him a pillar in that new Christian congregation. Also saved that night was Mrs. Harvey Grant.

In early summer, Mr. Sedore pitched a district tent in town and with Lottie Anderson Dixon as singer began an evangelistic concentration again. District preachers helped some, including Superintendent Daw. More good grain was harvested and a class of seventeen begun. (The membership was twenty-six by the following March.) One young man, Grant Hoover, sought the Lord after being smitten with unshakeable thoughts of final separation. They came at a communion service as the rest went forward and left him behind.

Despite the twenty-six-mile distance between towns, Mr. Sedore continued to come as able, local preachers or exhorters being in charge on Sunday nights. Said Fred Smith, a charter member who participated in those wondrous days and who furnished details for this story, "Attendance was always good, no matter who took the meeting."

In the fall of 1932 the present parsonage was bought. At first, its front rooms were remodelled for a chapel and the rest rented. Then in 1934 Orillia was given circuit status and Mr. Sedore became the full-time pastor. In early 1937 a vacant Methodist church in a neighbouring community was purchased and the salvage used to build the present church. Local and district volunteers led by Mr. Sedore completed the erection for the June opening by Rev. R. R. Blews.

Severn Bridge is the site of the present permanent district camp which will be described later.

Barrie, Hillsdale and Wyevale—The Barrie church dates from 1939 when the conference decided to open a mission there. R. B. Warren, who was just entering pastoral work after five years of teaching at Lorne Park College, was chosen for the task. An empty store near the main five corners was rented and fitted up for a chapel. A society was soon organized.

This official beginning had been preceded by an interesting sequence of events. Years before, nearby Crown Hill members, under the aggressive leadership of Mr. Thomas Luck who brought people in his democrat, had held prayer meetings in various Barrie homes. (The Charles Hickling home was one of the first to open.) The Year Books show Barrie listed as a point on the Crown Hill circuit as early as 1895. Converts of the beginning years include Mr. and Mrs. John Peters, Frank Perkins and

Harry Smith. In 1926 and 1927, while Rev. G. H. Bache and then L. S. Hoover pastored the Hillsdale-Crown Hill circuit, camp meetings were held at the east end of Barrie with Rev. F. Lincicome as evangelist. On the second occasion, several relatives of Rev. B. A. Sutton were converted. Later, the William Minos moved to Barrie. These people and others of Free Methodist persuasion deserved a pastor. After more prayer meetings conducted by Rev. Walker Skelding and then Rev. L. C. Ball (from Hillsdale-Crown Hill), the 1939 Warren appointment came.

Under Mr. Warren's pastoring, several Barrie people found the Lord and interest increased. Sara Gregory came for a revival campaign and the little chapel was filled at the last service.

Rev. J. F. Gregory was district superintendent during that first year and worked valiantly to collect funds over his two districts to pay the pastor's salary of $10 per week, leaving only other local expenses for the small congregation.

At the following conference with Mr. Gregory returning to a pastoral charge himself, Barrie was assigned to the Hillsdale pastor, Rev. F. Loft. In 1944, Rev. A. F. Ball was moved to Orillia with Barrie listed as an extra appointment. By 1946, the district superintendent Rev. C. W. Kay was instrumental in securing as pastor, Rev. P. L. Chase, who had been labouring as an evangelist in Western Canada. He had a new cement church completed and dedicated by May, 1948, and a parsonage built that same year. The parsonage was constructed in part out of materials salvaged from the Crown Hill brick church. Mrs. Chase, daughter of T. L. Fletcher and a capable preacher herself, helped her husband a great deal during the Chase stay there. During most of their Barrie years, the Chases lived in three little Sunday School rooms at the back of the church. They continued there even after the parsonage was built, letting the latter be rented as three apartments so the debt could be reduced faster.

Hillsdale was first listed in 1909 (and with Crown Hill) under Wilmott and Emma Harnden who presumably began this new work.

A Midland work was opened in the summer of 1912 when W. Zurbrigg of Hillsdale-Crown Hill, aided by L. Slingerland, pitched a tent in the town park and began an assault. Ethel Davey and Alberta Sims supplied until 1917, by which time a central church and parsonage property had been bought or built and the church dedicated.

Wyevale was first created an appointment in 1922 when Albert and Alvina Gunter were sent to supply it and Midland. The Wyevale Church was erected in 1936 under L. C. Ball's pastorate. Total cash cost: $405.

Timmins and Goldlands—In 1921 A. Sims, as a supernumerary preacher, went to the northern clay-belt community of Goldlands (forty-two miles northeast of Timmins) and held some schoolhouse meetings. For a time afterwards, the Myles Van Luvens, pioneer Free Methodists in the area, held Sunday School and preaching services quite regularly in their home and with some success. Not till 1927 did the first appointed pastor come—

N. F. Perry. He organized a class of eight and by the following spring had a church built. Off and on till 1936, various men and boys spent limited periods there. Then Elmer and Grace Goheen came north and for many years combined Sunday School work and preaching with local teaching, using dog sled transportation in the winter to get to their several points.

In 1943 the Goldlands circuit became Northern Ontario Mission. The next fall Superintendent C. W. Kay and Secretary of Evangelism R. B. Campbell toured the north at quarterly meeting time and asked the Goheens to move to the city of Timmins and begin a work. By April of 1945 a new Timmins Sunday School was in operation. Glen Elford and Clinton Bright later served short pastorates at Goldlands. Elmira Webb (later Freeman) assisted in children's work at Timmins for over a year.

By late 1946 a chapel-parsonage had been purchased with money from many sources—General Mission Board, General W.M.S., East Ontario Conference, Muskoka District and others. The chapel was dedicated in 1949 when Bishop Ormston and Missionary Secretary Lamson came north with Superintendent Daw on another survey. The following year, the Canadian Executive Board created a new Northern Ontario Home Missions District comprising mission work around Timmins and Fort William. Rev. Ross Lloyd was made superintendent.

Goheens at Goldlands church　　　　　　　　　　　Timmins Chapel

D. Peterborough District

Cordova Mines and Victoria—The first Free Methodist church on the Peterborough District is said to have been built at Victoria. Emerson Snyder, about 1894 or earlier, probably was responsible. Victoria is not mentioned in the Year Books till 1896 and then as a part of the Trent Bridge—Healey's Falls circuit.[8] Among early members were George Pounder, George Saunders, Ira Loucks and Grace Steenburg, the latter being class leader.[9]

Some time during the 1890's gold was discovered in the Cordova area. The prospects for profitable mining seemed so good that machinery was brought in and mills built. But because of mismanagement or miscalculations, the mines in a few years closed permanently.

Cordova community was annexed to the Beaver Creek circuit in 1903, then under Charles Babcock. Jane Rupert of the Beaver Creek society was made leader of Cordova's first class. In 1905 Mr. Babcock was moved to Cordova which was at that time linked up with Trent Bridge and Victoria. The Cordova Free Methodists worshipped in a vacant store, then bought the local Presbyterian church—for sale because of the closing mines. It gave them one of the largest church buildings in the conference. Since then a parsonage—directly across the street—has also been secured.

Marmora, North Marmora and Beaver Creek—Beaver Creek was first listed as a circuit in 1895 with Jennie Robinson named to tend it. Actually Louisa Free, a lay sister from Trent Bridge had previously held some winter services in the community and a Mr. Pack had fitted up his drive-shed for a temporary place of worship. Mr. Sims soon reported that a neat frame church had been erected and dedicated and a society of four had been organized. The Robinson-Free team had supervised the erection. William Peck donated the lot for the church and a cemetery. Those who came to the fencing bee were given a free burial plot. There was an early parsonage there too.

Charles Goodrich was stationed at Beaver Creek from 1900 to 1902. In June, 1901, he started a tent revival at North Marmora. So great was the conviction, that some would go to the altar while the sermon was still in progress. As the season grew cooler, a box stove was set up in the tent and later a tar paper shack was built. "The Sheep Pen," some unfriendly folk called it, yet as Sara Gregory points out: "It was a real Sheep-Fold to the Hawleys, Packs, Hamiltons, Airharts, Howes, . . . who met the Great Shepherd as their Saviour in this humble edifice." Mr. and Mrs. Charles Wells, whose family are active at Marmora and beyond today, were among the early members at North Marmora. (Mr. Wells, single till 1903, had been converted at his bedside a year before the revival.)

It was at a district meeting at Beaver Creek in 1906 that the W.F.M.S. for the then-called Havelock District was organized. A church was built at North Marmora that year, the lumber donated by Fred Wells (brother of Charles) who had it sawn for an earthly home and then discovered he was about to be promoted to a heavenly one.

During late 1921 just after Sperry Snyder had been assigned to Beaver Creek and Spring Brook, services were held in a hall in Marmora itself. Leonard Slingerland, the district elder, reported as many as sixteen seekers in one service and hopes for a class that did, in fact, follow soon.

In 1925 Roy Sedore came to this circuit as his first appointment. After a good revival in the Marmora hall where services had been held, he bought during the year the town's former Presbyterian church—a fine brick building. Rev. F. L. Baker, who came to Marmora for camp meetings in the summer of both 1926 and 1927, returned again in November of 1927 for the dedication.[10] (This church was unfortunately ruined by a nearby blast in March, 1960, but a new larger one is being built.)

The earliest parsonage was at North Marmora but more recently a town parsonage has been secured. In fairly recent years the Peterborough District superintendents have lived at Marmora, and even more recently C. W. Kay while supervising the whole conference.

Vennachar—Although Vennachar church and society existed before 1895, the circuit had its dark days in the early 1920's. For a time no pastor was sent and the church was closed. But three members, Mr. and Mrs. R. W. Connor and Mrs. Beatrice Ball, prayed on. Then in 1924 and 1925 C. V. Fairbairn and helpers saw God moving there again. Out of that revival came two preachers and two preachers' wives—Lorne Ball, Mr. and Mrs. John Martin, and Mrs. Nicholas Bosko. Two other local boys, Roy and Clarence Chatson, were to spend periods in the ministry also.[11]

The Vennachar parsonage was built in 1933 under William and Violet Mallory. About that time Denbigh, Plevna, and Northbrook were preaching points too. At intervals, Fernleigh belonged as well.

In September, 1944, Vennachar celebrated its Semi-Centennial under Nicholas Bosko as pastor. Numerous former converts and former workers were present or sent greetings, among the latter group being W. H. Gregory and Thomas Flake.

Gunter—Although a church had been here during 1894-95, there was still no parsonage when S. E. Ward arrived to minister in September, 1907. Undismayed, he partitioned off part of the church shed for his family and then went to work on a parsonage which was livable by December. Cost: $200. Barnett Babcock, there in 1913-14, reported the "misfortune" of losing this parsonage by fire, then added, "but still encouraged." It would appear that a replacement was built at once.

We have noted the preachers, including several Gunters, that came out of Emerson Snyder's early ministry. Some have said that all the Gunters were "born preachers." Of the talented lay folk, there is general agreement that Mrs. Sadie Gunter was the most fluent. Many a time she came to conference as delegate, pled for a preacher and then heard the bishop read: "Gunter—to be supplied." That meant her, so homeward she turned to resume the dual duties of farmer's wife and spiritual shepherd.

Gunter is said to have contributed a total of ten preachers to the church—an enviable record indeed.

Warkworth and Castleton—The Warkworth circuit may be considered as beginning with the appointment in 1894 of Samuel Rogers to rural Burnley (later called Zion) just east of Rice Lake in Northumberland County. At a quarterly meeting in the spring of 1896 Mr. Sims dedicated a new church that Mr. Rogers had just built. Great crowds attended and Mr. Sims wrote: "The whole country seems stirred and ready for the sickle."

In 1897 H. L. Miner was the appointee and the circuit read "Burnley and Warkworth." D. L. Gunter in early 1904 wrote of a district meeting in a Warkworth "mission room." Ira and Esther Brown evidently assisted in some services about this time. Two springs later a new "Mission Hall" was dedicated with District Elder C. Cunningham preaching the dedicatory sermon. Such large crowds attended the accompanying district meeting that the large local town hall had to be rented. The supply pastors, Amanda Hughes and Gertrude Pratt, having just conducted ten weeks of fruitful meetings, twenty people joined the church. A district camp there in the summer of the same year resulted in over one hundred seekers and another thirteen local members. At the conference that year, 1906, A. H. Norrington, as we have seen, married Miss Hughes and the whole trio joined battle locally. By January of the next year, 1907, Mr. Norrington had a new church ready for opening.

Above: 1906 Camp of former Havelock District at Warkworth under C. Cunningham.

Right: Mrs. Emma Richardson
"Her face shone with the presence of the Lord."

W. H. Gregory served from 1910 to 1913. Sara Gregory remembers fondly some of the saints of this period—Frank Miner who boasted of belonging to the Aristocracy of Heaven, Alex Harnden who not only exhorted but also sang and laughed joyously at church, George Harvey who boasted a letter every morning from his Heavenly Father, Emma Richardson (mentioned before) who seemed the ideal class leader, Mrs. John Kelly whose cookies thrilled the parsonage children, Will McNutt whose "democrat" carried his twelve children to the Lord's house each Sunday, Will Ireland who loved to share his home with the pastor's family,[12] Merton Spinks (the Sunday School superintendent) who loved to entertain young people at Sunday supper so they would be sure to go to service, . . . Many children from these homes were converted during Mr. Gregory's first year at Warkworth. In fact, he had twenty-three probationers within his first six months there.

In 1945 Burnley (Zion) church celebrated its fiftieth anniversary under pastor S. S. Bailey. Mrs. Norah Gunter of Castleton was one of those present who had attended the church as a child.

Castleton is a recent addition to the Warkworth circuit. A. F. Ball bought a vacant Wesleyan Methodist church in Castleton, only weeks before this writer went there in 1940 to his first school. A class had been organized in 1934 with services in the interval held in homes or halls.

Campbellford—This town is first listed in 1906 and as a part of the Warkworth circuit. As noted, Amanda Hughes and Gertrude Pratt had been supplying the circuit, but the marriage of A. H. Norrington to Miss Hughes warranted more battle ground for the party.

Behind this Campbellford opening was a small one-armed saint who prayed and sacrificed for a Free Methodist work there. With the lumber industry getting exhausted around Trent Bridge and Healey's Falls, the Loucks and Kellar families had moved to Campbellford and begun services in a hall. Little Mrs. Loucks especially carried the burden.

By 1909 Campbellford was listed as a separate circuit of seven members and assigned to Ethel Davey. (Actually some time during the previous conference year, Gertrude Pratt and Aggie Kearns had been placed in charge there under the official Warkworth-Campbellford pastor, C. Cunningham.)

Kate Clark supplied this mission from early 1915 to 1917 and supervised the erection of a $3,500 cement block church which lacked only $200 of being paid for at the time of dedication—probably in early 1917. (She died that November at only forty-five from rheumatic grippe and sciatica.)

At a camp meeting just out of town in 1925 one service was said to have continued for fourteen hours and to have produced about a dozen clear definite conversions.

Picton—One report tells of an unsaved Michigander coming to Prince Edward County about 1898 and telling his religious neighbours such favourable stories of Free Methodism that they grew hungry for a salvation that really saved. They sent word through to Elder Sims (then living at Kingston) to visit them. A drive-house at the back of a sap bush was fitted up with planks and lanterns and the people flocked in to hear his old-fashioned gospel. Another story by Mr. Sims himself mentions a Brother Robert Farring and wife moving to that area from Keith and starting cottage prayer meetings before he arrived.

Kingston District Camp at Picton, 1904

At any rate, the response to Mr. Sims' coming proved so encouraging he saw to it that the people were sent a pastor that fall—young Ira Brown whose wife was Verona's former talented singer, Esther Goodberry. The people soon began to seek the Lord in earnest. By December, when new Elder Norrington came for a quarterly meeting, he was able to enroll a class of seventeen, including the Hughes family. S. Rogers was sent as pastor the following fall, the circuit being called Picton and Bloomfield.

In the summer of 1901 the Kingston district camp meeting was held near Picton. (This Prince Edward circuit then belonged to that district.) The camp was so successful that Mr. Sims, now elder again, was able to enroll eleven new local members at its close. Another good camp meeting, of which we have a picture, came in 1904. Rev. Albert Bean of Pennsylvania was one evangelist. R. Burnham and C. Goodrich were elder and pastor respectively.

By the summer of 1905, two churches had been built in the country and a parsonage and church lot bought in the town. C. Goodrich and C. A. Fox who followed him, must have taken some initiative in these matters. Mr. Fox likely built the church about 1906.

The Gregorys were sent to Picton and Elmbrook in 1913. In the town they often resorted to street meetings and found the singing of the Hughes family attracted crowds. Some lasting conversions resulted from their two-year ministry. A union camp meeting for Kingston and Campbellford districts came to Picton in 1915.

From time to time, various communities in the county were listed as preaching points but their work did not become permanent. Demorestville, Bongard and Long Point were of this sort.

Consecon would seem to have been raised up by Barnet Babcock about 1931. For a time later it was part of the Frankford circuit. Point Traverse began appearing as a listing in 1941 and under E. S. Bull. Neither of these places now have churches.

Peterborough—H. B. Luck was sent here as first pastor in 1905. This man, who seemed to carry revivals everywhere, did not fail Peterborough. By conference he had fourteen members and a year later twenty-two, and a year after that thirty. Peterborough belonged to the Toronto District at first and had that district's camp in 1907.

Lottie Babcock and Kate Clark served the circuit for three years beginning in 1910. When they left, the society had a parsonage plus a stone and brick church (with basement Sunday School rooms) on Aylmer St. It was dedicated in August, 1910, just before conference.

A Toronto-Campbellford union camp was held at Peterborough in a grove opposite Jackson's Park in 1913. C. Cunningham was pastor and A. D. Zahniser the evangelist. During the camp Bishop Pearce made a surprise visit. W. B. Olmstead was the evangelist at a Peterborough revival just before or after this, at which time S. B. Griffith was entirely sanctified. Another camp was held near the city in 1925. At it, as wave after wave of seekers came forward, a final Sunday service lasted fourteen hours.

It was while he was serving this church during 1930-31, that still-young Roy Chatson died, a typhoid casualty.

Peterborough has had its "lows." Once Mrs. Ethel Griffith supplied while her husband S. B. Griffith, living locally, served as district elder. At other times no pastor was assigned. C. W. Reynolds, who willingly went to this weak circuit for two years beginning in 1945, did much to start it on a healthy upgrade again. And his successor R. E. Dargan continued the trend into the past decade.

Frankford and Trenton—George Overpaugh, who preached for years as a Free Methodist, eventually severed his church connection (about 1910) and began an independent work at Frankford under the name "Bible Christian." Later he went West and the orphan converts asked the Free Methodist Church to accept them and their property. This they gratefully did. The transfer must have taken place about 1917, since the circuit was first listed in that year and under J. W. Potter as pastor. A total of twenty-five members were already enrolled. Rev. and Mrs. R. L. Casement are fruits of early Free Methodist effort at Frankford. A. F. Ball, Barnet Babcock, Richard Babcock and W. H. Gregory all saw good revivals during their pastorates. Twiddys, Kemps and Morrows were among those who came into the church from other communions during the late 1930's. The new stucco church was built by pastor Roy Sedore during 1945-46 with

Dr. Byron S. Lamson conducting the dedication. This writer was principal of the local secondary school at the time and an "assistant" to the pastor.

Frankford has entertained at least three annual conferences—in 1921 with Bishop Warner, in 1931 with Rev. B. N. Miner, and in 1945 with Bishop Fairbairn—and for a time was the location of the district camp. The Trenton work has never had its own church.

Bellville—The Norrington-Cark team, we have seen, campaigned (evidently without success) in this area before going to Petworth in 1888. In the 1920's an Indian lady, Julia Smart, worked an Aldersville Mission somewhere on an Indian Reserve near Belleville and even attempted a footing in the city. But again nothing permanent resulted. Not till this past decade did Belleville really feel Free Methodism. But that story comes later in "Recent Review."

---

1. W. H. Linstead, father of Herbert and Eldon, was the Free Methodist pastor at Uxbridge from 1924 to 1927.
2. Cataraqui already had a church, the work there being an offshoot of the earlier Elginburg foothold.
3. Among other Verona young people at this time were Edna Carslake Burnham and Clark Reynolds. Mr. Ball was later to be an East Ontario district elder.
4. The Griffiths subsequently spent some thirty years in the ministry, part of which time Mr. Griffith was a district elder.
5. Mrs. Wartman at first was reluctant to go with her husband to this new point without class or church. But after getting sanctified at Godfrey camp the next summer, she found the rebellion gone. There were weeks, though, when fuel and hall rent took all but sixty cents of the offerings.
6. Mr. Fairbairn held meetings at Wagarville in .1919. For a time it had been attached to Verona.
7. Wrote Fred Smith of that memorable meeting: "I shall never forget His coming. We had been standing with bowed heads while the altar call was being given, when suddenly I heard and felt a mighty rushing wind which seemed to fill the house. I looked up thinking that all the windows were open but they were all closed (It was March) and there was not a sign of a breath of air. It was the windows of Heaven that were open. . . ."
8. Trent Bridge (south of Havelock) entertained the conference of 1897, the first one east of the Toronto District. This saw-milling centre has since faded out.
9. Mrs. Lily Whitney, a daughter of George Steenburg, still attends the Cordova Church.
10. District Elder E. J. Lee, in reporting the 1926 camp meeting, noted that street meetings were a prominent feature of it.
11. Roy Chatson, a gifted preacher, died shortly after entering the ministry.
12. Will Ireland later married Gertrude Pratt.

2.
FORWARD IN WEST ONTARIO

A. Sarnia District

Charlemont and Wallaceburg—The great Keith or Charlemont revival of 1888-89 and the local district camps of 1898 and 1899 (when the Haley brothers were saved) are mentioned elsewhere. On a Tuesday of the latter camp the altar service lasted seven or eight continuous hours and produced at least fifteen genuine converts, a number of them being children. Among them were Albert Haley, Eddie DeMille, Mary DeMille (later Roberts), Margaret Allan (later Stevenson) and her sister Annie, and Beatrice Robinson. Charlemont society alone gained eleven new members.

The Charlemont parsonage was the first built on the district. That came during 1895-96 when the Warren-Green team were there as pastors. The church followed in the spring of 1897 under John Timbers.

The Wallaceburg people bought a large brick church from the Baptists around the turn of the century but it burned in December of 1903. After that, a local hall was rented for a time.

There is a record of an encouraging revival at Charlemont in 1916 when E. E. Loveless was pastor. Over twenty, from among nearly twice as many seekers, were clearly saved. Many of the converts were Sunday School scholars.

Charlemont had a number of early district camp meetings and several annual conferences as well.

No services are held in Wallaceburg at present, although Free Methodist families have lived there and services have been held at various times in the past. It is only a short distance to the Charlemont church. Says J. A. Robb of this circuit: "It may well be that Charlemont has produced more preachers for Canadian Free Methodism than any other point in West Ontario."

Some West Ontario lady evangelists about 1920—Anna Botting, Effie Cowherd, Elizabeth Allan, Harriet Cowherd, Alice Walls.

Essex—This lovely town in the heart of Essex County is first mentioned in the Conference Minutes of 1911 as "Essex Center . . . To be supplied." The following year Alice Walls and Anna Botting are listed as doing the supplying. A note written in December of that year speaks of a "neat little cement block church near the centre of the town" that had been built during the previous summer, this despite the fact that Essex was a new work and a small class. F. L. Baker had just been there for a district meeting and dedication. For a time Essex was joined with Windsor to form a circuit.

In 1947, during J. Withenshaw's pastorate, a parsonage was built beside the church.

Goderich—The fine church and parsonage in this Lake Huron town are the fruit of a work began in 1934. Resident J. H. Millian came in contact with the Free Methodist paper and through it got in touch with R. H. Hamilton just back from Saskatchewan. Mr. Hamilton, aided by his wife, Elizabeth Allan, and Pearl Earl as singers, conducted a campaign in a basement lodge room and organized a class of six. Evelyn Dawson was put in charge. In 1935, Harold and Martha Marlatt were appointed to the new circuit. A house left to the society by the will of Mr. Millian soon became the parsonage in early 1936. During that same year, Mr. Marlatt built a church which was opened in December and dedicated by Claude A. Watson the following May. In 1947 during R. C. McCallum's ministry the earlier parsonage was sold and a new one built near the church. Besides the house which sold for $4,000, Mr. Millian left $6,000 to the Free Methodist Church to be divided among the local society, Lorne Park College and the ministers' Superannuate Fund.

London—Although an appointment existed here as early at 1876, the work, as we have seen, died out even in Mr. Sage's time. In 1925 it reappeared under Rev. H. G. Kent, father of Dr. Lois Kent. He moved there for two purposes: to have his future-missionary daughter attend medical school, and to see a work established in this fine city. Though busy (as a painter and decorator) to meet expenses, he was able to open a mission. The present church-parsonage building there, a former Presbyterian Church, was bought in 1930 when Olive Vail and Ruby Hicks served the circuit. At the conference held that year in Hamilton, $1,700 was given or pledged towards this new project. G. W. Stevens followed the lady workers and gave four fruitful years of service. The debt was cleared and the church dedicated in 1938 when J. A. Robb was pastor. For a number of years the circuit was financially assisted by the Conference.

Middlemiss—This circuit is a continuation of the one that first appeared under the name Iona in 1880. The new name came in 1886 at which time it was linked with Southwold.

We have seen that the church was built during 1884-85. The parsonage

THE BATTLE WAS THE LORD'S

is said to have been built during 1909-10, although no pastor was under appointment on the circuit that year.

At a camp meeting there in 1900, Mr. Sage, who had gone back to his homeland in 1887, returned for a visit. He brought blessing to the saints as he reminded them of the days when he had "underbrushed his way

Above: Group at Sarnia District Camp, 1911.

Left: Sarnia church and parsonage

Below: Annual Conference at Sarnia in 1920 with Bishop Pearce.

through Ontario." He was then about seventy-four but still preaching—at Marine City, Michigan.

When Alice Walls and Elizabeth Allan served Middlemiss about 1915, it was linked with St. Thomas, but this latter work seems to have vanished later.

For a few years Middlemiss was listed under the name Thames River.

Sarnia—Families, such as the Bottings, Mannings, Harrises, and Wilsons, moving from Charlemont helped to increase the infant Sarnia class whose organization was described earlier. The 1897 conference changed the name of this circuit from Point Edward to its present one, because, during the previous year, pastor John Timbers had built a church at nearby Sarnia and the congregation began worshipping there.

M. S. Benn, sent in 1901, completed paying off the church debt and built a fine parsonage. During his third year he saw the membership substantially increased after an excellent revival. A remarkable district camp meeting at Sarnia one summer at that time resulted in seventeen conversions from one morning service that lasted till five o'clock in the afternoon.

The present large brick Sarnia church was built towards the latter part of H. G. Kent's 1915-18 pastorate.

Sarnia was host to the historic All-Canada Conference in 1920. That story is told in another section.

Thedford and Sharon—About 1905 or 1906, J. A. Fletcher, the Thedford pastor, held an unsuccessful six-week tent meeting at Sharon. But he followed it with a successful fifteen-week revival in a vacant house belonging to a local preacher named Aaron Smith. Mr. Smith donated a lot for a church and before J. A. Fletcher left in 1906 a good building subscription fund had begun. (J. C. Gare was one early convert who was to become a class leader.) T. L. Fletcher followed his brother J. A. to the circuit and built the Sharon church. It was dedicated by W. B. Olmstead in 1908 (an American who first preached in Muskoka under Mr. Sage).

About 1914 or 1915 the old Primitive Methodist church, that had been purchased at Thedford in the 1880's to replace the original "cooper-shop" chapel, was torn down and rebuilt on the same lot. Isaiah Bailey, a local preacher, was supplying on the circuit at the time, and did much of the work.

During the pastorate of Rev. G. W. Stevens in the late 1920's, Rev. Levi Ecker[1] came to Sharon for an encouraging revival that resulted in twelve baptisms.

The West Ontario Conference of 1935 was held at Thedford, with F. L. Baker being in charge.

Thornyhurst—For many years previous to 1950 this community with Terminus constituted a circuit. Most of the early information available refers to Terminus, which was an outreach from Charlemont. There is, for instance, a record of twenty-three sound conversions in a six-week revival held by David Allan, the Charlemont pastor, in early 1899. It appears nearly all converts joined the church. By the next spring a new church had been built and dedicated. A second revival, just preceding the dedication, proved even better than the previous one, with at least fifty seekers and twenty-one more probationers. Several older men deep in sin were among the trophies.

Wabash, Chatham and Dresden—At various times since 1895, various combinations of the following places have been grouped into one circuit: Florence, Ousley, Croton, Oakdale, North Dawn and Dawn Mills, Dresden, Thorncliffe and Wabash. Wabash itself is first specifically listed as a conference appointment in 1914 under J. T. Abrams. Early Free Methodist families there included Wises, McQuarries and Shaws.

Miranda Coatsworth Wilson was a devout Methodist lady who early took her stand with the Free Methodists at Wabash. For years she contributed much as a class leader, song leader and Sunday School teacher.

Wabash society purchased a vacant Methodist church at nearby Thorncliffe about 1921 during J. H. Roberts' pastorate and moved this building to Wabash. Earlier churches at Florence and Ousley were sold to help bear the cost. In 1926 the Wabash church was moved to its present site under P. K. Smith. In 1929 the parsonage was bought, moved and remodelled under J. C. Gare.

The Chatham connection dates from 1940 when G. W. Stevens came for a year of aggressive effort. Actually it began earlier since, for the five previous years while stationed at Charlemont, he had conducted a well-received weekly broadcast over the Chatham radio station. Also a camp was held there in 1939. Since 1941 Chatham and Dresden have both been considered a part of the Wabash circuit.

Windsor, First—Windsor does not appear in the conference records till 1928. In that year R. G. Evans was sent to Essex and Windsor, but lived at the former place. During some of the intervening years Windsor has been joined to Essex, and during others it has been listed as a separate appointment. In 1947 a house was purchased with the intention of fitting up the main floor as a chapel and having living quarters upstairs. The arrangement evidently was not deemed satisfactory and since that time, the house has been rented out to tenants and the rental applied on a hall. The Windsor work has suffered by the removal of numbers of its members, by frequent part-time ministers, and by the absence of a suitable house of worship. A small but loyal band of pilgrims continue at the present and are served part-time by Rev. H. H. Hyndman, who labours at much personal sacrifice.

Zion—This church began, like Thornyhurst, as an outgrowth of the Charlemont circuit. In late 1900 a Miss Annie Knight Humphrey of Dawn Mills moved there, secured permission for the use of the local Beaver Meadow schoolhouse and called Rev. T. L. Fletcher of Charlemont for meetings.[2] Assisted by local preacher Neil McGugan, he had great success in a twelve-week campaign. It is said eighty-five people were at the altar; in one service, every unsaved person was there. Among the surnames of the early members at Zion appear the following: Dawson, Annett, Blacklock, Fader, Humphrey and Unsworth. Joseph Dawson was the first convert there. Mr. Fletcher organized a class of thirty-five and began at once to build a church. The dedication came in February of 1902, with W. B. Olmstead officiating.

A nearby point named Oakdale had a class of eleven organized in the fall of 1904, after a camp meeting and six more weeks of special meetings there. Zion, Oakdale and Ousley were constituted a new circuit that year under George Evans. Later, Zion, Unionville and North Dawn were the points on the circuit.

Zion's parsonage was built during 1923-24 while Rev. Wyatt Bates was on the circuit.

In early 1928 under Rev. J. H. Roberts a real moving of God took place at Zion. Esther Annett, who was one convert, has vivid recollections of the way the pilgrims set aside their work for the more important matter of the moment. When it was too muddy to drive to service, the people walked.

B. Sault Ste. Marie District

Sault Ste. Marie—About 1901 Mr. and Mrs. Alec Vallier, Free Methodists from the Kingston District, and a Mrs. Warren, also a Free Methodist, moved to the Canadian "Soo" and joined the church in the American "Soo." A few years later several Canadian Johnsons were converted and the American pastor J. E. Saunders began services on the Canadian side—first in homes, then in a rented hall. In 1905 a West Ontario Conference preacher was requested, and E. A. DeMille had the honour of being first pastor and organizer of the class.[3] Lurena Vallier was first class leader and Charles Eddy first local preacher.

In 1910 under the labours of Matilda Sipprell a Gore St. Mission was purchased. Two years later, P. K. Smith sold this property for almost four times its original cost, then bought another lot and proceeded to build a brick church. W. B. Olmstead dedicated this church about 1914 or 1915. Shortly afterwards a parsonage was purchased.

During 1921-22, when W. R. and Harriet McCready served the circuit, a lengthy revival resulted in a membership increase of eleven.

The Sault Ste. Marie circuit and St. Joseph Island were constituted a separate Sault Ste. Marie District in 1946. These two were near each other, but about three hundred miles from the other Lake Superior circuits.

St. Joseph Island—This island, some twenty-two miles by eleven miles, lies thirty miles from Sault Ste. Marie at the southeast end of the St. Mary's River where it empties Lake Superior into Lake Huron. At points the island lies close to the United States. About 1894 some islanders such as the Brownlees and Connells, visiting American relatives heard a young Free Methodist named B. H. Alberts preach. Hungry for salvation, they and others soon invited Mr. Alberts over to the Cheers log schoolhouse where, after a five-week campaign, he formed a class of seven with Ann Brownlee as class leader. That was April, 1895. The North Michigan conference in August sent Mr. Alberts back to serve the island calling the new circuit Richards Landing and Bethel. Crowds came to the services, but soon unpopularity forced them from the Cheers school.[4]

The Island's Mountain school opened, however, and by January a second class of thirteen existed under Fred Eddy as leader. One man brought his family to services driving a horse and a mule together. Among the many "Mountain" converts were Sarah and John Kirk and their two sons.[5] Mrs. Kirk was destined to spend many years as Sunday School superintendent and class leader, and Mr. Kirk as janitor. By the conference of 1896, "St. Joe" had thirty-six members and a church begun on an acre lot donated by a charter member, Octavius Lee.[6] Though called the "Mountain" Church, it was midway between the two schools and provided a place of worship for Guys, Brownlees, Watsons, Connells, Blacks, Sees, Reids, Farrels, Brayleys, Gilroys, Fishes, Eddys, Woods, Kirks and others from the two communities. The frame 28' x 40' building was completed in early 1897 and dedicated by Bishop Hart in July.

In 1900 the circuit assumed its present name but was divided into two classes, Cedar Grove and Mountain. Mrs. Ashur Smith was converted about this time under pastor N. J. Fuller. She became a loyal Christian and her family still support the church. Also about 1900 the Island's first camp meeting was held—in Andrew Black's maple grove. Curiosity brought people from all parts of the island. Some non-residents came by sailboat. Many from Michigan were present.

L. C. Fletcher, who followed Mr. Fuller, added Graces, Stemburgs, Archibalds and others to the church and in 1902 organized what was called the I Line Class. Mr. Harten, converted at seventy-four, was largely responsible for this new effort.

In 1907 with border regulations tightening and a Lake Superior District in West Ontario now functioning, St. Joseph Island was transferred to the West Ontario Conference. L. H. Isles, a Canadian, who pastored the circuit just before and after the transfer, built the parsonage on another adjacent lot (five acres this time) supplied by Mr. See.[7]

The Cedar Grove Church was built by J. M. Eagle around 1910 when he was both pastor and stationed elder there.

C. Lake Superior District

Hymers, O'Connor and Gillies—About 1903 the George Moore, George Mayo and David Youmans Free Methodist families from Walsingham came to the Lakehead area. A little earlier, other Free Methodists by the names of Earl, Denison and Waldron had come from South Dakota and

Camp of old Lake Superior District (now Sault Ste. Marie District) at Richards Landing in 1911 under J. M. Eagle.

Right: Fred Killins

a little later the Fred Killins family arrived from Bracebridge. A number of these people began homesteading in the timber territory around Hymers, some thirty miles southwest of Fort William.

The West Ontario conference of 1903 sent young Harry C. Freemantle as a pioneer preacher to this area listing it as New Ontario Mission. He held services in the Hymers village schoolhouse and the Hannit home, and also in Fort William where some of the Free Methodist arrivals were living. The Hymers society was organized in December, 1903, with Mrs. Sarah Earl the first class leader. There were nine charter members.[8] A little later a Sunday School was held in a widow Wright's log house with local preacher George Moore as superintendent.

R. A. Coates, sent to Hymers for 1906-07, built a lean-to shanty which served temporarily as church and parsonage. His successor, C. Fader, saw the present church erected in 1908. Oscar Earl cut logs, Mr. Fader skidded them, Fred Killins sawed the lumber, all the men left their work to attend the numerous "bees"; and when the building with its white pine seats and grained ash woodwork and Hannit-made pulpit was completed, Elder Eagle from the Tillsonburg District came for a service of dedication, offering at it a dedicatory prayer that people still talk about. The present parsonage was built by the next pastor, J. W. Peach, about 1910.

It was during his stay that George Bayes donated a lot from his farm for a Free Methodist cemetery. Even then, the mail train came to Hymers only once a week.

Services were begun about 1917 in O'Connor Township. At first they were held in a community church, later in a Township Hall, while prayer services were in the homes. J. A. Robb, on the circuit in 1934 began services in a school in Gillies Township and saw some converts in a revival. There are members in both communities now, but most area services are in the Hymers church.

Fort William and Port Arthur—The first Lakehead pastor (Mr. Freemantle) in 1903 organized, besides his rural church, an urban class of nine members. About 10,000 people lived in the Twin Cities then. J. H. Roberts in 1906 (the year the Lake Superior District was created) was the first full-time city pastor. Early Port Arthur meetings were held in the Howard Earl home. Often meetings were conducted at Slate River also in the Dennison home. Later, some of the congregation moved away and others that remained moved their membership to Hymers. For several years from 1921 on, Anna Botting, Olive Vail, W. R. McCready, R. H. Hamilton and others spent varying periods labouring in the cities but with limited success. After a second lull, Ella Lishman, sent in 1946, mustered another small class during her three-year assignment and began a church building fund. Norman Winslow, who followed for 1949-50 began a building program.

D. Hamilton District

Brantford—The church we have seen bought in 1891 on Market Street was torn down about late 1895 and rebuilt to produce a more substantial structure. George Taylor did much of the carpenter work. B. H. Roberts (son of B. T.) came in the spring of 1896 for the re-opening of the new attractive 35' x 60' white brick building. General Superintendent Sellew conducted the dedication in February of 1902. (B. R. Jones had presided at the first West Ontario conference here in 1896, J. M. Eagle being secy.

About this time, the pastor, Robert Hamilton, had an excellent revival with the aid of W. B. Olmstead as evangelist. Converts included Effie Cowherd and the pastor's son, R. H. (Henry).

In 1904, while Samuel Rogers served the society, a parsonage was bought.

For a short period beginning in 1906 a Brantford District, under M. S. Benn, existed.

Hannah Burkholder who died in 1933 was described as having been a faithful member at Brantford for forty years.

Caistor Centre and Kimbo—The first church and parsonage on this circuit were apparently built by David Allan during 1902-03. The church was at Caistor Centre and the parsonage at Kimbo. A notorious thief and drunkard named Peter Sammons was converted under Mr. Allan. (Watch for

Annual conference at Brantford in 1914 with Bishop Sellew.

him and proof of his transformation in the Welland story.) Kimbo was a German community, its name meaning *elbow* and given because of the location at a bend in the creek. Nancy Schantz, when there, preached in German. Among early members appear the names Zurbrigg, Hoffman, Wilcox, Muir, Evans and others. A church was eventually built here too, probably by George Overpaugh.

When Wyatt Bates was on the circuit in the early 1930's, the Kimbo parsonage burned and a new one was erected at the other point. Fire was to hit the circuit again in 1950.

Dunnville—Conference Minutes show Dunnville first as an appointment in 1918 under Levi Ecker. It was annexed to an existing circuit of Canboro and Montague. The Dunnville church was opened in March of 1928 and dedicated in August of the same year. (A church built at Canboro in 1897 by C. M. Smith and his still-living son A. E. provided materials.) Ruby Hicks was listed as supply pastor then. The annual conference of the next year met at Dunnville, Elizabeth Allan then in charge. The absence of a parsonage—until this last decade—made for frequent changes of personnel and, as a result, slow growth.

Galt—We have noted the early beginnings here and the historic conferences of 1880 and 1895. The first parsonage was built by M. S. Benn in 1904 on land donated by J. Ballantine.

Under J. A. Fletcher in 1909 the church and parsonage were sold and another church was built downtown beside a purchased parsonage. Rev. J. T. Logan came in August for the dedication.

At different times, Hespeler and Guelph were listed as appointments of the Galt circuit.

The latest surge of growth at Galt belongs to the decade just past.

Hamilton, West Ave.—The Hamilton society which had been begun as a Hannon off-shoot in early 1891, had been operated for a time as a separate circuit, and had been left "to be supplied" in 1895, was attached to Hannon again in 1896 under M. O. Coates. The affiliation lasted till the conference of 1900 when J. E. and Ada Foreman were sent as supply pastors. But the Hamilton work probably had not continued in a thriving state. At any rate, in early 1901 some scribe wrote of securing a "fine hall" at 39 King William Street in the heart of the city. It was to be operated after the fashion of the Free Methodist Olive Branch Mission in Chicago, and was, in fact, called "Canadian Olive Branch Mission." The Norringtons spent three weeks in opening the new project. A Mary J. Everhart and a Dr. Harriet Sheldon (later Barnes) were two early workers sent from Chicago.[9] The mission served the Hamilton members and others for several years, but when the rent became burdensome it appeared Hamilton was too small a city for the success of such a project. From 1904-07 the society had no appointed workers. About 1908 while Matilda Sipprell and Martha Mullen were stationed there and M. S. Benn was district elder, a $4,000 property at 102 Catherine Street N., was purchased. It provided facilities for both a chapel and living quarters. During H. G. Kent's 1918-20 pastorate, this building was sold for $7,000 and the present West Ave. church built. The dedication was by C. V. Fairbairn in late 1926 (this his last conference year in Canada). Mr. Fairbairn helped pastor David Allan in two weeks of revival before the historic district meeting dedication. In the early 1940's a large parsonage was bought across the street from the church.

For over forty years this West Avenue church has been one of the stronger ones in West Ontario. It has been host to at least four annual conferences, including both the 1930 and the 1945 anniversary occasions described in the "Milestones" chapter. One of its most noteworthy early members, from 1900 on, was Peter Sharp whose larger story is told elsewhere.

Hamilton (Parkdale) and Hannon—Rev. E. A. Cooper, the West Ave. pastor in May of 1939, began this "east-end" work as an afternoon Sunday School on the park grass. By fall, the original thirteen youngsters had become almost forty and a Scout cabin was rented for the winter. The next spring Mr. Cooper built a 20' x 30' chapel that in a short time was to have over one hundred people attending. In 1944 an extension at the back was necessary.

For several years in the middle 1940's, Mr. Cooper had charge of this new church while serving at the same time as director of the Canadian Church Council for Men in Service. Stanley Freeman was one layman from West Ave. who early and helpfully associated himself with this new project.

Hannon, begun so early, did not become a part of this circuit until the present decade. For some years during the first and second decades of the century, nearby Ancaster had a small Free Methodist work, a continuation of a class mentioned before.

Niagara Falls and St. Catherines—Josie Rusk (later Wees) and Mary Botting were sent to Niagara Falls' established church in 1894 and Miss Rusk stayed for two happy years. Wards, Newhams and Priors were numbered among her faithful members then. Leonard Slingerland, who was to become an effective evangelist, was a local preacher in her congregation. For a period Miss Rusk and her companion walked the fourteen miles to Niagara-on-the-Lake for a Sunday afternoon service in a third-storey room.

In late 1900, while local preacher George Teal of Ridgeway served the Falls as supply pastor, a church on Simcoe St. bought some time earlier, was dedicated by General Superintendent Jones. To help pay expenses, this church for a time was rented to the city on weekdays for a school.

In 1922 during the pastorate of Elizabeth Allan the present brick church on Huron Street was built. The congregation has had several genuine revivals. Wilbur Teal remembers its customary Sunday testimonies after morning sermons as times when the saints were blessed and the unconverted were made hungry.

The parsonage was built some time after the church, and by D. McGugan. The conference of 1936 in returning C. E. L. Walls to "The Falls" made St. Catherines a new appointment. (Many years before in the 1880's a non-permanent work had existed in St. Catherines, also linked with Niagara Falls.) It continued as a part of the circuit till made a separate charge during the past decade.

Ridgeway—When M. S. Benn came as pastor in 1894, he found a complicated debt on the old M. E. Church bought a few years earlier. But after a good revival, the people were able to pay it off. A church in Fort Erie was also acquired during his stay.

J. A. Fletcher, as pastor, held a revival campaign in the winter of 1900-01 that lasted twelve weeks. The large church was filled by the crowds and the whole community awakened.

Daniel and Hattie Toole assisted by Mrs. Mary Clink in the spring of 1905 saw another great moving of the Spirit. In one service, fourteen joined the church and eighteen more sought the Lord.

Ridgeway's church was dedicated in 1906 when her society played host to the 1906 annual conference with Bishop Sellew.[10] The same bishop was there in 1918 for another conference. A parsonage debt received a boost that time.

About forty people sought the Lord in a 1924 spring revival when H. H. Hyndman was pastor.

In the early 1930's the new smaller church at Ridgeway was built during the joint pastorate of Effie Cowherd and Ruby Hicks.

Fort Erie for a time was an appointment of the Ridgeway circuit.

Welland—J. A. Fletcher seems to have held the first services here—street meetings. Ira Brown in 1901 was the first pastor. He held services in an old church west of the canal and north of Chippawa Creek. Niagara Falls people helped pay early bills.

By December of 1902 Mr. Brown was advertising the dedication of a church. He had held a revival for twenty consecutive weeks with such excellent results that the vacant Methodist Church (with parsonage attached) in the centre of the town had been purchased. A month after dedication the membership was up to twenty-eight.

The present church at 39 Grove St. was built in 1919 and dedicated that October by Bishop Clark. The adjacent parsonage was bought about the same time from a faithful layman named Norval Lynn. Robert Bloye was pastor then.

The local W.F.M.S. is said to have been organized at a district meeting in 1910 by Mrs. Agnes Benn, conference president. Her husband was district elder then.

Peter Sammons, the Caistor convert of bar-room background, was an early local preacher and class leader at Welland. He came to be highly respected for his faithfulness.

For many years Wainfleet was an appointment on this circuit and some of the members today still live there.

E. Tillsonburg District

Norwich and Kelvin—Mr. and Mrs. Francis Lees, earlier converts of Merrill's Mills, moved to nearby Norwich about 1890, after Mrs. Lees had prayed much about the matter. In 1894 Kelvin's pastor, W. C. Walls[11] held some Sunday afternoon meetings in Mr. Lees' home. In 1896 while M. S. Benn was stationed at Kelvin, Mr. Lees persuaded him to come to Norwich for some street meetings. He preached from a platform in front of an implement shop standing on a large old-fashioned arm chair. Some indoor services here and there followed, but only for a limited time.

After a 1904 camp meeting at Norwich, pastor M. O. Coates of Kelvin began Sunday meetings in Norwich's town hall. H. C. Freemantle, who followed next, secured an upstairs hall, fitted it up with chairs and held regular services. Young George Lees was one convert. (Norman and Frank Lees now are grandsons of Francis Lees. Norman being a son of George and Frank of George's brother Wesley.)

The first Sunday School was held in 1905 with Mr. Lees as superintendent. J. T. Abrams was supply pastor then. J. A. Fletcher built the Norwich church during his 1906-1907 stay.

The Kelvin community experienced a true revival in early 1920. The following account is pieced together from versions submitted by Howard Hyndman, Mrs. B. E. Stevenson and Mrs. H. A. Marlatt:

A few pilgrims in Kelvin village prayed earnestly and regularly for a revival. Young Howard Hyndman, a relative of some of these "narrow" folk, developed a strange restlessness that took him to the faster life of Hamilton in search of satisfaction. Out of curiosity he attended a couple of Methodist evangelistic services, only to find his unrest deepening. In his hotel room he promised God to quit sin for good and do anything. Immediately he found peace. Howard returned home shortly, began family devotions and sang hymns instead of the former worldly songs. His mother, though a church member and Sunday School teacher, was smitten through his changed life and began, with his sisters, to seek the Lord in the home kitchen. (She did find the Lord privately a little later.)

About this time the local Methodist circuit decided to have its first revival campaign in over twenty years, engaging a London evangelist named J. W. Brown. Howard told the evangelist of his conversion and offered to help. He was asked to sing in the choir and "receive the converts" when the evangelist should give the invitation. During the first invitation, Howard's sister Meta joined him at the front. Without giving her a chance to pray, the evangelist invited the choir to march down and congratulate the young lady on her stand. The members did this formally and the meeting ended.

During an afternoon prayer service held shortly at another point on the circuit, Howard's father fell on his knees between the seats and cried to God for mercy. Although he had, in reality, only started to seek the Lord, the evangelist was soon making a stir in the neighbourhood with the announcement that John Hyndman was converted.

About the same time, B. E. Stevenson, the local Free Methodist pastor, began to hold special services also. When he learned of the Methodist meetings, he closed his own out of courtesy and began attending the others. Shortly, Howard, discovering who Mr. Stevenson was, began going to the Free Methodist parsonage seeking advice. He was assured his father could know his sins forgiven.

Howard continued "receiving the converts" though disturbed over the lack of prayer. When Howard's father came forward one night, Mr. Stevenson was melted to tears and sobbed aloud. Emboldened by this "support," Howard invited his father (along with his sisters Meta and Nora who had also come) to kneel at the front seat. While the evangelist on one side exhorted Mr. Hyndman to profess salvation, son Howard on the other side urged him in a whisper to pray till he knew for himself. Howard hardly needed to do this however, for, as he learned later, his father had once been converted before. It was probably this night that Mr. Hyndman under his burden of sin, cried out pitifully, "If there is anyone here who can pray, will you come and help me to get saved?" Before a special prayer meeting could be arranged, Mr. Hyndman was saved in his stable, getting victory even over his chewing tobacco.

The evangelist soon officially invited Mr. Stevenson and his congregation to participate in the services and Mr. Stevenson took charge of the altar services. Conviction was prevalent for miles around and even on stormy nights the church would be full before the service hour. Denominational lines were forgotten as strong men and youth knelt together and sought the Lord. Some converts were church members; others, like Mr. Hyndman, were "plain sinners." Some found the Lord at home but the emphasis was on knowing. There was much telling of friends and straightening up of earlier wrongs, this latter action often producing fresh conviction. Harold Marlatt and wife were converted because of Hyndman visits. Privately or publicly, about one hundred are said to have been saved in the revival.

Shortly after the services, numerous converts, without invitation, began attending Mr. Stevenson's church. Eventually he announced a coming opportunity to join. On a quarterly meeting Sunday morning when district elder J. M. Eagle was on hand to receive them, twenty-nine people trooped to the front and took the Free Methodist vows. In all, about thirty-six of the converts became Free Methodists. These included, besides the Hyndmans and Marlatts, such people as Henry Brown, Mr. and Mrs. Charles Almas, Mr. and Mrs. David Almas, several Almas children and a Mr. and Mrs. Crabbs.

The Free Methodist ministry did well by the revival too. Both father and son Hyndman were to hear the call and heed it, besides Harold Marlatt who was to become widely known for his evangelistic gifts. (This writer first found the joy of the Lord under his ministry at Lorne Park College.) Meta Hyndman was to become the wife of Rev. Peter Bodnar.

Port Burwell and Houghton—During the summer of 1895 while Matilda Sipprell and Alma Smith (the Ebenezer-Otterville supply pastors), aided by Miss Smith's father, C. M. Smith, were holding a tent meeting near Houghton, a vandal burnt up their tent. But some non-Christian men, sympathizing with them in their plight, took a collection, bought another tent, pitched it and offered protection. Among the converts of the meetings (or others soon afterwards) appear these names: West, Beech, Miller, Lucius, Rohre, Cockran. A year later the same ladies were stationed at Houghton by conference and the Houghton church was soon built on the first concession.

Meetings held in the Waggoner schoolhouse produced one convert named Henry Palmer. In early 1906, Mr. Palmer bought a vacant Methodist church in the area for a barn. His pastor, Robert Coates persuaded him to move it near the Claus cemetery and make it into a Free Methodist church. This was done just before conference creating a new preaching point called Bayham.

A different preacher, C. Fader, came to the circuit, after conference. He held extended meetings—some in a tent in Johnson's Woods and some in the Bayham church. A class was organized from the new crop of Webbers, McQuiggins, Palmers, Lawrences and others, that found the Lord, W. E. McQuiggin being its early leader. Later, fire destroyed the Bayham church. (For a time it had been linked with Ebenezer.)

Free Methodism was established in Port Burwell about 1910 after a

1911 Camp of former Brantford District (probably at Tillsonburg) under M. S. Benn

vacated Methodist church was bought by two men and deeded over. A couple of unworthy women who falsely called themselves Free Methodists were said to be an early hindrance to the cause in this town. But a camp meeting there in 1915 attracted about 4,000 people on its final Sunday.

The Houghton appointment enjoyed a gracious revival in the spring of 1927. According to Mrs. Bessie Grass Waring, the services had just started when the spring break-up made the roads so miry it seemed wise to close temporarily. But teen-age Sylvia Balcom (niece of Mrs. Waring and now the wife of Rev. Wilbur Teal), broke into sobs at bed-time because the meetings had closed and she had failed to get saved. The pastor, J. R. Lambert, although living eight miles away at Port Burwell, agreed to continue. The services, once started again, lasted till summer with whole families finding the Lord.

Port Rowan—This community first appeared as an appointment in 1908, along with Port Royal, under D. H. McCallum. Previously Mr. McCallum had been stationed at nearby Walsingham and probably began the Port Rowan work before moving. In the early spring of 1909, evangelist C. W. Stamp held a short but successful campaign at Port Rowan before being obliged to go on to western Canada. It appears there was already a new church built. W. J. Cowherd built the parsonage about 1916.

The names Howe and Countryman appeared among the charter members. Joseph Howe was cited for his faithful efforts and sacrifices in connection with the new church, and Agnes Countryman was first delegate to annual conference. They were converts of David Allan at Port Royal.

The 1913 and 1922 annual conferences were here, under Bishop Hogue.

Simcoe—Rev. George E. Mayo opened a mission in this town in May, 1931, and after a revival with evangelist Levi Ecker during the next year organized a small class. This work soon declined with no appointment again till about 1950 at which time we shall see a fresh foothold was gained.

Tillsonburg and Ingersol—After this area became popular in the 1930's for tobacco-growing, various Free Methodists living in the neighbourhood of the old Ebenezer church sold their farms and moved elsewhere. Consequently the church and parsonage were sold in 1942, and the next year a new church in the town of Tillsonburg was completed and dedicated. A parsonage was also built. Those changes occurred under J. A. Robb. Encouraging growth has followed since.

---

1. Mr. Ecker was known as the Canadian Bible Evangelist. He had been converted from a life of drunkenness.

2. As early as 1896 Charlemont pastor J. P Maitland and local preacher Jacob Hamilton had held a few Sunday afternoon meetings in this school.

3. He was evidently sent after conference time. The Lake Superior District was created a year later, including also Fort William and Hymers which had previously belonged to the Sarnia District.

4. Another version of the story says they held some services in a Bethel Methodist Church and then were forced out of it.

5. Mrs. Kirk was at first certain someone had told the preacher about her heart and life, but could remain away only a short time.

6. Mr. Lee was the father of Mrs. W J. Power of Sault Ste. Marie.

7. The district camp is now on this lot. See later details.

8. Fred Killins was one who remained a devoted member there for many years.

9. Dr. Sheldon eventually spent from 1909 to 1913 as a missionary in Africa under the Free Methodist Board.

10. A. H. Norrington had been a district elder but resigned at this conference. Be sure to note what happened to him at East Ontario's Bracebridge conference a week later.

11. In 1895 Mr. Walls was named elder for the Hamilton and Brantford districts but continued to live at Kelvin. Within a year, Mr. Norrington of the Sarnia district went west because of first wife's health, leaving the whole conference under Mr. Walls.

12. Kelvin had a resident minister at that time.

Section 5: Warfare in Western Canada

Migrated Easterners, homesteading in the religiously cold West felt the need of the fires of Free Methodism in their new homeland. They started Sunday Schools and did what preaching they could, while appealing to Ontario to send missionaries. Reinforcements began to come in 1898 and by 1906 they had carved out a Western Canada Conference. Further conquests over the second eight years warranted division into Saskatchewan and Alberta conferences in 1914. This section will trace the beginnings and progress of Free Methodism in all the western provinces. The saga of Saskatchewan, where the first western foothold was gained, is doubtless among the finest in our North American church's history. Manitoba, because so integral a part of the Saskatchewan work, will be treated under Saskatchewan.

1.
THE SWORD OF THE LORD IN SASKATCHEWAN

Free Methodism stormed Saskatchewan because a Muskoka business man got a vision of what he could do and should do, and then dared to do it. But first the background story.

In the closing decades of the last century, the prairie land now known as Alberta, Saskatchewan and Manitoba was then known as the Northwest Territories and Manitoba. This great region was passing from the regime of the great fur companies and was becoming recognized as a land of tremendous agricultural possibilities. Thousands of settlers swarmed westward to secure homesteads and grow wheat. Among these were Mr. and Mrs. Robert Green[1] and their relatives, Mr. and Mrs. Robert Elsom, who had been identified with Free Methodism in Thedford, Ont., and who settled near Moose Jaw, Sask.; the Travises, the Railtons, and the Cooks from Belhaven, Ont., who moved to the West and settled near Sintaluta; and the Seymour Babcocks who went to Ormiston. A few Canadian families had gone to what is now Alberta, among them William Whittaker from Brantford and a Brother D. D. Oughton. These settled in Calgary. Others, especially Americans, had gone into different parts of Alberta. From Muskoka went the Henwood family who had settled in northern Manitoba near Grandview. Also included were Mr. and Mrs. David Kirk (originally from Muskoka's Bracebridge) who had lived, and had helped to lay the Free Methodist foundation, in Toronto and from there in 1892

153

had gone West and settled at Belmont, Manitoba. They, in particular, wrote many letters to their Eastern friends telling of the needs of the great new land and asking for a minister to be sent out.

Mrs. Kirk's letters began to bear fruit. Mr. J. D. Shier, a lumber merchant and mill owner in Bracebridge, caught the burden and approached the local pastor, W. H. Wilson, making him the proposition to pay his family expenses if he would go West and endeavor to establish the Church in that land. He also offered to provide Mr. Wilson a gospel tent, family tent, and two hundred folding camp seats and pay him a stipend monthly until he became self-supporting. This meant real sacrifice for Mr. Shier at that time, as his business seemed to be in need of all the cash he could raise to carry it through a crisis. However, he and his good wife

Mr. and Mrs. J. D. Shier

Rev. and Mrs. W. H. Wilson and family

had made the proposition a matter of earnest prayer and were prepared to make this important sacrifice.

Mr. Wilson transferred his conference membership to West Ontario, because Western Canada seemed more logically to be in its territory, and in that same fall of 1898 was appointed a missionary to Manitoba and the Northwest along with his sister evangelist, Mrs. Jennie Robinson (later Mrs. Robert Elsom). Mr. Wilson went ahead; and his wife, three small children and Mrs. Robinson came the next spring.

Mr. Wilson spent two days at General Conference while passing through Chicago on his way to the West. On October 28, he reached Belmont, Manitoba, and was greeted by the David Kirks that he had known in Toronto. He preached in the local Methodist church a few times and in a nearby schoolhouse, but did not stay long. It was threshing season and the fall had been wet. Week-night services got little attendance. By November 15 he was at Sintaluta in Assiniboia, N.W.T. (now Saskatchewan). He stayed four weeks visiting among the people, some of whom had been Free Methodists in the East. Mr. Wilson preached several times there and also at Kenlis across the great Qu'Appelle Valley. The residents were eager to attend services.

By mid-December the new missionary had gone ninety-four miles west of Sintaluta to Moose Jaw. This town was on the mainline of the C.P.R. with a population of 1,200. Apparently prejudice among other Protestant churches was strong (seven or eight had already arrived in the West) and people in general showed more interest in amusement than in evangelical religion. One man and his wife, however, expressed a desire for salvation and the man soon allowed Sunday services to be held in a hall he owned. A schoolhouse seven miles out was shortly put to use also.

Mr. Wilson returned to Belmont the next June and found his 30' x 50' tent and other equipment had arrived by train from the East. By now his family had joined him, the group staying for a time with the hospitable Kirks. Meetings were held first in a schoolhouse, then for some weeks through the summer in the tent with the Wilson family living nearby in a tent themselves. Rev. W. B. Olmstead from Michigan joined them in this campaign staying for four Sundays. Seven people professed conversion, and others were seeking the Lord. It does not appear that a permanent work was established here, however, but a Sunday School was begun and Mr. Kirk put in charge. (Recall the earlier reference.)

The first two years were, in general, times of great discouragement. The following winter of 1899-1900, the Wilsons were back in Saskatchewan living at Boharm and holding schoolhouse meetings at Westview, near Grayburn.[2] They tell that when Mr. Wilson was about to cancel these services because of apparent failure, Mrs. Wilson had a providential dream. She seemed to be trying to dig a well in very hard ground and was almost at the point of quitting, when suddenly she broke through the hardpan and struck plenty of water. "Will, that's Westview," she insisted in the morning.

With renewed effort, Westview did respond and a permanent footing was gained. The society that resulted was the first in the Canadian West, except for a "floating" one Mr. Wilson had early organized from scattered Free Methodists that he visited. Westview is located in a splendid agricultural district and has assisted in a material way with several other fields. The Browns, Tanners, Wilsons, Nesbitts and Robsons were among the leading families in those early years. William Robson had known Free Methodism before, and, with the preacher "after him," became one of the first converts.[3] W. H. Brown and wife developed into sturdy members. Mr. Brown was to be delegate to both annual conference and General Conference and represent Saskatchewan at the Sarnia All-Canada Convention in 1920.

Young energetic J. W. Haley went West in the early summer of 1900 and was soon looking after Westview. The people he described as "real old-fashioned fire-baptized saints." That summer and fall, Mr. Wilson, now free, held an extended tent campaign at Sintaluta, some distance to the east, and began a society there. Less than a year later, in 1901, the settlement had Free Methodism's first Western Canada church and also its first official camp meeting. The Kirks came and Mrs. Kirk wrote that "great good was done." It closed with the old-fashioned march and song—

First official Western Camp Meeting at Sintaluta in 1901.

in this case the singers majored in "Away Far Beyond Jordan." The charge of discourtesy was commonly levelled by other church people when an effort was made in a new community. But Mr. Wilson was satisfied that the prevalent scarcity of real salvation justified these intrusions.

At Caron (near Westview) Mr. Haley aided by Mr. Wilson put on a 1900-01 winter drive and another society followed. Mr. and Mrs. H. A. Hurlburt who were to become the first native Western workers, were among those converts.

The 1901 session of the West Ontario conference listed a new Manitoba and Northwest District under Elder Wilson. Besides Sintaluta, which was to be under Mrs. Robinson and himself, and Westview and Caron under Mr. Haley, Greenville, Sask., and Belmont, Man., were two appointments "to be supplied."

But a jolt awaited the Wilsons; Mr. Haley, who had felt an earlier call to Africa, decided he should now go there.[4] Mr. Wilson thought his present field almost as challenging, but by the spring of 1902 the mission board had accepted him and Mr. Haley was on his way. An appeal to the 1902

Left: Rev. and Mrs. F. M. Wees and Family

Westview Church and Environs

West Ontario conference for reinforcements brought the couple of Mr. Wilson's choice for vacated Westview—aggressive and able Rev. and Mrs. F. M. Wees.[5] There Mr. Wees was to build a parsonage and church and in that pioneer country was to labour ruggedly as pastor or superintendent for over a quarter century.[6] There his wife was to stand beside him giving leadership in many ways, especially in missionary emphasis, and even pastoring herself. Mr. Hurlburt was given his first appointment (Alameda) by that 1902 conference.

Soon the Elsoms and Greens who farmed near Moose Jaw undertook to assist in opening a work in their town. Moose Jaw at the time was a centre for grain growers and cattle men, while nearby on South Hill camped 1,000 Indians, the remains of Chief Sitting Bull's Sioux band who had sought refuge in Canada after their historic massacre of American cavalry. Gaining a foothold was difficult, but a Mr. Robert Snowdry helped Mr. Wilson purchase the old Presbyterian church which was moved to a suitable lot.

About this time Rev. Robert Hamilton moved West and purchased a farm near Moose Jaw. He had spent many years in the ministry in Ontario, but through failing health had to give up the work. His presence greatly helped the struggling Moose Jaw society. During the next few years several other Ontario families moved to the city and district, among them Deyos, Bottings, Smiths, Priors, Bradleys, Arnolds, Nobles, Ruttans and Hannas.

In 1903, D. H. McCallum, having gone west from Ontario, was assigned to Ebenezer and Greenville in the Sintaluta community—the first stationed pastor there. By the next summer he had a society, a parsonage, and a church ready for dedication. At Alameda where Mr. H. A. Hurlburt had been sent, Mr. Wilson organized a class that came to be known as Roseview. The centre was located about twenty-five miles northeast of Estevan.

Moose Jaw Camp of 1906

First Western Canada Conference, organized at Moose Jaw Camp of 1906 by Bishop B. R. Jones. Seated—Robert Hamilton, J. B. Newville, B. R. Jones, W. H. Wilson, Mrs. Robert Green, O. L. King, F. M. Wees, E. L. Steer; Standing—Jennie Robinson Elsom, Robert Elsom, Jennie Hamilton, R. H. Hamilton, Theo. Sharp, Mrs. Theo. Sharp, Mrs. David Kirk, Mrs. W. H. Wilson, David Kirk, Mrs. Green, A. L. Haight, Mrs. J. W. Commodore, H. A. Hurlbut, J. W. Commodore, Mrs. Oscar King, Wm. Robson, Mrs. F. M. Wees, Geo. Cook, Mrs. Annie L. Steer.

Among the members were Sniders, Coles, Asseltines, Draders, Knoxes, Commodores and others from Verona and Oak Flats; Robinsons, Steeles and Dies from Fernleigh; and Joices from Bracebridge. This soon became a thriving and spiritual class and a little later under Rev. Charles Dierks from Muskoka, many souls found the Lord at "Old Roseview."

The year 1905 was significant. In it, what had been the Manitoba and Northwest District of the West Ontario Conference under Mr. Wilson became the Saskatchewan District under Mr. Wees, and a new Alberta District made its first appearance under Rev. O. L. King, previously of Michigan. The need for this latter new district—a "paper" one— and the stirring stories of what came of it are told in the next chapter.

But the new West Ontario Conference arrangement was to last only one year. With a total of 6 preachers, 9 circuits and 148 members, the two western districts were made a new Western Canada Conference by Superintendent Jones who come to Moose Jaw in the summer of 1906.[7] The action followed a request to the General Executive Committee, because the distance from Ontario was so great. Mr. Kirk's faith that Canada would some day have a western conference had now become sight.

This first conference in the West drew together people separated by 1,000 miles. For it, thirteen tents were pitched on the open Moose Jaw prairie. Eleven circuits were listed, five being in Saskatchewan. R. H. Hamilton, a young schoolteacher, took his first charge, Roseview, then,[8]

Rev. and Mrs. E. Steer who had come from Michigan the year before, continued looking after Moose Jaw. (Mrs. Steer was named president of the conference W.F.M.S.) Mr. Wilson continued at Westview. While her husband continued as superintendent, Mrs. Wees was assigned a new community—Hudmore and Blackheath near present Stroughton. The nomadic Kirks had arrived there and in their home had started a Sunday School that now begged a preacher. A two-room shack in the Kirk yard made a home for the Weeses and soon three appointments were flourishing.

Mr. Wees, with help from Mr. Hamilton, Jr., held a tent meeting that fall in the hitherto unworked centre of Estevan where the Almiron Snyders from Verona had settled. One of the few converts was a German washerwoman who, after sixteen years as treasurer of the new Estevan society, passed on, leaving a generous bequest to the church.

The 1907 conference met at Westview with Bishop Hogue.[9] He dedicated churches both there and at Moose Jaw that September. The Hamiltons were moved to Estevan after Mrs. Snyder found they were willing to go, and put a little pressure on the Stationing Committee. Charles Dierks took up a homestead in the Lowetown and Mount Green community southwest of Estevan to serve a few families (Joices, Robinsons, Rogers and Flakes) who had moved in there.[10] Mr. Wilson took the district eldership back again, and both Weeses laboured on at Hudmore. Robert Hamilton, Sr., died that fall shortly after conference bequeathing $1,000 to foreign missions and another $1,000 to the Western Canada Conference.

An early cottage meeting at Estevan was memorable. One person after another, beginning with a young bedridden rheumatic, was finding victory and praising God. This enraged a young man who had come with his lady friend and had sat up through the prayers. Finally he blurted out: "This is not the Holy Ghost, but hypnotism." When fresh prayers began bombarding heaven for him, he left. Twenty years later he wrote Mr. Hamilton to report that the power of that meeting followed him twelve years until he yielded to God.

Also that year Mr. Hamilton began a rural revival in Mizpah School to the north. Smallpox closed the meeting after nineteen had been converted in two weeks. The pastor moved on to another place only to hear a little later that, with the quarantine lifted, the young converts were carrying on again by themselves. On his return, Mr. Hamilton found services that consisted of a few songs, an altar call and an altar service. Yet some sixty people found God, among whom was a Mr. and Mrs. C. B. Garratt who were to spend a long period in the Saskatchewan ministry. Mr. Garratt was to become very successful as a personal worker among all classes, establishing a reputation for his home-visiting.

Evangelist C. W. Stamp came from the United States in early 1909 for Estevan winter services which ran five weeks long. Mr. Stamp described these in a March *Free Methodist* as "one of the greatest revivals we have

Rev. and Mrs. R. H. Hamilton

had since we began to travel for the General Church." Many Mizpah converts came in to boost the town congregations and attract town people.

Total membership for Estevan in 1908 had read thirteen. For Estevan and Mizpah in 1909, it stood at fifty-two. One convert named P. B. Holmgren has since served periods as mayor of the town, has given many years on the Moose Jaw Bible College board, and has represented Saskatchewan at General Conference. It was said a high percentage of the Mizpah conversions were lasting. This Estevan circuit work seems to illustrate what a man and wife could do. The Hamiltons were without church, parsonage or Home Mission fund when they went, but they had what were more important—ambition, faith, and God. And they had both a church and parsonage too before the first Christmas.

Manitoba's first class was organized at Benito in March of 1909. A Bro. and Sister Findlay and a Sister Free had held some meetings there. Mr. Findlay was appointed supply pastor at conference time.

After a third year at Estevan, a Westview conference in 1910 moved the Hamiltons to another previously nonexistent circuit—Weyburn.[11] A hastily built barn on a newly purchased lot made a temporary home. In winter weather twenty-five to forty degrees below zero, Mr. Hamilton and two Estevan brothers erected a small tabernacle on a lot leased downtown. Then Mrs. Wees and Mrs. Kirk arrived for opening services. And every night from the end of January to the end of March, new Bethel Mission had its meeting. Forty people sought the Lord and a new Weyburn society had seventeen members next conference.

At a 1911 Weyburn conference, F. D. Bradley transferred from East Ontario and was posted to Moose Jaw. Mr. Wilson transferred to Michigan to be financial agent at Spring Arbor Seminary. It was reported by the Committee on the State of the Work that both Weyburn and Moose Jaw now had parsonages.

The Hamiltons continued at Weyburn and supervised during the following winter that first experiment with a Bible School in Canada. Mr. Hamilton, Mrs. Lawrence Kirk and Mr. H. Spencer were teachers. Mrs. David Kirk directed the school home. Midford Kirk was one student.

Rev. F. F. Prior, Rev. T. L. Fletcher and Rev. J. A. Fletcher (his brother), all came west about this time and were to prove great assets. All the preachers' wives deserve honourable mention too, for the preachers could not have faced the rigours of pioneer work without their courageous assistance.

Rev. T. L. Fletcher

At the 1913 conference in Calgary—the only one under the Western Canada name that Alberta ever entertained—a five-whereas resolution to the General Executive Committee called for a division of the huge 700-mile by 350-mile field into two conferences. The request was granted and at Weyburn in September, 1914, the new Saskatchewan Conference under Bishop Pearce held its first session after eight years in the Western Canada connection.[12] At the time, there were nine preachers in full connection and five on probation in Saskatchewan. Lay members totalled 238. Mr. Hamilton became the new district elder of the one-district, thirteen-circuit conference. He had already held the Saskatchewan district office in the other conference one year, previous to which he had begun a district parsonage at Weyburn while resident pastor.

In the winter of 1914-15, Mr. Hamilton reported that "perhaps one of the greatest revivals we have had in this country is in progress near Weyburn." The pastor, T. L. Fletcher, had been driving about twenty miles a day for nearly three months of the northwestern winter. Layman homesteader Neil McGugan, just arrived from western Ontario the previous spring, was assisting and was having the joy of leading many of his neighbours to the Lord. The country was stirred for miles around and over one hundred sought the Lord. The Conference Minutes show an increase of thirty-three members on that circuit at the 1915 conference.

The same 1915 Minutes show two districts—Weyburn and Vanguard (a new southern area). Rev. F. F. Prior was made elder of the latter. A year later, there were three—a Southern one and a Western one, both under Mr. Wees, and a new three-circuit Northern one with nucleus at Durban, Man., under J. A. Fletcher. (As early as 1909 the Wm. Findlays from Ontario had settled in that area, supplied work, and got Sunday Schools and a class going.) The conference session in 1915 was held in July and the people were happy, for they could now make the single long trip to a combined conference and camp meeting. Bishop Sellew stayed for the entire period and preached once a day.

Six circuits show for the appointments on the new district a year later in 1917. Mention was made in the records of the "terrible war" on, and how that nearly every society had lost members or adherents because of it.

Some district shuffling occurred at the next conference—in 1918. Rev. J. A. Fletcher continued living and serving with his wife at Durban circuit but without his district responsibility. Mr. Wees became responsible for both districts. Apparently the army was taking young preachers and conference expansion was hindered. Miss Lottie Babcock who had earlier moved to Saskatchewan from Ontario was cited as doing good work as a conference evangelist. Hume had a new society and four other unnamed centres did also. Perhaps Battram was one, for it received its first preacher in 1918.[13] These additions helped to make the total membership of 406 in 1919. It represented an increase of almost 40 per cent over the figure of two years before. During this conference year Neil McGugan, aided by his noble wife Martha, joined the ministerial ranks supplying Weyburn and Riverview in his home area.[14]

In 1920 the conference voted $1,600 of Home Missions money towards opening work in the provincial capital, Regina. Miss Lottie Babcock was appointed to begin the mission and did organize a class of thirteen despite intense opposition. One early convert, Ben Smith, was to become a minister. In due time, a church was built and the Weeses took over. A better Regina church location has since been secured and the work, after a lull, revived. The W. E. Nixon family was one that lived in Regina and worked faithfully during some of the church's early struggling days.

This brings us to the point for the telling of the story of how Free Methodism providentially came to Saskatoon.

Mr. Hamilton took charge of a mission field called Brooking during the 1920-21 conference year. He organized a class there, and later held a tent meeting at Dry Lake assisted by Lottie Babcock and Edith Abbott. Among the nearly thirty converts was a young girl named Sarah Boyes whose family moved shortly to Saskatoon, about two hundred miles from our work. Saskatoon then had over 30,000 people.

A little later, when Mr. Hamilton was District Elder again, Sarah wrote asking when the Free Methodists planned to open a church in Saskatoon. An evasive reply was soon followed by another missive saying she could get a well located brick store rent-free for two months. When Mr. Hamilton visited her a few weeks later, this young high school girl who "had never been in more than half a dozen Free Methodist meetings in her life" was effervescent. "Oh, Brother Hamilton," she said, "God wants a Free Methodist Church here!"

Mr. Hamilton, through the press, invited adherents nearby to write him and went in to Hanley, seventy miles away, to spend a Sunday with a prosperous brother, Charles Jarvis. In casual conversation he discovered Mr. Jarvis planned to retire that fall to Saskatoon and was anxious to see a work opened there. The story of the empty store convinced Mr. Jarvis it was all of the Lord and brought a promise of the first one thousand dollars when the work should reach the stage for a church.

A three-week campaign in early 1921, a class of twenty-one, and a regularly rented mission hall came in quick succession as God's answer to a young girl's faith. A church followed in a few years. The Jarvises, Heises, Porters and our old friends, the Kirks (now retired) were all associated with the early work in Saskatoon. William Nixon, a Battram layman, is mentioned along with Mr. Jarvis as helping to open the mission.[15]

Mr. and Mrs. David Kirk

From here on, the records are somewhat irregular, but stories of new communities opening up keep appearing. Bield, Manitoba, was one that first showed as a preaching point in 1921. Two Chase families from Minnesota made a nucleus.[16] Rev. P. L. Chase who has since been a pastor and superintendent in several conferences came from one of them.

At Sprattsville, Conference Evangelist J. A. Fletcher reported a tent meeting in the fall of 1922 with one hundred at the altar and fifty-eight joining the church. This point was later joined up with Eyebrow under Rev. Neil McGugan. Eyebrow had been raised up by a Wesleyan Methodist, Rev. Adam Shea (father of George Beverley), but was handed over to our church because the Wesleyans had no other churches in the province. Mr. McGugan bought a fine church while at Eyebrow.[17] Mr. Fletcher saw scores converted about this time at other places. Sinclair, Estevan, Battram, St. Elmo, Weyburn and Pinkham all felt the impact of his evangelism.

Kindersley-Ormiston, a couple of hundred miles northwest of Moose Jaw, had its first stationed pastor, Rev. B. H. Robinson, in 1921 after a J. A. Fletcher tent meeting at Ormiston. Kindersley was where the Robinson family decided to live and the A. Andersons were among the first converts there. Mr. and Mrs. A. M. Carmichael of the Brethren in Christ and whose church was out of town, proved solid friends; he, as a member of Parliament later, being responsible for getting the Federal Act of Incorporation through the Commons. Kindersley saw an early District Quarterly Meeting after a mission building had been purchased and remodelled.

Roblin, Manitoba, first became an appointment in 1925 with W. A. Miller and his wife of nearby Bield as pastors. In June of that year the province's first camp meeting had been held there, T. L. Fletcher being the conference elder. Roblin was the last circuit served by Rev. A. A. Buffam before retiring about 1948 due to heart trouble. He, with his capable wife, had spent over twenty faithful years in the Saskatchewan Conference ministry.[18] Several sons are following him into Christian work.

THE BATTLE WAS THE LORD'S

There's an interesting story about some services Mr. Hamilton held near Grandview, Manitoba, in 1926 and how it precipitated a new Free Methodist society. It appears that some of the members of the old Riverview Methodist Church (or United Church, since the previous year) wanted a revival and held prayer meetings to that end. Free Methodists from Bield were holding cottage meetings there too. Albert Henwood, Riverview's S. S. Superintendent, approached his area superintendent and found he would permit a Free Methodist to come. Mr. Hamilton came for three weeks. One night nearly everyone in the church went forward as a seeker.

Mr. Hamilton soon had to get out because his kind of evangelism proved unpopular, but some of the people clamoured for a Free Methodist society. Mr. Hamilton consequently enrolled twenty-six members in the Henwood home. Margaret Henwood, who later became Mrs. Ronald Collett of Africa's Congo-Nile Mission Field, was one convert of that Riverview beginning. Five pastors were to come from Riverview too. A church was built in 1933 by Rev. Ross Lloyd, after the appearance of an earlier parsonage.

When Rev. F. Markell was on the circuit in 1942 he bought a vacant Baptist church in Grandview itself, moved it and fixed it up for services.

To the Davis area came retired Rev. James Evans from Nebraska; also a Breeden family from Oklahoma. J. A. Fletcher, the northern elder, then held some meetings and organized a Davis church. A little later, about 1926, Misses Ethel Fletcher and Daisy Langman were stationed there and bought the Methodist church. When R. H. Hamilton went to help in tent meetings, some Roman Catholic Ruthenian railroad workers attended. One was wrought on and two months later in a prayer meeting found the Lord. He went east to Lorne Park College, then attended McMaster University for his B.A. For years now, Rev. Peter Bodnar has been a valued minister of the West Ontario Conference.

The Davis work later centred in nearby Prince Albert on the North Saskatchewan River, with the church moved there and remodelled. This is one of our most northerly churches in Canada. A mission field was opened at Norbury and Spiritwood farther west, after several Prince Albert families moved there.

In 1927 the conference gained strong auxiliaries with the arrival of Rev. and Mrs. D. S. Wartman from East Ontario. They took charge of the Moose Jaw church first, but helped Mr. Hamilton in tent meetings at Avonlea during the next summer. A class of twenty-five and a church followed this Avonlea effort.[19] While Mr. Wartman was superintendent of the Southern District in 1940 and serving the Moose Jaw Church as well, the Moose Jaw Bible College was opened with much supervision from him. Its larger story comes in another chapter. Later on in the 1940's Mr. Wartman was to spend several years as conference elder over the three existing districts.

The three-district arrangement began in 1928 under R. H. Hamilton as conference elder when three circuits in Manitoba created a Yorkton

District. From 1931 on, it has been known as the Manitoba District but, with only a few irregularities, has been served along with the two Saskatchewan districts by one elder or superintendent at a time. Men who have supervised the whole conference at once from 1925-50 include T. L. Fletcher, R. H. Hamilton, F. M. Wees, C. B. Garratt, E. R. Orser, D. S. Wartman, and M. C. Miller.

The Hamiltons were hopeful that a Winnipeg work would follow a beginning they had made there. But their vision was not sufficiently shared and the project died. We shall see that the recent merger brought a work there.

Many more individual fields could be described—Davidson, Lone Rock, Birch River, Brandon,[20] . . . But these must suffice. The Saskatchewan rural work has ever had problems to discourage all but the stoutest hearts —drab, shadeless landscape, periodic drought,[21] soil drifting, sand storms, hail, early frosts, winter blizzards, distance, . . . These have tended to produce a constantly moving population which many a time has spelled the end of work started with great promise. Shaunavon and Canuck (or Climax) are two such that consolidated, then evaporated.[22]

What some ministers, their wives, and families endured is hardly conceivable for an Easterner. Take Rev. and Mrs. Fred Prior again, as one pair who spurned the easy life where they were stationed at Estevan to live in a two-room shack with their three children on the open prairies down Vanguard way south of Swift Current in 1914. They did it because a Divine call had come and they felt the tug. The settlers there had no one even to bury their dead.[23]

Everyone received the Priors well, but 225 miles was a long hot ride to conference the next summer—especially in an open buggy. Their baby took ill after sixty miles. The sun was too much. A settler's wife along the way did her best, but in vain. The child died and was buried at the foot of the garden. The brave parents drove on to conference. They reported with tear-filled eyes, but they were not discouraged. No other place in the conference appealed to them like their mission field.[24]

By valiant soldiers like these, the sword of the Lord was wielded not in vain in Saskatchewan.

By 1950, appointments existed in the following Saskatchewan centres: Moose Jaw, Westview, Eyebrow, Ames, Avonlea, Regina, Weyburn, Riverview, Hume, Estevan, Saskatoon, Kindersley, Prince Albert, Norbury, Spiritwood, Davidson and Lone Rock.

The Manitoba District of that conference in the same year showed appointments at Roblin, Bield, Grandview, Riverview, Rapid City, Birch River and McKinley School.

---

1. Mrs. Green's obituary called her "the first Free Methodist in Western Canada." The Greens had gone west from Michigan in 1887 but they had previously lived in Ontario where Mrs. Green had been converted under Jerusha Hagle in 1882.

2. Mrs. Robinson had previously directed a Sunday School there for a season. Religious devotion was such a lost art that no other person would attempt to pray in public.

THE BATTLE WAS THE LORD'S

3. He had gone from Port Burwell to the west thinking he would get away from religion.

4. Mr. Haley's immense contributions across forty years in Africa were to prove the genuineness of his call.

5. Mrs. Wees and their two children stayed with her Bracebridge parents, the James Rusks, till the next spring by which time a parsonage had been completed.

6. Shortly after the Wees family were settled, their home narrowly escaped destruction from a galloping prairie fire. Another time while the 1903 camp meeting was on, an electric storm flattened their tent along with the others. Mr. Wees, with babe in arms and wife behind, had to rush to the school house amid pelting hail that broke windows on three sides.

7. W. H. Wilson was secretary and Robert Hamilton Sr. was treasurer.

8. Mrs. Hamilton, who had been Jennie Walls in Ontario had travelled west by train in 1905 to marry "Henry." She recalls the unpredictable bronchos coming to church from all directions. Drivers had ropes to throw them, if they got too obstinate.

9. The title changed from General Superintendent to Bishop in 1907.

10. Thomas Flake, recently from Huntsville but mentioned earlier as a singer assistant to W H. Gregory at Denbigh, was one of God's early heroes at Mount Green. His influence over many years meant much to both local and conference. Zella Nixon of Moose Jaw Bible College is his daughter.

11. There is a record of a camp meeting there earlier in the summer with thirty-two tents pitched on a prairie fifty miles from any trees.

12. Fred Prior and F M. Wees were secretary and treasurer respectively.

13. In the hungry thirties the church group at Battram was forced to disband. The Nixons, formerly of Winnipeg, went on to Regina.

14. It was later in a rural schoolhouse revival on the Westview circuit that Mr. McGugan aided by his district elder saw a notable McGugan convert in the person of Ross Lloyd, a one-time successful ball player and, at that time, an addict of drink and drugs. His transformation was complete and led him into the ministry as an evangelist, later as a Superintendent in the Lake Superior area, and now as a west coast pastor.

15. Mr. Hamilton wrote in 1928 of dedicating a new handsome stucco church with basement in Saskatoon. It was on an ideal corner but cost with lot only about $8000.

16. A Mrs. Van Sickle has been mentioned as another early pilgrim here.

17. Mr. Hamilton dedicated this church about the same time as the one at Saskatoon.

18. Mr. Buffam was known for his "tender concern for the needy." They tell of his walking twenty-five miles in sub-zero weather to call on isolated families in the Kindersley area.

19. This was also a stucco church and was dedicated in the early summer of 1928, just after the Saskatoon and Eyebrow dedications.

20. In 1952 Rev. J. A. Tanner began one at Brandon and was stricken with polio before completing it.

21. During the drought years around 1930, farmers who had been well-to-do were often in a pathetic condition almost without food—this in sections of both Saskatchewan and Alberta.

22. The footholds were not failures because they did not last. Converts often turned up in other places, and many made heaven though lost by our church.

23. The Kirks, now here (before their last earthly move to Saskatoon), had begun another Sunday School and sounded a call for a preacher. When Elder Hamilton had arrived on his initial visit, Mr. Kirk, with his house full of Saturday-night neighbours organizing a new Sunday School for the morrow, met him at the door, hugged him and cried: "Mother, the church has come! The church has come!" The larger truth was this: the church had come when the godly Kirks had themselves arrived.

24. That was the year Conference made Mr. Prior a district elder there.

2.
THE ATTACK IN ALBERTA

Alberta, the foothill province, had a population of only about 185,000 when Free Methodism first moved that way in 1904-05, but in a dozen years the figure was to be tripled to over half a million made up of some forty-seven nationalities and sixty-five denominations.[1]

Mr. Frank B. Lewis, an Edmonton local preacher, wrote in the *Free Methodist* of Feb. 21, 1905, "The Northwest is settled by the oppresed of every nation, especially English. . . . We have Russians, Galicians, Half-breeds, Indians, Chinese, Germans, Boers, Jews, French, Welsh, Scandinavians, Italians and some from the States."

Like sturdy Saskatchewan, this was predominantly a land of farmers— farmers with big farms whose average size as early as 1917 stood at almost 350 acres. Calgary and Edmonton even then each had less than 60,000 people, while Calgary in 1905 had only a fifth of that figure.

The church pattern of development in that province resembled Saskatchewan's. Free Methodist laymen from the East began settling on Alberta homesteads.

Mr. Lewis, in particular, had gone to Alberta from Michigan. He claimed to be called West in a vision to help establish Free Methodism in Alberta. He and the others called for help to their home conferences in Ontario and Michigan and help came. Rev. O. L. King, a former schoolteacher, transferring from the East Michigan to the West Ontario Conference volunteered for the western work and was exported that summer of 1905—the very year the provinces of Alberta and Saskatchewan had to be carved out of the great Northwest Territories to keep pace with mushrooming population.

Rev. and Mrs. Oscar L. King

A few people must have tittered when the West Ontario appointments were read off that fall, for they intimated the existence of a whole new second western Canada district. The list read: "Alberta District, O. L. King, district elder; Edmonton, Lizzie J. King, supply; Calgary, to be supplied; Wetaskiwin, W. H. Black, supply; Vermilion Valley, to be supplied; Stoney Plain, to be supplied; Earlville, to be supplied." Here was evidence that the Stationing Committee, while lacking workmen, did not lack a knowledge of needy fields.

Mr. King, with his family, slowly worked his way west stopping at points in Western Ontario and Saskatchewan for services and finally settling in Edmonton, a town of 7,000, where a few Free Methodist families already were living. The first society was formed in November in a tar-paper shack at Hurry (now Bruce), sixty miles southeast of his base. These eleven were charter members: S. W. Cole, Dora Cole, Rickerson R. Haight,

Sidney Haight, Merrit S. Haight, Belle Haight, Arthur L. Haight, Ella Haight, Thomas Waldie, Lucy Waldie, Jesse Allen, Jay Allen. Jay Allen became class leader.

In January of 1906 a revival was held in the schoolhouse at Michigan Centre, a rural point southwest of Edmonton. Helping the Kings were F. B. Lewis, and a Rev. S. M. Henry. The *Edmonton Journal* reported these meetings but not with complete endorsement, for evidently secretism had been mentioned. A class developed at Michigan Centre and another apparently was organized somewhere nearby. Leduc shortly got some successful services; and an Edmonton congregation, recruited in cottage prayer meetings, began looking for a church site.

Mr. King started a Sunday School in his Edmonton home in April with Harry Smith as superintendent and F. B. Lewis as assistant. The charter members of the Edmonton society begun at that time included G. W. Smith, Harry Smith, F. B. Lewis, Lizzie J. King, Lily Austin and Jesse Allen. All but the last named person were made full members at once so must have been former Free Methodists in the East.[2] Right away a tabernacle was secured and during the warm months the services were held in it, these including a special evangelistic campaign and the first Alberta District Quarterly Conference.

A few figures on Mr. King's first eight months are revealing: miles travelled—2,500, pastoral visits made—233, times preached—87, other services attended—155, field support received—$140.75.

When General Superintendent B. R. Jones organized the Western Canada Conference in July of that year, 1906, at the Saskatchewan District Camp Meeting in Moose Jaw, Mr. and Mrs. King were on hand with a creditable report: forty full members, thirteen probationers, four circuits, two Sunday Schools. Mr. King's district appointments for the new year were quite altered and ran as follows: Edmonton, to be supplied; Hurry and Round Hill, A. L. Haight, supply; Michigan Centre, Conjuring Creek and Calmers, Thelia Champion, supply; Calgary, to be supplied; Earlville. F. B. Lewis, supply; Ranfurley and Denwoodie, to be supplied.

A driving-team the Kings had lacked. Consequently, while passing through Calgary on the way home, they secured, with the help of Mr. D. D. Oughton, a team of "cayuses," or small Indian ponies. These, Dick and Dan, were evidently somewhat unbroken. Dick soon proved nervous and Dan sulky. The two-hundred-mile buckboard jaunt to Edmonton took two and a half weeks and brought its share of rigor: rainstorms and runaways, sleeping on the ground and losing the trail. The Kings apparently were constant sowers of Gospel seed for whenever they stopped at a home they prayed and exhorted the settlers to seek first the kingdom of God.

Their handbill announcing a camp meeting at Hurry that summer had a blunt footnote relative to its purpose: "Come and get saved before it is too late." A few wise people did.

The Hurry class soon came up with a novel, but impractical, proposition to raise money for a church. Mr. King should take a homestead there, they would do the work to "prove up," he should then given them $400 to build. Seeing merit in the idea, the Kings filed on a homestead claim and left Edmonton for their new temporary Hurry home in tents. Lily Austin, Mrs. King's sister who lived with them, finding on arrival that her sickness while travelling had been typhoid, became bedfast for a time. Immediate rain shortages made stock watering a problem. An October prairie fire swept in, burning up one tent, $150 worth of goods, and some District funds earmarked for tabernacle and printing press. The contemplated frame house didn't get built that fall. As Mr. King wrote in his diary: "We have changed our plans . . . , the fire took so much that we must get a place to live as cheaply as possible." The winter home was a side-hill "dug-out."

Life was grim at Alberta District's Hurry hub that 1906-07 winter. Coal had to be teamed in from a mine about twenty miles distant. Four feet of snow on the level made roads sometimes almost impassable. Getting one ton often took four days. Mr. Sam Cole, a Hurry layman, let his place be a distributing centre for coal and other "needments." He also let Mr. King hold several winter meetings in his home. Of one, Mr. King wrote: "I preached and the Lord helped me greatly." One can almost believe the Lord was under obligation to honour such sacrifice.

That winter another family member joined the Hurry Haights—aged Rev. Walter (uncle Walter to all the community) from East Michigan. Though living distant from the meeting place he was nearly always there and preached often, assisting the appointed pastor, A. L. Haight.

At Bentley, a village near Lacombe, services were held that winter when Rev. R. H. Shoup, an Oklahoma Conference ordained deacon, came and took charge of a boarding house. His coming brought great cheer to Mr. King.

Hurry had another camp meeting the next July and at it the quarterly conference decided to invite Revs. Wm. H. and R. R. Haight to join them from East Michigan.[3]

Mr. Shoup, was received into the conference of 1907 and went to Hurry late that fall at the suggestion of the district elder to fill a vacancy left by conference. Mr. King was now living back in Edmonton, so the Shoups lived in his new homestead house. It was a dreary place for a home but a bunch of small willows nearby provided some consolation—a place for secret prayer. The poor but kind settlers of the area rallied well to the schoolhouse meetings.

Rev. R. H. Shoup

A profitable Harland camp meeting the next summer was held in a "bush" that consisted of "about an eighth of an acre of small brush about from six to ten feet in height to afford shade."

Shortly the Grand Trunk Pacific on its way from Winnipeg to Edmonton moved through the district just skirting Hurry. Bruce, a mile away, became the new town site and all buildings moved away. In July, 1908, the Free Methodists bought their first Alberta property, a lot for church and parsonage in Bruce. Mosquitoes were so bad because of the heavy rains that summer, that smudges had to be built at the meeting house to save the horses. Men and women both wore protective veils during travelling.

The 1909 Western Canada conference was invited to Bruce but stayed in Estevan. Six hundred miles was a long distance to come. It was also a long distance for Albertans to go and only two—O. L. King and R. H. Shoup—attended. The Alberta membership was coming up slowly but all "circuits" except Mr. Shoup's were read off "to be supplied." Rev. W. H. Haight did get from Michigan to Alberta that November and took Bruce. A little later, local preacher E. J. Draper of Vermilion was sent to Conjuring Creek. A keg of nails and one thousand feet of lumber were offered towards a parsonage there, but before the house arose, most of the people moved away and the preaching point was dropped.

Mr. King, however, soon had a society started at Wittenburg with Mr. Shoup transferred to that point. Back at Edmonton and Bruce, Rev. C. W. Stamp, General Conference Evangelist, held some meetings. The Shoups drove 144 miles in their spring wagon to a Tofield camp meeting during August, 1909. By living partly on wild raspberries that they picked en route, they still had $1.35 of their original $5.00 left when they arrived in time to help distressed Mr. King put up the tabernacle.

Up to this point growth had been very gradual but an extended meeting near Earlville at Concord schoolhouse early in 1910 produced twenty-six seekers, a class of more than twenty, and a Sunday School. Mr. King and Mr. Lewis had conducted this revival. W. E. Hunt was appointed supply pastor to aid R. H. Shoup.

Alberta membership stood at eighty-nine at the 1910 conference held at Westview. A petition asking for the creation of two Alberta districts was granted. Rev. W. H. Haight became elder for the Edmonton district, while Mr. King moved three hundred miles south to the new Southern District as Stationed Elder, sharing also with his wife the pastoral responsibilities at Winnifred.

This district had yet no class, but Mr. King organized two in March—at Carlstadt (later Alderson) and at Winnifred—and soon afterwards organized a district executive. Mr. Shoup in December, 1910, began publishing *Western Tidings* from Medicine Valley. It was a conference project edited by O. L. King.

Edmonton in the north had a camp meeting in July of 1911, held in a natural grove one block from the later site of the Edmonton Technical School. And Carlstadt in the south was treated to one in August. R. R. Haight, fresh from Michigan, helped in this latter one.[4]

The fall conference at Weyburn disclosed some interesting details of Alberta's progress: Bruce had a church nearly completed, Edmonton had a chapel-parsonage mission on the way, Kinnondale was ready for a pastor, and Calgary needed one greatly. R. R. Haight was sent to Calgary and

R. H. Shoup to Edmonton, which had had no pastor the year before.

During that following conference year Calgary people built a parsonage on a two-acre lot purchased at great sacrifice by Mr. King six years before. This house served as temporary meeting place. The Edmonton mission was also completed enough to use. Edmonton gained seven memberships at a July camp but some were by transfer. Over the conference that year, 1911-12, there were twenty-four membership additions.

Under Rev. W. J. Henderson and District Elder W. H. Haight, Ellice schoolhouse near Bashaw had a six-week revival in February, 1913, that produced twenty converts. Two of them, G. W. and D. S. Forrester, were to become ordained ministers. And Sunny Plains (later Armada) that same winter saw a new society formed after its school also had been turned into a revival centre.

In the fall of 1913, the Western Canada Conference came for the first and only time to Alberta—to Calgary. Rev. Alexander Beers presided in place of Bishop Jones.[5]

Meanwhile the Edmonton congregation had been growing and a white brick church was begun. It was completed in the summer of 1914, Mr. Shoup being the pastor. To its basement Purity Press, as it was called, soon moved to continue pouring out holiness literature of various kinds including *Western Tidings*.[6] Jay Allen did the printing.

In this new church, with nearly 70 per cent of the Alberta members on hand, the first annual gathering of the newly created Alberta Conference met that fall under Bishop William Pearce who carried out its organization and dedicated the building.[7]

This 1914 conference followed an earlier one the same year at Weyburn that saw the division of the Western Canada Conference into separate Saskatchewan and Alberta Conferences. The old conference had a year earlier petitioned the Executive Committee for permission to divide. In 1914 Alberta had 185 members and 8 ministerial members. With the new conference, it reverted to a one-district organization, W. H. Haight being the district elder. The appointments read as follows: Edmonton, R. H. Shoup; Bruce and Philips, F. B. Lewis; Lake Geneva, C. W. Cronin; Bartonville, A. C. Calhoon, supply; Gadsby, Alma Dies, supply; Sullivan Lake and Castor, D. Forrester; Lacombe, to be supplied; Sunny Plains, Ada Henderson, supply; Kinnondale and Wheat Centre, W. J. Henderson, supply; Carlstadt, to be supplied; Winnifred, to be supplied; Oscar L. King, evangelist; C. T. Dierks, supernumerary.

Records (apart from the conference minutes) of the years from 1914 to 1920 are spotty, but the followings facts emerge from them: An Ingleview society of twelve members was formed on the Armada circuit in the winter of 1914-15 following a six-week Henderson revival; a new mission began during 1915-16 at Alderson without a pastor, a Mrs. Nathan Bigger giving some local leadership; a 1916 camp meeting near Bashaw was well attended and converts included Streeter Arnett[8] and Mr. and Mrs. Peter Stewart and their three future-preacher sons, John, James and Charlie; the

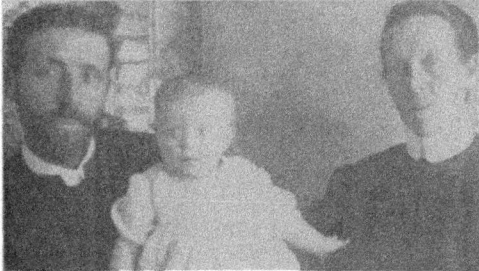

Above: Second Alberta Conference at Tristram (Ellice) in 1915, with Bishop W. T. Hogue.

Left: Rev. and Mrs. W. H. Haight and Burton

Bruce church was dedicated in April, 1917, by Bishop Sellew after a week of revival meetings in it;Ponoka had its first camp meeting in 1918; a 1919 conference-camp at Ponoka, where C. W. Cronin was pastor, attracted over three hundred campers who lived in sixty-five tents, one a tabernacle holding ten families; the 1920 dual meet—again at Ponoka—began a much-needed home mission program and subscribed $1,300 towards it.

Alberta's vital statistics for that year showed 14 circuits, 20 Sunday Schools, 294 members, 10 preachers, 25 local preachers and evangelists, 5 churches and 6 parsonages. By now there were two districts again, the two district elders being H. B. Luck for the north and C. G. Heath for the south.

To indicate the places and personnel at this time, we include the 1920 appointments:

Northern District: H. B. Luck, district elder; Edmonton, C. W. Cronin, H. A. Hammer, supply; Lake Geneva and Wildmere, Phil Denney; Bruce, Philips and Kinsella, E. C. Madsen; Delburne, D. S. Forrester; Lacombe Mission, R. R. Haight, Florence E. Haight, William Carmichael, supplies; Bentley, Meadow Brook and Medicine Valley, J. J. Ealker, supply; Tristram and Manfred, W. J. Henderson; Ponoka, Earlville and East Side, W. S. Walker; A. S. Stambaugh, superannuated; R. H. Shoup, granted certificate of standing with a view of transferring to the Oklahoma Conference; F. B. Lewis, granted certificate of standing with a view to transferring to another

Conference; Streeter Arnett, granted the privilege of attending school.

Southern District: C. G. Heath, district elder; Calgary, Wayne and Rockyford, to be supplied; Armada, Amethyst and Green Prairie, A. C. Calhoon, Bertha Calhoon, supply; Alderson and Jenner, James R. Stewart; Travers, Ingleview and Carl's Hill, G. W. Forrester, A. L. Taylor, supply; Foremost and Macleod, C. G. Heath, Lamorah Sellers, Lena Nelson, supplies; Medicine Hat Mission, C. S. Shaver, supply.

Early Albertans were poor but very big-hearted.[9] Rev. F. L. Baker, for years Field Secretary of the General Missionary Board, declared after a conference-camp visit that there was "no greater spirit of sacrifice anywhere in the church." There is a record of about $1,000 pledged in 1917 for Seattle Pacific College, $2,000 in 1918 for Woodstock Children's Home in Illinois, and $1,700 in 1919 for missions (this latter in a context of two crop failures). While these givings were leaving the conference, scarcely a preacher was getting $500 salary and practically everyone had to work on the side. Perhaps a combination of more local restraint on outgoing funds and earlier local emphasis on home missions would have made for a stronger Alberta conference by 1920 and during the years that followed.[10] For several years from 1920 on, Alberta had a Northern and a Southern District under H. B. Luck and C. G. Heath respectively. The recurring droughts at this time made life and progress most difficult.

In early 1923, Lacombe, under C. P. Stewart, secured a church.[11] This was an existing one purchased and moved into town to a good location. The Alberta conference that year added the Okanagan Valley of British Columbia to its Southern District and named John Smith to supply it. (See his story under British Columbia.) The Cascades provided a natural boundary between the Alberta and Washington conferences, the latter conference being at work on the British Columbia coast, as we shall see.

There is a report of a camp meeting of the Northern District at Clive in 1924 with twenty people baptized.

By 1925 Mr. Heath was in charge of both districts, and Elkhorn, north of Lacombe, was ready for a church.

In 1927, a recently purchased, centrally located church in Calgary had its opening. New pastor Luck was calling for addresses of local friends —and donations. At conference that summer the saints said a touching good-bye to the Heaths who were leaving for Kentucky-Tennessee. Rev. Streeter Arnett was now over both districts. Under his preaching in 1928, Floyde Coxson was sanctified. Mr. Coxson has since spent almost a quarter century in the ministry including ten years as superintendent.

In 1930 the two-district organization changed to a single district called Alberta-British Columbia. By now there were two Valley circuits: Kelowna-Peachland and Kamloops. More details on these Okanagan churches come in the British Columbia chapter.

The next year the beautiful conference camp ground at Alix was bought and used for the first time. The camp was good and seemed to

Alberta Conference group with Bishop R. H. Warren at Alix in 1935.

hold promise of a better day for Alberta. There was need of a better day, for the membership had dwindled to 195.

Evangelist A. L. Haywood and his wife spent an extended period in Alberta in 1932 and under God brought much new life. A May meeting in Lacombe was followed by a June campaign in Edmonton. The couple even remained for the summer conference-camp meeting. At Edmonton, seventy-five people sought the Lord and twenty-four joined the church. H. B. Luck was conference elder at that time.

He continued until 1936 when Rev. P. L. Chase, a prairie-raised boy mentioned earlier, came from the East Ontario Conference and assumed leadership. There had been a 60 per cent upswing in membership during that Luck eldership.

The next year a new two-circuit British Columbia District was created. Enlarged by 1938, this district was at that time placed under Mr. Arnett. The name of Rev. C. E. Coxson first appears at the district level in 1940 looking after Alberta itself. By 1942 the Valley District had five circuits and was under Mr. Chase.

In 1948, the year of semicentennial for Western Canada, there were still the two districts—Alberta, under Rev. Streeter Arnett, and British Columbia (its interior circuits) under Rev. C. E. Coxson.

1. This enormous population burst resulted from the imaginative immigration policy of Sir Clifford Sifton, a westerner named by Laurier to the post of Minister of the Interior.
2. Mr. and Mrs. John Arnett and Mrs. G. W. Smith were early members there.
3. A. L. that year received $23.85 as pastoral support.
4. A mild hurricane at Carlstadt blew the tabernacle down during a service but no one was seriously hurt.
5. Mrs. Beers who came with her husband wrote for *The Free Methodist* a vivid account of a train wreck in which she and her husband were involved enroute from Seattle. They miraculously escaped injury.
6. *Western Tidings*, begun in 1910, became an Alberta project after the division.
7. Oscar King was made secretary of the conference and R. H. Shoup its treasurer.
8. Mr. Arnett was to serve many years in the conference as both pastor and district elder.

9. Writing of early days at Bruce, Nellie Whittaker said: "Times were rather hard for the preachers who came first and I understand that one family ate gophers for meat."

10. One factor that did delay circuit development in early years was the constant moving of members and converts as they searched for better economic conditions. Some went to the towns; others, back East or to the West Coast. In contrast with this pattern, one finds the record of Nellie Whittaker who moved to Bruce in 1908 and lived there for many years.

11. Watch how often this builder-preacher and new churches are linked together later in British Columbia.

3.
THE BATTLE IN BRITISH COLUMBIA

Free Methodism in British Columbia began on the west coast. A Mr. and Mrs. Edgar Blewett of New York's Susquehanna Conference, had moved to beautiful New Westminster. Hoping to see Free Methodism established in B. C., they started cottage prayer meetings and invited Rev. T. H. Marsh, a district elder of the Washington Conference, to visit them. That was about 1907. A Rev. F. H. Harmer, recently moved from Michigan, helped with the prayer meetings for a time, but the visit led to a successful tent meeting the next year in New Westminster's Tipperary Park and the organization of a new society of twenty-two.[1] For a time Mr. Marsh (then a conference evangelist), or someone appointed by him, looked after the society. Rev. C. S. McKinley—one who had assisted in the services—became the new pastor in 1910 and served three years. A parsonage was already built and he completed a church in 1911. By 1913 the class included sixty-five full members and many more probationers. Ada Henderson was a stalwart member in those first years.

To fast-growing Vancouver a few miles away, Mr. and Mrs. Wm. Rennie and Mrs. Pearl Leise, of the Michigan Conference, came about 1914. They opened a downtown mission and formed a small society. A little later the Washington Conference bought, at a great bargain, a valuable piece of property with a large mission hall on it. Mr. McKinley looked after this for four years and raised up a good class. A notable revival occurred here in 1924 with crowds that made it necessary for seekers to kneel at their seats. It came just after the pastor himself had received the baptism of the Holy Spirit. His name was H. B. Taylor. Although the work suffered later reverses, a new church building was purchased in 1935 and a forward movement put into action during the four-year pastorate of F. M. Wees.

Later on, Rev. Myron Boyd and Rev. Layman Fletcher each served here one year. During the more recent pastorate of Ontario's Rev. J. E. Campbell, Sunday School rooms were built under the main church auditorium, and a house for a parsonage was secured and moved beside the church. There is now also a chapel in the Rupert Street district of the city where a Sunday School is held.

Victoria, on Vancouver Island, first shows up as an appointment in the Conference Minutes of 1941 with a Mrs. Alice Simpson supplying it. In 1944, Rev. Ben Smith (formerly of the Saskatchewan Conference) who had been serving Vancouver, was transferred to the island and remained there till 1948.

In 1941, the coastal churches which had been a part of the larger Puget Sound District were organized into a British Columbia Coast District but still remained a part of the Washington Conference.

Effort in Central British Columbia began at Kamloops along the C.P.R., just northwest of sunny fruit-growing Okanagan Valley.[2] Rev. Charles Dierks of the Saskatchewan Conference went there about 1913 because of his wife's poor health. Holiness preaching was not readily received at Kamloops, but when others came to the interior the Dierkses were there to aid.

It was a Vancouver layman who took Free Methodism to the Valley itself. In early 1922 John Smith had an impressive vision call to the Okanagan. He went the next year to Kelowna, a town on the east side of fifty-mile-long Okanagan Lake, where he became an instrument of the Lord in raising up two valley societies, helped by C. G. Heath, a district elder from Alberta.

Mr. Smith was left in charge for five years, preaching in schools and halls. General Conference of 1923 decreed that the Cascades should be the boundary between the Washington and Alberta Conferences. That meant this area would be Alberta responsibility.

In 1927 the Ellis Hughes family came from Westview, Saskatchewan, to Kelowna. They had been attracted there by a *Herald* report of weather so fine you could have tent services even in winter. Pastor Hamilton at Westview had reminded Mr. Hughes on leaving that he would be expected to produce. He not only took turns with others in preaching at Kelowna, but went on soon to Kamloops and helped the Dierks get a mission started. The Penticton work was begun in 1930 by a Rev. J. M. Vines.

The first interior church was at Kelowna, built with assistance from Elder Arnett after the meeting tent had burned and the insurance company had paid $170. Later in 1931 Rev. C. P. Stewart, a preacher-builder, added living rooms at the back to make a parsonage.

During the depression an interesting ministry was added to the Kamloops Mission. Unemployed men passing through the railway centre had no place to sleep. With town help, Mr. Dierks and Mr. Hughes directed a program of providing for these men both physically and spiritually using a partitioned-off part of the mission. They supplied a floor for the men to sleep on and several thousand meals.

Mr. Dierks did not live to see a longed-for church there, but about 1935 his wife donated a lot and Rev. C. P. Stewart erected the building. Taylor and Miller families moved in and soon Elder Luck from Alberta had a small class started.

By early 1938, John Smith felt the pillar of fire moving towards West Summerland, another Valley town, and found there Christians of several denominations praying for a revival. A Fletcher-Chase party, on invitation, came in May for a tent campaign and the result was a twenty-nine-member Free Methodist class, with a basement church and parsonage soon afterwards. The Charles Wesley James family, that has since become such a decided asset to the church, had been a part of the welcoming committee and joined the new society with others.[3]

In 1940 Mr. Stewart completed the church and improved the parsonage at West Summerland. W. S. Angell, C. E. Coxson and George Schnell were other pastors there in the program's infancy.

A Mr. and Mrs. J. W. Hackett who were converted in nearby Peachland under C. G. Heath donated property for a slightly later Stewart-built church in Kelowna. Rev. C. B. Garratt from Saskatchewan served as pastor at Kelowna for a time and later retired there before his recent death. Several Coxson brothers served pastorates there.

Right: Kelowna Church, completed about 1946. Rev. and Mrs. C. B. Garrett in front.

Below: Ministers and wives who have served in Canada attending a Minister's Conference at Seattle Pacific College about 1945.

THE BATTLE WAS THE LORD'S

A work was started in the Cariboo Country, but was discontinued. Hope, on the upper Fraser and Penticton at the south end of the lake, had Free Methodist works for a time. The one at Hope (begun by J. E. Campbell) was taken over by a Holiness Band from Vancouver. A Sandford family helped to get a work started at Grindrod in the northern part of the valley. It does continue.

Winfield, in a fruit district not far north of Kelowna, eventually became a society attached to Kelowna. Later it was a separate circuit but more recently has been linked with Grindrod some distance north.

In "Progress Across the Provinces" you will read of changes of supervision plus encouraging expansion in the coastal province during the last decade.

---

1. The charter members included Mrs. J. Mercer, Mrs. J. Sincock, Mrs. J. Davis, the Misses Rose and Maude Sincock, Mrs. E. Blewett, Mr. and Mrs. Lou Henderson, Mr. O. C. Abrams, Mr. E. J. Gaudin, a Mrs. Hall, and a Mrs. Mack. Helping in the campaign had been the E. E. Shelhamers and the Alexander Beerses. Mr. Shelhamer was a widely known evangelist and Mr. Beers Seattle Seminary's principal.

2. Okanagan Valley with irrigation is a veritable Garden of Eden, famous for its peaches, cherries and Macintosh and Delicious apples. Deer are plentiful in the mountains nearby. The dry mountain air and mild climate make it one of Canada's most charming and healthy areas for living.

3. Brother Joe and sons Joseph and Kenneth served as pastors while daughter Frances became the wife of Rev. Lloyd Mino of West Ontario. Frances, Kenneth and Grace all came East to attend Lorne Park College.

Section 6: Giants... In Those Days

Behind every advancing enterprise stand people, individuals who were prepared to assume the lonely responsibilities of leadership so necessary in that success.

This section provides sketches of a few of those who, through devoted services as leaders, became great in Canadian Free Methodism—men and women, clergy and laity, foreign missionaries and home missionaries. It is climaxed with the story of the General Church's only Canadian-born bishop.

Here is one of the hardest portions of the book to handle. Ferreting out enough significant facts is difficult. But deciding who to include—and not include—is delicate. The writer is no more satisfied with this section than many readers will be. But limitations of space and time prevent a more complete coverage. The running history has already disclosed dozens of others (some equally worthy) in action. In fact, the lives of many prominent people seem most easily treated that way.

1.
SOME MILITANT MEN OF THE MINISTRY

C. H. Sage—Charles Sage was Canada's first conference-appointed Free Methodist pastor, being sent by North Michigan in 1876. Born in 1825 in New York State, he grew up sceptical about religion until his mother found the Lord in a Methodist camp meeting. At fourteen, conviction that followed the death of a friend took him to a protracted meeting. There he sought the Lord, with assurance coming just as he started for home. Following the example of a light-talking young minister, he lost his witness for a time. Having learned the blacksmith trade as a boy, he set up a business for himself in manhood. Mr. Sage gradually grew disgusted with local Methodist shallowness and what he called money-raising "sprees." While away from home once, his wife wrote that the holiness-preaching Free Methodists had come to town and that he would probably like them. He did. After seeking several weeks and consecrating to leave the popular Methodist church for these despised people, he found the blessing of holiness himself.

Mr. Sage's new life soon led him into considerable persecution. Later he moved to Michigan and began homesteading. Though his boyhood education had been most limited, he soon started a Sunday School and prayer meeting in this community and others near, a discipline that was to help prepare him for his rugged regime in Canada. Discovering that the fruit of his winter revivals needed constant attention, he felt called to full-time work, joined the North Michigan Conference in 1870 and accepted appointment to his home area. A year later, having paid up his debts and built a barn, he left the farm in care of his sons and joined the itinerant ranks. The story of his heroic mission to Canada (at age fifty) and his success there in Canada has been told in other places; also the account of his efforts in Tennessee and his later year in Canada.

Undoubtedly a major part of Mr. Sage's genius was his ability to enlist and his willingness to use lady preachers, when men in only limited numbers would heed the call. His dedication is well reflected in the words given in his autobiography as quoted by a Negro: "I heard him say he would go anywhere this side of hell, if he could get a soul saved." His humility comes out in a reason given for not attending a General Conference once: "I did not think myself capable of doing anything at such a gathering where there were so many learned and talented men. I had never felt myself capable of being a chairman (district elder) and when I would be introduced as a chairman I would feel like sinking out of sight." He seems to have often been embarrassed over his lack of education, but found it difficult to master studies at the mature age he entered the ministry. Mr. Sage's clear forthright style of writing—and he wrote extensively—does indicate a fine mind.

After his first wife died, he married, in 1894, Maggie Jerusha Hagle, one of the first lady evangelists he had sent out in Canada. She came south to Dakota after receiving his mailed invitation, arriving while he was in a camp meeting. (The marriage took place the day after the camp closed.) After more labouring in Idaho, Washington, and Michigan, Mr. Sage retired in 1901, a worn-out warrior. (At the age of 73 he had been sent to Bay City, Michigan, to get a church and parsonage out of debt, which chore he did, along with accomplishing and paying for needed repairs. At the next session, suffering from erysipelas, he told the stationing committee his work was done. Yet they read him off for Bay City again. Of this action he wrote: "For the first time in my life I backed up and would not go; and I felt perfectly clear." As a result he was sent to an earlier-served and easier circuit.)

He lived till 1908 to know that the Canadian work which he had pioneered on full-salvation lines had swollen into three conferences. To many in his day he was affectionately known as "Father Sage." Canadian Free Methodists have yet to devise adequate means of honouring their debt to this simple, earnest soldier of the cross who left wife and child behind to plant the church banner in their spiritually needy land.[1]

James Craig—Mr. Craig was born in Scotland in 1844, the eleventh child in a family of twelve. At ten, with his mother and family (the father had died) he came to Maryland. For years he and his brothers worked in the coal mines of various states. At twenty-one he was converted in Methodist meetings but joined the Free Methodists in Illinois three years later. His first circuit was at Jacksonville in Illinois but a little later he was serving a circuit in Kansas. After a year and a half at Spring Arbor Seminary, during which time he was entirely sanctified, he married Mary Davenport, who had been one of his Spring Arbor teachers. That fall of 1876 he joined the new North Michigan Conference (the year Mr. Sage first came to Canada) and in 1878 was ordained a deacon. The conference of 1879 sent him to Galt under Mr. Sage as chairman. A year later he was ordained an elder. For eighteen consecutive years from 1882 on, he served as a chairman of various districts. For twelve years he was secretary of the Canada Conference. Four times he went to General Conference. Four years he was on the Executive Committee of General Conference. Twice he superintended the business of having an annual conference incorporated. In 1900 he transferred from the West Ontario Conference back to Michigan. Later he transferred again to Southern California where, after superannuation and a long period of patient suffering, he died in 1919.

Mr. Craig's decision to follow the ministry was not an easy one. When he made it, an attractive business future was bidding. The Canadian Church may be thankful for the choice he made. Hogue's *History of the Free Methodist Church* evaluates him thus: "He was a man of ability and thoroughness . . . , an excellent preacher, a fine disciplinarian, a dignified executive officer, and a man of positive convictions. . . . In fact, he was just such a man as the Canada work needed to help give it shape and strength in its formative period." [2] His wife proved a most capable helper in Canada, she herself serving a time as a conference evangelist. Her promotion of missions and her office as the first president of the W.F.M.S. have been told earlier. Mr. Craig strongly endorsed women's right to preach.

Albert Sims—Mr. Sims was born in Gloucestershire, England, in 1851, claimed conversion at eighteen, and came to Canada as a missionary. His first appointment was the Primitive Methodist Church at Sydenham. A little later, to keep popular with his wealthy Etobicoke congregation, he softened his message. While he was at Scarboro in 1877, Robert Loveless, using the medium of good books, enlightened him on his compromised position. Condemnation followed, but decline in worldly Toronto continued until 1879, when, on the invitation of Mr. Loveless, he attended a Free Methodist camp meeting at Tonawanda, N.Y. It appears that he went to seek holiness but discovered himself in need of forgiving grace first. At any rate, though he, on invitation, preached an early sermon there, he was a seeker himself before the camp ended.[3] That fall he joined the North Michigan Conference, was accepted as an elder, and sent to Woodstock to open work. Shortly he married a Kelvin convert, Elizabeth Hutchinson. He was the first secretary of the Canada Conference. For many years from 1883 on, we find him as a travelling chairman. He had the honour in 1909 of preaching Robert Loveless' funeral sermon. He attended the Sarnia All-Canada Convention in 1920 to represent West Ontario and went to General Conference on numerous occasions.

Mr. Sims wrote and published over fifty books and booklets and over one hundred tracts. The Sims autobiography was called *Yet Not I*. For some time he edited and published a stirring holiness magazine. Mr. Sims was a godly, efficient labourer in his Lord's vineyard.

W. C. *Walls*—Wesley Walls grew up in the Scarboro area where he was early converted among the Primitive Methodists. His ministry began in early 1881 when, shortly after joining the Free Methodists, Mr. Sage invited him to look after Huntsville circuit. That fall he joined the Canada Conference and married Mary Alice Loveless, daughter of Robert. He was ordained as deacon and then as elder in 1884 and 1887, respectively. Because of his practical preaching and wholesome teaching, Mr. Walls was often appointed to circuits to follow the revivals of women evangelists. He was one of the first two district elders in the West Ontario Conference when it was organized in 1896. Earlier he had served a period as treasurer of the Canada Conference. Although he was superannuated in 1897-98, he later served on two circuits before his death in 1900. Mrs. Walls was one of the best singers in the church of her day and was frequently called upon by the district elder to lead the hymns in general gatherings.

Three of Mr. Walls' children have given conspicuous service to the church: Jennie, the oldest daughter married R. H. Hamilton and shared with him, a ministry that lasted nearly thirty years in Saskatchewan and twenty in Ontario; Alice was an ordained Ontario minister for forty years before her recent passing (see larger story later); and C. E. L. (Emerald) has already given nearly forty years of service in the Canadian church as pastor, superintendent or evangelist.

Right: Rev. and Mrs. W. C. Walls

Below: Rev. and Mrs. J. M. Eagle

J. M. Eagle—Mr. Eagle was born in Yarker and as a young man learned the harness-making trade. He was converted in the Verona-Norrington revival of 1889-90. In the spring of 1891, he and Petworth's Alfred Wattam were sent by Mr. Craig to look after work at Toronto and Port Credit, the former just beginning. At Armadale's May District Meeting he gained a Local Preacher's License. The 1891 Canada Conference sent him to Hannon. He was a charter member of the West Ontario Conference when it was organized in 1896, and served twenty-nine years alone as a district elder. Several times he attended General Conference as a ministerial delegate. He also represented West Ontario at the All-Canada Sarnia Convention and on the Canadian Executive Board. For one quadrennium he was a member of the church's General Missionary Board. He was Lorne Park College's Financial Agent when the school opened as well as president of its Board of Trustees. He died in 1936 while serving Hamilton's West Avenue Church. His wife was the former Hannah Loveless, daughter of Robert Loveless. A daughter Ora married Rev. R. C. McCallum.

Richard Burnham—Mr. Burnham's boyhood home was at Uxbridge but he was converted at age twenty-three in early 1880 during a gracious revival near Armadale where he was working. After eight years as a busy layman —class leader, Sunday School superintendent, local preacher—he heeded a call to leave the farm for full-time service and gave some thirty-six years to the ministry in East Ontario, the time divided about equally between circuit and district work. We shall see that his invitation to attend a conference was a factor in C. V. Fairbairn's decision to become a Free Methodist. Mr. Burnham's first wife, the former Charlotte Ball of Uxbridge, toiled with him for nearly thirty years. She has been described as one of the most saintly women of early Free Methodism. A son, Fletcher, is a pastor in the East Ontario Conference now.

Rev. and Mrs. Richard Burnham   Rev. and Mrs. Emerson Snyder

Emerson Snyder—Born at Yarker in 1868, Mr. Snyder received a call to preach while reading the Bible at family prayers the morning after his Verona conversion in the Norrington revival of 1889-90. In the spring of 1892 at age twenty-three he was sent by Rev. A. Sims to Gunter where the people were calling for a preacher. The story of his successes there is already told. His marriage to helpful Mary Milliken came just before conference that summer. She had been serving circuits for several years already. Mr. Snyder gave nearly forty years to the East Ontario ministry as pastor or District Superintendent during which period he moved twenty-five times. Someone described him in the words applied to New Testament Barnabas, "a man . . . full of the Holy Ghost and of faith." Mr. Snyder spent his retirement days at Verona, passing on during the 1956-57 conference year.

David Allan—Mr. Allan belonged to a family of Scotch Presbyterians who lived near Barkway in Muskoka. While working as a foreman in a Bracebridge lumber camp in 1889 he was invited by the Free Methodist cook to attend a nearby revival being conducted by Rev. R. Burnham. He went, was convicted, and shortly converted. A little later, he walked twenty miles to a Craig quarterly meeting to join the church. Home at Barkway, he set the community on fire. His first circuit—Barkway, Housey's Rapids, and Severn Bridge in 1891-92—was shared with Robert Hamilton, the two men forming a "David and Jonathan" friendship. Most of Mr. Allan's ministry was in West Ontario (he was a charter member of that conference), where he spent many years as both a pastor and a district elder. He was a member of the Sarnia All-Canada Convention and a General Conference delegate. He was superannuated in 1935, because of poor health and died in 1940. His life story is in book form: *From Lumber Camp to the Ministry*. Mr. Allan was fearless, deeply spiritual, and apt in illustration—a natural leader. Two of his daughters, Elizabeth (later Mrs. J. P. Foy) and Margaret (Mrs. B. E. Stevenson), were both able workers in the church. Another daughter, Frances, was the first wife of Rev. P. K. Smith.

Rev. and Mrs. David Allan

M. S. Benn—Miles Benn was born at Petworth in Addington County in 1867. His conversion story has been told. In 1890 he married Agnes Moir, a young teacher who had come to the community and found the Lord. With leadership qualities, she was to prove a strong helper and a great missions promoter at all levels. (She was, in fact, the first Canadian to serve on the Executive Committee of the General W.M.S. and, for at least three quadrenniums from 1899 on, was an associate editor of the *Missionary Tidings*.) The Canada Conference of 1892 sent Mr. Benn to his first circuit, Bracebridge. In 1899, feeling a hunger for more knowledge, he left the itinerancy for two years to attend Spring Arbor Seminary. During this time his wife taught school. Mr. Benn then served the Canadian church till 1938 with pastorates and district elder responsibilities in both East and West Ontario and secretarial service in the latter conference. In

GIANTS ... IN THOSE DAYS

his nineties now (in Florida), but still with a keen mind, he is the only ministerial survivor of that 1892 conference which first stationed him. Besides conducting a number of successful revivals as revealed earlier, Mr. Benn cultivated a decided aptitude for money-raising, making him repeatedly in demand for financial urgencies. For a short period before the Lorne Park College property was actually purchased, he served as part-time Financial Agent and secured substantial pledges for the school about to be started. His record (largely told already through the running story) of buying and building parsonages, of buying churches, and of paying off existing debts is an impressive one indeed. In the case of Toronto Eglinton, he was transplanted there from a short term in Kingston, when its lot and new basement chapel were in danger of being lost. How varied are the gifts that God gives for the establishing of his church!

Rev. and Mrs. M. S. Benn

W. H. Wilson—Mr. Wilson's story has been largely given in scattered fragments but because of his immense contribution we give it again in a connected version with a few details added at the end. Converted in the Keith revival of 1889-90, he left his profession of teaching to enter the ministry in 1890, being assigned to Walsingham. Eight years later, while at Bracebridge and after having served periods on several circuits including Armadale, Toronto and Brantford, he accepted a West Ontario appointment to Western Canada as the first Free Methodist missionary there. His wife, the former Martha Page, had been an evangelist under Mr. Sage. The couple's heroic pioneer work in that new land need not be retold. When they left in 1911 to go to Spring Arbor Seminary where Mr. Wilson was to serve as financial agent, the Western Canada Conference that they had founded had grown to three districts, sixteen circuits and nearly three hundred members. His picture will always have an honoured place in Moose Jaw Bible College. He retired in Seattle where he was killed by a car while en route to do some hospital visiting. Mr. Wilson had the distinction of being secretary of the dividing Canada Conference of 1895.

F. M. Wees—Mr. Wees was born in Stratford in 1874 but grew up in the Sarnia area where he was converted in his father's home at age twenty-two. A few months later, district elder W. C. Walls appointed him to the Shetland circuit. In 1902, after having served on four circuits, he volunteered for pioneer service in Western Canada to fill the gap created when J. W. Haley left there for Africa. In Saskatchewan he served numerous circuits for ten years (see Saskatchewan story) and spent twelve years directly afterwards as district elder. He was a delegate to the Sarnia All-Canada Convention, a long-term member of the Canadian Executive Board and a representative of the Saskatchewan Conference at several General Conferences. His wife, the former Josie Rusk, was a very effective preacher too—so effective that a separate story is given on her. In 1924 for family health reasons, Mr. Wees transferred to the Washington Conference but returned later to Saskatchewan as district elder. The Weeses retired eventually in Regina, with intervals at a daughter's home in California. Mr. Wees is still alive in Regina, though in failing health.

William Zurbrigg—Mr. Zurbrigg was born in Perth County in 1873 and was converted in 1896 after an unsatisfactory boyhood attempt to be a Christian. He claimed to have a call to the ministry some six years before his conversion. At twenty-six, two years after his conversion, he was assigned to supply Middlemiss circuit in the West Ontario Conference. A year later we find him attending Spring Arbor Seminary. After schooling, a thirty-two-year ministry was served in the East Ontario Conference beginning with a period as Uxbridge pastor. While there, he married Minnie Rusk. His ordination as elder came in 1905. Mr. Zurbrigg was a member of the trustee board of Lorne Park College for twenty-five years and for a time was resident there as Business and Farm Manager and Field Representative. For thirty-three years he was East Ontario Conference treasurer. For twenty-four years he was president of the Canadian Executive Board and had much to do with the 1927 incorporation of the church in Canada. After retirement, Mr. Zurbrigg lived in Toronto affectionately looking after his invalid wife, till his death in November, 1958, at age eighty-five. Mr. Zurbrigg was especially known for his kindly and cheerful spirit.

O. L. King—Oscar King was an East Michigander. He was born in 1872, converted and sanctified in 1892 while teaching school, and sent to his first circuit in 1897. A missionary at heart, he could not resist F. B. Lewis' calls for help from Western Canada. In 1905 he volunteered to go via the West Ontario Conference and was sent to Alberta as her first appointed missionary. His status was that of district elder while his wife Lizzie was created supply pastor for Edmonton. The story of their early hardships and pony travels has already been related. They stayed in Alberta only ten years but during that time Mr. King helped organize the Western Canada Conference in 1906, serving for a time as its secretary. He edited the *Western Tidings* for the first few years after it was begun in 1910, and helped organize the Alberta Conference in 1914. During 1914-15 he ministered as an evangelist. R. H. Hamilton described him editorially as "one of the truest Canadian pioneers Free Methodism has ever produced." Jesse Allen wrote of him: "He was a very kind man and always seemed to be afraid of hurting other people's feelings."

After a few years in Washington, the Kings went to Alaska as government teachers, seeking an opportunity to establish a Free Methodist work among the needy natives. He never saw his dream accomplished. Mr. King's early death in 1925 was the result of a fever he contracted after falling through the ice while crossing an unbridged stream. He was obliged to go miles in frozen clothes to reach a settler's home where he could warm and dry. The natives, for whom he had poured out his heart, conducted a simple funeral. His wife wrote: "We buried him among the sand dunes on the most westerly point of the American continent."

R. H. Hamilton—Mr. Hamilton was born in Kent County, Ontario, in 1883 and spent his boyhood in pioneer parsonages as his pastor father, Robert, moved from place to place. He was converted in early 1902 and sanctified soon afterwards. In 1905 he married Jennie Walls who travelled to Westview in Saskatchewan, where he was then teaching, for the marriage. Henry, as they called him, taught a year more, then took his first circuit—Roseview—just as the Western Conference was being organized in 1906. After opening work at Estevan and Weyburn, Mr. Hamilton was made superintendent of the Saskatchewan Conference. He stayed in the West until 1934 pastoring other places (including Moose Jaw) and serving as conference evangelist and conference superintendent. Back in West Ontario, his further service included being pastor of the Brantford circuit, superintendent of the three western districts, pastor at Sarnia, and conference evangelist. While evangelist (with consent of his stationing committee) he also served as pastor for the Gospel Workers in the Georgian Bay area. He died in late 1954 while serving the Welland circuit.

Mr. Hamilton represented Saskatchewan at the Sarnia All-Canada Convention in 1920, and was a member of the Canadian Executive Board from its organization almost to his death, part of this time as president. He founded the Canadian *Free Methodist Herald* and despite a busy schedule of other activities edited the paper, with the help of his wife for its first twenty-five years. (Earlier, Mr. Hamilton had begun a *Saskatchewan Tidings*.) He helped secure the first Federal Act of Incorporation. He represented Saskatchewan four times at General Conference and served four years on the General Board of Administration. For a time he was a Lorne Park College Trustee. The formation of the Canadian Holiness Federation was to a great extent the result of his vision. He was first president of this organization serving five years.

With his passing, Canadian Free Methodism lost one of her stronger leaders in fairly recent times. Vision, aggressiveness, administrative ability, and adaptability were among his gifts during forty-eight years in the ministry.

At present, a son Burton is a member of the Canadian Executive Board for Saskatchewan, one daughter Hazel teaches in Roberts Wesleyan College, and another is a nursing instructor in the Christian Medical College Hospital at Vellore, South India. Mrs. Hamilton is still blessing the church with her cheerful youthful spirit. She lives in Oshawa where she proved a handy "unofficial" helper in this history's preparation.

H. B. Luck—Mr. Luck spent the early years of his ministry serving circuits in East Ontario. At Peterborough Mission, his first assignment in 1905-08, he raised up thirty members. In 1914-15, while stationed at Newmarket and Holt, he conducted (without an evangelist) a Holt revival that resulted in eighty conversions. In 1919, because of asthma, he transferred to the Alberta Conference. By 1920 he was district elder of the Northern District and represented his conference at the Sarnia All-Canada convention. More circuit service which included a period at Calgary, another spell as elder over the whole Alberta Conference (which included then interior British Columbia), and Mr. Luck was ready for retirement—in 1936. He passed away in the spring of 1960 at West Summerland in British Columbia's beautiful Okanagan Valley.

Mr. Luck lived a life of personal discipline that included early rising and abundant pastoral visitation. His ministry was strongly evangelistic with little inclination to compromise. Sara Gregory wrote of him: "Brother Luck seemed to carry revivals everywhere." A study of Conference Minutes reveals that he was in the habit of leaving a circuit or district or conference healthier membershipwise than he found it.

W. H. Gregory—"Will" Gregory was a Verona boy who without knowing "what was wrong" with him began to feel the convicting power of the Holy Spirit while playing cards on a Sunday afternoon eight hundred miles from home. Quitting his job he went home and began reading his Bible and John Wesley's sermons. He felt his sins pardoned while praying alone beside his bed. That was September, 1890, and before he had ever heard of the Free Methodists. The next July at a Verona camp meeting he was entirely sanctified, and began witnessing whenever an opportunity arose. In 1892 with the aid of a singer he conducted his first campaign in the Orange Hall at Denbigh in north Addington County. Elder Norrington in March of 1893 or 1894 asked him to go to Vennachar and the conference of 1894 returned him. Shortly he married Carolyn Brisco, one of his northern converts. Wesport, Odessa, Belhaven, Bracebridge, Kingston, Gananoque, Warkworth, Picton, Odessa again, Verona, Toronto (Broadview), Frankford, have all since had him at some period for a pastor. On several of these circuits he has served twice. There was also a period as district elder. Mr. Gregory retired in Verona in 1948 after fifty-five years in the ministry—an extraordinary record. Though extremely aged (he is in his nineties), both husband and wife are still active and blessed.

The Gregorys were kingdom builders wherever they went. Mrs. Gregory's Sunday School and youth work have been touched on already. Their family has been a pronounced asset to the church. Their son James F. is now editor of the *Free Methodist* in Winona Lake, Indiana, after periods of service as a pastor, district elder, Christian college professor and president. Their daughter Sara is also known church-wide. She has earlier been a Greenville professor and a pastor, and in more recent years has worked with notable success as an evangelist. She collected much helpful data on East Ontario for this history and assisted in checking the manuscripts.

Rev. and Mrs. W. H. Gregory

Rev. and Mrs. F. A. Daw

F. A. Daw—Francis Ambrose Daw was born in London, England, in 1894. At nine, he came to Canada having already been confirmed in the Church of England. At thirteen, he went to work for a Wesleyan Methodist farmer near Ottawa and, after learning the way of salvation, found the Lord in the haymow. He was soon made superintendent of the local Wesleyan Sunday School and granted a Local Preacher's License. In 1915 he married Margaret Jackson. Mr. Daw's introduction to Free Methodism came in 1920 when Rev. C. V. Fairbairn invited him to help in tent meetings at Newburgh, while he left to attend annual conference at Bracebridge. The next year he joined the East Ontario Conference. By 1925 he was ordained an elder. From then on, he was to give conspicuous service in many areas until his early death in 1951 while pastoring at Newmarket. A summary of that service runs thus: pastor at Gravenhurst, Peterborough, Warkworth, Kingston, Verona and Newmarket; district superintendent for sixteen years including supervision at some time on all East Ontario districts; representative of his annual conference at five General Conferences; member of the General Board of Administration and the Commission on

Missions for twelve years; member of the Board of Directors of the latter for eight years; member of the Canadian Executive Board and editor of the *Canadian Free Methodist Herald* for four years; corresponding editor of the *Free Methodist* for sixteen years; secretary of the East Ontario Conference for twenty-six years; assistant secretary at three General Conferences. Other important offices held include that of treasurer of his Conference Sunday School Board and president of district branches of the Canadian Holiness Federation. At one time he held thirty-two greater or lesser offices in religious organizations. Once he received twelve votes at General Conference for bishop.

Other evidences of spiritual leadership include his building of a church at Pine Lake on the Bracebridge circuit (See romantic story in section on circuit development), his sponsoring of a weekly "Light and Life" radio program at Kingston before the church-wide broadcast under that name appeared, the purchase of present camp ground sites on both Kingston and Peterborough districts during his superintendencies, his crowded church at Kingston, and his common altar services when preaching.

A deep student (see reference in chapter "They Went to College at Home"), Mr. Daw died as he would have wished—in his study among his books.[4] The tribute given by Dr. J. F. Gregory at the next annual conference read in part: "As an administrator he was wise, tireless in labours.... In the pulpit he handled the Word as a student, with dignity and fervour. As a writer, he gave evidence of a well-ordered mind . . . his editorials were read widely. In personality he was modest, deliberate, not talkative, a man of prayer, full of faith. He had no time for any work except that of the kingdom of God."

Today his younger son, William, is an elder in the East Ontario Conference serving Napanee. His oldest daughter, Joanna Harnden, has for years been active in Y.P.M.S., F.M.Y. or W.M.S. work.

---

1. Since the lines above were written, approval has been given to the suggestion to make Sage Publishers, Oshawa, the trade name for the now-necessary book business of Free Methodism's Canadian Executive Board. This decision (in keeping with widespread denominational practice) will provide reviewers with a distinctive publishing name for reference, will encourage the production of more books in Canadian Free Methodism, and best of all, will immortalize a man who both valiantly made church history and vividly wrote it.

2. Henry Mellor, who heard him preach the same sermon four times on a quarterly meeting tour, wrote of him: "I think he was the best all-round man that ever travelled in Canada."

3. His text was "Let your light so shine." Someone raised the question in his testimony: how could one let his light shine if he didn't have any. Mr. Sims took the hint.

4. His daughter Joanna wrote, "He seldom . . . sat down to relax without a book in his hands."

2.
SOME WORTHY WOMEN ALSO

Maggie J. Hagle—Maggie Jerusha Hagle's story is largely told but here is a list of the highlights: conversion in Primitive Methodist meetings, membership in the new Jericho Free Methodist class organized by Mr. Sage in the summer of 1877 near the end of the first year in Canada, sanctification that fall in Sage meetings; assistance shortly in Thedford services, then in London where she offered herself for the regular work, assignment to Muskoka with Martha Thomas (the first pair of ladies so sent out), transfer to Ellesmere, then Hannon, Iona, Shetland, and Galt. Sometimes she served with another worker, sometimes alone. About 1882 she suffered a broken hip in a buggy accident and thereafter was always lame. Miss Hagle went to Dakota in 1894 to become the second Mrs. Sage. She la-

Some early lady evangelists (taken 1891): Back Row—Maggie Crittenden (later McKay), Laura J. Warren (later Coleman), Mrs. Mary Norrington, Nancy Schantz; Middle Row—Mrs. Mary Taylor, Mrs. Mary Craig, Matilda Sipprell (later Taylo); Front Row—Martha Page (later Wilson), Olive Diller, Annie L. Green (later Steer).

boured with her husband in various states before his retirement and outlived him about fourteen years. As a preacher she was evangelistic in her emphasis; as an individual she was saintly.

Matilda Sipprell Taylor—Matilda Sipprell was born near Otterville of devout Christian parents. She was converted at home at thirteen but later went to the city to be a dressmaker and became worldly. Her sick-bed conversion, her light on holiness in the Sims-held Northfield wagon-shop chapel revival, and her sanctification at Hannon Camp have been told. By 1880 she was helping Valtina Brown begin a work at Uxbridge. In all, she laboured on ten fields in the Canada Conference and eight in West Ontario after the division—a thirty-year service. She shared her last charge, Sault Ste. Marie, with Alice Walls in 1910-11. She had been responsible for purchasing a mission building there. Miss Walls described her as "a woman of deep spirituality, utterly sincere, . . . a true saint." It was her custom to rise at five A.M. and spend hours in prayer for the salvation of souls. After the Sault ministry, she went to California and married George Taylor, formerly of Brantford. She died at ninety-two, after two years of patient near-blindness. Still available is her Evangelist's License of 1882 signed by Rev. C. H. Sage.

Laura Warren Coleman—A New York State girl, Mrs. Warren lost her husband, Rev. F. H. Warren, in early 1881 during his first year at Chippawa in the Genesee Conference. Perhaps through services her husband had held on the Canadian side of the Niagara River, she developed an interest in Canada. At any rate, she attended an 1881 camp meeting at Armadale where Mr. Sage asked her to join a Miss Hoffman at Severn Bridge. This proved to be the beginning of a lengthy period of effective service in Canada. It later was to include labouring in many places, first with Martha Stonehouse and then with Annie Green. Her part in the Charlemont revival is told already. In 1897 she married General Superintendent Coleman with whom she travelled across the church till his death in 1907. After that, she returned to Canada again and served circuits in both East and West Ontario. It appears she was sent to Charlemont and several other places several times each. Two different late team-mates were Flossie Teal and Anna Botting. Her days of final retirement were spent in Lockport, N.Y.

Martha Stonehouse—As a young Agincourt lady, Miss Stonehouse was converted along with her father in the Silas Phoenix home in the early part of the great Armadale revival of 1879-80. Ambitious and talented, she took an accelerated course at a ladies' college in Hamilton planning to teach. Then feeling a call towards Christian service, she was resolved her training must not be used for secular purposes. Her first assignment by the Canada Conference was in 1882 to Gananoque, a circuit she shared with a Maggie Draper. Later teamed with Laura Warren she served at Kelvin, Port Royal and Marston, Galt, Waterloo and Rockwood and Hannon.

Miss Stonehouse was very devoted and was developing into an able preacher, but her health gave way while at Hannon during 1887-1888 causing her to leave the itineracy. Eventually she went to the Craig home in Stouffville where she passed away triumphantly in June, 1889. Interested in a well-trained ministry, she had vision that a Canadian Free Methodist school would exist, and left $1,000 in her will to help worthy students prepare there for Christian work. Her picture still graces the walls of Lorne Park College.

Martha Stonehouse

Annie L. Green Steer—As a young girl, Annie Lizzie Green came from England to Canada with her parents about 1875 and in her early twenties found the Lord at a Florence camp meeting. After a period of visiting and praying with her neighbours, she became an evangelist labouring nine years with Mrs. Laura Warren. Their part in the Charlemont revival is given elsewhere. Miss Green had a very tender appealing spirit in contrast to Mrs. Warren's more authoritarian manner. After marrying Rev. Edward Steer of East Michigan she served in that conference for a time with her husband and then went to Saskatchewan the year the Western Canada Conference was organized. After labouring on three circuits there, the couple in failing health moved to Florida and pioneered holiness work before Mrs. Steer's death in 1922. A great promoter of foreign missions, Mrs. Steer served periods as W.F.M.S. president in several conferences.

Elizabeth Mackness—Mrs. Mackness was born of Wesleyan Methodist stock in England and with her husband John came to Canada in 1841 settling at Thedford. After some years in the Primitive Methodist Church there, she joined the Free Methodists, the first in her community to open her home for services. Through reading holiness literature she had been led into the experience of heart purity before the Free Methodists came. James Craig who travelled over three hundred miles to preach her funeral sermon in 1896 counted her among "the most devoted and deeply spiritual persons" that he ever knew.

Nancy Schantz—Miss Schantz came from Waterloo County of German parents who belonged to the New Mennonite Church. Her inviting of Mr. Sage to preach in Woodstock and her outstanding revival after Mr. Sage sent her to her first circuit, Belhaven, have already been mentioned. Brantford, Ridgeway, Kelvin, Lansdowne, Kimbo and other places also shared her ministry. Her last appointment was Middlemiss in 1901. She retired in Michigan with relatives. Miss Schantz was a natural leader, able to manage camp meetings, entertain conferences, and travel and preach without a co-labourer. She had a commanding appearance but always spoke with an accent. Resoluteness was among her distinguishing traits. When the man in whose home she first stayed at Belhaven would keep her no longer, she said: "The Lord sent me here and I shall stay," meaning in that community.

Mary Scott Norrington—After her marriage in 1887 to Rev. A. H. Norrington, this lady travelled and laboured with her husband in at least ten Free Methodist conferences, including both East and West Ontario where he spent part of the time as a district elder. She had previously spent some years as evangelist herself in the United States, although born in South Crosby, Ontario. The Norrington ministry at Petworth and Verona and later in West Ontario is already told. At one time Mrs. Norrington supplied Lansdowne while her husband served as conference evangelist or pastor elsewhere. Mrs. Norrington was especially effective in exhortation and song, and had a gift for inspiration. When a mob threatened once to hang her husband, she courageously stood beside him. Her itinerant way of life meant she knew little of the comforts of a home. With failing health, Mrs. Norrington was taken by her husband to the Pacific Coast from West Ontario. After intense suffering from Bright's disease, Mrs. Norrington died in 1904. Wrote R. H. Hamilton of her: "Among the excellent women who helped to turn many to righteousness in our Canadian work, possibly few will shine brighter."

Josie Rusk Wees—Miss Rusk of Bracebridge was converted in Burkholder meetings in 1885-86, sanctified a little later in Burnham meetings and at sixteen began taking services. Her first conference assignment (assisted by Mary Milliken who later became Mrs. Emerson Snyder) was in 1890 in the Huntsville area where three appointments had to be covered on foot—sometimes by wading deep snow. A later ministry at Point Edward was discontinued because of illness from overwork. After a rest period at home, during which time "Uncle Shier" was converted in the big revival, she continued at Orillia, then Niagara, then Ebenezer. In 1898 she married Rev. F. M. Wees. After four years together on two more West Ontario circuits, the preaching team went west to Saskatchewan's Westview. The western story is told in other places except that for nearly four years while the Weeses were in Washington, Mrs. Wees served as matron and preceptress at Ladies' Hall of Seattle Pacific College. R. H. Hamilton has described hers as "a life filled with intense service." There are many indications that she was an extremely vital personality.

Alice E. Walls—A daughter of Rev. W. C. Walls, Miss Alice was born at Walsingham Centre in 1887. She was converted at eleven at the family altar and shortly after was sanctified wholly and joined the church.

Desirous of thorough preparation to serve the Lord, she completed high school, and later the Bachelor of Arts degree at Toronto University. After two years of public school teaching, she served her church in many

Rev. Alice E. Walls

capacities: thirteen years of pastoral service in the West Ontario Conference—Sault Ste. Marie, her first appointment, and Middlemiss, her last (this shortly before her passing); eighteen years of Christian education at Lorne Park College, five and one-half of those as principal (this writer both studied under her as a teacher and taught under her as a principal); nineteen years as W.M.S. treasurer; three years as W.M.S. president; and seven years as Y.P.M.S. superintendent—all these in the West Ontario Conference; twenty-eight years in various General W.M.S. offices—recording secretary, first vice-president, missions study secretary, and editor of the *Missionary Tidings* (this latter office for twelve years at Winona Lake, Indiana).

Miss Walls enjoyed the distinction of being the first woman in the Free Methodist Church in Canada to be ordained a minister. (She was probably the second of any denomination in Canada.) The ordination—at Ridgeway conference in 1918—was by Bishop Sellew.

Because of her distinctive achievements, her name is included in the following annuals: Biographical Encyclopedia of the World, 1945, 1946, 1947; Who's Who in the Middle West, 1950; and Who's Who in Methodism, 1951.

For nearly thirty years before her passing on February 1, 1959 (the last several years in failing health), she had laboured towards the completion of the history of the Free Methodist Church in Canada. As indicated in the preface, this work involved extensive research. The West Ontario Conference gave the first assignment in 1929 while the Canadian Executive Board placed her in charge of the larger project about 1952. Had it not been for her painstaking work and voluminous correspondence growing out of intimate acquaintance with many of the personalities involved, the history would have been a threadbare volume indeed. It is a solemn trust to build the superstructure on her soundly laid foundation.

Miss Walls died at London and was buried at Armadale. Her life was radiant; her service was joyous; her deeds do follow her.

3.
SOME LOCAL LAYMEN WHO COULD LIFT

This chapter will mainly cover those men whose stories, unlike those of say Robert Loveless or David Kirk, have not been told in sufficient detail in other parts of the book. Nor is it in any sense a complete list. Let these people be considered as a few representative members of the laity on whom enough details were available to make a short story without undue repetition.

Thomas Clark—"Happy Tom," as he was affectionately called in late life, was born in Gloustershire, England in 1837. With his mother and step father, he moved at six to Gormley and early took up with drinking and other bad habits. Later he got in the saloon business in Buffalo and himself became such a drink slave that they named him "Drunken Tom." After a period in the U. S. Army during which time he saw service in the South, his mother's prayers resulted in a degree of reformation, and then complete deliverance in a Buffalo Pearl Street Free Methodist church. Following marriage to a Buffalo girl, he came back to Agincourt near relatives and later lived at Stouffville, Uxbridge and Toronto. He was sanctified at a Primitive Methodist camp meeting and testified to the experience for about fifty years.

Tommy, the first Free Methodist in Canada, played a significant part in bringing the church to Canada as we have seen in the chapter "How It Happened." His ministry of visiting has also been told. For many years he worked in the building trades—stone-mason, plasterer, paper hanger—while in slack seasons he sold Bibles and religious books, visited jails and hospitals, and even preached. His life story mentions Shetland, Severn Bridge, Bracebridge and Port Credit as preaching points served, although these do not all seem to have been conference appointments. There is a 1904 report by him in the *Free Methodist* telling that in the previous year (he was then living in Toronto) he preached 40 times, exhorted and testified 181 times, made 515 visits and travelled 2,134 miles. Another year he talked and prayed with 264 hospital patients and distributed 6,000 tracts and papers.

Tommy Clark's religion seemed to be the kind that spilled over. This white-whiskered man knew a salvation that delivered completely, and he never grew tired of testifying in church or out of church about the pit of sin from which he had been dug. He spent his last years in California with a son. At eighty-two, he was still doing "mission work."

J. W. Stuart—Despite even pulpit persecution of early Free Methodism in Northfield, former Methodist class leader Stuart and his wife were one couple who attended the Sims meetings and became so interested they went on to the Hannon camp. There, discovering they knew not saving grace, they sought and found it. Back at home they identified themselves with the Free Methodist Church, and despite gossip and charges of hypocrisy held fast. Mr. Stewart developed into the pillar type, being always ready to encourage his pastor by his hospitable door and sanctified purse. Once he bought an extra horse for Mr. Sims to use in his circuit travels. It is said that the Kelvin church was built largely through his liberality and influence.

Rufus Stewart—This Mr. Stewart belonged to the Hannon society. He had the distinction of being made a full member of the church without serving a probationary period because of a need for trustees at the 1881 dedication. He proved worthy of the confidence; he was on hand for every quarterly meeting for fifty years, during which time he served continuously as trustee. He also knew periods as local steward, class leader, Sunday School

Rufus Stewart

superintendent, and even janitor; and represented the circuit at annual conference forty times. Mr. Stewart was described as a man of few words, but of helpful counsel and deep spirituality.

Harry Bray—Mr. Harry Bray of Huntsville was nearly conscripted for the ministry, but felt clearly that God wanted him to fill the local gaps as they developed. He often walked twenty-five miles or more on a Sunday and took three services when the pastor was not available. Two periods as Sunday School superintendent covered forty years in that office. He held Local Preachers' License for about forty years. Although he passed on in 1944, his aged wife is still triumphantly awaiting her crossing and kindly sent this information in the summer of 1959 from her Muskoka Sunset Lodge quarters. His son Gordon served East Ontario circuits from 1917 to 1925 and now is widely known as the manager of the retail department of the United Church Publishing House.

Eugene Smith—Mr. Smith was one of the persecuting Orangeman at Petworth in its early Free Methodist days, but after his conversion he became a strong local preacher and was used of the Lord in the conversion of others at Verona, Odessa, and Napanee. He supplied Napanee on occasion. A blacksmith by trade, he carried his witnessing to his shop where loitering young men heard many a gospel message between anvil strokes.

At the 1920 All-Canada Convention in Sarnia, Mr. Smith was one of the two East Ontario delegates, having represented his Odessa home church at annual conference that year.

William Goodberry—Though born at Dresden in western Ontario, this brother spent most of his life at Verona where his parents, Mr. and Mrs. Lorenzo Goodberry, were charter members. There he came to be recognized as a local preacher of exceptional ability. In testimony and song few laymen could excel him. For years he filled the offices of class leader and adult Sunday School teacher and was known as a delegate at both annual conference and General Conference. He helped the Gregorys serve Cole Lake in its infant days.

Sara Gregory refers to him as a "powerful local preacher and wise class leader . . . whose influence still lives on." This writer remembers him as his godly great uncle. A son Cecil is well known today across East Ontario.

William Franks—Born in a wealthy English family with brothers who went to British East Africa and Brazil, Mr. Franks came to Canada and became a prosperous land owner in Saskatchewan. Frugal and shaggy he was induced to attend the Westview Free Methodist Church and under Rev. R. E. Slingerland's pastorate was soundly converted. For some years this unassuming but intensely loyal man conducted a Sunday evening service for the people of a poor community near his land.

Mr. Franks developed a strong interest in Missions giving at one time $1,000 to open work in Urundi, Africa. At his passing, he left a legacy of several thousand dollars for the church. A substantial grant of this was used towards the opening of Moose Jaw Bible School. In recognition of his stewardship, the main Moose Jaw building is called Franks Hall.

F. B. Lewis—Layman Frank Lewis in the early 1900's travelled from Michigan to Alberta because of a vision. He considered himself called of God to help establish a Free Methodist conference in that province. The trip West was spectacular in several ways: His wife was healed of a fever at the time of departure; he received needed money just in time for the trip; he contracted smallpox while travelling on an immigrant train and with his wife and baby spent thirty-seven days of Calgary winter quarantined in a tar-papered shack. Mr. Lewis' father-in-law, George Smith, was already in Edmonton. He had less faith for an Alberta conference, though he agreed to help. He had an Exhorter's License but Mr. Lewis had a Local Preacher's License. Glowing letters back to Michigan telling of opportunity for land and evangelization accomplished the desired end. Rev. O. L. King came first and the Haights and others followed. Mr. Lewis held revivals in Conjuring Creek and Michigan Centre even before Mr. King arrived.

For a number of years Mr. Lewis served circuits himself. The year the Alberta Conference was organized, he supplied his first circuit, Bruce and Philips. Later he joined the conference and was under appointment till 1920. After a period in the Washington Conference he retired in Seattle where he still lives. F. M. Wees wrote of him in the *Western Tidings* that as a layman "he did more than any other . . . to plant Free Methodism in Alberta." One who has read the Lewis memoirs can readily believe this statement.

Isaiah Bailey—Mr. Bailey was saved near Parry Sound after prolonged private seeking and before he met the Free Methodists. Soon he went to Thedford where he joined the infant Free Methodist class. He became a local preacher and became known favourably for his prayers, testimonies, exhortations and song leading. He often supplied outlying posts, as Klondyke, and twice was left in charge of the local circuit including the time, as already noted, when the church was rebuilt. Mr. Bailey also gave service as Sunday School superintendent and conference delegate. His son, S. S. Bailey, became a minister in East Ontario.

Peter Sharp—A sailor in early life, Mr. Sharp was angry when he returned home in 1882 and found his Methodist choir-member wife had become the first convert in Matilda Sipprell's Port Credit meetings. But he soon asked forgiveness, got saved himself and joined the church. A little later he moved to Galt. After thirteen faithful years there, he moved to Hamilton just before the Canadian Olive Branch Mission experiment began.

Through many trying years he faithfully stood by the Hamilton work as a trustee, steward, Sunday School superintendent, class leader, local preacher and delegate to annual conference (often serving on stationing committee). Once he represented West Ontario at General Conference. A daughter Ethel became the wife of Rev. P. K. Smith; Rev. G. W. Stevens is the son of another daughter.

George Fuller, Sr.—This prosperous but humble business man was associated with Free Methodism in Toronto even before the first Broadview church appeared about 1900. Besides holding numerous local offices, Mr. Fuller was a delegate to the Sarnia All-Canada Convention of 1920, a delegate to General Conference three times, and for eight years a member of the General Church's Board of Administration. His son, George, Jr. is perhaps the Canadian church's best-known layman, and continues the tradition of service at all levels from local to general. (At the general level he belongs to the Board of Administration, the Commission on Missions and the Investment Committee and was once a delegate to the World-Wide Methodist Conference at Oxford, England. Working too on the Canadian Executive Board he has been responsible for winning significant degrees of independence for the Canadian church.)

Peter Sharp

John Whitfield Featherston—This man, a descendant on his mother's side from the famous English evangelist, was born on a farm near Bracebridge in Muskoka. His conversion was the indirect result of a Free Methodist schoolhouse revival near his home, a conversion that was to result in most of his nine brothers and sisters becoming Free Methodists. Mr. Featherston served as pastor at Port Credit for a time but later went to the West where he farmed at Belmont in Manitoba and at Blackheath and Tisdale in Saskatchewan. At both latter places he helped as a local preacher to establish Free Methodism. Wherever he lived he won the respect of his community as an honest God-fearing man. He attended the same Muskoka school and church as Josie Rusk. She and her husband F. M. Wees, were later associated with him in the Lord's work on the prairies.

4.
SOME CANADIAN FIGHTERS ON FOREIGN SOILS

This chapter will outline the life and work of Canadians who went out under the Free Methodist Board before 1950. The later ones will be mentioned briefly under "Recent Review."

J. W. and Esther Jane (Hamilton) Haley—Mr. Haley was born in Muskoka where his parents had met and united with the Free Methodists. When he was a boy, the family moved to Thorncliffe community in Lambton County of western Ontario. In his twentieth year at a camp meeting on his father's farm he was converted. A month later he was entirely sanctified. That was 1898. We have seen that by 1900 he was en route to western Canada to assist newly sent W. H. Wilson in missionary work of the West Ontario Conference. But Mr. Haley had felt his ultimate work was to be in Africa. In March of 1902 he was accepted by the General Missionary Board and was soon afterwards on his way to the dark land. His wife-to-be Esther Jane Hamilton, followed him to Africa in 1905.

The Haleys laboured in Portuguese East Africa for a time and later spent periods in both the South Africa and the Transvaal fields. (In 1926 he had published a book called *Life in Mozambique and South Africa*.) But a burden for the heathen of the interior continued to grip him. In 1929 he wrote to West Ontario about this concern and about his plan for a trip north to the Belgian Congo the following year. Eventually in 1935 the Board assigned him to Ruanda-Urundi, a healthy mile-high region near the equator where lived about half a million people without the gospel. As other workers joined him, this Congo-Nile Mission developed into the fastest growing of Free Methodist fields. Mr. Haley died in 1951, having spent forty-three years in Africa, but today there is an 8,000-member conference there as a monument to his pioneering spirit. Six schools and a hospital aid the work of evangelizing. About two dozen missionaries are

J. W. and Jennie Haley   Albert E. and Matilda (Deyo) Haley

now assigned to the field. At one time both of the Haley's two daughters, Dorothy and Peace, and their husbands, Burton McCready and Oddvar Berg, were serving there.

From the beginning, this Congo-Nile Mission has been run on indigenous principles, that is, the people were taught to support their workers. John Wesley Haley will ever be remembered for his advocacy of this method, and his ability to prove that it worked. Truly, to Ruandi-Urundi, he was "a man sent from God."

Albert E. and Matilda (Deyo) Haley—Converted on the same campground as his older brother (but a year later), A. E. Haley, after a brief pastoral ministry in West Ontario, followed J. W. to Africa in 1905 as an evangelistic missionary and gave forty-seven years of service under the General Missionary Board. Matilda Deyo, who was soon to become his wife, went out in 1906. This Haley couple's missionary years were spent in South Africa and in Portuguese East Africa developing an agricultural program at the Fairview Mission in Natal, and a technical program at Edwaleni, and more recently doing ground work for the Greenville Mission Hospital. Although Mrs. Haley died in 1947, Mr. Haley is still alive and since 1954 has been serving pastorates in his home conference of West Ontario. At present, with his second wife, he is stationed at Welland.

C. Floyd Appleton—Mr. Appleton was born at Vivian in 1881, graduated from Seattle Pacific College in 1903 and the following year left, after a farewell from his home church at Bracebridge, for a pioneer mission ministry in China's Honan province. After the death in 1905 of Clara Leffingwell, the founder of China's Free Methodist Mission, he became the Mission's superintendent, started a Bible Training School and served, except for a furlough period of poor health, till 1920. In 1907 he had married Laura Millican. After returning to America he earned a Master's and a Doctor's degree from the University of Washington. From the completion of this training in 1924 until his death in 1932, he was in charge of Seattle's Bible Department. Mr. Appleton was the East Ontario Conference's first foreign missionary and the first missionary to reach China sent out by our Board.

C. Floyd Appleton

Lucy Tittemore

Effie Cowherd

Lucy Tittemore—Little information was available on this missionary beyond the facts that she was Maritimes-born and North Chili-educated and served in China from 1907 to 1920. This would identify her as among the earliest missionaries in that country and as serving under Mr. Appleton.

J. W. Winans—Mr. Winans was born in North Cayuga township in 1864 and converted at Canboro in 1898. He served pastorates in West Ontario and then in 1907 began a twenty-year missionary career in the Dominican Republic of the West Indies. For part of the period he was superintendent of the Mission there. His mastering of the Spanish language during a period in the South before his conversion is believed to be a factor in his choice of mission field. Ill health forced him home. After an operation he hoped to return to his mission where "no one is doing my work," but he died in a Hamilton hospital in 1929. It would appear that Mr. Winans was the first Free Methodist missionary to the Dominican Republic. Carrie Turrell Burritt wrote of him in *The Story of Fifty Years*: "He loved the poor neglected people of the Dominican Republic and was used of God in the salvation of many."

Effie Cowherd—Born at Brantford, the sister of W. J. Cowherd and Harriet Cowherd (later McCready), Miss Cowherd, after attending the seminary at North Chili, served effectively on the India mission field from 1914 to 1927 as an evangelistic missionary. Famine conditions during part of her period made it necessary for her to care for native children, a ministry that has since paid off through its producing of fine Christian workers. For several years after her final return from India and before her death in 1950, Miss Cowherd did some supply preaching at Ridgeway and London and served her conference as an evangelist.

I. S. W. Ryding—Mr. Ryding was born in Manchester, England, and later came to Canada. In 1918 he joined the East Ontario Conference and left for mission work in China where he was to engage in teaching and literature distribution. In recent years after being forced out by the Communists he transferred to congested Hong Kong island, a British possession on the doorstep of Red China. When he died in 1956, his chapel mission was transferred to the Holiness Movement Church under Rev. and Mrs. Alton Gould who were working on the island. Since the merger, it is a thriving Free Methodist Mission again. Mr. Ryding was a quiet man who never married and who took few, if any, furloughs. Said F. A. Daw of him once: "If there is such a thing as apostolic succession, he was in it."

I. S. W. Ryding

THE BATTLE WAS THE LORD'S

Ethel (Davey) Ryff—Ethel Davey was a Verona (Oak Flats) girl who before her passing in 1949 at age sixty-two spent thirty-one years in southern Africa. After attending Sydenham High School and Kingston Model School, she taught elementary school, then pastored in East Ontario at Gananoque and a Midland Mission. Appointment to Portuguese East Africa came in 1918. In 1923 she married Jules Ryff, another Free Methodist missionary. For a quarter of a century, in the Johannesburg mining district of the Transvaal Mission, she ministered in such ways as supervising Sunday Schools, organizing a Women's Missionary Society and a Women's Christian Temperance Union and editing the *Inhambane Tidings*. Her husband was superintendent of the Transvaal Mission for many years. (In all, he gave fifty years of mission service.) A step-daughter, Lois, married George Fuller, Jr. of Toronto who is well known in both the Canadian and the American Church. A step-son, Frederick is now under missionary appointment in Transvaal after an earlier period as superintendent of the South Africa Mission. There are two daughters also in Africa.

Mrs. Ryff visited her homeland only three times after leaving in 1918. On the last occasion, her former pupils arranged a special session at the Oak Flats school and showered their beloved teacher with gifts. It is this writer's boast that his mother was a close girlhood friend of "Ethel" (the two girls supplied Westport together for part of 1908-09), and that he had personal correspondence with this great lady not long before her passing about 1945.

Bessie (Reid) Kresge—Born at Kingston in 1897, Bessie Reid was converted under C. V. Fairbairn while teaching school in the Desert Lake community. After pastoring at Frankford and Peterboro for a total of three years, she attended Greenville College, graduating Magna Cum Laude in 1925. That same year she began a mission career in China that extended to 1940. About 1939 she narrowly escaped death in Japanese bomb raids on Chengchow. During furloughs from the China field, she completed the B.D. degree from Greenville and in 1934 was ordained a deacon, one of East Ontario's first among women. Later she attended New York's Biblical Seminary. From 1945 to 1953 she served in South Africa, then the wife of Luther Kresge. While her husband assumed the principalship of the Edwaleni Technical College, she pastored the local mission church, taught Bible classes, and organized evangelistic teams of Christian students to preach in heathen villages. For some years now she has been on the world executive of the Women's Christian Temperance Union. Since 1955 she has been editor of the *Missionary Tidings* at Winona Lake. She is listed in *Who's Who of American Women*.

Lawrence E. Arksey—Mr. Arksey was born in North Gwillimbury township near Belhaven in 1898 but moved to Toronto with his parents, Mr. and Mrs. John Arksey, in 1907. He attended Broadview church as a boy and graduated from Greenville College Cum Laude in 1924. (In 1922 he

Ethel Davey Ryff

Bessie Reid Kresge

Lawrence E. Arksey

Pearl Reid

had married Ruth Secord of Oklahoma.) After a short period of East Ontario service, the Arkseys sailed for Africa in 1927. From 1928 to 1946 (except for furloughs) they laboured in Portuguese East Africa. Mr. Arksey's accomplishments and responsibilities included building a training school for African Christian leaders and serving as its principal; pastoring, superintending and supervising a mission farm; securing at Lundi in Southern Rhodesia a site from the government. Mrs. Arksey assisted her husband in his many duties, taught women and worked in the dispensary.

Since 1951 Mr. Arksey has been pastoring in the Presbyterian Church in the United States. He had served at Toronto Broadview, for nine months after returning to Canada in 1946. Seattle Pacific College gave him the honorary D.D. degree in 1948.

Pearl Reid—Miss Reid was born in Kingston and converted at an Odessa camp meeting. She took nurses' training at the Kingston General Hospital. After periods of nursing and then further schooling at Lorne Park College and Greenville College, she sailed for China in 1934 with her sister Bessie who was returning to that mission from a furlough. During her fourteen years there she taught in the Kaifeng Bible School and the Paoki Bible School and served also as school nurse in each. She did rural evangelism as well. For a time during war, she worked for the American Army and supervised Chinese nurses. She left China because of war conditions, but in 1950 received appointment to Japan where she has since laboured, teaching in the Osaka Christian College, conducting Bible classes in churches, and preaching. During periods in the homeland she has completed the B.A. degree at Greenville and the M.R.E. degree at John Wesley Seminary. She was ordained by the East Ontario Conference in 1950.

Ronald and Margaret (Henwood) Collett—Mr. Collett was born in London, England, and educated in the William Booth Memorial College of Winnipeg. He married Margaret Henwood of the Saskatchewan Conference in whose bounds he ministered six years before joining J. W. Haley's

Ronald Collett   Margaret Henwood Collett

pioneer Ruandi-Urundi Congo-Nile Mission in 1936, only one year after its founding. For some years now he has been superintendent of this indigenous but fastest-growing field that contains Free Methodism's largest church and largest hospital. Mr. Collett's work has included the directing of educational, medical and evangelistic programs. The educational program alone involves at least 138 day schools with more than 10,000 students and six boarding schools (one a Bible School for graduates and sponsored by three denominations), with over 1,500 students. Mr. Collett is the church's official representative with the government which subsidizes the school program. Mrs. Collett, besides raising her family of four, has worked extensively in instructing women in homemaking and in teaching in the Kibuye mission school.

Wesley C. and Lela (Swayze) DeMille—This couple attended Lorne Park College, participated in pastoral work in their home Saskatchewan Conference and in West Ontario, and since 1937 have served the church in Africa. Their first term was in Portuguese East Africa, but more recently they have been in the Transvaal where Mr. DeMille is now superintendent. He directs mission work among the miners and cooperates in a literacy campaign that includes Bible translation. Mrs. DeMille has been active in evangelistic and educational work among African women, directing kraal and mine hospital visitation. Besides, she has organized many new Sunday Schools, distributed gospel literature and participated in the Laubach literacy campaign. Mr. DeMille is a grandson of Charlemont's Fannie DeMille. His son Clarke now labours in Southern Rhodesia.

GIANTS ... IN THOSE DAYS

Wesley C. DeMille

Lela Swayze DeMille

Lois E. Kent—Miss Kent was, until 1959, the Canadian church's only medical doctor ever sent abroad.[2] Born at Wellandport, the daughter of Rev. and Mrs. H. G. Kent, and educated at the University of Western Ontario in London, she spent from 1938 to 1942 as a medical missionary in India assisting at the Umri Hospital. Serious illness forced her return before the completion of her first term. Since returning, she has received a special certificate in Internal Medicine from the Royal College of Physicians and Surgeons of Canada, and has enjoyed membership in various medical societies. She resides now in Brantford.

Marjorie (Peach) Rice—Marjorie Peach was born in Brantford, the daughter of Rev. and Mrs. J. W. Peach. She trained locally as a nurse and later attended Spring Arbor Junior College. From 1938 to 1941 she served as a nurse in the Congo-Nile Mission and since then, as the wife of Dr. J. Lowell Rice, has worked in the South Africa Mission. Mr. Rice has recently been superintendent of the new Greenville Mission Hospital in Natal and Mrs. Rice, besides caring for their four children, has assisted in supervising mission churches and has conducted women's classes in Bible study, homemaking and health.

Burton A. and Dorothy (Haley) McCready—Mr. McCready is the son of Rev. and Mrs. W. R. McCready, former missionaries in India, and Mrs. Haley the elder daughter of our first Africa missionaries. They were appointed to the Congo-Nile field in 1939 shortly after their marriage. Mr. McCready's work included supervision and teaching in the Union Bible School, holding prison services, directing construction, opening rural pri-

THE BATTLE WAS THE LORD'S

Lois Kent

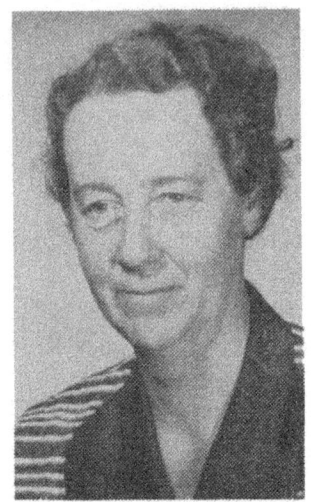

Marjorie Peach Rice

Burton A. McCready

Dorothy Haley McCready

Peace Haley Berg
and husband

Florence Carter

mary schools and teaching women by the Laubach method. Mrs. McCready supervised the dormitory of a school for missionaries' children and worked among the women whose language and customs she had learned as a girl. Although at present the McCreadys are on extended furlough in America, they are still listed with missionary status under West Ontario. Mr. McCready is a graduate of Greenville College and this spring expects to have the Master of Arts degree from the University of Michigan.

Peace (Haley) Berg—Mrs. Berg, the younger daughter of J. W. Haley, was, like her sister Dorothy, born and educated in South Africa. She began missionary work in the Congo-Nile as a nurse and evangelist in 1940 and three years later married Oddvar Berg, a missionary from Norway working in the Belgian Congo. Until 1958 the Bergs continued to work in the Free Methodist mission.

Florence Carter—U. S.-born, she is of W. Ont. stock being a granddaughter of Brantford's Teresa Botwright. She is probably a descendent also of James Carter, Kelvin's early lay church builder. Miss Carter is a nurse with extensive education, training, and experience on this continent before going to Africa (Portuguese East) in 1948. She is still serving there.

Edna McQuiggan—A daughter of W. Ontario's W. E. McQuiggin, she worked a period among the Japanese of New Mexico and California from 1938.

---

1. Church membership in the Congo—Nile stood at over 8,000 in 1959, registering a gain of over 3,500 in the previous five years.
2. In less than a year before his scheduled graduation from medical school, West Ontario's Eldon Meredith, who was preparing for a medical mission career in India was murdered—it is thought by hitchhikers he had picked up.

5.
BURNISHING A BISHOP—SOME BISHOP!

C. V. Fairbairn was born at Ventor (near Kemptville) in Eastern Ontario in 1890 and grew up in an environment of family altars, sing-songs and Bible quizzes. Of Scotch Baptist background, father Fairbairn saw to it that in his home the Sabbath spirit had well set in by Saturday night.

As a lad of nine, Charles "went forward" at a children's meeting and earned the school nick-name of Preacher Dick. As early as ten, he was lining up dolls and preaching to them. When he was thirteen, to keep a vow, he went to the mourners' bench at a Wesleyan Methodist holiness camp meeting conducted by Rev. A. J. Shea, father of singer Beverly. When he was fifteen, he experienced a truly awakened sense of sin and kneeling at a chair in a cottage prayer meeting, received an assurance that enabled him to say "I am saved."

A tug towards the ministry came shortly, but he resisted the prospect of identification with these unpopular Wesleyans until he found himself running away from God. A fresh surrender at twenty-one followed the sudden death of a minister friend who had just before tried to warn him of his waywardness—a surrender big enough to include the pulpit if necessary. In three months Charles was recommended for Local Preacher's License.

During his last year in high school, Charles preached his first sermon before a large local congregation including some of the dreaded high school crowd. Soon an invitation came to look after Portsmouth (suburb of Kingston) Methodist church while attending Queen's University. His mother would wisely give no advice, but in prayer the decision to go was made.

Leaving Kingston station for Portsmouth, Charles' carter proved to be Asa Amey from the little Free Methodist church on Colborne Street. By the end of the second year at Queen's, Charles' faith had fled. Social life, sports, faculty skepticism, student agnosticism, and certain reading had combined to slowly drive it away. Yet he preached on and shortly married Lena Vannest, a nurse-in-training who sang in his choir. Though not saved at the time, she had attended Verona's Free Methodist church and found herself out of sympathy with some of her husband's activities, both religious and social. Presently she found the peace and joy of the Lord at home, and her husband, smitten with conviction, dropped his doubts and followed suit.

Soon after this, Mr. Fairbairn was transferred to the Verona circuit where his preaching took on an evangelical note uncommon in Methodist churches at that time. He even proposed at the Godfrey appointment that they have such an out-of-date thing as a revival. The more serious members agreed on a need, and in early 1916 the effort was on, with souls being garnered in for God.

A little later, Ernest Campsall, one of the converts, dedicated his grove to the Lord and for eight years Mr. Fairbairn held summer meetings at what was named the Bethel Camp Ground. Visiting singers included Beverly Shea's grandmother Mary and aunt Marion Whitney. Visiting speakers included Beverly's father, as well as Peter Wiseman, R. H. Hamilton and the Cowmans and Kilbournes who had founded the Oriental Missionary Society.

Shortly after the first Godfrey revival, Mr. Fairbairn tried in vain to have a revival at another point, Bellrock. Then it was he realized fully his personal need of that second experience of cleansing and power emphasized earlier by the Methodists and even at that time by the Wesleyans, the "Hornerites" (Holiness Movement), and the Free Methodists. Before his wife at the Verona parsonage family altar, Mr. Fairbairn confessed his need, and there received assurance that he was sanctified wholly. From then on, he preached the experience constantly and was soon affiliated with an organization called the Canadian Methodist Holiness Association which helped to provide the Bethel talent mentioned earlier.

Free Methodists were suspicious at first that Mr. Fairbairn's deeper-than-ordinary preaching was largely a bid for popularity in their community. But personal attendance convinced them that here was a Methodist truly in earnest. For 15 months in 1917 and 1918 he campaigned steadily in one community after another around Verona-Desert Lake, Thirteen Island Lake, Deyo's Corners, Godfrey, Newburgh, Wilmur, Wilton, Sydenham, Harrowsmith, Verona. Only the outbreak of the deadly Spanish flu in mid-December stopped the tide and that only temporarily. Hundreds were swept into the kingdom; others rejected the call. Many of both groups never saw spring.

Before the story of the following spring's renewed evangelism is continued, Mr. Fairbairn's denominational developments should be brought up to date. The news of what was happening at Verona reached conference ears and one evening the president and another senior minister visited an evangelistic service. What they saw was too like a "Hornerite" meeting to please them much.[1] Soon a letter came suggesting Mr. Fairbairn should go back to college and offering to arrange a charge near Montreal's McGill University. The Fairbairn resignation that had already been begun was finished and sent as a reply; but, on invitation, the circuit was occupied till conference time in June, 1918.

Even after the invitation was sent, a senior minister visited Mr. Fairbairn and threatened to have another preacher in his pulpit on the Sunday following if he did not withdraw the resignation. But the threat was ineffective and the preacher never came anyway.

A new baby had just arrived at the parsonage. Mr. Fairbairn still had no clear plans for the future. Some converts and other friends sensing his need of encouragement met at the parsonage and gave or pledged a total of $365 to help him get started into whatever new venture he should feel led. The present leading was towards more nearby evangelism and through that summer Mr. Fairbairn continued tent meetings.

211

THE BATTLE WAS THE LORD'S

Rev. Richard Burnham was the Free Methodist elder for the eastern half of the East Ontario Conference in 1917-18. Perhaps he sensed a possible recruit. At any rate, before the August conference of 1918, Mr. Fairbairn received a letter inviting him to attend it—that year at Newmarket.

He went and liked it, especially the way Bishop Sellew and Rev. E. J. Lee handled the questions on holiness as the latter was about to be ordained deacon. In his heart there welled up a desire to be one of them. Mr. Fairbairn preached at conference that night and soon had an invitation to be one of them, with the promise of all the elbow room he needed as an evangelist. In prayer together it seemed that this was the proper future. The campaigns continued again till stopped by December flu. It was in December that Mr. Fairbairn actually joined the Free Methodists.

Hardly over the flu himself, Mr. Fairbairn was preaching for the Free Methodists at Kingston early in the new year. On he went: to Toronto Broadview, to Westport, to Harrowsmith again (its society was organized after this effort), to North Toronto, and back to Godfrey. Though only a conference evangelist, he felt pressing responsibility to get done what others seemed not too concerned about. Bands of workers under his supervision were soon holding meetings (some simultaneously) here and there—Wagarville, Elginburg, Newburgh, Lansdowne, Deyo's Corners, Flinton, Bracebridge. These meetings sometimes went on while he participated in official district camp meetings. Into 1920 they ran—Northbrook, Warkworth, Odessa—until his district elder (and family health problems home at Newburgh) began to suggest that he might be more zealous than wise. But the lull was only temporary. Inkerman, Westport (Mrs. Fairbairn had to be rushed to Kingston hospital from there with appendicitis), Godfrey Camp again, Winchester Wesleyan Camp, Flinton and Newburgh again, Bracebridge Conference (there he was ordained deacon), Sarnia All-Canada Convention, Spring Brook, Warkworth, Campbellford, and Ottawa—all followed in quick succession.

Came 1921, and the schedule roared on. A strange epidemic of some sort hit Glendale (Kingston District) Camp that July and nearly took his helpmate and the oldest child, Jean. In August a personal weariness matured to typhoid fever and laid Mr. Fairbairn aside for nearly two months. To allow ample time for recovery, the conference at his suggestion named him to Westport. With eight members it was the smallest circuit. But he rested no more than necessary. Although starting to preach from a chair, by the third year he was almost as busy as before with revivals going for miles around, aided by Mrs. Fairbairn, Mabel Hughes, Wilhelmina Goodberry, Stanley Donnell, Neil Stoness, R. J. Whaley, Dr. W. D. Stevens, Abe McEwen, Sidney Sully, Elwood Orser, Nicholas Bosko and others many of whom also participated as pulpit supplies when the revivals stopped. At conference time in 1924 there were seven preaching appointments (one was Maberly) and the original membership had quadrupled.

That conference both ordained him as an elder and appointed him to

Peace Haley Berg
and husband

Florence Carter

mary schools and teaching women by the Laubach method. Mrs. McCready supervised the dormitory of a school for missionaries' children and worked among the women whose language and customs she had learned as a girl. Although at present the McCreadys are on extended furlough in America, they are still listed with missionary status under West Ontario. Mr. McCready is a graduate of Greenville College and this spring expects to have the Master of Arts degree from the University of Michigan.

Peace (Haley) Berg—Mrs. Berg, the younger daughter of J. W. Haley, was, like her sister Dorothy, born and educated in South Africa. She began missionary work in the Congo-Nile as a nurse and evangelist in 1940 and three years later married Oddvar Berg, a missionary from Norway working in the Belgian Congo. Until 1958 the Bergs continued to work in the Free Methodist mission.

Florence Carter—U. S.-born, she is of W. Ont. stock being a granddaughter of Brantford's Teresa Botwright. She is probably a descendent also of James Carter, Kelvin's early lay church builder. Miss Carter is a nurse with extensive education, training, and experience on this continent before going to Africa (Portuguese East) in 1948. She is still serving there.

Edna McQuiggan—A daughter of W. Ontario's W. E. McQuiggin, she worked a period among the Japanese of New Mexico and California from 1938.

---

1. Church membership in the Congo—Nile stood at over 8,000 in 1959, registering a gain of over 3,500 in the previous five years.
2. In less than a year before his scheduled graduation from medical school, West Ontario's Eldon Meredith, who was preparing for a medical mission career in India was murdered—it is thought by hitchhikers he had picked up.

5.
BURNISHING A BISHOP—SOME BISHOP!

C. V. Fairbairn was born at Ventor (near Kemptville) in Eastern Ontario in 1890 and grew up in an environment of family altars, sing-songs and Bible quizzes. Of Scotch Baptist background, father Fairbairn saw to it that in his home the Sabbath spirit had well set in by Saturday night.

As a lad of nine, Charles "went forward" at a children's meeting and earned the school nick-name of Preacher Dick. As early as ten, he was lining up dolls and preaching to them. When he was thirteen, to keep a vow, he went to the mourners' bench at a Wesleyan Methodist holiness camp meeting conducted by Rev. A. J. Shea, father of singer Beverly. When he was fifteen, he experienced a truly awakened sense of sin and kneeling at a chair in a cottage prayer meeting, received an assurance that enabled him to say "I am saved."

A tug towards the ministry came shortly, but he resisted the prospect of identification with these unpopular Wesleyans until he found himself running away from God. A fresh surrender at twenty-one followed the sudden death of a minister friend who had just before tried to warn him of his waywardness—a surrender big enough to include the pulpit if necessary. In three months Charles was recommended for Local Preacher's License.

During his last year in high school, Charles preached his first sermon before a large local congregation including some of the dreaded high school crowd. Soon an invitation came to look after Portsmouth (suburb of Kingston) Methodist church while attending Queen's University. His mother would wisely give no advice, but in prayer the decision to go was made.

Leaving Kingston station for Portsmouth, Charles' carter proved to be Asa Amey from the little Free Methodist church on Colborne Street. By the end of the second year at Queen's, Charles' faith had fled. Social life, sports, faculty skepticism, student agnosticism, and certain reading had combined to slowly drive it away. Yet he preached on and shortly married Lena Vannest, a nurse-in-training who sang in his choir. Though not saved at the time, she had attended Verona's Free Methodist church and found herself out of sympathy with some of her husband's activities, both religious and social. Presently she found the peace and joy of the Lord at home, and her husband, smitten with conviction, dropped his doubts and followed suit.

Soon after this, Mr. Fairbairn was transferred to the Verona circuit where his preaching took on an evangelical note uncommon in Methodist churches at that time. He even proposed at the Godfrey appointment that they have such an out-of-date thing as a revival. The more serious members agreed on a need, and in early 1916 the effort was on, with souls being garnered in for God.

A little later, Ernest Campsall, one of the converts, dedicated his grove supervision of the Kingston District.² In less than a year's time the northern circuits were organized into a new Maberly District still under him. This would make possible more thorough evangelism by way of local district and camp meetings.

Even before the 1925 conference, with his new authority he was writing stirring copy for the *Canadian Free Methodist Herald*, copy that unbared his burden for advance. We quote from his "Open Letter to Canadian Free Methodists" in the May 1925 issue: "We are right now at a critical place in our history. Stagnation threatens our life. We are barely holding our own, if we are actually doing that. . . . We are practically getting nowhere. Something must be done at once or we will have to haul down the flag in defeat. God never intended the Free Methodist Church in Canada to haul down her flag in defeat. . . . We have the right doctrine. . . . The fault is elsewhere."

As chairman of the Board of Aggressive Evangelism of the East Ontario Conference, Mr. Fairbairn came up with some pointed suggestions. Free Methodists should pray for a revival that would begin in their own hearts. It was imperative that the revival begin at once among the parsonage people. There needed to be more definite preaching on what real regeneration would do for a man. There needed to be soul-searching holiness preaching that would "drag out and expose carnality." Carnality was labelled "the biggest block in the way of a revival in Ontario."

Some of its manifestations were identified. Selfishness, for instance. "Our own interests are so precious to us that God's interests are relegated to the relation of . . . side lines, our main line being our own peculiar selfish interests or business. . . . Preachers become selfish and do not like to stir themselves. Preachers' wives become selfish and will not let their husbands answer some Macedonian call. Pilgrims become selfish, . . . and . . . refuse to turn out, if a local preacher is to take the service, while the preacher is trying to open up some new field." Covetousness among laymen, pastors and evangelists, got detailed treatment.

But back to the recommendations. Each conference should have a reliable spirit-filled, zealous man in the field as evangelist. He would be well looked after by free-will offerings. Finally, an earlier recommendation made at Sarnia in 1920 in a paper submitted by F. F. Prior, a district elder of the Saskatchewan Conference, was renewed: That the Canadian Executive Board be urged to engage "a general evangelistic party to consist of an evangelist and one or more singers and workers." There is every indication that Mr. Fairbairn was ready to take on such evangelistic responsibility, if invited. But alas, the Canadian Executive Board of that period "knew not the day of their visitation."

East Ontario Conference kept him in the quarterly meeting routine for two more years till 1927. But even at that, he held some good revivals and tried to impart vision to the pastors.³ Then General Conference, recognizing his potential, snatched him away as one of its evangelists and Canadians said good-bye to a man too progressive for them. Since then, the

Fairbairn family about time they left Canada
for Kansas

Fairbairns have lived in McPherson, Kansas, and their four daughters have married Americans. After four years as general conference evangelist, Mr. Fairbairn spent one year as a voluntary general evangelist, four as McPherson pastor, and three years as a Kansas Conference superintendent.

The big honour and responsibility came at the General Conference of 1939—election to the church's four-man Board of Bishops. This was the first time a Canadian had been selected and no other has since been selected.

The work load and routine associated with this office have been staggering—summer conferences across the continent, winter visits to points in the conferences assigned, more evangelistic campaigns, participation in interdenominational meetings, seminars in Wesleyan doctrine, youth group speaking, board meetings and more board meetings at church headquarters, consultation on problems here and there, copious writing for church papers, correspondence unlimited, long periods away from home. (For one year in the 1940's he was home six weeks.) The sound health maintained through the years on this rugged program bespeaks an iron constitution and disciplined living. A genius for detailed planning is doubtless a leading reason why he accomplishes so much. A passion for progress is behind it all.

Bishop Fairbairn's heart is still in his native land and the Canadian Free Methodists love him still as their own. His memory for old names and faces is uncanny and he does not hesitate to call out names when preaching. A speaking appointment in Canada ensures a full house wherever he goes. When God especially blesses, few can excel him in the pulpit. Human interest characterizes his approach. Probably his greatest sermon is one he calls "Why I Believe the Wesleyan Message." He gives it again and again, and it is printed in a book with other holiness addresses given at a Greenville College Ministers' Conference.

Actually he has written several books, the list including *A Primer on Evangelism*, *Purity and Power*, and a popular booklet, *What We Believe*. His autobiography *I Call to Remembrance*, carried recently in the *Free Methodist*, has met with tremendous response and has since been published in book form by Light and Life Press.

As Bishop Fairbairn surveys his years of evangelism, he has, like Paul, much about which he can boast in the Lord. It is estimated that over 1,500 people found God at the Bethel Camp alone in the eight years it operated. Some of his better known converts from early years were Bessie Reid and D. S. Wartman. The East Ontario Conference of 1958 contained ten preachers who directly or indirectly came out of the Fairbairn campaigns. Five churches were built and, another bought to look after converts he won. In more recent years his impact for God has been continent-wide. How far from the truth were the predictions of some Methodists that he would be destined to obscurity if he left them.

Yes, Charles Victor Fairbairn has been some Methodist pastor, some camp meeting sponsor, some tent meeting holder, some Free Methodist pastor, some district elder, some general conference evangelist, and, for the last twenty-one years, some bishop!

Had the Canadian church been able to contain him, had she, recognizing his gifts of evangelistic leadership, created for him evangelistic tasks commensurate with those gifts, she might have been coming up to Centenary with her growth graph for the last third-century less level.

---

1. Mr. Horner, we shall see, had made himself very unpopular in the Methodist Church before his expulsion and his subsequent formation of the Holiness Movement Church.

2. Mr. Fairbairn had been president of a Camp Meeting Association founded to conserve the results of tent campaigns. With his new responsibility, he had to give this office up and the organization soon folded.

3. During this period he held in the Houghton College Church (Wesleyan Methodist) near Buffalo, a meeting that the pastor called "the mightiest revival in the history of Houghton."

Section 7: Strategic Twentieth-Century Instruments of War

The Canadian church, once established, was never content to be a mere auxiliary of the parent American church. While recognizing the values of affiliation, she has from early years striven after denominational adulthood in an ever-increasing sense. That is understandable strategy. Her successes in autonomy could be said to date from the formation of the first Canada Conference in 1880, a story earlier told. The significant later developments began in 1920 at the so-called Sarnia All-Canada Convention. The Canadian Executive Board emerged from that meeting and close after it in the same decade came the Canadian Free Methodism Herald, Lorne Park College, and a Dominion Act of Incorporation, all indications of increasing maturity. More recently Moose Jaw Bible College began. Permanent camp grounds with valuable facilities are now general. And only last year, the Canadian Free Methodist Church welcomed by merger almost all congregations of the Holiness Movement Church of Canada. The increased membership resulting from this influx will surely make for greater vigor and independence in the future. Here is the account of these twentieth-century instruments, the means by which the battle in Canada has been and can continue to be fought more effectively.

1.
A CANADIAN HIGH COMMAND

During the forty-year interval from 1880 to 1920, the original Canada Conference of thirteen circuits had multiplied into four conferences of ninety-one circuits, an increase of 700 per cent, while the original membership of 324 had swollen to 2,614, an increase of over 800 per cent. But the Canadian work was not yet consolidated nor sufficiently nationalized. By 1920 it seemed time to act.

For the first time since Western Canada had decided to "go it alone" in 1906, the Sarnia Convention of 1920 brought together representatives from all four conferences. After a period of correspondence between conference leaders, it had been called to consider matters of special interest to Free Methodists in Canada.[1] The annual conferences in the summer of 1920 named their delegates: A. Sims, E. Snyder, C. V. Fairbairn, George

Fuller Sr., D. E. Smith from East Ontario; J. M. Eagle, D. Allan, W. J. Cowherd, W. F. DeMille, G. A. Lees from West Ontario; F. M. Wees, R. H. Hamilton, W. H. Brown from Saskatchewan; H. B. Luck (unofficial) from Alberta. Mr. Luck, F. C. Wilson, and Nellie Whittaker (all of Alberta) were made honorary members. The group met in the Sarnia Church Oct. 13-17. A. Sims, the last surviving member of the first Canada Conference at Galt, forty years previously in 1880, was named chairman. J. M. Eagle, who had called the meeting to order, became secretary.

Nineteen petitions and memorials were drawn up and presented. Only the most significant are summarized here:

1. That steps be taken to secure a Canadian Executive Board consisting of one elder and one layman from each annual conference to care for Finance, Education and Evangelism and that a bishop be invited to preside at the annual sessions. (This was all subject to the approval of General Conference with arrangements made for a provisional board temporarily.)

2. That steps be taken toward securing a Canadian school.

3. That a committee be appointed of two members from each conference to arrange for the drafting and passage of a Dominion Act of Incorporation.

4. That arrangements be made for an evangelistic party to work under the direction of the Canadian Executive Board.

5. That the General Conference be petitioned to make such changes in the constitution as will permit the Canadian Executive Board to elect its own Treasurer, and retain in Canada all funds except Bishops' salaries, General Conference expenses and Foreign Missions. (This, since "our people . . . have already sent . . . thousands of dollars out of their country . . . whereas a vast tract . . . is yet untouched . . . and many of our towns and cities are not entered because of a lack of funds.")

Delegates to first all-Canada Convention at Sarnia, Oct. 1920. Back Row—W. A. Brown, F. M. Wees, Eugene Smith, David Allan, H. B. Luck, W. C. Cowherd, Wm. DeMille, Emerson Snider. Front Row—Geo. Fuller Sr., A. Sims, Geo. Lees, R. H. Hamilton, J. M. Eagle, C. V. Fairbairn.

6. That the General Conference Executive Committee be requested to establish a branch publishing house in Winnipeg or Toronto. Failing this, the Canadian Executive Board should be empowered to establish a Canadian book room.

7. That a custodian of Canadian records and significant photos be appointed, these to be held "until such time as a history of Canadian Free Methodism shall be written."

The Provisional Executive Board was set up with the following names appearing on it Sims, Smith; Eagle, Lees; Hamilton, Brown; Luck, Wilson. Mr. Sims, Mr. Eagle, and Mr. Lees were made chairman, secretary and treasurer, respectively.[2] The latter three were named a committee to locate a site for a school. The whole board was authorized to act as a Board of Education and a Board of Evangelism and Home Mission. Mr. Sims was appointed custodian of historical data.

An evangelistic service was held each evening. Preachers, in order, at these services from Wednesday to Sunday were R. H. Hamilton, E. Snyder, W. Zurbrigg, C. V. Fairbairn, and H. B. Luck, with A. Sims speaking Sunday morning. People were seeking and finding the Lord at each service. C. V. Fairbairn, who had been a Free Methodist for only two years now, reported on the religious services and wrote: "We have attended many conferences, conventions and assemblies of the saints . . . but we fail to recall one on which God so manifestly set His seal as He did on the All-Canadian Free Methodist Convention held at Sarnia . . . God was in it from beginning to end."

A. Sims, the chairman, edited a thirty-page booklet on the proceedings of the convention calling it *Free Methodism in Canada*. Several bonus features were added in the booklet: an essay, "Who Are the Free Methodists"; details of the first Canada Conference of 1880; appointments of the four conferences of 1920; some 1920 statistics; a list of the six Canadian foreign missionaries at the time (Appleton, Ryding, Davy, Winans, Haley and Haley); and a paragraph on the Canadian church's healthy progress over the first forty years.

Some follow-up decisions and activities growing out of the convention should now be noted. At the General Conference of 1923 the request to hold certain budget funds in Canada was granted and provision was made for a permanent Executive Board with its own treasurer. The Board would care for the budget funds, Canadian Conference Claims and other matters of a purely Canadian nature. The Canadian Board was granted $2,000 to start a Superannuate Permanent Fund. Meanwhile, Alberta decided temporarily to remain out of the Canadian Executive Board.[3] Saskatchewan decided, because of distance, not to share in establishing a school. Mr. Sims was soon busy with an appeal in a November *Free Methodist* for items for that some-day-to-be-written history.

The Executive Board has numerous later achievements to its credit. The story of launching a Canadian magazine in 1922, of securing a Federal

STRATEGIC TWENTIETH-CENTURY INSTRUMENTS OF WAR

Act of Incorporation in 1927, and of receiving by merger the Holiness Movement Church in 1959—these are all of such significance that individual chapters have been written on them. A chapter appears on the establishing and developing of two schools, but these were really conference projects.

The Executive Board has through the years handled the superannuate program for ministers. Prior to the annual conferences of 1936, a new plan, related to Dominion Government Annuities, was developed but failed to get the necessary approval. In 1937 the Board adopted another plan that had been suggested by some of the conferences. Under it, each minister paid $5.00 per year into the fund and the full claim was $300—that after thirty years of recognized service.

By 1948, the number of superannuates and dependents of deceased ministers had increased until the plan was inadequate to care for its responsibilities. At this time the maximum claim was raised to $360 per year and the minister's contribution raised to $10.00 annually. Also the Board launched a campaign to raise $10,000 to augment the fund. George Fuller, Jr. was appointed Canadian Field Secretary of Superannuates to spearhead the drive. It was so successful that $12,000 resulted.

Another change was made in 1955 when each participating minister was required to contribute to the fund one per cent of his salary. (This was changed the following year to read, salary and other income as reported to annual conference.) At this time the amount collected for the Superannuate Fund, through the Canadian Service Fund, was increased to $3.00 per member.[4] Two significant changes were made in 1958: the maximum claim was raised to $560 and the name was changed to Ministers' Pension Fund.

During World War II, the Executive Board established a Canadian Church Council for Men in Service. Rev. E. A. Cooper, as director, gave outstanding service.

More recently, a scholarship plan has been set up to aid Canadian students attending John Wesley Seminary Foundation.

Sponsored by the Executive Board, an All-Canadian Convention was held in Toronto, November 12, 1947, one day prior to the Annual Meeting. All four Canadian conferences were represented. Matters given special study at that time were: The Superannuate Plan, Finances, Home Missions and Evangelism, and a Home for the Aged.

Following the securing of a new Federal Charter in 1959 (this charter made necessary because of the Holiness Movement merger), the Canadian Executive Board at its annual August meeting in Toronto, appointed a committee to prepare a draft of a constitution and by-laws for the Board to operate under. Dr. C. A. Watson, a Los Angeles attorney and secretary of the General Conference, rendered valuable service in the preparation of such a document.[5] This was formally adopted by the Directors of the Board, on December 7, 1959, subject to ratification by a majority of the Canadian conferences at their 1960 sessions and the next meeting of the

Canadian Executive Board. Basically this constitution is patterned after the Constitution of the Free Methodist Church of North America. The by-laws may be amended at any annual meeting by a majority vote of those present and voting, except as to the matter of conference representation and the manner of their election. Changes here can only be made when approved by a majority of the annual conferences.

Article X of the by-laws reads as follows: "The Ecclesiastical affairs of the Board shall be governed by the Discipline of the Free Methodist Church of North America, except as to those matters reserved to the Canadian Executive Board and the Canadian Conferences, and such matters as have not been specifically delegated by the Canadian Executive Board and Canadian conferences to the Free Methodist Church of North America and its Board of Administration, in so far as the same are not inconsistent to the laws of Canada, the Articles of Incorporation as enacted by Parliament of Canada or the Constitution and by-laws of this Board." This statement is considered very significant.

Both the old charter of 1927 and the new one of 1959 give the Free Methodist Church in Canada full powers to set up and hold its own General Conference anytime it may become necessary or advisable. Headquarters for the Canadian Executive Board is at Lorne Park College, Port Credit, Ontario.

Members of the Canadian Executive Board are elected for a four-year term, by ballot, by the annual conferences. Each annual conference is entitled to elect one ordained elder and one layman to the Board. When a conference reaches eight hundred full members it may elect two of each, and shall be entitled to an additional ministerial and lay delegate for every subsequent six hundred full members. The Directors of the Executive Board are elected by the Board, from its own number, at its annual meeting.

The following composed the personnel of the Board in 1959: East Ontario—L. C. Ball (President),[6] R. L. Casement (Secretary), Bruce Reid, George Fuller, A. B. Moffatt, L. F. Warren, C. W. Reynolds, Ritchie Wells; West Ontario—L. A. Freeman (Treasurer), J. A. Robb, G. W. Stevens, T. M. Wilson; Saskatchewan—G. S. Jenner, Burton Hamilton; Alberta—F. W. Coxson, George Wolfe.

The three officers with Mr. Jenner comprise the Directors. Presidents before Mr. Ball have included Albert Sims, William Zurbrigg, R. H. Hamilton, and J. A. Robb.

While the 1920 ideal of a Canadian book room has never been realized as visualized, the decision to release this history under the trade name of Sage Publishers marks a forward step in literature distribution. What happens with regard to handling or even publishing other books or supplies under this fitting label will doubtless depend on popular demand.

---

1. One factor that spurred the agitation for a Canadian Executive Board was a decision of the 1919 General Conference to launch throughout the church a General Budget that would provide money for education, charities, missions and evangelism. Of

STRATEGIC TWENTIETH-CENTURY INSTRUMENTS OF WAR

the $2,000,000 required, Canada's portion, based on membership, would be $114,000.

2. This board was to be subject to the approval of the several annual conferences in 1921, awaiting the final approval of the General Conference of 1923.

3. Alberta stayed out till 1948 at which time C. E. Coxson and G. F. Shay became members. Since then there has been continued co-operation. Perhaps the American background of so many early Albertan Free Methodists made it difficult for them to think nationally in their new homeland.

4. The Canadian Service Fund is an annual assessment to the circuits based on the local membership.

5. Dr. Watson's larger assistance in working out details of the merger are dealt with in the "Reinforcements" chapter.

6. Rev. L. C. Ball gave substantial and greatly appreciated help in the development of this chapter.

2.

A NATIONAL LINE OF COMMUNICATION

No mention of a coming Canadian magazine appears in the Sarnia Convention report, but the Provisional Canadian Executive Board formed there in 1920 was soon thinking magazinewise. On November 1, 1922, even before that board was made permanent by General Conference, Volume I, No. 1 of the eight-page monthly *Canadian Free Methodist Herald* was out, edited by R. H. Hamilton of Moose Jaw.

An editorial on page 1 told of the conviction that "the interests of God's work in Canada demanded a monthly periodical of our own devoted to matters of spiritual interests." Some of its specific aims were mentioned: to keep the people in touch with a Bible Training School and Seminary soon to be established, to help the conferences co-operate in opening up missions in needy parts of Canada yet "untouched by our Holiness workers," to help dispel prejudice that Free Methodism is "an American Church," to provide a Canadian channel to "open doors of service before us," to encourage our people to "use their pens and give expression to truth." The article appealed for "one thousand subscribers at once" and for manuscripts. Young people might write "letters, testimonies, reports or articles on various themes (go easy on poetry)." Pastors, district elders, "capable laymen," "our dear missionaries"—all were encouraged to write.

Apart from the news published, much wholesome material was always present. Among interesting articles in that first issue were ones entitled "The Unity of Canadian Free Methodism," "The Canadian School," and "Do Your Own Thinking." This latter one included a humorous Sam Walter Foss poem telling how the wandering homeward woodland trail of a calf grew to a beaten human path, because of the ease of being a follower.

R. H. Hamilton, aided much by his talented wife, edited the paper for twenty-five years. In completing the thirteenth annual volume in 1935, he wrote: "It is scarcely thinkable that you have continued me in the editorial office all these years. Our first thought was that if we could carry the paper over for the first year we would then, without doubt, be relieved."

There was rich evidence that the paper he produced was meeting a real need as letters from the mission fields and the West sang its praises. It appears the early subscription goal had soon been reached but the trying depression years of the early thirties "cut deeply into the subscription list." Instead of a thousand subscribers as in the peak years the number dipped to about six hundred. It sagged at another time when some East Ontario voices began scattering seeds of no-need about their conference.

From 1947 until his death in 1951, Rev. F. A. Daw edited the "Herald" and heightened the reputation already established. He saw the subscription list increase by about one third.

Since 1951, Rev. R. B. Warren has carried the editorial responsibility. Circulation has continued to grow each year with a new peak in 1959 when *The Holiness Era* merged with it. It stands at over 3,000 now. In some early years the magazine had to be subsidized from the Executive Board funds. (In 1934-35, $120 was needed.) But for many years now, it has paid its way.

The *Canadian Free Methodist Herald* is intended to supplement rather than to supplant the church-wide *Free Methodist* published at Winona Lake, Indiana. As such, it is proving decidedly successful. It is no small responsibility to be Canada's only Methodist magazine, a distinction it has enjoyed for all but the first three years of its publication period.[1] It will surely fill an increasingly large place in the national life of the church in the years ahead.

---

1. The Methodist Church's *Christian Guardian* ceased with the formation of the United Church in Canada in 1925.

3.
A DOMINION GOVERNMENT CHARTER

Before the Dominion Charter was gained, several provincial charters had appeared.

The Canada Conference, we have seen, was organized in Ontario in 1880. By 1884 a Standing Committee on Incorporation (J. Craig, B. T. Roberts, R. Loveless, J. Eckardt, A. Sims, Wm. Stonehouse were the members) reported they had succeeded in getting a Bill of Incorporation through the Legislative Assembly of Ontario and had secured a "Model Deed."

Again after the division of 1895 with its creation of two Ontario conferences, new legislation was needed. Both conferences were incorporated provincially in March of 1897.

Eventually with Free Methodism established in several provinces the need for a Dominion Charter arose. That was obtained in the session of 1927. But what an effort it took!

Credit for the Bill's passing goes to persistent efforts of a Brethren in Christ Member of Parliament named Mr. A. M. Carmichael from Kindersley, Saskatchewan, along with the cooperation of Mr. Mackenzie King, then Prime Minister. The story which was largely supplied by Mr. Carmichael to a Mrs. M. E. Robinson who wrote it up for the *Herald* in August, 1927, runs like this:

A bill was introduced in 1924 but withdrawn. Another was introduced in 1926, reached second reading, then failed to pass. In 1927, upon invitation Mr. Carmichael consented to let the Bill go in under his name as a Private Bill. He was very friendly towards the Free Methodist Church because its Kindersley Mission had been of great spiritual help to members of his family.

The procedure for such a Private Bill was a complicated one. Only on certain days at certain hours would one be considered. A Private Bill had first to be advertised in certain papers, then a petition made to the House of Commons. It was carefully scrutinized by an examiner then introduced with first reading. After that, it was printed in both English and French and posted on the Members' files. After a set time it was given second reading, then was referred to the Private Bills Committee who reviewed every clause. If satisfactory, it returned to the House for detailed consideration by Committee of the Whole House. After third reading it might be finally passed. In the Senate, much the same procedure was followed again.

For Bill 177, as the Incorporation Act was called, there was considerable objection to the Articles of Religion, by the chairman of the Private Bills Committee who was a French Roman Catholic. But it eventually got by the Committee and to the House. Article 20 proved very objectionable to some members. Mr. Carmichael, after being advised by a cabinet minister that there was little hope of getting it through on account of certain wording, decided to leave out all the Articles of Religion and substitute a statement saying the Articles would be those contained in the latest Discipline on certain pages.

With Easter near and the customary rush to get the season ended, the Bill would surely have got pushed aside had not Mr. King listened to a plea of Mr. Carmichael and helped get an extension of time. It passed the final stages hastily, and in the Senate under the sponsorship of a Senator W. B. Willoughby of Moose Jaw carried unopposed. 'Tis said Mr. and Mrs. Carmichael spent a night in prayer for this Bill's success. The battle was the Lord's. God bless their memory!

After Bill 177 had passed, heated opposition developed denouncing its claimed insult and promising a petition to the government for the striking out of objectionable clauses in the incorporation papers. But the Bill stood.

In 1958, because of the Holiness Movement merger, a new Act of Incorporation was prepared. This was passed by Parliament in 1959. More details follow in a later chapter.

4.
REGIONAL TRAINING CENTRES

A. Lorne Park College

We have seen that the vision of a "salvation school" in Ontario came early, but lacked vitality then to materialize. We have noted the later revival of the school interest in the appointment at the 1920 Sarnia Convention of a committee to locate a school site and in the 1922 aim of the *Herald* to keep the people in touch with the coming school.

The 1921 Ontario annual conferences appointed committees to work together toward establishing a school and this joint committee first met in the "Old Broadview Church" on Nov. 15 of that same year. It included A. Sims, W. Zurbrigg, R. Burnham, W. J. Cowherd, J. W. Peach, Thomas Loveless, C. A. Prior, Geo. A. Lees, Wm. DeMille and W. D. Ferguson. Mr. Sims was made president, Mr. Peach secretary and Mr. Zurbrigg treasurer. They decided to establish a school in the area bounded by Toronto, Hamilton and Newmarket.

After visiting some prospective properties, the committee met at C. A. Prior's Toronto home on Dec. 7 and decided on a Taylor property northwest of Port Credit. It was purchased a little later for $21,250, a twenty-six-acre block with a large brick and stone building (a farm house and annex), a small stone house and an old barn. The Seventh Day Adventist people had earlier used it as a school campus before moving to Oshawa. And before that, it had been the old Shaver farm mentioned already.

We have noted, too, that Martha Stonehouse in 1889 left in her will $1,000 to assist worthy students preparing for the ministry in a Free Methodist school in Canada. This action was thirty-five years before Lorne Park began. It is said that her step-mother, who was to get the interest on the money while she lived, died the year Lorne Park opened.

School opened Sept. 16, 1924, with James F. Gregory as principal and Miss Alice Walls as assistant, J. M. Eagle being financial agent and president of the twelve-man Board. Mr. Gregory was newly wed at the time and newly graduated from Greenville, although with teaching experience in Ontario schools. A special convocation, to which two hundred visitors came, marked the opening. Rev. B. W. Huckabee, Rev. C. V. Fairbairn and Rev. Geo. Mitchell all participated. There were twenty-five students that first year with a jump to fifty-two the second.[1]

In 1927 the school's name which had been Lorne Park Seminary was changed to Lorne Park College following the discovery that Protestants in Canada seldom used the term Seminary. In 1928 Lorne Park was incorporated under a Provincial Charter.

To keep the Lorne Park story intact, we now bring it up to the present. The next four paragraphs are quoted almost verbatim from a manuscript contributed by Rev. Lorne Ball who has been closely associated with the school for many years.

First Ministers' Conference, Easter Week, 1926. Bishop Pearce and Doctor Wiseman were guests.

"In the year 1925 a frame house was erected which has been used across the years for staff and students. For many years both boys and girls were housed in the main school building, and most of the staff lived in the same building. The early years were characterized by water shortages, and an effort (not always successful) to make the land pay off by growing general farm produce and keeping cows, pigs, chickens and horses. In October 1948 it was decided to sell the horses, harness and hay. For a number of years after Mr. Eagle's period, Wm. Zurbrigg served the school as financial agent and farm manager. Mrs. Zurbrigg rendered many years of service as chief cook for the school.

Crowded conditions made it necessary in 1944 to turn a four-car garage into a boy's dormitory, but during Christmas vacation time of that year, this building burned to the ground. (No lives were lost and the building itself was covered by insurance.) This forced immediate action in securing accommodations,

Original Lorne Park building

Part of school family the first year.

225

THE BATTLE WAS THE LORD'S

and a large brick home with about two acres of land was bought for $11,500 on what is the present campus. Dalton Kirk was principal at the time, and F. J. Jones, business manager. Soon after, it was thought best to gradually move the entire operation to the south side of the newly constructed Queen Elizabeth Highway. An adjoining ten acres of land was purchased for $10,000, and a little later another one and one-half acres was bought for $1,500 making a total south-side campus of thirteen and one-half acres.

Lorne Park family, 1941-42

J. F. Gregory Hall

The new Administration Building had its beginning with a sod-breaking ceremony at the Easter-time Ministerial Conference of 1954. Bishop C. V. Fairbairn laid the cornerstone at the Annual L.P.C. day, May 24, 1954. This building cost a total of $166,443.72 (without furnishings), and was opened for classes in September of 1955. (K. Lavern Snider was principal during the construction, and L. C. Ball, business manager.) At the Annual Lorne Park Day in 1957 this building was officially named J. F. Gregory Hall and, appropriately, Dr. Gregory was the guest speaker for the day.

On the present campus, the principal's house was built in 1948 while Rev. R. B. Warren was principal. In 1949 a duplex cottage was built, primarily for married students. In 1952 a bungalow was built with L. C. Ball, business manager and field representative, being the first occupant. In the summer of 1957, two large nearby houses were purchased from the Department of Highways for $525 and moved onto their present sites for staff houses. These are each two-family dwellings.

The sale of lots on the northside property up to 1955 netted almost $70,000, and a recent sale to the Department of Highways of the remaining north-side assets has brought in another $55,000.[2] Besides this, the Department of Highways in 1957 paid $11,500 for a strip of land along the edge of the south-side property on which to build a service road for the Queen Elizabeth Highway. A new dormitory is already begun, its name to be Annesley Hall in appreciation of a promised grant from the sale funds of the former Holiness Movement Annesley College in Ottawa.

The present campus has in its favour a central location, an abundance of water (both natural and piped), first-class transportation facilities by bus and train, and excellent work opportunities for students.

Lorne Park has been characterized by frequent changes in principals, staff, business personnel and board members—perhaps too frequent for a strong, continuing program. James F. Gregory served as principal for eight years.[3] He was succeeded by the following people in the order named: Alice Walls, Herbert Linstead, Alice Walls, Harold Loveless, Alice Walls, Dalton Kirk, R. B. Warren,[4] K. L. Snider, J. Leon Winslow (first president), C. H. Zahniser and Byron Withenshaw.

This next list includes most of those who have been regular assistant teachers at some time in the past, the names arranged roughly in order of their beginning of service: Fredrea Gregory, Olive Hicks, G. A. Mitchell, Ethel Fletcher Chase, Lillie Walker, Lottie Anderson, Leila Fletcher, Harold Loveless, Herbert Linstead, Olive Teal, Alice Kirk Linstead, Peter Wiseman, Dalton Kirk, R. B. Warren, Wymund Kirk, Ronald Bock, Grace Bock, Ruth Cresswell, Ruth Cooper, Edith Goldthorpe, Irene Lockie, Ella Lishman, John Sigsworth, Kenneth Seale, Irene Kirk, H. M. Fletcher, Elmira Webb Freeman, Alice Burleigh Foley, Donald Bastian, Mary Irwin, J. L. Wheeler, Evelyn Moffett, Miss B. Major, Grace Smith, K. L. Snider, Lois Snider, Harry Swallow, Eldon Kay, Marion Bright, Florence Pickert, Mary Wallace, J. Leon Winslow, Violet Campbell, Garnet Dickinson,

THE BATTLE WAS THE LORD'S

Hazel Hamilton, Marvin Munshaw, Norma Smart, Ellen Winslow, John Knott.

These teachers make up the present staff of 1959-60 under President Byron Withenshaw: Charles Grandfield, Wilson Stein, Jay Stein, Melville Elliott, John McFarlane, Douglas Wilson, Fred Jobson, Magdalena Banning, Edward Davis, and Irene Lockie.

Looking after money matters and related interests, these men, at least, have served as financial agent, farm manager, business manager, field representative, or public relations director, or with some combination of these responsibilities: M. S. Benn,[5] J. M. Eagle, W. Zurbrigg, F. J. Jones, Donald Bastian, L. C. Ball, Harold McNutt, Francis Casement, and R. C. McCallum.

These men have sat on the Board itself, directing the program through the years:

East Ontario—Rev. M. S. Benn, Rev. Wm. Zurbrigg, Rev. R. Burnham, Thomas Loveless, Joseph Arksey, Wm. Goodbury, J. Clark Swart, Rev. C. V. Fairbairn, W. R. Aylesworth, C. A. Scott, W. W. Wrightman, Rev. E. J. Lee, Geo. Fuller, Sr., Rev. W. H. Gregory, John A. Ball, John Tidball, W. N. Ireland, Rev. F. J. Jones, H. M. Wilkins, W. L. Smith, Rev. L. C. Ball, Geo. Fuller, Jr., Rev. C. W. Kay, Frank Barkey, Rev. R. G. Babcock, Leslie Clark, Rev. D. S. Wartman, Rev. A. B. Moffatt, Ritchie Wells, Rev. W. J. T. Hicks, Rev. R. B. Warren, Eldon Kay, Rev. W. J. Stonehouse.

Early Lorne Park Board: Back Row—Joseph Arksey, J. W. Peach, Geo. Lees, J. Clark Swart, Wm. DeMille. Front Row—Thomas Loveless, M. S. Benn, J. M. Eagle, R. Burnham, Wm. Zurbrigg.

West Ontario—Rev. J. M. Eagle, Rev. W. J. Cowherd, Rev. J. W. Peach, Geo. A. Lees, W. D. Ferguson, W. E. DeMille, Rev. E. A. DeMille, Wellington Hamilton, Rev. D. McGugan, Delmar Ecker, Rev. P. K. Smith, James Freeman, Gordon Vance, Rev. R. H. Hamilton, Rev. C. E. L. Walls, L. A. Freeman, Morley Wilson, Rev. G. W. Stevens, Ernest Campbell, Rev. W. H. Hobbs, W. D. Brown, Rev. R. C. McCallum, Irvine Martin, Rev. B. Withenshaw, Rev. W. C. Cowherd, Merlin Coates, F. E. Lees, Rev. J. A. Robb.

Mr. L. A. Freeman currently serves as president of the Board and has done so for some years.

From the first, Lorne Park has been a combination high school and Bible training centre. (For several early years elementary education was given too under Mrs. Gregory.) For some time now, high school work up to and including grade thirteen has been offered. The Bible program at the Junior College level prepares academically for ordination. Several senior church colleges in the United States will recognize up to two years of work from Lorne Park-trained students. A B.Th. degree is in planning.

In 1945, with twenty years of history behind it, J. F. Gregory wrote of Lorne Park:

"The school has had two main objectives, the education of young men and women for the Christian ministry, and the education of high school students in a thoroughly Christian environment. The accomplishment of the first objective may be seen in well trained ministers, and ministers' wives, in all our Canadian conferences, and in missionaries now serving in China and Africa. Those of us who have had a share in the training of these men and women watch the extensive growth of Lorne Park's influence with warm hearts, and all others who have helped to build and

Lorne Park Board with Principal and Business Manager at time of building Gregory Hall
(Frank Barkey and Geo. Fuller absent)

maintain this school must feel how profitable is their investment. No less has been the returns from the hundreds of young people of secondary school age who have not only found knowledge and training for life here, but through Christian experience have found the power to do that which is right. These have made their influence felt as leaders in Free Methodist Churches on every district."

Hundreds who have gone there since have been blessed and made a blessing around the world. A large portion of those who, in recent decades, have served there were once students. If, as many discerning people believe, a church's future is wrapped up in the character of its schools, Ontario Free Methodists must insist that Lorne Park's standards of leadership, scholarship, discipleship, and idealism are high ones, and must furnish the funds to make its necessary ministry possible.

B. Moose Jaw Bible College

In the early days of Lorne Park College, numbers of young people from Western Canada made the long costly trip east for either high school or Bible work. A few went to the United States. Some followed another unsatisfactory course—attendance at schools of a different theological persuasion. In Saskatchewan the conviction grew that a Wesleyan Bible school was imperative and the conference of 1937 set up a planning committee composed of Burton Hamilton, H. Whiting, Marian Walrath and J. Kelt, with Rev. C. B. Garratt as chairman.

Two years passed with no school in sight. Then some forty or fifty young people, confident it was coming but anxious to speed up matters, decided on a very unorthodox means of getting action. Into a conference session just after recess they disturbingly trooped, singing a parody composed for the occasion: "I Know the Lord Will Send a Bible School." Bishop Fairbairn gave them a hearing and the outcome was a new committee, with a member from each of the larger centres to look for a suitable building.

This group got busy. D. S. Wartman, its chairman as well as Moose Jaw pastor and local district elder, found during the year a promising sixteen-room brick house in his city. He summoned the committee. They liked its location on University Heights overlooking the city, river valley and parks; they prayed about it on the spot; and they bought it at a bargain price. Happily, by then the generous bequest from the William Franks estate was available to the conference for just such a need. It was fitting that the building was named Franks Memorial Hall.

The Wartmans, with help, speedily fixed up classrooms and secured the needed furnishings. Fifteen students had already enrolled, but one important element was lacking: teachers. A special prayer meeting around the Moose Jaw church altar was quickly answered by the securing of two Cleveland Bible College graduates—Miss Florence Pickert to be principal, and

Photo at left: Lorne Park family, 1953-54

Miss Della Holdsworth (later Mrs. Lightle) to be assistant. Both had the Bachelor of Theology degree. It is evident these ladies did not come for money, for salaries were set at $20 per month each, plus board and room. Mr. and Mrs. Wartman moved into the school too, and for six years, besides carrying on their church and conference duties, gave their services as business manager, preceptress and secretary—this in exchange for room and board.

The school opened November 1, 1940, with an impressive curriculum and has continued since with growing strength and effectiveness. A three-year Diploma Course has been the regular offering, but a one-year Christian Workers' Course has also been provided. It is said that after eight years of operation, half of the Saskatchewan appointments were pastored by ordained graduates of Moose Jaw. Besides, some were serving in the Alberta Conference or making better laymen locally. Some graduates since have continued to Seattle Pacific College, Greenville College and John Wesley Seminary, most to return to their home conference. By 1954 about seventy-five young people had completed the regular course, and as many more had taken a partial course. Others from out of town had lived at the college, taking advantage of its Christian environment, while attending the local high school.

In 1959 the program was extended to offer also a Bachelor of Theology degree which includes all work needed for Elder's Ordination and entrance to seminary.

Miss Pickert gave strong leadership till 1947, when she resigned as principal in favour of mission service. M. C. Miller, Wilfred Kinney, and L. A. Smith each held the office for a time. In 1957, when Rev. L. A. Smith[6] was in charge, the title of the college head was changed to presi-

Class of 1942-43. All nine students of back row were in first graduating class

dent.[7] Since 1958, Rev. J. Wesley Stewart has filled the office. He is a son of Rev. C. P. Stewart, a veteran Western Canada pastor already familiar to the reader. Present assistants on the faculty include Paul Buffam, Verna Gray, Zella Nixon, Vera Forrest, and Doreen Flesher.

Other earlier assistants through the years (besides Miss Holdsworth), included Miss Hublard, Helen Markell, Cecil Driscoll, Elaine Walrath, Verna Smith, Bernice Tanner, Wilfred Kinney, Glen Buffam, Eunice Buffam, Eileen Moore, Alice McDonald, Mrs. Laura Buffam, Douglas Walrath, Elnora Hunter, Lillian Plum, and Dorothy Smith.

The present eleven-man Board is composed of Hugh Alexander, E. H. Childerhouse, Lyle Garratt, Mel Hammond, George Harriman, Harold Lees, H. Meeds, Douglas Russell, and J. L. Walrath Sr., with G. S. Jenner and J. L. Walrath as chairman and secretary respectively. There is now representation in the group from both the Alberta Conference and the former Holiness Movement Church.

Saskatchewan people who served on earlier Boards included Leonard Rusk, A. A. Buffam, P. B. Holmgren, Burton Hamilton, Margaret Wartman, Elsie Hindmarsh, D. S. Wartman, Margaret Miller, Harold Riddell, J. A. Tanner, L. Henwood, Walter Cooke, W. Kinney, J. E. R. Greenshields, J. D. Kennedy.

Building changes have occurred through the years too. In 1947, a building across the street from the main one was purchased. This annex was used as principal's residence, girl's dormitory, library and reception room.

Sod turning ceremony, July, 1954, for new annex building. Bishop L. R. Marston, Trustee P. B. Holmgren, Principal W. Kinney, Trustee L. Henwood, Trustee W. Cooke, Trustee G. S. Jenner.

Franks Hall and new annex building

In 1953 it was sold in favour of centralization and planned enlargement on the main thirteen-acre campus. In the summer of 1954 Bishop Marston participated in a sod-turning ceremony for a new three-floor 32' x 62' school building. Though constructed largely with volunteer labour and on a pay-as-you-go basis, it is now completed and in use.

Moose Jaw is already studying further expansion through a recently appointed ten-year planning committee. Needed especially are more living quarters, an assembly hall, a gymnasium, and a president's residence.

With the recent closing of the Holiness Bible College in Winnipeg, Moose Jaw inherited a quantity of furniture, about 1,700 books, and some extra students. Yearly payments from the proceeds of the sale of the Winnipeg building are also planned.

Moose Jaw Bible College has made a creditable beginning in her two short decades. With a continuing objective of "quality before quantity," it looks as if she is destined to play an increasingly significant role in the perpetuation of Free Methodism in Western Canada.

Note—Apart from taking training in our own national schools, numerous Canadian students still cross the border for further study in one of the church's several degree colleges including the John Wesley Seminary Foundation (affiliated with Asbury Seminary) which offers graduate degrees in theology.

---

1. Among those first year students were Philo Chase, Crawford Cowherd, and Herbert Linstead who are all ministers today.
2. Much credit for this sale goes to Dr. C. H. Zahniser, president of the college at the time.
3. Dr. Gregory reports he was also full-time teacher, bookkeeper, secretary, treasurer for budget, dean or proctor of boys, supervisor of student labour and pastor.

Faculty and graduating class of 1959

STRATEGIC TWENTIETH-CENTURY INSTRUMENTS OF WAR

"I did anything that needed to be done," he says, adding that he also "built roads, dug ditches, repaired water pumps, cleaned cesspools, planted trees, skated with the students, went toboggan-riding and snowshoeing, prayed with the students, counseled, did much field work, covered the camp meetings and conferences in the summer, and had time for a few mistakes." The wonder is that he lasted eight years.

4. For one year during Mr. Warren's principalship, 100 per cent of all Grade thirteen papers written were passed, and many with honours. This was a provincial record.

5. Mr. Benn as Financial Agent did an excellent short-term piece of money-raising even before the school opened and on a part-time basis.

6. Mr. Smith was born in South Africa, the son of Free Methodist missionary Nathaniel B. Smith.

7. About the same time the words Bible College replaced Bible School in the name of the institution. Work then offered was considered to be at college level.

5.
PERMANENT CAMPS

We have seen how Methodism's camp meeting was copied by Free Methodism and played a significant part in the church's Canadian growth. We have seen that the locale for early camps tended to move from year to year. Slowly since 1900 the trend has been towards church-owned properties with buildings added. This chapter will relate what has happened in each conference and in some cases on each district.

East Ontario Conference—Kingston District folk have met annually since about 1944 at their Light and Life Campground near Glenvale on No. 38 Highway, ten miles north of Kingston.[1] The present huge cement block tabernacle, built in 1952 under the supervision of Stanley Donnell of the Kingston society, will hold 1,000 people. The property was owned formerly by Herbert Curl of the Harrowsmith society. With a fine dining hall, twenty cottages, about fifty motel rooms, a W.M.S. chapel and a water-pressure system, the ten-acre property is said to be worth approximately $80,000.

Light and Life Camp Tabernacle under construction

Before moving to this site the district camp for several years was near Harrowsmith on Joseph Storms' farm, and named, by Rev. C. V. Fairbairn, Ebenezer Park. Verona area had some of the earliest camps with others later at such places as Odessa, Wilton and Elginburg. An F.M.Y. camp property for the conference now exists on the Kingston District. (See details later.)

The Peterborough District camp is now located at Orland on No. 30 Highway, seven miles north of Brighton. The grove of pine-surrounded maples was bought in 1946. It has four motels, twenty or more cottages, a large dining hall, and a permanent tabernacle built in 1959. The property with its water-pressure system is worth perhaps $70,000. Earlier camps had been held at Picton, Warkworth, Frankford and other centres. A C.Y.C. camp for several districts is held at Orland annually in August.

The Toronto District camp called Pine Orchard is a ten-acre lot six miles east of Newmarket. It has been in use since 1947 and is now equipped with a 50' x 100' tabernacle, a dining hall, two dormitories with twenty rooms, fifty cottages, a prayer chapel and water-pressure system. The district property, apart from the many personally owned cottages, is worth at least $25,000. A lot near Holland Landing was used for seven years before 1947, while earlier camp meetings were scattered about the district at such places at Ravenshoe, Baldwin, Toronto, Armadale, Uxbridge and Belhaven.

Muskoka District people since 1950 have had a permanent ten and one-half-acre camp at rustic Severn Bridge only a few rods away from No. 11 Highway leading from Toronto to North Bay. Here again there is a permanent tabernacle that seats four hundred, besides adequate dining and sleeping facilities. Recently an industrial firm donated two C.Y.C. units where boys and girls, a dozen of each, can stay. Some cottages are privately owned. The district property is valued at about $12,000. Muskoka's camp meeting before 1952 moved from place to place, almost every circuit getting a turn at some time. The last location before going permanent was on the William Goheen farm at Housey's Rapids.

West Ontario Conference—Except for the two smaller more westerly districts, there is now one camp for the whole conference. The ground, a nineteen-acre block on the No. 2 Highway near Thamesford, was bought about 1944 for $1,800. As presently developed, the camp is considered worth $125,000 and operates under a Provincial Charter. Facilities include a large tabernacle, a children's chapel, a dining hall, a store, a refrigeration unit, washrooms with septic tanks, C.Y.C. dormitories, about a dozen special cabins, and another one hundred cabins owned by individuals on leased lots. The summer annual conference is now always held here just before the main week of the summer camp. Before this present property was purchased, conference camps were held for some years in a beautiful donated grove on the Edward Mudford farm near Walsingham. The 1934 gathering here with evangelist Elmer McKay was rated one of West Ontario's greatest. There are records earlier still of camps at such places as Charlemont, Zion, Middlemiss, Norwich, Kelvin and Niagara Falls.

Although some early camps were at other island locations such as Marksville, the Sault Ste. Marie District has for more than thirty years now had its camp on a portion of the St. Joseph Island church property, now a lovely second-growth maple grove. In 1958 a permanent tabernacle was built on this hill-top location by the pastor, John Knoll. About a dozen cabins and a dining hall have been added.

The Lake Superior District owns a whole eighty-acre block on the Trans-Canada Highway between Fort William and Hymers and about a mile from the scenic village of Kakabeka Falls. The front twenty-five acres is covered with Jack-pine, despite enough timber being taken off the lot earlier to pay for it. The camp here, one of the newest, has a dining hall and about a dozen cabins, but a canvas tabernacle is still used for a place of worship. This district has had camps since 1918, the first being held near Slate River when Rev. David Allan was superintendent. The present property was bought in 1952 during the superintendency of Rev. Ross Lloyd.

Saskatchewan Conference—Groves suitable for camp grounds are scarce in many parts of Saskatchewan but in 1919 a beautiful grove on the Moose Jaw River near Moose Jaw was "discovered" by R. E. Slingerland and was soon secured as a permanent conference camp. Since then this camp has been developed to a high degree with approximately fifty cabins. The permanent tabernacle was built in the early 1940's under D. S. Wartman, Conference Superintendent. It is used for the annual conference as well, with the two meetings running consecutively. Negotiations for the purchase of a second property will be described in a later chapter.

Alberta Conference—Alberta has had one central camp at Alix since 1931. The nine-acre property contains a 60' x 60' tabernacle, a dining hall with dormitory above and kitchen with built-in freezer below, and numerous other dormitory rooms and cabins. Many of the cabins are privately owned. The district parsonage and the local parsonage are both on the same property. Before the permanent spot was bought, camps had been held at such places as Clyde, Bashaw, Ponoka, and Lacombe.

On *British Columbia's* Interior District, Grindrod is now the home of a permanent camp. A beautiful tabernacle was recently built on the grounds. Early camps were held at Kelowna, Penticton, Vernon, Enderby and West Summerland. The Coast District has no camp of its own.

Note—Mention will be made later of four additional campgrounds resulting from the merger. Three are in eastern Ontario and one in Manitoba.

---

1. C. W. Reynolds ranks the 1953 camp here (with M. E. Andrews as evangelist and the Wilson Trio as singers) the best to date. Blessing and conviction were extraordinary. Unsaved observers stood on seats to watch altar developments.

6.
WELCOME REINFORCEMENTS

On January 1, 1959, the merger of the Holiness Movement Church in Canada into the Free Methodist Church in Canada became effective and a Private Bill at the spring session of Parliament provided for the necessary changes in the Act of Incorporation.[1] A Proclamation of the merger was made to all Free Methodist churches throughout the world on March 22 and read in part: "It is an occasion for great rejoicing that these churches of like precious faith have thus attained organic union."

Thoughts of some such action had been entertained for years. As early as 1953 there is a substantiated report of a secret ballot among the Holiness Movement people of the Eastern Conference to discover which holiness denomination they would prefer to affiliate with, should they feel it in their interest to approach any. The vote was strongly in favour of joining the Free Methodist Church. In September, 1957, the General Conference of the Holiness Movement Church meeting in Winnipeg went on record as favouring union, and in 1958 the annual conferences approved.

To understand the significance of this influx of reinforcements we need to review the history of the Holiness Movement Church and its status at the time of entry.

Ralph C. Horner, the founder, was born near Shawville, Quebec, and converted in 1872 at the age of seventeen at a Methodist Camp Meeting near his home. Two months later at another camp he was entirely sanctified.[2] He entered the ministry and was ordained in 1887 in the Montreal Conference. Even during his probationary period he carried on a very effective evangelistic ministry with emphasis on Wesleyan doctrine. While doing special evangelistic work on his first assignment at Shawville he took in 230 members. Soon church leaders became antagonistic and assigned him to a circuit. Ultimately, after tent campaigns continued, his name was dropped from the conference roll. That expulsion came in 1895.

Ralph C. Horner

With this turn of events Mr. Horner and some sympathetic workers organized at Ottawa the same year a "Wesleyan Connection." This work spread to Quebec, Manitoba, Saskatchewan, Alberta, British Columbia, New York State, Ireland, Australia, Egypt, Sudan, and China and eventually Hong Kong and Brazil. When incorporation was achieved in 1900, it was decided to change the name to the Holiness Movement Church in Canada. (The first bill to have it incorporated as the Wesleyan Methodist Connection of Canada or even the Christian Connection of Canada had been blocked in 1896 by Methodist pressure—this despite its 36 circuits, 1,090 members and 4,553 adherents.)

Mr. Horner was designated Bishop of the new church, later to be succeeded by Rev. A. T. Warren. About 1926 the term General Superintendent was adopted instead of Bishop, and, from then on, three such officials were to serve—one in Eastern Canada, one in Western Canada and one in Egypt. The superintendents in these fields at the time of merger were W. J. Stonehouse, E. H. Childerhose, and Norman E. Cooke, respectively.

Although an unfortunate split occurred in 1916 with the emergence of the Standard Church, the "Movement," as it was commonly called, continued to grow. To help ensure a trained ministry and missionary force, Annesley College flourished for years in Ottawa and another school in the West in various centres. The Holiness Bible College in Winnipeg operated in recent years until 1957. (This college has since united with Moose Jaw Bible College.)

Mission work received special emphasis. The first foreign work was in Egypt, begun in 1899 by Rev. Herbert Randall. By the time of merger this had expanded to the second largest Protestant mission in the country, a self-governing conference of 5,000 members in eighty churches. Most were in the Nile Valley with several in Cairo.[3] The mission work has included a girls' school and a training centre for ministerial students. It is noteworthy that the first new missionaries going to this field after the merger (they left in Sept. 1959) were Earle and Doreen (Babcock) Hawley, he a former Holiness Movement from Ottawa and she a Free Methodist from Verona.

During the days of Japanese aggression in China, Rev. and Mrs. Andrew Caswell became war casualties there (June 23, 1939), and Rev. William Dickson survived a bombing raid by jumping into a well where he remained in cold water until his rescue seven hours later. The Chinese Mission is still active in Hong Kong where Rev. Alton Gould is in charge. On invitation, he had already taken over the Free Methodist mission on the island after the aged Canadian missionary, I. S. W. Ryding died there in 1956. The new mission in Brazil, opened by Rev. and Mrs. M. A. Campbell, has recently been manned by Greenville-trained Roy Kenney and his wife. The church in Belfast, Ireland, became an appointment of the East Ontario Conference at the 1959 conference, but later the General Commission on Evangelism accepted Ireland as a church extension district.[4]

For many years a publishing program was centred in Ottawa with a book store, a Sunday School paper, and two magazines—the *Holiness Era* and the *Missionary Challenge*. In the merger Rev. Arthur Voteary, editor of the *Holiness Era*, was named associate editor of the *Canadian Free Methodist Herald*.

THE BATTLE WAS THE LORD'S

At Kingston church on October 7 and 8, 1958, a meeting of leaders of the two churches (including Free Methodist bishops and several other Board of Administration members) took place to work out details of the merger. Dr. Claude Watson acted as attorney. Heavily attended worship services were held in the evenings. Four Holiness Movement representatives attended the annual Board of Administration meeting in Winona Lake the following week. At a December meeting in Ottawa, with the help of Dr. Watson, a final agreement was made, approved and signed.

Personnel at the Kingston merger meeting in October, 1958. Kneeling: R. B. Warren, C. W. Kay, Murdo Campbell, R. Boston, B. S. Lamson, Hugh White, Roy Harrington, W. A. C. McFarlane. Standing, first row: J. S. Mitchell, Bishop W. S. Kendall, Bishop J. P. Taylor, E. H. Childerhose, Bishop C. V. Fairbairn, W. J. Stonehouse, Bishop L. R. Marston, W. A. McMillan, A. Wilkins. Second row: Asa Smith, Harry Hawley, H. Lees, R. L. Mainse, W. J. Parmerter, J. A. Robb, J. R. Woodland, R. L. Casement, A. S. Hill, Lloyd Warren, C. W. Reynolds, C. A. Watson, George Fuller.

It is gratifying that locations of numbers of the various new Free Methodist Churches arising from the merger are such as to fill in some of the previous geographical gaps in Canadian Free Methodism. The church can now be said to have a much greater national coverage. For instance, a better foothold now exists in Quebec (several churches in the Shawville area), while both northeastern Ontario and previously vacant parts of the West are represented. The large cities of Winnipeg and Ottawa now have established Free Methodist churches for the first time. Ottawa has two,

STRATEGIC TWENTIETH-CENTURY INSTRUMENTS OF WAR

in fact. Smiths Falls, with population 9,000, and Prescott, over half as large, are two eastern towns that now have churches. There are four extra campgrounds now—at Stittsville near Ottawa, at Cobden near Renfrew, at Shawville, Quebec, and at Killarney, Manitoba. This Killarney Camp has been continuous since 1896 (except for two years) and has had a permanent tabernacle for over fifty years. Killarney had Western Canada's first holiness camp meeting.

At its June, 1959, commencement program, Greenville College of Greenville, Ill., the church's senior degree college, awarded Mr. Stonehouse the honorary degree, Doctor of Divinity. The citation mentioned his work as pastor, superintendent, and chairman of the Holiness Movement Missionary Board and his leadership in effecting the merger. It read in part: "The recent merger . . . is in a large measure due to the vision and understanding of this man." President Long who conferred the degree said it was Greenville's way of welcoming not only the man, but the entire Holiness Movement Church into the merger. Rev. R. B. Warren, once a minister and teacher of the Holiness Movement Church received the Doctor of Literature degree at the same time for his work as edtior of the *Canadian Free Methodist Herald*, newspaper columnist, and author. His citation mentioned also service as liason officer in negotiations for the merger. There are many reasons to believe that the merger will be a healthy development for each communion involved.[5]

Note: This chapter should not close without at least a brief salute to the several Georgian Bay Gospel Workers congregations which with less fanfare recently became Free Methodist. See further details in the West Ontario portion of the chapter "Progress Across the Provinces."

---

1. The Bill, # S-27, was passed by the Senate on June 17 and received Royal Assent on July 9. It was kindly presented to the House by Mr. M. D. Morton, Member of Parliament for Davenport, Toronto, and introduced to the Senate by Honourable Senator Lambert. Technically the two churches merged with each other but continued under the name of The Free Methodist Church in Canada.
2. While taking his theological studies at Methodism's Victory College, 1883-85, Mr. Horner used to be a trial to his professors when he would look them in the eyes and ask them if they had this experience.
3. The Egyptian conference voted unanimously to become Free Methodists. There are probably 9,000 or 10,000 adherents in Egypt besides the 5,000 members.
4. At the August, 1959, East Ontario Conference, Rev. R. Boston, Sec. of the General Conference of the former Holiness Movement Church, was appointed to Belfast and a $1200 subscription taken to help build a new church there. That conference saw other ample evidence that God was blessing the merger.
5. Dr. H. W. Pointen, now pastor of Wesley United Church, Ottawa, who prepared a thesis in 1950 on *The Holiness Movement Church in Canada* for his Bachelor of Divinity degree at Victoria University was so impressed with Holiness Movement doctrine and standards of conduct and living that he wrote: "These characteristics associated with the Holiness Movement Church in Canada and written into the texture of their Discipline, might well become the norm for every branch of the Evangelical Church. Through the eyes of the world, it may appear a 'narrow way,' but it holds forth the assurance that it is the 'only way' to the abundant life."

Section 8:
Meaningful Twentieth-Century Milestones

Milestones were early associated with the military. The famous Appian Way leading from Ancient Rome and built for the rapid movement of troops had its milestone every "mille-passus" (thousand paces) to mark off the interval. Figuratively speaking, history has its milestones too—its anniversaries when a pause is in order to recall a movement's origins and to review its growth.

Five significant markers can be discerned dotting the roadsides as one retraces the course of Canadian Free Methodism in this century. The Hebrew fathers in Joshua's time were commanded to have an answer when their children should ask them "What meaneth these stones?" Our children need one too. This section, though brief, will point out our twentieth-century milestones and, by noting how they were handled, will re-emphasize their significance.

1.
CANADA CONFERENCE'S SEMI-CENTENNIAL, 1930

Fifty falls after the first Canada Conference met at Galt, the West Ontario folk, in whose area Galt is located, commemorated that early event in a Thursday evening service at their Blews-held thirty-fifth annual conference at Hamilton.

The only conference survivor across the fifty years at the ministerial level was Rev. A. Sims. He, along with Rev. J. M. Eagle, Rev. D. Allan and Rev. R. Burnham, reminisced or reviewed the interval, then the four warriors stood while the congregation sang "Faith of Our Fathers." The service concluded with further remarks by Rev. G. W. Stevens and Rev. Alice Walls on the present and the future respectively; Rev. P. K. Smith, as secretary, wrote up the *Herald* record.

The East Ontario Conference seems to have had no special service, but the anniversary was noted in Secretary Daw's *Herald* report in the sentences: "Free Methodism has now been established in Canada fifty years and still adheres to the principles on which it was founded. Opportunities for growth and achievement were never greater than at present."

MEANINGFUL TWENTIETH-CENTURY MILESTONES

2.
ARMADALE'S SIXTIETH ANNIVERSARY, 1940

At a May district meeting held at Armadale in 1940, special recognition was given to the sixtieth anniversary of the erection of the church in this cradle of Canadian Free Methodism. Among those preaching were W. H. Gregory, pastor for 1899-1901; Lottie Babcock, conference-appointed pastor for 1903-06 and elder-appointed on other occasions; A. F. Ball, pastor for 1909-11; M. S. Benn, pastor for 1919-20; F. J. Lee, pastor for 1920-22; and S. S. Bailey, pastor for 1935-38.

District Elder J. F. Gregory, who had arranged the program, furnished an "Anniversary Review," while Mrs. J. M. Eagle, daughter and only remaining child of Robert Loveless, and Mr. John Beare, a layman who had been present at the 1880 dedication, both gave "Reminiscences." Aging W. H. Wilson mailed in from Seattle his memoirs of an 1891-93 Armadale pastorate.

Bishop Marston, whose uncle D. D. Marston had served Ellesmere for 1883-84 and had died just a few years previously, sent greetings. Speaking of "Uncle Dan," he said, "I recall him as a vigorous dynamic preacher, and have no doubt he made a good pioneer in the establishing of Free Methodism in Canada."

John King was Armadale pastor at the time of the anniversary. A large number of the Loveless connection attended from widely scattered points.

3.
EASTERN CONFERENCES' GOLDEN ANNIVERSARY, 1945

West Ontario went "all out" in '45 to remember this milestone using two evening services at the annual conference held, like the 1930 anniversary, at Hamilton, but presided over this time by Bishop Fairbairn.

To be sure the event lived on, pastors Stevens and Cooper of West Ave. and Parkdale respectively had prepared a thirty-six page orange-covered booklet for the guests. In keeping with the two special services developing the themes "Free Methodism in Retrospect" and "Free Methodism in Prospect," the booklet carried a double dedication: "to those noble warriors of a former day who by their godly lives, deep spirituality, fervent zeal and faithfulness in precept, bequeathed to us a lofty scriptural standard of pure and undefiled religion" and "to those young people among us, upon whose shoulders rests the responsibility of lifting high the torch. . . ." The editors hoped that through the loyalty of these young people the next fifty years would "record the greatest era of genuine spiritual advancement in our history."

The booklet contained everything pertinent, it seemed—a Fairbairn foreword, Hamilton church stories, the conference program, pages for recording the new appointments and officers, the "Denominational Origin" story, appointments of 1895, comparative statistics for 1895 and 1944, a Stevens survey of the fifty years, some biographies, a ministerial conference roll, a ministerial honour roll, lists of lady evangelists, missionaries and conference session locations, three looks at the future with emphasis on Lorne Park and the permanent campground, a host of pictures, and, as in regular school yearbooks, pages for autographs and "ads" to pay for the project.

There is no record of any special East Ontario observance.

4.
WESTERN CANADA'S SEMI-CENTENNIAL, 1948

In this year, 1948, R. H. Hamilton, for the Saskatchewan Conference, prepared a dainty brown-bound anniversary booklet. It recalled the Western Canada beginnings and first fifty years; it displayed pictures of Rev. W. H. Wilson, the first missionary, and Mr. J. D. Shier, who sent him; and it included as well the program of a special anniversary service (held during the summer conference-camp) in which Rev. D. S. Wartman, the conference superintendent, Bishop Taylor, the conference president, Rev. and Mrs. F. M. Wees (he, the camp evangelist), and many others took part.

Since the work in Alberta and British Columbia began later than 1898, those provinces did not join Saskatchewan in any 1948 observance.

5.
CHURCH-WIDE CENTENARY (CANADIAN VERSION), 1960

In 1960, the year of this book's publication, the world-wide Free Methodist Church celebrates a century of activity. The quadrennial General Conference which, in the pattern of recent years, would have come in 1959, was delayed a year so its date could correspond with this magnificent milestone. Well ahead, a general Centenary Observance Committee under Rev. Charles W. Kingsley was set up to offer leadership in plans for all levels—General Conference, annual conference, and local society. Through articles in the *Free Methodist* and repeated releases to annual conference Centenary Committees, Mr. Kingsley has developed detailed plans and church-wide anticipation.

There was to be, in fact, a year of commemoration, beginning with a special Pre-Centenary service at each 1959 annual conference, continuing up to the June General Conference at Winona Lake and on to the various 1960 annual conferences. A Centenary slogan was adopted: "From Age to Age a Living Witness." [1] Two-colour banners, large and small, bearing the slogan and a suitable design were made available for church displays. A church calendar was planned with provision for a Superintendents' Convocation, a Covenant Sunday, a visitation program, and pilgrimages to centres of local historical interest.

But we are mainly concerned with Canadian observance. At the Canadian Executive Board level, there emerged early a suggested program for Canada which included cooperation in the general Centenary plans; sermons on our origins, development, doctrines and opportunities; F.M.Y. and C.Y.C. study along similar lines; a Centennial Week at each Canadian school; an early 1960 evangelistic campaign on each circuit; completion of this history before General Conference; an appropriate Centennial Service at each annual conference; a special General Conference message in each church immediately after General Conference; and a dedication of all resources to the great unfinished task.

And the various Canadian conference committees have been busy too. The Pre-Centennial service at East Ontario's 1959 annual conference on the Light and Life Camp Ground included a testimony of reminiscence by ninety-one-year-old Rev. W. H. Gregory; a development of the Witness theme—launching it in the United States by L. C. Ball, extending it to Canada by E. S. Bull, and preserving it in print (a progress report on this book) by the writer; and finally an impressive youth consecration occasion under the burning challenge of Sara E. Gregory.

The 1960 session of this largest of the conferences is scheduled for the Pine Orchard Camp Ground from which a special evening pilgrimage is planned to the nearby Ellesmere-Armadale area. Here the old Loveless homestead will be visited and a service held in the Armadale churchyard among the gravestones of Loveless, Stonehouse, Underwood, Beare, Walls and other worthies. Rev. E. S. Bull, local pastor under whose leadership this Armadale society is seeing new life, is chairman of the Conference Centenary Committee. He and Bishop Marston are to speak.

Other conferences are making their plans. West Ontario has named P. K. Smith as historian to report on significant events at a special 1960 conference service. District Meetings and other general gatherings are to have a Centenary emphasis. And pilgrimages to such places as Galt, Hannon, Ridgeway, Thedford, and Charlemont are being considered. From Saskatchewan comes word that local circuits are to hold Centenary services and that the spring district meetings are to include Centenary observances as well. And Alberta will doubtless give its salute to the past. It is expected that each conference will have display booths in the tent-city to be called Centenary Exhibit Circle at Winona Lake in June.

As these lines are being hurriedly written in January, there is still hope that this project of thirty years, which sets forth in word and photo the story of over eighty years of Canadian Free Methodism, can actually be in print for the great summer celebrations. Surely the completed book will itself be a reason for rejoicing.

---

1. This is also the title of an interpretive book by Bishop Marston.

Section 9: Recent Review

Under this caption and before the challenge section is attempted, three final areas of concern will be examined. They are: signs of progress during the decade just ended, scope of outreach beyond our Canadian communion (including latest missionary movements), and extent of change within the present church when such church is compared with that of former days. The writer is very aware that this last is a bold topic for a layman to tackle. Yet he feels that the compelled scrutiny that preceded, and the labour pains that have attended the birth of this book may entitle him to make some comparisons for those readers not familiar with Free Methodism today. The others will have made them already.

1.
PROGRESS ACROSS THE PROVINCES

It is intended that this chapter be a rapid look at advances, both material and spiritual, across the various conferences during the 1950 to 1960 period. It is based largely on information hastily solicited from superintendents or former superintendents and a few pastors. For omissions existing or great accomplishments understated, pardon is pled.

A. *East Ontario*—On the Toronto District, Holt, under R. J. Slack, has renovated its church; Uxbridge, under W. S. Lyons, renovated its parsonage; and Newmarket, under R. G. Babcock and C. W. Reynolds, has built Sunday School rooms and remodelled its parsonage. At West Toronto, the church, begun earlier, was completed by A. J. Thaxter and had its mortgage-burning ceremony in 1957. At Toronto Eglinton about 1950 a regular church was erected over the earlier basement, and a parsonage begun. L. E. Fletcher, himself a builder, deserves greatest credit for these accomplishments. In 1958 under R. B. Warren all debts were paid on this completed $80,000 property. At Richmond Hill, E. S. Bull of the Armadale circuit began a new work and built a church in the early fifties. This foothold started with an open-air Sunday School in the summer of 1952, continued through the following winter in the home of Mrs. Lela Finch, blossomed out to a tent program in the summer of 1953, hibernated to a new church basement in December of that year and by the spring of 1955 had a completed church to its credit. G. W. Stevens opened and dedicated the church in May. The class was organized in June of that year.

East Ontario Conference group at Toronto, Broadview, in 1951, with Bishop Ornston

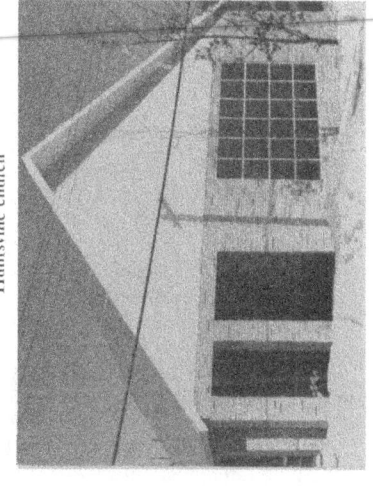

Huntsville church

Toronto Warden Ave. church

THE BATTLE WAS THE LORD'S

The fairly new Oshawa foothold has continued to expand under S. B. Griffith and now for eight years under R. E. Dargan. A new Sunday School wing has been added to the church to accommodate an attendance that sometimes exceeds 250. The membership has increased to approximately seventy. During 1958 a fine replacement parsonage was purchased. Almost $4,000 was raised for missions in 1959. This city has doubled in population during the past ten years and offers unlimited opportunity. Plans are on foot to begin a branch work shortly at city's edge. One of the Free Methodist churches resulting from the merger is located on Warden Avenue in the Scarborough area of Toronto's east end. This Wesley Chapel, as it is called, was built in late 1954 and is a very modern building accommodating a large Sunday School.

On the Muskoka District, Gravenhurst has remodelled its parsonage and is putting a basement under its church. B. E. Dawson has been pastor since 1953. The old Huntsville property has recently been sold and Gerald Sedore is now giving leadership in the erection of a new, centrally located building that includes a large auditorium, a six-room apartment and numerous other rooms for Sunday School and youth activities. The Orillia work, begun only in 1932, has become the strongest on the Muskoka District. Its Sunday School attendance exceeds one hundred[1] and its C.Y.C. under Harold Hoover and Dorothy Smith shows the largest membership in the conference. The Northern Ontario Goheen pioneers continued at Timmins until transferred to Barrie in 1956. (They had been in the mining city for eleven years and in the northland a total of twenty years.) The Clinton Brights serve both Timmins and Goldlands now. As noted under West Ontario, the Northern Ontario Home Missions District which began under Ross Lloyd no longer continues under a separate superintendent.

In Peterborough city on the district named after it, the society under A. J. Thaxter has bought a better parsonage and now a lot to relocate its church. At Warkworth the old rural Zion church has been sold and the village church improved by basement Sunday School rooms. Gerald Kemp has been minister since 1952. Picton, under H. A. McLeod; Cordova Mines, under Nicholas Bosko; and Marmora, under G. H. Bache have all added Sunday School rooms to their properties, in some or all cases adding basements. (While C. W. Kay served as conference superintendent, he lived at Marmora.) Two new churches have been built: one in the town of Campbellford, under Nicholas Bosko, following a fire; the other in the city of Belleville, under Edith Mainprize, following the opening of a distinctly new work there by the P. L. Chases.

This Belleville beginning deserves more detail. About 1952 the Chases, while stationed at Frankford, felt led to extend a ministry to a number of Free Methodist friends in Belleville. At first, the Sunday School and worship services were held in the home of Mr. and Mrs. Louis Greitrix. Increasing attendance emboldened the pastor and people to buy a double lot. On this, led by Mr. Chase, they erected a building whose basement was fitted up as an auditorium and whose upper stories were finished as apartments to rent as debt reducers. (The Chases had worked that plan successfully at Barrie.) The six-member society organized in 1955 has now grown to at least thirty-three members. Since 1957 Miss Edith Mainprize has capably served as resident pastor. In April, 1959, the society began building a church on another large lot bought a year earlier. Located on Anandale Road in a new subdivision, this grey block edifice will be, in Miss Mainprize's words to the *Free Methodist*, "the only church within a radius of two miles." Centennial Free Methodist Church, for that is what it is fittingly being named, had its first basement services on January 10 ("wonderful day") of this Centenary year. May it be the harbinger of a host of additional second-century churches in cities long lacking or lean on the essential message of Methodism.

Belleville's Centennial Free Methodist Church (nearly completed)   Verona church

From this district comes one final encouraging word. Frankford, under F. L. Burnham and assisted by West Ontario's W. N. Teal, experienced an old-time revival during the fall just past. In the pastor's words to the *Herald*, ". . . many were saved and sanctified. . . . The whole church has been renewed and encouraged."

Since the merger, a former Holiness Movement church in Kingston has been sold. The congregation has transferred to the large Colborne Street church nearby where Dr. R. B. Warren is the pastor. A new lot for a second church in the city's western suburbs has already been secured and a new Sunday School begun in the Polson Park Public School adjacent to the purchased lot. Verona (about 1953 to 1955) built a new large brick church under P. O. Miller followed by W. S. Lyons. It is said that at the opening service in the upper auditorium the saints were unusually blessed, and seven people sought the Lord without preaching. The building was dedicated in October, 1959, by Dr. Claude Watson. Deyo's Corners, of this circuit, and Holleford, of the Harrowsmith circuit, were last year grouped into a separate circuit. Under E. S. Bull, the Harrowsmith church early in the decade was remodelled, with Sunday School rooms added. At Odessa under G. H. Bache, rooms were added also; Cole Lake, under

R. G. Babcock, has purchased a parsonage. Napanee church in early 1958 was extensively renovated and enlarged under William Daw. (Mr. Daw in 1959 was awarded an honorary Doctor of Divinity degree by an American educational institution for outstanding work among youth in his conference.) Membership there has shown an encouraging upswing since 1950. Gananoque is in healthier shape since layman Walter Twiddy served several years there as a supply in the early 1950's.

A flourishing new work now exists at Perth. C. V. Fairbairn held tent meetings in the town in the early twenties but, in his words, "Perth never really opened its heart to us." In 1953, pastor Donald White of Mississippi and district superintendent C. W. Reynolds held meetings in a school for a month. (The Perth interest grew from the moving there in 1944 of Mrs. Lila Hannah, a Mississippi woman.) While Lorne Casement served the area next, a class was organized in late 1954 and a church was completed on Gore Street in Perth by 1959. Much of the work was done by skilled tradesmen of the congregation, these sometimes working evenings after the long drive to Ottawa and back. The official opening came in May, 1959, by Dr. Claude Watson. A parsonage is now completed also. Membership and Sunday School attendance are increasing encouragingly and the various missionary and youth organizations are functioning well. Perth now belongs to the new Ottawa District resulting from the merger. With Richmond Hill and Belleville, this makes three new East Ontario centres to get Free Methodist churches in five years. Renfrew, in the Ottawa District, is soon to have a fourth.

Clarenceville, Quebec, welcomed for the first time in 1958 an East Ontario pastor in the person of A. H. Perry. Despite the necessity of services being held in a home, gratifying community interest and some conversions resulted. The effort continues this conference year under R. J. Slack. Recently several thousand dollars from a Clarenceville Hawley estate was left to the General Missionary Board. This circuit is also now attached to the new Ottawa District.

Rev. R. McCaw, the new Quebec pastor of the Shawville-Campbell's Bay circuit, now conducts his own weekly broadcast from Pembroke.

East Ontario, though large, was from 1955 to 1959 under one superintendent, C. W. Kay. With the addition of the Ottawa District, it was necessary to divide the heavy responsibility. A. B. Moffatt is now in charge of the Kingston and Ottawa Districts and lives at Ottawa. Dr. W. J. Stonehouse serves the Toronto, Muskoka and Peterborough Districts. A superintendent's residence was purchased in Uxbridge in late 1959, just seventy years after a similar purchase there for Chairman James Craig.

A progressive step was taken by the 1959 annual conference in setting up a loan fund for use in buying or building church properties. Members may lend at $4\frac{1}{2}$ per cent and churches may borrow at 6 per cent. This plan should make for general advance. W.M.S. giving to missions for the conference year was nearly $19,000—a record, according to Conference President Mrs. Margaret Wartman.

B. *West Ontario*—At London in 1956, a parsonage was purchased to replace inadequate living quarters in the rear of the church building. More recently, pastor E. A. Cooper began a Sunday School in the city's northwest part called Merwyn Heights. Thedford, under Sterling Hicks, is moving its church and fitting up a new basement with Sunday School rooms. At Thornbury, Peniel and Williamsford in the Georgian Bay area—groups of Christians formerly belonging to the Gospel Workers were organized as Free Methodist societies about 1958. Property that included two frame churches, one brick church, and a parsonage was transferred with them. Also on the Sarnia District across most of the last decade, an interesting ministry has been carried on among the coloured folk of Windsor. Leaders in the movement have been a loyal coloured family—Gordon Johnson, his wife and children. In a rented hall, a Sunday School has been held and occasional evangelistic services. This program has operated under the name Second Church.

At St. Joseph Island on the Sault Ste. Marie District, a basement is being constructed under the existing church. John Knoll serves there.

Following a survey conducted by Bishop Ormston and Missionary Secretary Lamson, the Lakehead area, along with Timmins and Goldlands of East Ontario, was constituted in 1950 a Northern Ontario Home Missions District. Both the Canadian Executive Board and the General Commission on Missions were partners in this arrangement. Ross Lloyd was named superintendent. This arrangement continued for about five years only. During this time Mr. Lloyd was responsible for securing the Kakabeka Falls camp property already mentioned, also a Fort William property where a chapel was built. During 1955-56, J. A. Tanner led in the erection of a fine corner-lot church, leaving the original chapel beside it to be converted into a parsonage. At Dryden, 230 miles farther west, Mr. Tanner held a weekly service for a time, but distance has made continuance impractical. All points on the Lake Superior District are now under one pastor. The

West Ontario W.M.S., 1954

West Ontario Conference members, 1954, with Bishop Taylor
Saskatchewan Conference group, 1953, with Bishop Ormston

Light and Life Men's Fellowship is said to be active in the Fort William church.

During 1953-54, the Hymers society celebrated its semi-centenary. Under the title *These Our Fifty Years*, Charles Grandfield, the supply pastor, intimately and beautifully recreated the circuits' half-century in a mimeographed thirty-nine-page volume. Probably no other individual society in Canada has its past so well preserved. The Hymers people have recently added a basement to their church.

At Hamilton city itself, a building site has been purchased in Buchanan Park in a new housing area of Hamilton Mountain's west section. Here a very modern church is scheduled for erection this year. Plans for this West Avenue relocation were begun under Byron Withenshaw and are being carried out under the present pastor, Arthur Voteary. About 1951 the Parkdale people under C. A. Horton bought a parsonage. In 1953 Parkdale and Hannon were made one circuit. Very recently, pastor Fred Buchanan has given leadership in moving back the ancient Hannon church and building a basement under it.

Brantford completed and dedicated in 1956 a new brick church in a new residential area. R. C. McCallum, as pastor, supervised the erection. (The D. S. Wartmans, there from 1949 to 1953, had been responsible for the purchase of a better parsonage and the beginning of a church building fund looking towards relocation.) Already Sunday School space is crowded. The 1950 church fire at Caistor Centre seemed calamitous. W. N. Teal had found the work in 1948 nearly expired; but enthusiasm, paint, and revival had combined to make it flourish again, especially in a Sunday School way. After the fire came, however, unsaved men quickly turned in to help build a modern two-storey edifice that was ready for dedication in about a year. Revival has continued, and the Sunday School under Lloyd Mino has become one of the conference's largest. Mrs. Harriet McCready has pastored Dunnville across most of the past decade and seen encouraging growth in Sunday School and church membership. A better parsonage has been purchased and the church improved. Galt,

Brantford church

St. Catharines church

under the pastorate of J. A. Campbell, has changed location to a housing development on the city's south side and built by 1955 a brick and block church. Mushrooming membership, finance, and attendance have combined to justify basement enlargement already. At Ridgeway church the George Teal family has donated a beautiful solid oak set—communion table, pulpit and flower pedestal—in memory of "Mother and Dad." These sturdy Christians, we recall, were responsible for bringing Free Methodism to the town in 1883-84, besides both providing early leadership—she as class leader and he as local preacher. During his several years of pastoral service at Welland before leaving for Jamaica in 1953, Glen Pelfrey saw Sunday School attendance almost tripled. The upward trend has continued. St. Catherines, we have noted, was separated from Niagara Falls during this past decade. The new society was organized in 1957 and a beautiful brick church built and dedicated in 1959. Carl E. Chatterton has been pastor during the construction. This new program has had substantial assistance through the General Commission on Evangelism.

On the Tillsonburg District at least three progress signs are noteworthy. C. A. Horton in 1955 was obliged to enlarge the Tillsonburg church to accommodate an expanding Sunday School. Trends point towards the need for further enlargement soon. Sterling Hicks built a modest church about 1956 at Simcoe where the Chases are continuing to see the work grow. Neil McQuarrie added a basement with extra Sunday school facilities to the Port Rowan church in 1952.

For thirteen seasons now, E. A. Cooper has directed C.Y.C. camps on the district camp property at Thamesford. Over 1,700 boys and girls have attended and nearly 1,000 have professed conversion and received instruction.

West Ontario Conference membership and average Sunday School attendance are said to stand now at an all-time high. In 1959 W. C. Cowherd, previously of the Niagara Falls circuit, was named new conference superintendent succeeding J. A. Robb. W.M.S. money raised for the previous conference exceeded $10,000, according to the Conference President Mrs. Alma Haley.

C. *Saskatchewan*—This conference has made an impressive list of advances across the last decade. Moose Jaw, Estevan, Brandon (Manitoba), and Kindersley all boast new churches built, and Kindersley has a new parsonage as well. Brandon appears to be a fresh work. Grandview (Manitoba) has a new church under way and Cannington Manor and Melfort are each planning one. Birch River, Weyburn, and Eyebrow churches have all seen renovation programs and the former Holiness Movement congregation at Killarney (Manitoba) plans a renovation or building program. A new conference superintendent's parsonage has been bought in Moose Jaw. The building program at the Bible College has already been noted. Winnipeg's Wesley Chapel (formerly Holiness Movement) is of recent construction. Since the merger, the Bible College building beside it has become an educational unit of the chapel. Several new churches and congregations have been added to the Manitoba District as a result of the merger. In 1951 an interesting mission program began within the conference with the appointment of Lloyd and Bessie Robertson to work among the Cree and Chippewa Indians living on reservations in southwest Saskatchewan. The Broadview Indian Mission, as it is called, consists now of a farm (between reservations) with church and mission houses. Although the work was slow and discouraging at first (three and one-half years before a convert among the men), a recent year's progress included

Saskatchewan W.M.S., 1953

twenty-five baptisms and a gain of ten members. Besides, trained converts are returning for mission work among their people. Each summer of late, a camp is held among the Saskatchewan Indians. Over one hundred were registered in 1959 and most of the seventy children present sought the Lord. Unsung assistants in the mission's development were aged Mr. and Mrs. William E. Sweigard, he helping especially with the building and she with the visitation. Keith and Jean Taylor, trained at Winnipeg's former Holiness Bible College and at Seattle Pacific College, are now relieving the Robertsons, on furlough since October, 1959.

Latest conference plans are for the purchase of a seventy-acre property at Arlington Beach about seventy miles north of Moose Jaw near Liberty. It would be used as an Indian camp, youth camp, C.Y.C. camp and either a ministers' or a laymen's retreat. Centrally located in the conference, the property with one-half mile of lake front, recreational facilities and eighteen buildings (including a 300-capacity tabernacle) is available for only $14,000.

J. L. Walrath, a Moose Jaw, Greenville and John Wesley Seminary Foundation graduate, succeeded G. S. Jenner as conference superintendent in 1959.

D. *Alberta*—New churches have been built during the past decade in each of Alberta's two major cities, Edmonton and Calgary. The new Idylwylde Church, as it is called, in Edmonton was a district project with Rev. Douglas Russell supervising it while in charge of the Edmonton Parkdale church. The building is 36' x 62' with seating capacity for 185. The new Calgary church much like Edmonton's, is a replacement for an earlier but poorly situated one. Rev. H. J. Schnell was in charge of building it. Both buildings were begun in 1956 with the Calgary church being dedicated in December, 1957. A parsonage was bought in Calgary in 1956. The Calgary work is showing very encouraging growth with thirty-eight child conversions during the D.V.B.S. of August, 1959. Both new churches now have expanding Sunday Schools.

As the British Columbia paragraph explains, the Alberta Conference since 1955 has embraced less territory than formerly because of four British Columbia circuits being annexed to Washington. In 1959, Douglas Russell[2] was appointed Alberta superintendent succeeding Floyde Coxson. Though small, as conferences go, Alberta looks to the future with an undeniable optimism.

Above: Edmonton Idylwylde church

Right: New Westminster church

E. *British Columbia*—The Coast District of this province, still a part of the Washington Conference, has shown remarkable readiness to go forward during the last decade. New Westminster's membership now stands at 102 or more, an increase of almost 40 per cent, and its Sunday School attendance exceeds two hundred. In 1956, a beautiful new church was completed there. Bishop Fairbairn conducted the dedication in May, 1957. Don Bastian, a product of Moose Jaw, Lorne Park, Greenville and John Wesley Seminary has been pastor since 1956. He was preceded by C. P. Stewart who, as in so many other centres, built the church. At Forrest Road is a recently organized class that grew out of the New Westminster church.

Courtney, on Vancouver Island and 140 miles north of Victoria, has a new work entirely developed since 1956. It has a booming Sunday School and a fine parsonage, plus a $40,000 first unit of a church building that was dedicated in October, 1959. J. E. Campbell (originally of West Ontario) took the initiative in this planting, after a resident heard the Light and Life Hour and asked the Free Methodists to come.

At bustling cosmopolitan Vancouver, a former Holiness Movement society has now merged with the Free Methodist one, producing a relatively strong church. Rupert Chapel represents a second point on the Vancouver circuit and has its own Sunday School.

Victoria, on Vancouver Island, is considered on the upgrade after a slow beginning. J. E. Campbell began the Courtney circuit while serving here. He has ministered to coastal congregations since 1945.

The Washington Conference session of 1945 welcomed into its area what was formerly the British Columbia Interior District of the Alberta Conference. The same district name continues. Four circuits are included: Kamloops, Kelowna, West Summerland, and Winfield-Grindrod. Major recent advance on this district has been the building of the district camp tabernacle at Grindrod. Rev. C. W. Burbank of East Stanwood, Washington, has been superintendent of both British Columbia districts since 1955, along with others in Washington itself. One British Columbia circuit, Golden-Donald (straight west of Banff and over two hundred miles from the Alberta border) remains in the Alberta Conference.

* * * * *

To summarize the present nation-wide picture, Canadian Free Methodism represents nearly two hundred congregations scattered from Vancouver Island to Quebec province. With the recent additions from the Holiness Movement Church and the Gospel Workers Church, total membership stands at about 4,400. An extension of the census figures of 1951 would indicate that, counting also adherents; almost 11,000 Canadians today count themselves Free Methodists.

Sunday School enrollment approaches that figure also. Church property, including churches, parsonages, campgrounds and school campuses, has a value somewhere between $3,000,000 and $4,000,000.

As this chapter testifies, and the next one with it, the decade has indeed seen progress across the provinces. W. L. Smith, president of East Ontario's Light and Life Men's Fellowship, recently noted it in this picturesque fashion: "As we are girding for our second century, we seem to be getting our second wind."

---

1. Only one of its original Sunday School children is not now a church member.
2. Douglas Russell is a former Y. P. M. S. regional director of the General Church.

2.
IMPACT BEYOND OUR BORDERS

Although the Canadian Free Methodist Church is small as denominations go, her outreach is encouraging, and is constantly expanding. For convenience, we shall consider the recent contributions of Canadian Free Methodists and Free Methodism beyond their immediate membership circles under three geographical groupings: in Canada, in the United States, and around the world.

We have seen that by Sunday School and other connection the Free Methodist Church today ministers to, or is church home to, nearly 11,000 Canadians, a figure about two and one-half times as great as her membership of 4,400. This is encouraging.

In Ontario, many Free Methodist pastors extend their ministry by conducting weekly classes in religious education in the local elementary schools in accordance with provincial laws allowing clergymen to so teach. It is noteworthy too that R. E. Dargan, while president of Oshawa's Ministerial Association about 1955, was responsible for a brief to the Ontario Government seeking the right to add religious education in secondary schools. The necessary legislation was passed, and again as a member of the Oshawa Board of Education Mr. Dargan won permission to have religious education introduced in Oshawa's collegiates.

Various individuals in Canada minister widely too. Dr. R. B. Warren, editor of the *Canadian Free Methodist Herald*, besides sending his magazine to numerous libraries and non-Free Methodist homes, has developed a weekly writing ministry that results in a column on the Sunday School lesson or other religious topic appearing in some two hundred newspapers weekly. His devotional book, *Spiritual Strength for Today* (Thomas Nelson) is being well received also.

Free Methodist minister R. L. Casement of Toronto was in 1959 appointed President of the Canadian Holiness Federation.

Free Methodists have, in fact, contributed largely to this organization from its founding in November, 1943, when R. H. Hamilton served as chairman of the organizing convention in Toronto and was named its first president. Free Methodism being the oldest holiness church in Canada, her Canadian Executive Board had taken the initiative in calling this convention that attracted leaders from the following churches: Wesleyan Methodist, Holiness Movement, Church of the Nazarene, Reformed Baptist, Pilgrim Holiness, Standard, Gospel Workers, Mennonite Brethren in Christ (now United Missionary), and Salvation Army.[1] Free Methodist E. A. Cooper served several years as president of C.H.F.'s affiliate, the Canadian Youth Holiness Association.

One could mention that the founder-director of Oshawa's Christian Youth Centre which ministers to young people of many denominations is Free Methodist James Aldous;[2] and that the author of this history has had previous experience in writing, as outlined in the front of the book.

Not to be forgotten are former Free Methodist boys who are enriching other Canadian denominations. In this class are Reginald Holton with the Pilgrim Holiness people, and Herbert and Eldon Linstead and Arthur Creswell, all three ministers now in the United Church. Here, too, belongs Gordon Bray, for nine years a Free Methodist minister, but now manager of the United Church Publishing House's huge retail department. Several Free Methodists have served circuits in recent years among the Gospel Workers of the Georgian Bay area. These include R. H. Hamilton, R. C. McCallum and Stanley Dyer. Some of the Gospel Workers congregations, as shown already, have since become Free Methodist.

Numerous Canadians continue to serve the American Church and some even at the General level. Too numerous to name are those who received their advanced education (and often their wife) in the Republic and stayed for "greener fields" or other reasons. Mr. Fairbairn's assignment that began in General Conference evangelism and led to the bishopric is told. So also is Alice Walls' twelve-year editorship of the *Missionary Tidings*. At present these other Canadians (or former Canadians) hold key positions in the General Church: James Gregory, editor of the *Free Methodist*; Bessie (Reid) Kresge, editor of the *Missionary Tidings*; G. W. Stevens, General Conference evangelist; Claude Horton, assistant to the director of the Light and Life Hour. And Lloyd Knox, church publisher, has distinctly Canadian roots. The lay representation of George Fuller, Jr., on so many Winona Lake councils entitles him to mention again here. Also somewhere here should be mentioned the contribution of E. A. Cooper in developing the Manual and principles of C.Y.C. for the General Church.

Two former Lorne Park students are now filling large places in prominent American education institutions beyond the Free Methodist Church. They are James Robertson at Asbury Seminary in Kentucky and W. J. Power at Southern Methodist University in Texas.

Beyond the North American continent, Canadians have continued to feel and accept responsibility. Result: veteran missionaries returning, new volunteers being accepted and sent, and congregational mission gifts increasing—in one case to the point where they earned for a Canadian pastor a mission field visit.

A listing of missionaries leaving Canada during the past decade runs like this: In 1955 and 1956 the Moore Sisters, Eileen and Doris, left Saskatchewan for nursing ministries in the Belgian Congo. Laverna Grandfield, another Saskatchewan nurse, left for South Africa in 1956.

In early 1957 Western Ontario's Dr. Melvin Pastorius and nurse wife Betty headed for the Umri Mission Hospital in India on a short assignment. (They have since decided to stay longer.) Later that year Pearl Reid returned to Japan accompanied by first-timers Rev. K. Lavern and Lois Snider of East Ontario. Much of the Sniders' work will be teaching at the Osaka Christian College. Also in late 1957 Olive Bodtcher from New Westminster left Canada to serve as a nurse in a leper colony in the

Congo. A year later, Canadian Clarke DeMille, son of Rev. and Mrs. Wesley DeMille of Transvaal, returned to Africa with his American-born wife for a first assignment in Southern Rhodesia. In the fall of 1959 Earle and Doreen Hawley began a mission assignment in Egypt while Irma Ergezinger and Rev. and Mrs. Torance Alexander returned to Egypt and Rev. Alton Gould to Hong Kong.[3]

Serving some years now in India with the World Gospel Mission have been Rev. and Mrs. W. A. Smith of West Ontario. Glen and Dorothy Pelfrey left the West Ontario Conference about 1953 to work with the Missionary Bands of the World in Jamaica. Earlier, W. R. McCready and his wife, the former Harriet Cowherd, had served a time in India with the Pentecostal Bands of the World. They also were from West Ontario. Stanley Dyer, an East Ontario Lorne Park graduate, recently spent an effective short term with the Oriental Missionary Society in Japan and Okinawa. Kelly Toth of West Ontario is only now on his way home from such a mission entirely in Japan.

It is indicative of the quality of Canadian missionaries, that on the church's fourteen non-North American mission fields, five of the present superintendents are Canadians—Egypt and Hong Kong have Norman E. Cooke and Alton Gould, respectively, because of earlier Holiness Movement foundings, but Ronald Collett of Ruanda-Urundi, Wesley C. DeMille of Transvaal and K. Lavern Snider of Japan are Canadians as well. Mr. Collett had special responsibility among Christian Missions when Dr. Billy Graham visited his country in early 1960.

The mission field visit was won by pastor R. E. Dargan of East Ontario's Oshawa church in 1959. It was one of four awards across the North American church based on superior local giving per member.

Before this book is printed, Canadians George Fuller, Jr.,[4] and Dr. W. J. Stonehouse, as part of a nine-man North American Panel, will have participated in an Asia conference in Osaka, Japan. There they will have met representatives from Japan, Formosa, Hong Kong, the Philippines, India and Egypt in a study whose purpose Bishop Marston has described as "looking toward the organization of largely autonomous national churches within the various countries now controlled in large measure by mission extensions of the home church."

Canadian Free Methodists, though a small group, like to feel themselves a part of the world-wide Free Methodist fellowship of nearly 100,000 members scattered through nearly twenty countries and representing every continent but Australia.[5] The weekly church magazine, the *Free Methodist*, whose circulation exceeds 31,000; the top-rating weekly radio broadcast, the Light and Life Hour, that "girdles the globe" with full salvation's message (the new 100,000-watt Monte Carlo station of Trans World Radio alone carrying it in six languages);[6] the over two hundred missionaries under appointment, the missionary budget that is fast approaching $1,000,000 annually; the record of per member general giving that exceeds that of any other denomination in America[7]—these and other ministries make

Canadian Free Methodists not ashamed of their associations and their name.

---

1. It appears that Mr. Hamilton's deep interest in such a convention was related to his long-cherished hope that a union of the various holiness churches in Canada might some day be consummated. As early as 1931 he had presented to the Canadian Executive Board a resolution listing at least a dozen reasons why such a union seemed desirable.

2. Mr. Aldous is a producer of choice poetry. *The Motorist's Prayer* which he penned is known continent-wide (unfortunately without his name). A National Safety Council official estimates several million copies of one version have been circulated. The "Haven of Rest" gospel broadcast of California has recently made the poem up on a free windshield sticker.

3. Since returning, Mr. Gould has baptized fifty-two recent converts in one service.

4. Ill health prevented Mr. Fuller's going, but the conference was a great success.

5. The most recent figures show a total of 97,000 with 54,500 in the United States, the rest being in Canada and the various mission fields.

6. The Light and Life Hour is currently on six Canadian stations, nearly 150 American ones and a dozen or so missionary channels. Dr. Myron Boyd, the director, has been in Christian radio work for twenty-five years and with the Light and Life Hour for most of its more than fifteen years. For several successive years the Light and Life Hour won top honours from the National Religious Broadcasters. Before the new multiple-language Monte Carlo station opened in May, 1960, the listening audience was distributed over at least seventy countries and estimated at 10,000,000.

7. The latest Free Methodist figure released by the National Council of Churches in its annual series was $243.95 per member. The Canadian giving for 1958-59 (without the Holiness Movement figures) exceeded $700,000.

3.
HAS FREE METHODISM CHANGED TOO?

Abundant evidence was given in the early sections of this book to show that significant changes had come in Ontario Methodism between, say, the first and fourth quarter-centuries of the 1800's and that these changes were, in fact, partly responsible for Free Methodism's favourable reception. Free Methodism appealed to a generation that had known or knew about better days spiritually. It seems proper to discuss, then, the subject of Free Methodism and change.

Has Free Methodism changed too? Some changes are inevitable in a century that has seen man move from the horse-and-buggy era into a jet, atomic and even space age. But what about our basic beliefs? Do we still believe them? And standards of conduct? And methods of maintenance? What follows is an attempt to give a kindly but for the most part objective treatment of this delicate topic.

It can be stated confidently that the theological position is intact. Universalism, liberalism, and even neo-orthodoxy may be examined in an academic way,[1] but these counterfeit religions make little headway in our camp. Muddy pools tempt not those who have drunk of the living waters; gaudy fool's gold glitters in vain before those who have found the true riches; phosphorescence is not enough for men and women who have warmed at the fires of Pentecost; marshy paths have little pull to them who walk the highway of holiness. Free Methodism is still in the Bible-believing, life-changing, God-honouring evangelical tradition—Arminian, Wesleyanic, and Robertsian.

Many of her standards of conduct are still unpopular with the world and even numerous other churches. Using tobacco and alcoholic beverages; dressing and adorning lavishly; attending the dance, the theatre, and the card-party; joining the secret order—these are a few of the practices from which members are still expected to refrain, restrictions that mean Free Methodism still offers no cheap ticket to heaven and is still not easily sold to today's religious bargain-hunter.[2]

In some areas there is apparent change. The wedding ring, for instance, was once banned because of Scriptural reference to adorning with gold. Because of its symbolic significance to many in the church and without, this ring is becoming common and is not now specifically mentioned in the Book of Discipline. Some other earlier emphases are tending also to be classed as non-essentials and consequently receiving less stress or none at all. Whether to be welcomed or deplored, this two-pronged fact stands out: persecution is much less intense than it once was, and the reproach of being a Free Methodist is on the wane.

In general methods of strategy, change is apparent at almost every point. The itinerant system has by degrees been revised until no pastoral time limit now exists. Already some ministers have remained on one circuit for eight years and more. While few rich are numbered in the congregations, members could be said to belong mainly to the middle class, or at least its lower layers. Few of the real poor are among us.

Revival efforts are still conducted regularly, but greatly shortened in length, (the ten-day crusade is very common) and often limited in effect. Without disparaging the "mercy drops" still falling, let it be said that it is doubtful whether the Canadian church has experienced during the last quarter-century a truly great revival shower with decidedly permanent results.

Testimonies are still regular features in most Sunday evening services and at prayer meetings. (It might be argued that they tend to be less definite, particularly with respect to the Pentecostal cleansing and infilling.) Prayer meetings are universal, but not as well patronized as the occasional fellowship banquet in some places. Class meetings are not as general as once, although valuable preparatory classes are required before new members are received into full connection. Street meetings are gone. Changes in campgrounds have been described already. Perhaps, with cars, a smaller percentage of the people actually camp. Those who do may sometimes tend to regard the experience as more of an outing than their camping predecessors did. Quarterly meetings are still held, but because there has been a trend towards large areas (sometimes a whole conference) under one superintendent, a neighbouring pastor who is an ordained elder occasionally gets appointed to conduct the meeting. District meetings continue too, but do not attract the crowds or the Sunday pastors as they once did (this largely because of local Sunday pressures).[3] Congregational singing is now supplemented much more than it once was by "special songs." The old custom of the spontaneous starting of hymns is all but gone in some congregations. Musical instruments, which were originally excluded for "prudential" reasons, are now used in practically all churches.

Of household devotions this must be admitted with regret: we hear echoes that today's feverish family is not always winning the battle to maintain them. Private devotions, we hope, are faring better. Less stress is given to fasting; even less practice is probably resulting, this in spite of an evident physical need for dieting on every hand.

Visitation programs, especially in connection with Sunday School effort, are being renewed. Visitation evangelism in the old-fashioned style is rare.

Most circuits have good parsonages and more attention is being given to church architecture with adequate Sunday School rooms. Educational standards for ministers have been raised. Increasing numbers of candidates are earning college degrees and an encouraging number of Canadians have already graduated from the church's John Wesley Seminary. While sermons today are generally more homiletical, it is hard to insist they are more effective. Old timers will tell you there is less "awakening truth" coming from the pulpit now. By this phrase would be meant preaching on the judgment and eternal punishment. Or they will say that sermons do not "scrape the bone" as they once did. By this phrase would be meant the bold attempting to name sins more and to define what is meant by "the world" in terms of contemporary living.

Exhorters and local preachers are still licensed but, in general, are far less active in the ways that such officeholders were formerly. Newcomer in the field for organizing lay activities (including service outlets) is the Light and Life Men's Fellowship. With its strong emphasis on visitation and personal evangelism as reflected in its slogan MEN WIN MEN, this new arm has possibilities unlimited. There are signs that the lay potential is becoming kinetic, that the "Sleeping Giant" is awakening. Lady preachers, who featured so forcefully in the first half of our Canadian history, have become almost a breed extinct, this despite a continuing shortage of qualified male ministers. And despite also the fact that one is now proving in Belleville City that women can still be effective and even supervise the building of a church.

J.M.S., C.Y.C., and F.M.Y. (new name for Y.P.M.S.) organizations exist on many circuits to serve the needs of the junior members of the congregations. Special camping programs for youth at both C.Y.C. and F.M.Y. levels have been mentioned elsewhere. East Ontario F.M.Y. has its own camp property now at Echo Lake north of Verona.[4] The tent-to-permanent-tabernacle trend in district and conference camps needs no further word. Sunday Schools are more departmentalized than in early days and, as seen already, minister to many far beyond the church families.

THE BATTLE WAS THE LORD'S

The church's two residential day schools need not be touched on again. It is likely that, on the whole, a higher percentage of church children are being held in the church than formerly.

We have told of the Canadian church's distinctive magazine. Canadian Free Methodists still proudly patronize the denomination's Light and Life Press whose fine line of Sunday School supplies, magazines, and books are known and used far beyond the denominational confines.[5] The new Canadian history outlet has been mentioned already.

Missionary going and giving have intensified, as seen elsewhere. The annual missionary convention is gaining in popularity. On most circuits the W.M.S. is still the main mission-promoting agency. Church money continues to be raised without resort to supper sales. While more money is collected for the various needs, it seems unlikely that, with today's income levels, many members are denying themselves as those of earlier generations did.[6] Pastors' incomes have increased with the cost of living, but too often, even with allowances for free residence, are still below the average income among the church families. Budgets which provide a uniform weekly wage are prevalent and make for more security than the old days with their frequent lean offering plate weeks.

With all the improvements and progress, it is difficult to affirm that the militant spirit is, in general, as pronounced in either pulpit or pew as it once was. The war may not seem quite as real or the issues quite as urgent as in days of yore. Have the years and prosperity done to Canadian Free Methodism what they did to Canadian Methodism almost a century ago? Certainly not. At least not nearly as much. Still, in the light of the way Methodism went and some of our own tendencies now, who will deny that, should the Lord tarry, the next quarter-century will be a most critical period. Well may ours and succeeding generations tread cautiously when tempted to stray far from the Biblical beliefs and careful standards and even certain of the proven methods of those early saints. They had so much of God in their lives and in their efforts. So much more than most of us have.

God grant that twentieth-century Free Methodism may conquer this coming crisis.[7]

---

1. Walsh in *Christian Church in Canada* admits that "the liberal interpretation of Christianity with its faith in progress and evolutionary providence has received rough handling by history in recent years."

2. It is to be deplored that increasing numbers of Free Methodists with television sets, through the programs they watch regularly, are welcoming into their homes the very "world" that the church has traditionally discounted.

3. The old-time district meeting was geared to a great extent to a rural economy that is fast disappearing.

4. Frances Casement and Harold Sutton have been leaders in this project.

5. Sunday school supplies produced at Winona Lake include the famous Arnold's Commentary, lesson quarterlies in both the International and Graded Series, and weekly papers called *Evangel, Teen Time, Story Trails* and *Primary World*. Magazines include the weekly *Free Methodist*, the monthly *Missionary Tidings*, the *Sunday School*

(Continued on page 265)

Section 10: The Battle is the Lord's

The story is finished. It only remains to survey the present Canadian situation and "make the rousement." We hope the reader concurs that the theme and title were actually embedded in the content of the chronicle, and that this content rates worthy of inclusion as one chapter in the larger history of "the church militant" upon the earth; that the battle was indeed the Lord's.

But the war is, or should be, still on. The battle is not ended, nor will it end till the Lord Jesus Christ returns. And Professor Richard Traver of Roberts Wesleyan College accents our part in the battle by declaring that when that moment of return comes, He will want to find us "up to our elbows in life."

Our day and our opportunity and our responsibility get clarified in this postscript portion of the book. God told Habakkuk to "write the vision and make it plain." This writer will try to do just that for the Centenary vision that is his. Surely the trying needs no apology. The section ends with a prayer for divine leadership. It is hoped that every Canadian Free Methodist will, from his heart, offer some such supplication.

1.
RECONNAISSANCE—CANADA, 1960

By September of this Century year, 1960, Canada's population is expected (according to the Bureau of Statistics) to reach 18,000,000.[1] Noting a 1945 figure of little more than 12,000,000, we can see that this 1960 statistic represents an almost 50 per cent increase across the last fifteen years. And the figure predicted for 1980 by the Royal Commission on Canada's Economic Prospects (commonly called the Gordan Report) is 27,535,000—another full 50 per cent increase across the next twenty years.

(Continued from page 264)

Journal, and the popular new monthly Youth in Action. Among the numerous superior Light and Life books appear such volumes on Wesleyanism as Tenney's Blueprint for a Christian World and Turner's The More Excellent Way.

6. As A. C. Forrest, editor of the United Church Observer recently suggested, it is difficult to sing sincerely, "Jesus, I my cross have taken, All to leave and follow Thee," with an expensive auto parked outside the church door.

7. In commenting on the Methodist decline, C. H. Sage wrote in 1881: "I hope when members of the Free Methodist church lay the discipline and the Bible aside and do as they like, that the earth will open and swallow us up and give us a decent burial."

THE BATTLE WAS THE LORD'S

Geographer Griffith Taylor has suggested a population of 40,000,000 to 50,000,000 by the year 2000. Clearly, if the Lord tarries and nuclear bombs do not bury us, Canada is destined for a great growth.

Fortunately in this 3,500-mile-wide country (despite our barren North) we have the space for a huge population. Canada's area of 3,845,000 square miles makes her the second or third largest country in the world (even larger than the forty-eight States to the south, plus the new states of Alaska and Hawaii). We have the resources for a robust nation: abundant minerals, renewing forests, fur-bearing animals and fish, rich agricultural lands, hydro-electric potential, industrial capacity, enlightened and industrious citizens.

Two major factors account for Canada's recent population swell. One is the immigrants who have streamed in steadily because Canada is recognized widely as a goodly land. The other is the present high birth rate. (For the country as a whole, the annual average rate of population increase is 3 per cent. Ontario's figure of 3.2 per cent makes hers one of the world's highest.)

Since Free Methodism's strength is greatest in Ontario, some special facts for that province seem justified. In the fall of 1959 her total population passed the 6,000,000 mark.[2] This gives Ontario over one-third of the country's total people. (Her rate of growth is exceeding that of most of the other provinces partly because of many migrations to Ontario from those other provinces—about 10,000 a year.) The immigration statistics for Ontario are interesting, both as to totals and to countries from which the immigrants come. For the 1,000,000 who entered during the period from 1945 to 1949 the breakdown ran thus: United Kingdom—340,000; Germany, Austria and Netherlands—195,000; Italy—143,000; Poland—38,000; other European countries—164,000.

Tables of immigration figures for the whole country in most recent years reveal that Italy has consistently run closest to the United Kingdom in supplying new Canadians. And with the large numbers from other non-British countries as well, it is apparent that the percentage of British people in Canada is dwindling.[3] (It was about 60 per cent in 1876. Now it is less than 46 per cent.)

Canada is moving rapidly in the direction of an urban and industrial economy. Most of the immigrants and many of the one-time farmers are pushing into the cities. House-building in suburban areas is booming with many city families moving into these less-crowded suburban subdivisions. Metropolitan Toronto is one of the world's fastest growing centres with a present population of 1,600,000.[4] A surprising number of farmers who live within commuting distance of cities do shift work—and carry on farm operations at the same time as best they can. Those who stay full-time in agriculture are, with power machinery, working bigger and bigger acreages.

Moneywise, Canada is more prosperous than ever before. Her standards of living are close to those of the United States, which enjoys the highest in the world. Opportunities for careers in business, industry, and the professions are unlimited. There is a shortage on almost every hand of trained Canadians for the professional world. Increasing scholarships, bursaries and loan funds promise to make possible a university education to an ever-larger proportion of those capable enough and ambitious enough to absorb it.

Regarding the country's educational future, Wilbur Sutherland, General Secretary of the Inter-Varsity Christian Fellowship of Canada notes: "Both high school and university populations are expected to be more than doubled by 1980. . . . It is anticipated that we will need at least the equivalent of twenty-five new universities of 3,000 each by 1980." York University in the Toronto area and the Laurentian University of Northern Ontario at Sudbury are two that have just been born.

Politically, though with British traditions still strong, we enjoy as much freedom as perhaps any country on earth. Since the passage of the Canadian Citizenship Act in 1946, it is proper to speak of being a Canadian citizen as well as a British subject. A Bill of Rights is promised. Many Christians in Canada rejoice that the present Prime Minister, Rt. Hon. John Diefenbaker, is the product of a godly Baptist home[5] and that he displays both a strong appreciation for spiritual values and an inclination to reverse some trends (disturbing to Britishers and Protestants) that began to develop during the previous regime. His sturdy Minister of Finance, Hon. Donald Fleming, might be cited commendably also for his identification with such Christian movements as the Upper Canada Bible Society and Toronto Bible College.[6] Known throughout the continent, especially in evangelical circles, is Alberta's Bible-believing radio preacher-premier, Ernest C. Manning, and the way God has prospered his province since the discovery of oil in 1947.

Religiously, Canada is moving fast towards a point where the percentage of Roman Catholics will equal or even exceed the percentage of Protestants. Quebec with over 5,000,000 people is almost solidly Roman Catholic, while Protestant action there still remains spotty and very limited. It has been claimed that in the whole province there are less than one hundred full-time evangelistic Gospel workers among the French-speaking people. Some sixty towns and cities can be pointed out where no truly evangelical witness exists. Evangelistic groups most active among French-speaking people are the Fellowship Baptist, Brethren, and Pentecostal Assemblies. Most effective workers are said to be converted French-Canadians themselves. Ontario itself has a French Canadian population (mostly in the north) that numbers nearly 500,000. Only about 60,000 are Protestant.

The United Church is Canada's largest Protestant church with almost a million members.[7] Its weekly magazine, *The United Church Observer* edited by A. C. Forrest, enjoys a circulation that ranks it among the most widely read religious periodicals on the continent. Disturbing to many Canadian Christians were the contents of a recently appearing booklet prepared by a United Church Committee under the title "Life and Death —A Study of the Christian Hope." Too many traditional interpretations of Scripture were tactfully but certainly revised or called in question to make this a safe guide or to warrant continued theological confidence in some of the church's leadership. In contrast with such ultra-progressiveness, it is said that the United Church in rural Newfoundland (Canada's newest province, which entered Confederation in 1949) still bears numerous definite resemblances to old-time Methodism.

Among the nations that call themselves Christian, Canada is probably one of the most religious. Unfortunately, many operating groups offer the public something less than a New Testament standard. But on the other hand, a growing number (many as inter-denominational churches) teach the second birth and more (besides Free Methodists) than formerly, are of Wesleyan persuasion. It is encouraging to note that McGill's H. H. Walsh, after surveying widely the national church world, concluded his recent book *The Christian Church in Canada* with these words: "It would seem that activism, born of frontier revivalism, is still the authentic note of Canadian Christianity." [8] Such conclusions carry implications that dare not be overlooked, especially by Free Methodists. It looks as if F. A. Daw's thirty-years-ago observation expresses even stronger truth in 1950: "Opportunities for growth and achievement were never greater than at present."

---

1. The population by provinces and territories in 1960 would run close to these figures. Newfoundland—445,000; Prince Edward Island—102,000; Nova Scotia—725,000; New Brunswick—600,000; Quebec—5,170,000; Ontario—6,175,000; Manitoba—905,000; Saskatchewan—925,000; Alberta—1,285,000; British Columbia—1,600,000; Yukon—13,000; North West Territories—21,000.
2. It is expected to reach 7,000,000 as soon as 1966 and be at 9,620,000 by 1980.
3. Quite a sprinkling of Oriental peoples now live in coastal British Columbia.
4. Estimated population for 1980 is 2,800,000, with two-thirds of the increase due to immigration.
5. John the Baptist, he gets nicknamed.
6. Mr. Fleming was the featured speaker at a recent annual convention of the Bible society and gave an impressive Christian testimony on the occasion. He is a member of the Board of Toronto Bible College.
7. Anglicans are second strongest.
8. This country still has no Canadian Association of Evangelicals (except the Canadian Council of Evangelical Christian Churches which has a limited membership), but according to a recent article in *United Evangelical Action* such a fellowship seems shaping up.

2.
THE PRESENT ISSUE

Is the mission of Methodism in Canada ended? In a great front page editorial for the *Herald* (issue of June, 1925), R. H. Hamilton told of one Methodist Conference that, some time before the swallowing-up union of that year, had evidently thought so and had moved a resolution accordingly. But in the light of Methodism's mission as conceived by her founder, such a resolution would be a serious concession. That mission, it must be remembered, was "to spread scriptural holiness."

How providentially was Canadian Free Methodism prepared in the 1920's to take enlarged responsibility! An Executive Board, a magazine, a school, and a Federal Act of Incorporation—all developing within a period of seven years. Has Canadian Free Methodism made ample use of these tools or, as earlier labelled, these instruments of war? Has the Executive Board sometimes marked time when it should have marched forward? Has the school been sent adequate recruits from the circuits, and have those sent been hardened in high proportion into disciplined soldiers for both the front fighting and the supply lines? Has the Federal Charter's authority impelled the church to become both national-wide and nation-deep, "terrible as an army with banners"? Has the magazine—since 1925 Canada's only Methodist mouthpiece in journalism—sounded incessantly that loud and clear bugle call that has been its prerogative?

There will be wide variation among the answers formulated to these questions. Armchair analysts who have themselves done little or no personal fighting will especially need to exhibit unlimited charity toward those who did participate. The Hamilton editorial, referred to above, was entitled: "Shall Methodism Be Sustained in Canada?" The Hamilton answer suggested the matter lay largely with the Free Methodists. There could be general agreement on this conclusion—both then and now. Wesleyan Methodists work in Canada, but only in a very limited way and in limited areas.[1] There are other groups, as we have seen, that hold distinctly Methodist teachings, but they battle under other banners. Most of these are in no sense national in their coverage. If the glorious name *Methodist* ever again in Canada bursts out of the pages of history and parades across the columns of current events, it will likely be because the Free Methodists (the country's chief "continuing Methodists")[2] have formed some new vanguards and have done no little of some fresh field fighting.

Canada's population, and prosperity, and prospects, and persuasions were treated in the last chapter. But like every other country on this planet, Canada has something else that is less pleasant to mention; she has SINS.[3] And her sinners need a Saviour. And Free Methodists boast a Saviour that saves to the uttermost. With all the country's religiosity, probably those who seldom or never attend any church number into the millions. And of those who do attend, millions more testify by their lives that they have never been to Calvary, let alone Pentecost.

The present issue is whether we are going to accept the challenge before us; whether we are going to take the Centenary slogan, "From Age to Age a Living Witness," as our second-century battle-burden; whether we are going to be content to comfortably "hold the fort" or, impelled by the Spirit of God, are going out to do exploits.

When a national writer of Bruce Hutchinson's stature and knowledge says of Canadians in Maclean's Magazine,[4] "We're being corrupted by our boom," we probably are. And Christian people, including Free Methodists, are not untouched. The present issue is whether we are going to be (perhaps unconsciously) devotees of the gods of materialism—such deities as the god STANDARD OF LIVING, the god CLOTHES, the god HOLIDAY, the god SECURITY, and especially "the great god CAR"—or whether we will truly serve the Lowly Nazarene, of whom it was said that He "pleased not himself." Anything less than the latter begins to be idolatrous.

In his *The Screwtape Letters*,[6] C. S. Lewis makes Screwtape, a senior demon in hell, subtly explain what prosperity does in his letter to Wormwood, a working nephew on earth: "Prosperity knits a man to the World. He feels he is 'finding his place in it,' while really it is finding its place in him." The present issue is whether we are going to let our comfortable citizenship in this country fade our consciousness that our real citizenship is in heaven and that we are here only as pilgrim ambassadors; whether we are going to be so earth-bound and self-focussed that we will not be expendable for God.

The changes that came to Canadian Methodism between, say, 1840 to 1875 seem to have been tremendous. The present issue is whether Canadian Free Methodists will avail themselves of the resources in the Holy Spirit and the lessons in history, and doing so, not only withstand today's more intense temptations and pressures, but aggressively launch new invasions and engage in new raids for the honour of King Jesus.

---

1. In 1957 the Wesleyan Methodist Superintendent in Canada reported some sixteen congregations and some six hundred members. These were largely in the Ottawa and St. Lawrence valleys. No schools or magazines were mentioned for Canada.

2. The writer of this history at the invitation of the editor prepared an article for the *United Church Observer* of January 15, 1958, under the suggested caption, "Canada's Continuing Methodists."

3. Delinquency, divorce, heavy drinking, desecration of the Lord's Day, crime—all are on the increase.

4. See issue of April 13, 1957.

5. John Wesley found prosperity was creating problems among Methodists even before he died. Recall his famous steadying formula: "Earn all you can; save all you can; give all you can."

6. *The Screwtape Letters* by C. S. Lewis was published originally by Geoffrey Bles Ltd. of London, England. Permission to quote granted.

3.
THE ENGAGEMENT MUST INTENSIFY

The engagement must intensify. The rate of ground-gaining over the last forty years has satisfied no one—except the Enemy. Percentage gains in the first few years of the Canada Conference seem almost phenomenal. Percentage gains in membership for the first forty years of Canadian conferences (1880-1920), if continued through the past forty years would have yielded nearly 20,000 members by now.[1] It would be gratifying to be able to say we had kept pace at least with the growth in population since 1920. We cannot. The facts are: national population has increased slightly more than 100 per cent;[2] national membership has increased (without the merger) by scarce 50 per cent. Within the first forty years of activity in Canada four conferences were formed. None has been organized since 1914. The battle somewhere has bogged down. God has had to raise up others to share the evangelization that Free Methodists might have done.[3] The engagement must intensify.

There would be general agreement that evangelization was relatively easier forty to eighty years ago. Free Methodism filled a spiritual vacuum developing in Methodism. Preachers "got by" with less education because the masses were less educated. Fewer forms of community or home entertainment made religious services a place to go, a rural economy gave people more time to think. . . . Such arguments could continue lengthily, but they would hardly tell the whole story. Laodicean lukewarmness must have played a part in the levelling off. Some territory having been taken, the primal passion must have passed. Perhaps, too, fewer giants germinated.

It seems relevant here to note that, apart from the special Free Methodist picture, there is one most distressing fact about the Canadian situation revivalwise. Dr. Oswald J. Smith in his book *The Revival We Need* points it out. After recalling incidents from several widespread and deep movements of God in modern times he says: "When I remember that such an Outpouring has come to China, India, Korea, Africa, England, Wales, the States, the Islands of the Seas, and many other places, but that Canada, Our Dominion, our own beloved country, has never in its history experienced a national Revival, my Heart cries out to God for such a Manifestation of Himself." Here is another reason why the engagement must intensify.

There are populous centres still without one Free Methodist church. Sad to say, even Montreal, our largest city, belongs in this class. Clarenceville, to the south, could provide a base for entry. The whole Quebec province, in fact, is scarcely touched yet. Specifically needed in Quebec are teachers who know the French language to teach in French Protestant schools, so French-speaking families who become evangelicals need not cut themselves off from the rest of their culture. Northern Ontario is a vast mission field. The Lakehead district has 100,000 people. With the completion of the St. Lawrence Seaway, cities all along the route to Fort William and Port Arthur now are ports for small ocean vessels. That fact spells opportunity and responsibility. Sudbury and North Bay and Kirkland Lake are all virginal. (It is estimated that population in the Sudbury area will exceed 300,000 by 1975.) Mission Secretary Lamson's optimism a decade ago that "one of the denomination's greatest advances in the next ten years may be registered in the Northern Ontario Home Missions District,"[4] has not been vindicated. Membership during the past five years there has actually dwindled. The Maritimes are still waiting. Church expansion in cities and towns everywhere has not kept pace with their growth. Numerous villages and towns that once had Free Methodist societies no longer do. We must recapture the genius for multiplying. The engagement must intensify.

No plans have yet been formulated to minister to the various non-British groups filling up many of our cities. Some other Evangelicals have done so. The engagement must intensify.

In welcoming the Holiness Movement militia into the Free Methodist fortress we have gained no actual increase for God in enemy territory. We have only consolidated earlier-won victories that all may now wage war more effectively. As Arthur Voteary, new associate editor of the *Herald* has pointed out, the merger itself will neither bring revival nor deepen the individual's life.

Responsibility for the new offensive will have to be felt and shouldered at all levels. According to *World Vision Magazine* (May, 1959) the Commission on Evangelism of the Church of England in a published report claimed, "... if the church ... is to become a weapon for evangelism, the clergy are, and must be, the key to the situation. ... The awful responsibility is his ... and he cannot escape it." The minister will need to put at least as much time and energy into his labours as the average business or professional man, and unhampered by petty home chores. (Some preachers would even be paid more if they organized themselves and produced more.)

It will take leading leadership. The superintendents will have a key part to play in any new offensive. The new men in these offices in almost every conference will doubtless bring fresh viewpoints to their tasks. Worthy projects will need to be initiated and the money and methods and men found to carry them through.

The Executive Board, the *Herald*, the schools,[5] the conference boards and committees, the individual societies, the homes—each will need to prayerfully examine its particular place in the over-all strategy. Surely, for instance, the Light and Life Hour should be put on many stations in hitherto unreached sections of the country as public relations projects.

Other sects and evangelical groups, the cults and Communism are crusading. Their followers are out-studying, out-witnessing, out-sacrificing, out-working, out-believing, out-committing, out-glowing and consequently, greatly out-growing us. We ought to contemplate the consequences should our crusade not come. God can find others, even with a less pure doctrine, if necessary, to do His work. As for us, would the solemn words of Fulton Oursler to the whole Christian western world—written in the face of Communist zeal—echo particularly in the direction of Canadian Free Methodists in the face of their opportunity and responsibility? He wrote "We are crusaders today—or we are corpses."[6]

We may be, as G. W. Stevens believes, at our Kadesh-Barnea NOW.

---

1. This is not an unrealistic figure in the light of far greater gains by the comparatively new Pentecostal Assemblies of Canada who, though having begun since 1900, have grown to at least 130,000 members and adherents.

2. The 1921 census figure was 8,787,949.
3. It is not flattering to discover that Walsh's recent history *The Christian Church in Canada* does not even name Free Methodism. This omission is, however, hard to excuse, while other lesser groups are included. Yet many people on every hand are unaware of Methodist bodies still in Canada.
4. See *Lights in the World* (Light and Life Press), by Byron S. Lamson. Permission to quote granted.
5. With some others, this writer emphatically believes that the schools in particular have an awesome responsibility in maintaining standards, in teaching the meaning of discipleship to an indulged generation, in training the leaders that are so desperately needed, and in imparting vision.
6. See *Why I Know There Is a God* (Permabooks).

✝.
"YE CHRISTIAN SOLDIERS, RISE!"

We have the message;[1] we have the machinery; and we have the money (if God can get it). Do we have the methods for this hour? Particularly, do we have the men? Perhaps it could be affirmed that if we have the men we have the methods also, for that spiritual giant, E. M. Bounds, declared, "Men are God's method. The church is looking for better methods. God is looking for better men . . . men whom the Holy Ghost can use." Let the church return to the custom of putting its hand individually on those men it thinks worthy. General invitations are too often not enough.

An article in the *Free Methodist* of May 1, 1956 by H. H. Smith, Sr., quoted Dr. Nolan B. Harmon from the *Christian Advocate* thus: "If the church is short of preachers, the reason is we have relied on divine calls and neglected to give human ones." The article described vividly how Peter Cartwright and William Taylor of early American Methodism were pushed . . . into the ministry."

New sources of manpower for the ministry will have to be tapped. Some in lay circles may need to hear and heed a call to fuller service—at costs that are crushing. (Those who remain lay will somehow need to grasp more fully the fact that God has one standard of discipleship and that their responsibilities to sacrifice with more and more dedicated dollars,[2] to witness with their words, to lift in the Sunday School and the various church departments,[3] and to pray and study God's Word[4] for strength and direction, are just as great.)

But in our youth, guided by our elders, lies our main hope. West Ontario's E. A. Cooper has written recently and significantly in the *Free Methodist* on the role of different age groups in any offensive. Using army language and basing his thought on army strategy, he said: "I emphatically see that the devising and launching of a daring crusade program . . . should not be the responsibility of youth, but of more mature minds . . . who lay out the objectives . . . along with the plan of action . . . and then call on youth to respond to the challenge." Then Mr. Cooper adds, quoting another minister of insight, ". . . it is the blitzkrieg daring of sink-or-swim dependence on faith that appeals to the fire and enthusiasm of youth." Let our "mature minds" do this kind of planning.

And while the seniors plan, let the juniors, male and female,[5] prepare. Let them prepare by vigorous discipline—the discipline of frugal living, of personal witnessing, of hard studying. In particular, let them take time for a year or more of Bible study, regardless of career intentions. Let all capable of a college education then get it to equip them for whatever larger service they can render. Let them prepare by giving more early attention to finding God's plan and launching into it, and less to finding a mate before they are mature enough to discern the kind of mate their tasks will require.[6] Let them prepare by learning to discern the true nature of "the world" in its hostility to spirituality. Especially let them prepare by prayer and by receiving the Holy Spirit in Pentecostal fullness. They will need such preparations to make them a generation that senses again a war is on.

The Battle is the Lord's. Who will volunteer? Who are ready even for conscription, if necessary? "The Son of God Goes Forth to War, Who Follows in His Train?" "Ye Christian Soldiers, Rise!" "Militant Men for Jesus, Fall in Line!"

"Canada has hardly begun to see the power that will shake the Dominion," wrote Mr. Sims in 1884. It is unthinkable that his vision provided for that power petering out in a few decades. But if Walsh is right, that "activism, born of frontier revivalism, is still the dominant note of Canadian Christianity," then our prospects are bright still—bright if we catch the vision and pay the price. Free Methodism can yet have a large part in making that dominant note ring out across the Dominion and even re-echo around the world.

---

1. It is reported that Torrey Johnson, first president of Youth for Christ International, said to a leader of a sister Holiness Church: "You people have had this teaching on the Holy Spirit a long time and you haven't done much about it."

2. The sums we have to spend on ourselves are proof we are not denying as our forefathers denied. Why not a revival of individuals sponsoring Christian workers to new areas as J. D. Shier did? Or sponsoring the Light and Life Hour in new regions?

3. "Not adequate, but available" will need to become the prevailing philosophy.

4. A revival of nothing but teaching and studying God's word in the days of Jehosophat had the remarkable effect of producing the fear of the Lord in all the kingdoms about Judah so none dared make war. See II Chronicles 17:7-10.

5. While men continue in short supply and women are receiving more and more acceptance in public life, should not the girls be encouraged to train theologically for sending out in pairs in the itineracy as before, and as the Salvation Army still does.

6. Qualified exponents of the disciplined life such as Oswald Smith and L. E. Maxwell agree that present-day marriages contracted much before, say, age 25 tend to be hasty and ill-advised and that a man who truly wants to be at his Christian best today needs to first concentrate on preparing for and getting started in his life's work. In a similar vein, Mel Donald, formerly of I. V. C. F. and now Canadian General Secretary of S. I. M., advises that the "entanglement" of "going steady" is best deferred until the 20's.

5.
"LEAD ON, O KING ETERNAL"

Lord of Hosts and Eternal King of the whole universe, for that broad branch of Thy church on earth called Methodism, we give Thee thanks. For that century-old section called Free Methodism, we offer particular thanks. That it chose to come to Canada at a critical time is evidence to us of the workings of Thy Sovereign will. With its pure doctrines and and brave standards, it has moved in the main stream of salvation. But oh, how slow has the current flowed of late. Entrusted with the task of spreading a witness, we have settled for little more than preserving it.

Give us a divine discontent with our status. Let this story—though hastily and incompletely and imperfectly told—be one means of jarring us loose from our lethargy. In the words of Shakespeare: "Now, let it work." Forgive us our flabbiness. Help us to remember the ancient days. Make the faith and the love and the zeal and the success of our fathers ours also. Make us to recognize good human leadership when it appears, and to follow it. Let tasks be delegated in keeping with the gifts among our group. But be Thou ever our Divine Leader, lest we head off from the highway of holiness into some byway of our own building.

We thank Thee for this good country, Canada. Its spaces, its resources, its liberties, its God-fearing leaders, its stature among the nations of the world—all are of Thee and through Thee. "Lord of the Lands, make Canada thine own." Help us to manfully tackle our tasks in the fulfilment of this prayer. Help us to realize that if the people are not confronted with this prayer. Help us to realize that if the people are not confronted with and enamoured of the Pearl of Great Price, they will surely fall for some gaudy fool's gold instead, and we will be responsible.

We thank Thee for the signs of new life through the decade just past. If Thou dost tarry, continue this vitality and heighten it through the whole century ahead. Renew Thy work and restore Thy grace and pour Thy Spirit on us mid-twentieth-century Canadian Free Methodists to make us adequate. And the glory shall be Christ's—"whenever, wherever, and forever." [1] Amen.

"Lead on, O King Eternal,
The day of march has come;
Henceforth in fields of conquest
Thy tents shall be our home.
Through days of preparation
Thy grace has made us strong,
And now, O King Eternal,
We lift our battle song.

"Lead on, O King Eternal,
Till sin's fierce war shall cease,
And holiness shall whisper
The sweet Amen of peace;
For not with swords loud clashing,
Nor roll of stirring drums;
With deeds of love and mercy,
The heav'nly kingdom comes.

"Lead on, O King Eternal,
We follow, not with fears;
For gladness breaks like morning
Where'er Thy face appears;
Thy cross is lifted o'er us;
We journey in its light:
The crown awaits the conquest;
Lead on, O God of might." [2]

---

1. Apologies to Jack Miner's parody on the 23rd Psalm.
2. Hymn by Ernest W. Shurtleff.

Section 11: Appendices

1.
SUMMARY OF HISTORICAL HIGHLIGHTS

First Free Methodist in Can.	early 1870's (Thomas Clark)
First preaching visit to Can.	1873 (B. T. Roberts to Ellesmere)
First Canadian to become Free Meth.	1874 or 75 (Gilbert Showers)
First pastoral appointment to Can.	1876 (C. H. Sage of North Mich.)
First Canadian society organized	1876 (at Galt)
Creation of Can. District	1877 (under C. H. Sage)
First camp meeting in Can.	1879 (at Hannon)
Organization of Can. Conference	1880 (at Galt)
Incorporation of Can. Conf. in Ont.	1884
Organization of E. Ont. and W. Ont. Confs.	1896 (at Armadale and Brantford)
Provincial Incorp. of Ont. Confs.	1897
First missionaries to W. Can.	1897 (W H. Wilson, of E. Ont. and Jennie Robinson of W. Ont. from W. Ont.)
First Sask. society organized	1900 (at Westview)
First Que. societies organized	1900 (at Clarenceville and St. Armand Center)
First camp meeting in W. Can.	1901 (at Sintaluta)
Creation of Man. and Northwest Dist.	1901
First foreign missionary	1902 (J. W. Haley to Africa)
Organization of Western Can. Conf.	1906 (at Moose Jaw)
First missionary to Alta.	1905 (O. L. King, of E. Mich. from W. Ont.)
Creation of Alta. Dist.	1906 (under O. L. King)
First Alta. society organized	1906 (probably at Edmonton)
First B. C. society organized	1908 (at New Westminster)
Organization of Sask. and Alta. Confs.	1914 (at Weyburn and Edmonton)
First All-Can. Convention	1920 (at Sarnia)
Creation of Prov. Canadian Exec. Bd.	1920
Beginning of Canadian F. M. Herald	1922
Opening of Lorne Park College	1924 (at Port Credit)
Incorp. of Church by Dom. Gov't.	1927
Semi-Centenary of Can. Conf.	1930
First All-Ont. Youth Rally	1939 (at Toronto, Broadview)
Opening of Moose Jaw Bible College	1940
First Missionary to Que.	1958 (A. H. Perry of E. Ont.)
H. M. Merger and new Dom. Charter	1959
Church-Wide Centenary Celebrations	1960

APPENDICES

2.
LISTS OF LABOURERS
DISTRICT OR CONFERENCE CHAIRMEN, ELDERS, AND SUPERINTENDENTS

(Names in brackets denote newcomers from the Holiness Movement Church)

North Michigan Conference (Canada District)—C. H. Sage.

Canada Conference—C. H. Sage, Albert Sims, James Craig, D. D. Marston, A. H. Norrington.

East Ontario Conference—Albert Sims, James Craig, W. H. Reynolds, A. H. Norrington, R. Burnham, C. Cunningham, E. Snyder, L. Slingerland, C. V. Fairbairn, E. J. Lee, W. H. Gregory, F. A. Daw, A. F. Ball, S. B. Griffith, M. S. Benn, J. F. Gregory, C. W. Kay, R. L. Casement, C. W. Reynolds, L. C. Ball, R. G. Babcock, A. B. Moffatt, [W. J. Stonehouse].

West Ontario Conference—W. C. Walls, A. H. Norrington, J. M. Eagle, James Craig, W. H. Wilson, F. M. Wees, O. L. King, M. S. Benn, D. Allan, L. H. Iles, S. Rogers, E. A. DeMille, L. E. Loveless, W. R. McCready, J. W. Peach, S. S. Bailey, P. K. Smith, R. H. Hamilton, C. E. L. Walls, G. W. Stevens, J. A. Robb, Ross Lloyd, W. C. Cowherd.

Western Canada Conference—F. M. Wees, O. L. King, W. H. Wilson, W. H. Haight, R. H. Hamilton.

Saskatchewan Conference—R. H. Hamilton, Fred F. Prior, F. M. Wees, J. A. Fletcher, T. L. Fletcher, C. B. Garratt, D. S. Wartman, R. Lloyd, A. Summers, E. R. Orser, M. C. Miller, G. S. Jenner, J. L. Walrath.

Alberta Conference—W. H. Haight, R. H. Shoup, H. B. Luck, C. G. Heath, A. S. Stambaugh, Streeter Arnett, P. L. Chase, C. E. Coxson, L. L. Lupton, Floyde Coxson, George Schnell, W. S. Angell, Douglas H. Russell.

Washington Conference (B. C. Coast and/or Interior District)—C. W. Burbank, F. J. Archer, A. S. Hill, B. T. Root.

ORDAINED MALE MINISTERS WHO HAVE SERVED CIRCUITS

North Michigan Conference (Canada District)—C. H. Sage, D. D. Marston, Wm. McKay, A. Sims, J. Craig, T. Carveth.

Canada Conference—C. H. Sage, J. Craig, A. Sims, T. Carveth, Wm. McKearnin, A. Allguire, W. C. Walls, Jos. Bretz, C. M. Smith, D. D. Marston, W. T. Hogue, W. S. Sansom, Richard Burnham, A. H. Norrington, W. H. Burkholder, W. H. Wilson, J. M. Eagle, G. A. Prior, W. H. Reynolds, Robt. Hamilton, D. Allan, Edward Walker, J. H. Winter, L. A. Sager, Geo. Overpaugh, W. J. Campbell.

East Ontario Conference—A. Sims, Wm. McKearnin, L. A. Sager, Ed. Walker, A. H. Norrington, W. H. Wilson, S. Rogers, S. T. Gunter, M. S. Benn, R. Burnham, W. H. Gregory, W. H. Reynolds, E. Snyder, H. L. Miner, Chas. Cunningham, A. Allguire, Geo. Overpaugh, J. W. Commodore, D. L. Gunter, C. Goodrich, C. A. Fox, S. Walker, Sperry Snyder, W. Zurbrigg, L. Slingerland, H. B. Luck, A. F. Ball, Miles Babcock, F. F. Prior, B. E. Stevenson,

THE BATTLE WAS THE LORD'S

Richard Babcock, E. J. Lee, I. M. Loucks, Walter Brown, B. C. Cunningham, C. V. Fairbairn, G. H. Bray, R. Bloye, J. F. Gregory, G. A. Mitchell, C. H. Cronin, W. H. Linstead, F. A. Daw, S. B. Griffith, Albert Gunter, I. S. W. Ryding, Frank Loft, J. W. Corey, H. J. Crowder, N. F. Perry, J. W. Potter, T. C. Hutchings, D. S. Wartman, Philo Chase, T. L. Fletcher, R. L. Casement, S. S. Bailey, E. R. Orser, C. R. Chatson, R. Sedore, F. Roy Chatson, C. W. Kay, B. A. Sutton, A. B. Moffatt, L. Arksey, B. Babcock, F. J. Jones, N. A. Bosko, L. C. Ball, G. H. Bache, C. W. Reynolds, E. S. Linstead, R. G. Babcock, J. T. King, H. D. Booth, W. H. Mallory, Wesley Armstrong, J. T. Martin, W. W. Simpkins, R. B. Warren, W. J. T. Hicks, C. Stephenson, G. D. Kirk, B. E. Dawson, E. S. Bull, Elmer Goheen, R. T. Holton, A. J. Thaxter, F. L. Burnham, Donald White, K. L. Snider, L. E. Fletcher, R. E. Dargan, A. H. Perry, P. O. Miller, W. S. Lyons, H. A. McLeod, K. B. Bauder, Paul N. Ellis, Clinton Bright, W. J. E. Daw, Harold McNutt, Gerald Kemp, L. E. Casement, J. W. Johnston, R. J. Slack, R. Thompson, Roy Goodrich, J. N. Patterson, W. L. Thomlinson, C. H. Zahniser, [R. L. Mainse, R. W. McCaw, E. H. R. Hawley, D. W. Eyre, G. A. Hammond, R. H. James, W. A. McMillan, R. C. Raymond, A. Wilkins, T. W. Alexander, R. Boston, S. A. Graham, A. Moors, W. C. A. McFarlane, M. J. Gilmer, A. W. Voteary, J. Poynter, T. J. Riddall].

West Ontario Conference—W. C. Walls, W. J. Campbell, A. H. Norrington, Robt. Hamilton, J. M. Eagle, David Allan, Jos. Bretz, C. H. Reed, M. S. Benn, J. P. Maitland, M. O. Coates, W. H. Wilson, F. M. Wees, J. W. Haley, T. L. Fletcher, John Timbers, A. E. Haley, Thomas A. Drury, Alpheus Tice, W. R. Pattison, Samuel Rogers, J. H. Winter, Ira Brown, J. A. Fletcher, R. A. Coates, E. E. Loveless, L. H. Iles, H. C. Freemantle, B. E. Stevenson, Wm. Hoffman, J. H. Roberts, H. G. Kent, E. A. DeMille, W. J. Cowherd, James Clink, C. Fader, Ed. Slingerland, G. W. Freeman, J. T. Abrams, J. H. Stewart, J. W. Peach, J. E. Ayre, J. W. Winans, Robert Bloye, Charles F. Snow, Peter Smith, Miles Babcock, W. E. McQuiggin, Thomas Robb, S. S. Bailey, Levi Ecker, W. R. McCready, Donald McGugan, C. E. L. Walls, J. W. Haley, R. G. Thompson, Wyatt Bates, J. C. Gare, D. H. McCallum, G. W. Stevens, H. A. Marlatt, J. R. Lambert, J. A. Hyndman, W. A. Miller, W. C. Peach, J. W. Corey, James R. Robb, G. F. Armitage, J. H. Withenshaw, Peter Bodnar, H. W. Loveless, E. A. Cooper, W. A. Smith, J. E. Campbell, W. C. Cowherd, B. McCready, W. A. Coates, J. W. Fletcher, D. S. Wartman, R. C. McCallum, E. J. Myatt, L. W. Mino, M. O. Nelson, Robt. Gordon, Ross Lloyd, C. F. Lyons, R. Glen Pelfrey, J. M. Winslow, C. A. Horton, A. E. Haley, N. A. McQuarrie, N. W. Winslow, H. W. Hobbs, Mel Prior, W. N. Teal, J. A. Campbell, R. S. Hicks, J. A. Tanner, G. E. Babcock, Byron Withenshaw, P. L. Chase, J. W. Joice, Fred Buchanan, K. L. Snider, [A. W. Voteary].

Western Canada Conference—W. H. Wilson, E. Steer, Chas. Dierks, Theo. Sharpe, F. M. Wees, J. B. Newville, O. L. King, R. H. Shoup, W. H. Haight, R. H. Hamilton, F. G. Matthews, R. R. Haight, F. D. Bradley, F. F. Prior, J. E. Ayre, T. L. Fletcher, A. E. Warren.

Saskatchewan Conference—F. M. Wees, J. B. Newville, W. A. Miller, E. Steer, F. F. Prior, F. D. Bradley, R. H. Hamilton, T. L. Fletcher, J. E. Ayre,

J. A. Fletcher, C. B. Garratt, R. E. Slingerland, B. C. Cunningham, H. A. Hurlbut, C. Cunningham, B. H. Robinson, J. T. Abrams, J. E. Evans, Neil McGugan, B. Smith, Arthur Buffam, J. F. Airhart, D. S. Wartman, A. Summer, P. L. Chase, W. C. DeMille, Ross Lloyd, R. H. Collett, J. A. Tanner, F. Markell, J. M. Winter, M. J. Hindmarsh, E. R. Orser, J. E. B. Cowan, T. J. Ellis, G. S. Jenner, M. D. Cole, W. H. Byggdin, R. E. Byggdin, L. Henwood, M. C. Miller, J. L. Walrath, Jr., P. S. Garratt, D. M. Hammond, L. E. Robertson, E. H. Hammond, J. Joice, K. Burton, Glenn Buffam, D. Bastian, W. A. Liddle, W. D. Kinney, Charles Little, J. W. Stewart, P. H. Buffam, K. R. Taylor, [E. H. Childerhose, W. H. Moore, H. E. Flesher, J. W. Babcock, R. S. Caswell, Jewell Snowden].

Alberta Conference—O. L. King, C. T. Dierks, R. R. Haight, R. H. Shoup, W. H. Haight, A. S. Stambaugh, B. H. Green, C. W. Cronin, C. G. Heath, F. B. Lewis, E. C. Madsen, G. W. Forrester, D. S. Forrester, H. B. Luck, W. S. Walker, J. R. Stewart, L. E. Barnes, C. P. Stewart, Streeter Arnett, Gilbert King, J. J. Walker, W. P. Carmichael, C. E. Coxson, Louis Freitag, J. M. Vines, F. W. Coxson, C. R. Brewer, P. L. Chase, Floyde Coxson, J. D. Kennedy, L. L. Lupton, W. S. Angell, J. N. Walker, D. H. Russell, C. F. Lyons, R. H. Pollock, G. Schnell, C. Kaiser, J. P. James, E. A. Sagert, A. E. Brown, K. H. James, C. B. Garratt, J. H. Coxson, R. J. Rogers, Frank W. Coxson, J. H. James, J. E. Larwill, H. R. Larwill, Henry Schnell, D. G. Harriman, K. A. Kennedy.

Washington Conference (B. C. Coast and/or Interior District)—T. H. Marsh, P. H. Griggs, C. E. McReynolds, C. S. McKinley, J. D. Marsh, Wm. Rennie, J. M. Clos, J. A. Logan, F. W. Cathey, O. F. Defoe, B. H. Alberts, M. C. Clarke, E. A. Haslam, H. B. Taylor, A. E. Stickney, F. M. Wees, J. K. Root, W. W. Dexter, E. H. Harmer, S. E. Fosket, Myron Boyd, Ben Smith, E. R. Bishop, L. E. McKeown, C. P. Stewart, J. E. Campbell, E. R. Streutker, F. W. Coxson, L. Whitehead, Geo. Leasor, E. Lee. W. S. Angell, J. H. James, Geo. Schnell, Don Bastian, F. Bunger, Ross Lloyd, W. Sooter, [Roy Caswell].

ORDAINED LADY MINISTERS WHO HAVE SERVED CIRCUITS

East Ontario Conference—Sara Gregory, Bessie Reid Kresge, Delia Potter, Pearl Reid, Edith Mainprize.

West Ontario Conference—Alice E. Walls.

Saskatchewan Conference—Lottie Babcock, Marion W. Larson.
Alberta Conference—Mrs. Ada Foreman Henderson.

MALE SUPPLY PASTORS AND PROBATIONERS WHO HAVE SERVED CIRCUITS

North Michigan Conference—George E. Shorter, Gilbert Showers, J. W. Banta, J. H. Winter, Wm. McKearnin, C. M. Smith, J. Richardson.

Canada Conference—C. M. Smith, A. C. Leonard, M. Harrison, J. Wright, J. A. Adams, C. Schantz, D. Fletcher, G. Bullard, A. Elsom, G. Gardiner, D. Burkholder, G. T. Coates, C. D. Ward, G. Gordanier, J. A. Prosser, J. Sullivan, Chas. Reed, J. S. Bradley, J. Ruttan, Thos. Clark, E. C. Best, J. Cronin,

J. A. Learn, W. R. Pattison, T. McAuley, J. Leeder, J. J. Loat, J. E. Clink, D. Campbell, Hector Gibbs, E. C. Smith, Wm. Gribble, Edward Slingerland, A. Wattam, A. A. Kelley, H. Mellor, James Bretz, J. E. Foreman, J. W. Sexsmith, Miles Benn, W. H. Gregory, J. W. Commodore, Stewart Walker, H. Rogers, H. L. Miner, L. Snider, S. Rogers, W. J. Shay, Wm. Miller, J. Mudge, J. Rebman, T. Fletcher, E. J. Draper.

East Ontario Conference—G. D. McBride, J. W. Sexsmith, J. Foreman, J. W. Featherston, J. Clink, T. A. Drury, B. Boone, J. Shay, E. J. Draper, J. W. Potter, M. Howard, Ira Brown, F. D. Bradley, J. Montgomery, C. A. Babcock, Geo. Alton, Chas. Chamberlain, C. Cassell, Chas. Dierks, M. Babcock, D. Brown, F. E. Hind, R. Slingerland, W. P. Harnden, F. F. Prior, Norman Harp, Wm. Findlay, J. D. Cowan, A. M. Gunter, S. E. Ward, Henry Smith, Arthur Harp, S. Lashan, H. J. Crowder, D. Crowder, M. Simpson, Gerald Dyer, D. W. Skelding, H. Goodrich, W. M. Simpkin, Ephraim Babcock, Norman Eastman, R. O. Anderson, Wm. Goodberry, Roscoe Hawley, Williard Reid, S. H. Jeffries, D. E. Smith, Walter Wood, H. L. Strapp, J. W. Haywood, N. Hoover, Basil Shaver, R. E. Davey, A. Halliday, A. Cresswell, K. L. Harnden, Ross Crowder, Elmer Olmstead, Damon Ball, John Sigsworth, Adam Chisholm, J. G. Elford, Stanley Campbell, Norman Hart, James Austin, Albert Muir, Walter Twiddy, Gerald Sedore, Ira Leeder, Richard Haggarty, Harold Sutton, Wesley Lohnes, George Sanders, C. H. Gilchrist, Clarence Mills, K. J. Snider, P. Mainprize, James Stewart, Donald John.

West Ontario Conference—Charles Singer, F. Gallettly, Wm. Miller, J. E. Foreman, J. A. Hamilton, G. H. Potts, J. A. Fletcher, Geo. B. Teal, Geo. Evans, Robt. Earl, Wm. Zurbrigg, R. A. Coates, Wm. Nix, Robt. Elsom, H. A. Hurlbut, R. E. Nichols, Chas. Dierks, D. Toole, J. B. Newville, C. Fader, E. Steer, Geo. Cook, W. H. Black, F. B. Lewis, A. L. Haight, J. T. Abrams, C. Eaton, R. Slingerland, Isaiah Bailey, E. Stevenson, Warren DeMille, H. Scarrow, Arthur Brown, Oliver Fairbanks, Francis Lees, G. E. Mayo, J. A. McClung, L. W. Waldron, G. Miller, Earl Knox, H. H. Hyndman, Paul S. Ecker, J. G. Purdy, R. Solomon, R. O. Anderson, A. G. Hartle, Clifford Lee, W. A. Coates, Leonard Moore, W. C. DeMille, C. E. Parker, Roscoe Cowherd, J. Shepherd, H. L. Parker, G. M. Powers, Murray Hewgill, E. H. Pelfrey, Gordon Johnson, Melvin Pastorius, Ed. Brown, Chas. Grandfield, Ernest Lucas, T. J. McMichael, Jas. Carne, John Knoll, Asa D. Leedy, A. S. Barker, Verlyn Schnell, J. Leon Winslow, Ray Sider, Carl Chatterton, H. O. Alward, Burton Hamilton.

Western Canada Conference—F. B. Lewis, A. L. Haight, H. Hurlbut, Chas. Babcock, Wm. Findlay, Chas. Garratt, W. E. Hunt, Howard Traxler, R. Elsom, Chas. Cronin, B. H. Green, Daniel Barr, J. F. Airhart, Wm. Miller, Wm. Wilkinson, W. J. Henderson.

Saskatchewan Conference—Wm. Wilkinson, Oren Tallman, W. E. Hunt, John Elsom, G. A. Prior, John W. Featherston, C. E. L. Walls, Harry Brown, Wm. Donaldson, H. E. Traxler, Jos. Jones, Leonard Rusk, R. J. Laing, C. Knowles, E. C. Mitchell, Haley Tanner, Ernest Myers, Gordon Mitchell, J. Pritchard, Floyd Cornish, H. Whiting, John Rodine, A. A. Powell, H. Cox, W. D. Walrath, F. W. Coxson, W. Bassingwaite, Louis A. Smith, F. Steinke, Wayne Brimner, Glenn Joice, K. Plum.

APPENDICES

Alberta Conference—A. C. Calhoun, W. J. Henderson, J. W. Arnett, A. L. Taylor, G. G. Delamarter, Philip Denney, G. Attrell, H. A. Hammer, C. S. Shaver, F. C. Wilson, John H. Stewart, Elmer Pearson, Peter Roesti, Fred Gardner, Ryley Walker, Ross King, T S. Hutton, Otto Pearson, J. E. Smith, Laughlin McLean, Carl Malmberg, Sprague Taylor, David Attrell, Bartlett Attrell, R. C. Arnett, I. A. Gleddie, Ellis Hughes, A. M. Sharp, Ira B. Luck, Elmer Greanya, D. D. Oughton, Luther Somerville, George Kaye, Lloyd Mack, L. E. Fletcher, Wesley Bonter, J. E. Campbell, J. H. James, E. Roesti, Jake Miller, M. E. Lee, Sheldon Robb.

Washington Conference—J. R. Elsom, T. L. Fletcher, L. E. Fletcher, Arthur Champion.

LADY SUPPLY PASTORS AND EVANGELISTS WHO HAVE SERVED CIRCUITS

North Michigan Conference (Canada District)—Valtina Brown, Jerusha Hagle, Frankie Davis, Arlette Eddy, Maggie Crittenden.

Canada Conference—Jerusha Hagle, Martha Thomas, Maggie Hoffman, Mary Alice Loveless, Nancy Schantz, Laura J. Warren, Mary Hutchinson, Katie Epps, Matilda Sipprell, Eva Wicker, Martha Stonehouse, Maggie Draper, Mary Craig, Jemima Hutchinson, Miss Merritt, Mary Keeler, Mary Milliken, Olive Diller, Millie Lapp, Maggie Boyd, Jane Hill, Mary Bretz, Kate Booth, Phoebe Avery, Mary Taylor, Nellie Fulton, Emma Woodcock, Eliza Wees, Valtina B. Harrison, Martha Page, Annie L. Green, Maggie Crittenden, Josephine Rusk, Mary Norrington, Jennie Robinson, Annie Robertson, Lydia Bortz, Emma Snider, Almira Hogle, Minnie Bauder, Mary Botting, Jemima Macklin, Alma Smith, Ada Slingerland.

East Ontario Conference—N. Schantz, Emma Buck, Mary Diller, Jennie Robinson, Emma Snider Harnden, Esther Goodberry Brown, Lottie Babcock Ada Foreman, Eliza Free, Gertrude Pratt, Louise Hicks Findlay, Kate Clark, Amanda Hughes Norrington, Frances Botting, Caroline Gregory, Sadie Gunter, Laura J. W. Coleman, Ethel Davey, Georgia Wilkins, Nina Green, Ella Luck, Edith Sears, Annie Slack, Maud Everson, Olive Butcher, Edna Redner, Effie Gibson, Pearl Rebman, Annie Stark, Alberta Sims, Gertrude Patterson, Alvina Sine Gunter, Florence Potter, Edith Draper, Pearl Rye, Julia Smart Grey, Agnes Benn, Violet Gunter, Iva Snider, Violet Mallory, Edith Snyder, Edith Jones, Myrtle Halliday, Luella Ball, Lulu Halliday, Ethel Griffith, Gladys Miller, Grace Goheen, Neva Kemp, D. M. Wolsey, Audrey Robinson, Elmira Webb, Ila Hart, Ethel F. Chase, Lois Kemp, Helen McNutt, Muriel Darling, Bertha Mills.

West Ontario Conference—L. J. Warren, A. L. Green Steer, J. Rusk Wees, J. Macklin, M. Sipprell, A. Smith, Ada Slingerland, Alice Underhill, N. Schantz, Jennie R. Elsom, Mary Toole Clink, Emma Geary, Hattie Toole, Delia Sinden, Harriet Sheldon, Mary J. Everhart, Emma Green, Bertha Purdy, Flossie Teal, Maggie Allan, Lizzie J. King, Mabel Pett, Lillian Beirge, Effie Cowherd, Ada Foreman, Martha Mullen, Emily Kent, Lillian Briggs, Nellie Smith, Annie Botting, Alice E. Walls, Elizabeth Allan, Alma Scott Haley, Jane Hill Coates, Harriet Loveless, Harriet McCready, Mabel Peach, Grace Hyndman, Olive Vail, Myrtle Halliday, Martha Marlatt, Margaret Allan

THE BATTLE WAS THE LORD'S

Stevenson, Ruby Hicks, Hazel Arnold, Minerva McQuarrie, Edna Riblett, Sarah Miller, Evelyn Dawson, Katie Burton, Ella Lishman, Pauline Avey, Kathleen Garland, Muriel Darling, Jennie Hamilton, Kaye B. Mitchell.

Western Canada Conference—Josie Wees, Annie L. Steer, Thilia Champion, Hannah Lawrence, Lizzie King, Agnes Cronin, Florence Haight, Nellie Hunt, Ada Foreman, Alma Dies.

Saskatchewan Conference—Josie Wees, Sarah Miller, Edith Abbott, Eliza Fletcher, Victoria Ayre, Eliza Free, Alma Dies, Laura Gibbs Buffam, Nettie Raymer, Pearl Rusk, Eva Bradley, Myrtle Smith, Edith Sutherland, Hazel S. Knowles, E. C. Mitchell, Grace L. Summers, Ethel F. Chase, Lela DeMille, Margaret Collett, Ina Byce, Myrtle Moor, Verna Smith, Florence Moreside, Luella Dies, Helen Markell, Ina Miller, Doris Gray, Bernice Tanner, Lois Wheeler, Ruby Beckstead, Doreen Wilson.

Alberta Conference—Florence Haight, Alma Dies, Lizzie L. King, Alice Heath, Bertha Calhoon, Leila Ferguson, Lena Nelson, Leila Taylor, Lamorah Sellers, Flora Wilson, Katherine Shaver, Nina Taylor, Margaret Taylor, Vivian Madsen, Irene Kaye, Dora Eckert, Mildred Mottet, Betty Mack, Ethel Chase, Ella Somerville, Maude Rogers.

Washington Conference (B. C. Coast District)—Marion Rennie, Eva Alberts, Josie R. Wees, Alice Simpson, Mona McKeown.

W.M.S. PRESIDENTS

Canada Conference—Mrs. Mary Craig.

East Ontario Conference—Mrs. Mary Craig, Lottie Babcock, Agnes Benn, Caroline Gregory, Margaret Stevenson, Annie Ball, Mary M. Shier, Margaret Wartman.

West Ontario Conference—Mary Walls, Mary Rogers, Mary T. Clink, Agnes Benn, Lydia M. Birdsall, Harriet McCready, Harriet Loveless, Effie Cowherd, Alice E. Walls, Ethel Smith, Alma Haley.

Western Canada Conference—Annie L. Steer, Jennie Elsom.

Saskatchewan Conference—Annie L. Steer, Josie R. Wees, Edith Brown, Margaret Wartman, Hazel M. Crocker, Laura Buffam, Florence Hamilton.

Alberta Conference—Ada Henderson, Alice Heath, Florence E. Haight, Martha Wilson, Agnes Morin, Grace Wiancho, Reno Short, Ethel Dickson, Winnie Brewer, Ruth James, Ruth Russell, Della Kennedy.

Note—Until 1923 the organization was named Women's Foreign Missionary Society (W.F.M.S.).

APPENDICES

3
ACKNOWLEDGEMENTS

Books Consulted—The Bible, Free Methodist Hymnal, Worship in Song, Annual Conference Minutes and Yearbooks 1879-1959 (Light and Life Press), Earnest Christian—C. H. Zahniser, History of the Free Methodist Church—Hogue (Light and Life Press), Autobiography of C. H. Sage—(Light and Life Press), Story of Our Church—Howland (Light and Life Press), Why Another Sect—Roberts (Earnest Christian Publ.), Ordaining Women—Roberts (Earnest Christian Life Press), Free Methodist Books of Discipline (Light and Life Press), The Story of Fifty Years—Burritt (Light and Life Press), Plain Account of Christian Perfection—Wesley (Nazarene Publishing House), Life in Mozambique and South Africa—Haley (Light and Life Press), Lights in the World—Lamson (General Missionary Board), The More Excellent Way—Turner (Light and Life Press), The Wesleyan Message—Fairbairn Chapter (Light and Life Press), Wesley and Democracy—Bready (Thorn Press), A Tale of Two Brothers—Brailsford (Rupert Hart—Davis), Living in Two Worlds—Tenney (Light and Life Press), The Revival We Need—Smith (Marshall, Morgan and Scott), Why I Know There is a God—Oursler (Permabooks, Doubleday), Screwtape Letters—Lewis (Geoffrey Bles Ltd.), History of Methodist Episcopal Church in Canada—Webster (Canada Christian Advocate), The Methodist Church and Missions in Canada and Newfoundland—Sutherland (Methodist Church of Canada), First Century Methodism in Canada—Sanderson (Briggs), Egerton Ryerson, His Life and Letters—Sissons (Ryerson), Our Living Traditions—Egerton Ryerson chapter—Harris (Toronto University Press), Christian Church in Canada—Walsh (Ryerson), Julius Caesar—Shakespeare (Copp Clark), New Practical Standard Dictionary (Funk and Wagnalls) and others.

Booklets Consulted—Free Methodism in Canada—Sims (Report of 1920 Sarnia All-Canada Convention); Canadian Year Book of Free Methodist Church of North America, 1935; 50 Years of Progress—Golden Anniversary Issue of the West Ontario Conference, 1895-1945; Semi-Centennial Anniversary of Free Methodism in Western Canada, 1898-1948; These Our Fifty Years (Hymers History)—Grandfield; The Holiness Movement Church—H. W. Pointen (Thesis); Bill S-27 (Incorporation Act, 1959); Quick Canadian Facts, Fifteenth Annual Edition.

Periodicals Consulted—Earnest Christian, Free Methodist, Western Canada Tidings, Saskatchewan Tidings, Canadian Free Methodist Herald, Missionary Tidings, Light and Life Hour Transmitter, Moose Jaw Bible College Newsletter, Annual Free Methodist World Missions Report, Canadian Holiness Federation News, World Vision Magazine, People's Magazine, Missionary Standard, High Magazine, United Church Observer, Pentecostal Testimony, Maclean's Magazine, Ontario Government Services, Kingston Whig-Standard, Oshawa Times, Toronto Globe and Mail.

Lengthy Manuscripts Prepared Especially for This Book—Early History to 1895—Alice E. Walls, East Ontario Survey—Sara E. Gregory, Free Methodism in Western Canada—R. H. Hamilton and Zella Nixon, History of Central British Columbia—J. E. Smith and C. P. Stewart, West Ontario Camp

THE BATTLE WAS THE LORD'S

Grounds—J. A. Robb and L. E. Freeman, History of Housey's Rapids Church—L. C. Ball, History of Orillia Church—Fred Smith, History of Oshawa Church—R. L. Casement, Toronto Experiences—Mr. and Mrs. Henry Mellor, History of Hannon Church—G. W. Freeman, History of Brantford Church—Mr. and Mrs. Henry Mellor, History of Church on St. Joseph Island—P. K. Smith and Florence Power, History of Grandview Church—R. H. Hamilton, Origin of West Summerland Church—Frances (James) Mino, Sketches of Life and Experiences—David Allan, Life Story—F. B. Lewis, Autobiography—W. H. Gregory, Life Story—M. S. Benn, Biography of F. A. Daw—W. J. E. Daw, Lorne Park College—L. C. Ball, Moose Jaw Bible College—Mrs. D. S. Wartman and J. Wesley Stewart, Kelvin Revival—H. H. Hyndman, Keith Revival—Leticia Nelson DeMille, Canadian Executive Board—L. C. Ball, The Holiness Movement Church—E. H. Childerhose, Population and Immigration Figures—Dominion Bureau of Statistics.

Other Lengthy Manuscripts Consulted—Old Time Primitive Methodism in Canada—Mrs. Agar Hopper, Church Properties of Sarnia District of W. Ontario—C. E. L. Walls, I Call to Remembrance—Bishop Fairbairn's Autobiography, Jottings by the Way and Itinerating—James Craig, History of Alberta Conference—Shoup, Haight (R.R.) and Lewis, Woman's Work in Canadian Free Methodism—Mary C. Craig, Happy Tom—Thos. Clark.

Writers of Pertinent Short Reports, Press Articles, Letters, etc.—*General*—Alice E. Walls, W. C. Mavis, Byron Lamson, R. B. Warren, J. F. Gregory, Geo. Fuller, Jr., L. E. Maxwell, Bishop C. V. Fairbairn, Wilbur Sutherland, and others. *East Ontario*—James Ireland, C. H. Sage, A. Sims, James Craig, David and Mrs. Kirk, Henry Mellor, A. H. Norrington, M. S. Benn, T. A. Shaver, Annie S. Ball, R. Sedore, W. J. E. Daw, A. H. Perry, R. G. Babcock, Alberta Sims Webb, Margaret Bray, Dan Zurbrigg, Edith Goheen, Jennie Hamilton, Minnie Bauder Crimmins, B. A. Sutton, Mary Shier, R. E. and Grace Goheen, Minnie Hickley, Josie R. Wees, Wm. Zurbrigg, Emerson Snyder, Elizabeth Dierks, R. H. Hamilton, L. E. Casement, Bruce Reid, Nora Perry, Chas. Sigsworth, R. W. McCaw, Mrs. C. R. Elford, E. S. Bull, C. W. Reynolds, C. W. Kay, R. E. Sedore, Winnifred Bailey, J. T. King, James Aldous, Philo Chase, Mabel Luck Gleddie, Maude Bovee, Mabel Lyons, John A. Ball, W. J. E. Daw, Joanna D. Harnden, Edith Mainprize, R. L. Casement, E. A. Cooper, William Fell, Mary Crittenden, Mrs. E. C. Smith, and others. *West Ontario*—C. H. Sage, A. Sims, J. Craig, T. P. Jarnigan, J. W. Banta, Thos. McClive, A. H. Norrington, Laura J. Coleman, Matilda S. Taylor, J. W. Haley, A. E. Haley, E. E. Loveless, Mrs. Chas. Earl, Cornelia Beckham, J. W. Winans, S. H. Williams, R. Slingerland, M. S. Benn, Mary R. Whitmore, D. Burkholder, W. J. Campbell, Mrs. L. C. Fletcher, B. E. Stevenson, Josie R. Wees, Martha Marlatt, Margaret Stevenson, W. E. McQuiggin, P. K. and Ethel S. Smith, Earl Fiddler, Ada Foreman, Jennie Agar, Mary Botting, Sarah Miller, Geo. E. Mayo, Bessie G. Waring, Edna Riblet, W. J. Cowherd, Florence Power, G. A. Lees, Frank Lees, G. W. Stevens, C. E. L. Walls, L. E. Freeman, Harriet McCready, J. A. Campbell, James Robb, W. C. Cowherd, and others. *Saskatchewan*—W. H. Wilson, D. S. and Margaret Wartman, R. E. Slingerland, Minnie Bush Robinson, Josie R. Wees, M. J. Hindmarsh, Mrs. Edith Green, Midford Kirk, F. M. Wees, Zella Nixon, J. L. Walrath, and others. *Alberta*—Grace A. Wiancho, Nellie Whittaker, A. L. Somerville,

APPENDICES

Jesse Allen, O. W. Lyons, H. J. Schnell, Floyde Coxson, Douglas Russell, and others. *British Columbia*—C. S. McKinley, Cora Abrams Prior, Ida Townsend, J. E. Campbell, Don Bastian, C. W. Burbank, and others.

Individuals Who Gave Valuable Oral Information—M. S. Benn, E. A. DeMille, Chas. Wells, W. H. Gregory, Allen German, Wm. E. Sweigard, Jennie Hamilton, Rhoda Sims Rupert, A. E. Smith, W. L. Smith, Geo. Fuller, Jr., Robert Lightle, and others.

Individuals Who Made Helpful Criticism of Certain Portions of the Manuscript—R. B. Warren, Sara E. Gregory, Jennie Hamilton, Zella Nixon, J. Wesley Stewart, E. H. Childerhose, L. C. Ball, J. F. Gregory, Bishop C. V. Fairbairn, Bishop L. R. Marston.

Individuals Who Furnished Photos and/or Cuts—Alice E. Walls, C. E. L. Walls, Jennie Walls Hamilton, Minnie Bauder Crimmins, Sara Gregory, Alice Shillington Woods, Chas. Wells, Alice Lyons Dyer, W. J. E. Daw, Joanna Daw Harnden, Annie Slack Ball, Don Bastian, L. C. Ball, S. B. Griffith, R. E. Goheen, Edith Goheen, F. W. Coxson, Frank Lees, J. L. Walrath Jr., Carl Chatterton, Edith Mainprize, Reta Beare, L. E. Freeman, G. W. Stevens, Dorothy Wilkins Walker, Bruce Reid, Lyle Garratt, Ethel Hartford, Ruby Grant Kennedy, Mabel Denne Lyons, Gerald Sedore, Toronto Telegram, Lorne Park College, Moose Jaw Bible College, Standard Publishing House and others.

Lenders of Books, Manuscripts or Clippings—Jennie Hamilton, Rhoda Sims Rupert, Bishop C. V. Fairbairn, H. W. Pointen, S. B. Griffith, R. E. Dargan, Carman Gilchrist, Mrs. J. T. Ball, Minnie Bauder Crimmins, Lorne Park College Library, Oshawa Public Library.

Designer of Cover (including new publishing emblem)—Elmira Webb Freeman.

4.
INDEX

A
Abbott, Edith, 162
Abrams, J. T., 140, 148
Abrams, O. C. & Mrs., 178
Adams, J. A., 76
Adolphustown, Ont., 30
Africa, 53, 87, 89, 114, 116
Agar, James, 18
Agar, Jennie Milton, 80
Agincourt, Ont., 85, 192, 197
Alameda, Sask., 157
Alamonda, Mich., 93
Alberta B. C. District (Alberta Conf.), 173
Alberta Conf., 48-52, 152, 167-175, 176, 186, 188, 199, 218, 221, 232, 237, 245, 256, 257
Alberta Dist. (Alberta Conf.), 174

Alberta Dist. (Western Canada Conf.), 168
Alberta Dist. (West Ontario Conf.), 158, 167-169
Alberts, B. H., 142
Alderson, Alta., 170-4
Aldous, James, 110, 258, 261
Alexander, Torance & Louisa, 260
Alix, Alta., 173, 237
Allan, Annie, 136
Allan, David & Mrs., 35, 38, 54, 85, 92, 98, 103, 106, 123-125, 140, 144, 146, 184, 217, 237, 242
Allan, Elizabeth (see E. A. Foy)
Allen, Jesse & Jay, 168, 171, 186
Allguire, Austin, 20, 39, 76, 78, 91, 97, 105
Almas, Charles & Mrs., 150

285

Almas, David & Mrs., 150
Alton, George, 122
Ames, Sask., 165
Amethyst, Alta., 173
Ancaster, Ont., 69, 146
Anderson, A., 163
Andrews, M. E., 237
Angell, W. S., 177
Annesley College, 227, 239
Annett, Esther, 141
Appleton, C. Floyd & Laura M., 34, 53, 83, 123, 202
Arksey, Lawrence & Ruth, 53, 204, 205
Arlington Beach, Sask., 255
Armada, Alta., 171, 173
Armadale, Ont., 20, 27, 44, 61, 85, 92, 93, 105, 107, 183, 192, 196, 23, 242
Arnett, Streeter, 171-6
Arnette, John & Mrs., 174
Arnold, P. B., 50, 51
Asbury, Bishop, 14, 17, 52
Asbury Seminary, 234, 259
Assiniboia, Sask., 154
Austin, Lily, 168, 169
Avonlea, Sask., 164, 165

B
Babcock, Barnet, 115, 130, 134
Babcock, Charles, 87, 104, 120, 129
Babcock, Lottie, 105, 121, 122, 134, 162, 243
Babcock, M. S., 95, 120
Babcock, R. G., 120, 246, 250
Babcock, Richard, 118, 134
Babcock, Seymour, 153
Bache, G. H., 119, 120, 127, 248, 249
Bailey, Isaiah, 139, 199
Bailey, S. S., 132, 199, 243
Baird, Crawford, 82
Baker, F. L., 129, 137, 139, 173
Baker, Michael & Mrs., 80
Baldwin, Ont., 108, 236
Ball, A. F. and Annie Slack, 55, 59, 110, 115-17, 121, 127, 134, 243
Ball, Beatrice, 130
Ball, L. C., 103, 124-30, 220-7, 245
Ball, Simon, 59
Ballantine, J., 145
Bangs, Nathan, 22, 25, 30, 40
Banta, J. W., 65-8
Baptist Churches, 23, 136, 164, 258, 267
Barkway, Ont., 44, 85, 91-3, 106, 124, 184
Barnell, John, 68
Barnes, Dora, 120
Barnim, Edward, 81
Barrett, C. B., 81, 82, 99

Barrie, Ont., 90, 126, 127, 248, 249
Bartonville, Alta., 171
Bartonville, Ont., 29, 68, 69
Bashaw, Alta., 171, 237
Bastian, Donald, 256
Bates, Wyatt, 141, 145
Battram, Sask., 46, 162, 163, 166
Bauder, Minnie, (see M. B. Crimmins)
Bayes, George, 144
Bayham, Ont., 150
Bay of Quinte, 18, 31
Baysville, Ont., 85, 95, 125
Bean, Albert., 97, 133
Beare, John & Mrs., 103, 243
Beaver Creek, Ont., 105, 129
Beckham, Maria, 72
Beers, Alexander & Mrs., 171, 174, 178
Belfast, Ireland, 239
Belgian Congo, 53, 98, 201, 259, 260
Belhaven, Ont., 20, 23, 27, 44, 77-80, 91-4, 101, 102, 107, 153, 193, 194, 236
Belleville, Ont., 86, 135, 248
Belmont, Man., 47, 154-6, 200
Benito, Man., 160
Benn, Agnes Moir, 51, 98, 148, 184
Benn, Isaac, 86
Benn, M. S., 24, 38, 41, 55, 86, 95, 98, 102, 106-14, 139, 144-8, 184-5, 235, 243
Bentley, Alta., 169, 172
Benzinger, John, 91, 103, 124
Berg, Peace Haley, 53, 202, 209
Bible Christian Church, 17, 18, 134
Bield, Man., 163-5
Bigger, Mrs. Nathan, 171
Birch River, Man., 165, 254
Black, Andrew, 142
Black, W. H. 167
Blackheath, Sask., 159, 200
Blewett, Edgar & Mrs., 175, 178
Blews, R. R., 126
Bloomfield, Ont., 133
Bloye, Robert, 148
Bodnar, Peter & Meta, 149, 150, 164
Bodtcher, Olive, 259
Boharm, Sask., 155
Bolingbroke, Ont., 120, 121
Bongard, Ont., 134
Boone, Bernard, 106, 124
Booth, Kate, 20, 82
Bosko, Nicholas & Mrs., 130, 212, 248
Boston, R., 241
Botting, Anna, 89, 137, 144, 192
Botting, Mary, 106, 147
Botwright, Teresa H., 73, 102, 209
Boyd, Myron F., 175, 261

INDEX

Boyes, Sarah, 162
Bowman, Ephraim & Mrs., 58, 73, 75
Bracebridge, Ont., 19, 20, 27, 28, 34, 35, 48, 56, 69-71, 78, 79, 83-6, 90, 95, 98, 106, 113, 123-5, 143, 152-4, 166, 184, 185, 194, 200, 202, 212
Bradley, Frank D. & Eva Breeze, 107, 113, 123, 160
Brandon, Man., 165, 166, 254
Brantford Dist. (West Ontario Conf.), 97, 106, 144, 152
Brantford, Ont., 36, 38, 39, 44, 52, 82, 84, 92, 94, 97, 100, 102, 106, 144, 153, 187, 193, 203, 207, 253
Bray, Gordon, 112, 198, 259
Bray, Harry, 198
Bray, Margaret, 123
Brazil, 239
Bready, John Wesley, 13
Brethren in Christ Church, 223
Bridge, Amos, 102, 105
Bright, Clinton, 128, 248
Bright, Marion Roberts, 103
Brisco, Carolyn (see C. B. Gregory)
British Columbia, 173, 175-8, 188, 238, 256, 257, 268
British Columbia Coast Dist. (Wash. Conf.), 176, 237, 256, 257
British Columbia Dist. (Alta. Conf.), 174
British Columbia Interior Dist. (Alta. Conf.), 257
British Columbia Interior Dist. (Wash. Conf.), 237, 257
Broadview Indian Mission, 255
Brooking, Sask., 162
Brooks, C. D., 15
Brown, Dr., 34, 67
Brown, Esther Goodberry, 87, 131, 133
Brown, Henry, 150
Brown Hill, Ont., 108
Brown, Ira, 121, 131, 133, 147, 148
Brown, J. W., 149
Brown, Valtina, 69-71, 75, 192
Brown, Walter, 117
Brown, W H., 155, 217, 218
Brownlee, Ann, 142
Bruce, Alta., 52, 167-72, 175, 199
Buchanan, Fred, 253
Buckley, Arthur, 117
Buffalo, N. Y., 54, 61, 65, 70, 81, 91, 124, 197
Buffam, A. A., 163, 166
Bull, Earl S., 110, 124, 134, 245, 246, 249
Bunce, George, 51, 66, 67, 74
Burbank, C. W., 257

Burkholder, David, 90
Burkholder, Hannah, 144
Burkholder, W. H., 83, 90
Burnham, Fletcher & Edna C., 35, 135, 183, 249
Burnham, Richard & Charlotte B., 20, 35, 38, 71, 85, 89, 99, 100, 105, 118, 133, 183, 184, 194, 212, 224, 242
Burnley, Ont., 98, 105, 130-2, 248
Burridge, Ont., 120

C

Caistor Centre, Ont., 144, 253
Caledonia, Ont., 18
Calhoon, A. C. & Bertha, 171, 173
Calgary, Alta., 153, 161, 167-73, 199, 256
Calmers, Alta., 168
Campbell, Annie Robertson Walls, 95
Campbell, J. E., 175, 178, 257
Campbell, John A., 254
Campbell, M. A. & Mrs., 239
Campbell, R. B., 128
Campbell's Bay, Quebec, 250
Campbell, W. J., 58, 94, 100, 106, 111
Campbellford, Ont., 123, 132-3, 212, 248
Camp Grounds, 235-37
Canada Conference, 26, 44, 51, 52, 77, 81, 88, 95, 104, 181-5, 192, 216, 270
Canada Dist. (North Mich. Conf.), 26, 66, 70
Canadian Executive Board, 5, 6, 41, 128, 183-90, 196, 200, 216-22, 245, 251, 258, 261, 269, 272
Canadian Free Methodist Herald, 57, 176, 187, 190, 213, 221-4, 239-42, 249, 258, 272
Canadian Holiness Federation, 187, 190, 258
Canadian Methodist Holiness Federation, 211
Canadian Service Fund, 219, 221
Canboro, Ont., 34, 145, 203
Cannington Manor, Sask., 254
Canuck, Man., 165
Carl's Hill, Alta., 173
Carlstadt, Alta. (see Alderson)
Carmichael, A. M., 163, 223
Carmichael, Wm., 172
Caron, Sask., 156
Carter, Florence, 209
Carter, James, 72, 77, 78
Carter, Mr. & Mrs. (Galt), 32
Carter, Wm. & Isabel, 32, 65
Cartwright, Peter, 73, 273
Carveth, Thomas, 71, 76

287

Casement, Francis, 263
Casement, Lorne, 250
Casement, R. L. & Olive, 5, 6, 109, 110, 124, 134, 220, 258
Castleton, Ont., 130, 132
Castor, Alta., 171
Caswell, Andrew & Mrs., 239
Cataraqui, Ont., 99, 100, 105, 113, 135
Cedar Grove, Ont., 142
Centenary General Conference, 7, 244, 245
Champion, Thelia, 168
Charlemont, Ont., 27-31, 44, 87-90, 92, 106, 125, 133, 136, 139, 140, 152, 185, 192, 236, 245
Charters (see Incorporations)
Chase, P. L. & Ethel F., 127, 163, 164, 174, 177, 234, 248, 249, 254
Chatham, Ont., 97, 140
Chatson, Clarence, 120, 130
Chatson, Roy, 130, 134, 135
Chatterton, Carl E., 254
Childerhose, E. H., 8, 239
China, 35, 53, 114, 123, 202-5, 238, 239
Chippawa, Ont., 31, 67, 70, 79, 192
Christian Guardian, 118, 222
Christie, J. D., 97
Church of England, 17, 23, 268, 272
Church of the Nazarene, 258
Clarenceville, Quebec, 115, 122, 250, 271
Clarendon, Ont., 57, 87, 92-100, 105
Clark, Bishop W. H., 148
Clark, B. P., 20, 41, 86, 102, 135
Clark, Kate, 48, 132, 134
Clark, Thomas, 38, 61, 63, 74, 79, 196
Clifton, Ont., 79
Climax, Man., (see Canuck)
Clinesville, Ont. (see Elfrida)
Clink, James, 75, 83, 97, 105, 107
Clink, Mary, 147
Clive, Alta., 173
Clyde, Alta., 237
Coates, George, 73
Coates, Marcus O., 106, 145, 148
Coates, Robert A., 74, 143, 150
Cobden, Ont., 241
Cole Lake, Ont., 117, 119, 198, 249
Cole, Sam W & Dora, 167, 169
Coleman, Gen. Supt. G. W., 70, 101, 105, 123, 192
Coleman, Laura Warren, 79, 81, 88, 90, 92, 97, 106, 123, 136, 192, 193
Collett, Ronald & Margaret H., 53, 205, 206, 260
Commodore, J. W., 87, 97-105, 113, 121
Communism, 56, 272

Confederation, 16, 268
Congo-Nile, 53, 164, 201, 206, 207, 209
Conjuring Creek, Alta., 168, 170, 199
Connor, R. W. & Mrs., 130
Consecon, Ont., 134
Cook, Norman E., 239, 260
Cooper, Annie M., 112
Cooper, E. A., 48, 146, 219, 243, 251, 254, 258, 259, 273
Cooper's Falls, Ont., 93, 98, 124
Cooper, Wm., 72
Coopersville, Mich., 26
Cordova Mines, Ont., 128, 129, 135, 248
Corey, J. W., 108, 121
Countryman, Agnes, 151
Courtney, B. C., 257
Cowherd, Effie, 38, 53, 144, 147, 203
Cowherd, Grace, 38
Cowherd, Harriet (see H. C. McCready)
Cowherd, Mrs. Thomas, 82
Cowherd, W. Crawford, 82, 234, 254
Cowherd, W J., 203, 217, 224
Coxson, C. E., 174, 177, 221
Coxson, Floyde W., 173, 220, 256
Crabbs, Mr. & Mrs., 150
Craig, James, 20, 23, 25, 32, 39-44, 49, 57, 58, 76, 78-81, 84-105, 181, 184, 193, 222, 250
Craig, Mary D., 42, 51-3, 70, 106, 180
Cresswell, Arthur, 259
Crimmins, Minnie Bauder, 87, 90, 95, 100, 102
Crittenden, Maggie, 68
Cronin, C. W., 171, 172
Cronton, Ont., 140
Crowder, Ross, 113
Crown Hill, Ont., 19, 20, 83, 90, 93, 95, 105, 126, 127
Cunningham, Charles, 94, 98, 105, 113, 124, 131, 132, 134
CYC, 48, 236, 245, 248, 254, 255, 259, 263

D

Dargan, R. E., 134, 248, 258, 260
Davey, Ethel (see E. D. Ryff)
Davey, Ira, 91
Davidson, Man., 165
Davis, Frankie, 68, 74
Davis, Mrs. J., 178
Davis, Sask., 164
Daw, F. A. & Margaret J. 41, 114-20, 125-8, 189, 203, 222, 268
Daw, Wm., 190, 250
Dawn Mills, Ont., 100, 106, 140
Dawson, B. E., 248

INDEX

Dawson, Evelyn, 137
Dawson, Joseph, 141
Day, R. E., 22
Delamarter, George, 259
Delburne, Alta., 172
DeMille, Benjamin, 74, 75, 87
DeMille, Clarke, 103, 260
DeMille, Edward A., 103, 136, 141
DeMille, Fannie, 88, 103, 206
DeMille, Wesley C. & Lela S., 53, 103, 206, 260
DeMille, Wm. E., 217, 224
Demorestville, Ont., 134
Denbigh, Ont., 98, 130, 166, 188
Denney, Phil, 172
Denwoodie, Alta., 168
Desert Lake, Ont., 27, 117, 204, 211
Devoist, M., 82
Deyo, Clara, 89
Deyo's Corners, Ont., 87, 115, 117, 211, 212, 249
Dickson, Wm., 239
Diefenbaker, John, 267, 268
Dierks, Charles T. & Mrs., 124, 125, 158, 159, 171, 176
Dies, Alma, 171
Diller, Mary, 97
Diller, Olive, 19, 82
Dixon, Lottie Anderson, 126
Dominican Republic, 53, 66, 203
Donald, B. C., 257
Donnell, Stanley, 212, 235
Draper, E. J., 170
Draper, Maggie, 192
Dresden, Ont., 80, 87-9, 106, 140
Dryden, Ont., 251
Dry Lake, Sask., 162
Dry Town, Ont., 80, 108
Dulmage, Wm., 94
Dunham, Darius, 32
Dunham, F. J., 97
Dunnville, Ont., 145, 253
Durban, Man., 161, 162
Dyer, Stanley, 259, 260

E

Eagle, J. M. & Hannah Loveless, 87, 91-4, 101, 103, 106, 142-4, 150, 183, 217, 218, 224, 225, 242, 243
Ealker, J. J., 172
Earl, Howard, 144
Earl, Oscar & Sarah, 143
Earl, Pearl, 137
Earlville, Alta., 167, 168, 170, 172
Earnest Christian, 50, 51, 61, 72, 74
East Mich. Conf., 167, 169, 186

East Ont. Conf., 5, 25, 44, 47, 48, 52, 75, 104, 107, 113, 128, 152, 174, 184, 186, 189, 190, 202-5, 212-5, 235, 239-51, 259, 260, 263
East Side, Alta., 172
Ebenezer, Ont., 44, 106, 150, 152, 194
Ebenezer, Sask., 157
Echo Lake, Ont., 120, 260
Eckardt, J., 222
Ecker, Levi, 139, 145, 151, 152
Eddy, Arlette, 71, 73
Eddy, Charles, 141
Eddy, Fred, 142
Edmonton, Alta., 5, 51, 167-72, 174, 186, 256
Edmonton Dist. (Western Canada Conf.), 170
Edmonton, Idylwylde, 256
Edmonton, Parkdale, 256
Egypt, 238, 239, 241, 260
Elder, William, 126
Elford, Glen, 128
Elfrida, Ont., 69
Elginburg, Ont., 92-4, 99, 105, 113, 135, 212, 235
Elkhorn, Alta., 173
Ellesmere, Ont. (see Armadale)
Elmbrook, Ont., 133
Elsom, Jennie Robsinson, 45, 51, 88, 97, 103, 129, 153, 154, 156, 165
Elsom, Robert, 153
Embury, Philip, 17, 80
Enderby, B. C., 237
Enterprise, Ont., 87, 120
Ergzinger, Irma, 260
Essex, Ont., 137, 140
Estevan, Sask., 27, 50, 57, 157, 159, 160, 163, 170, 187, 254
Evans, George, 141
Evans, James, 164
Evans, R. G., 140
Everhart, Mary J., 146
Eyebrow, Sask., 163, 165, 166, 254

F

Fader, C., 143, 150
Fairbairn, Bishop C. V. & Lena, 18, 27, 58, 112, 117-9, 121, 130, 135, 146, 183, 189, 210-16, 218, 224, 227, 231, 235, 243, 250, 256, 259
Farring, Robert, 133
Featherston, John Whitfield, 200
Fell, Wm., 67, 75,
Ferguson, W. D., 224
Fermoy, Ont., 39, 40, 56, 87, 105, 120, 121

Fernleigh, Ont., 130
Fifth Lake, Ont., 87, 120
Finch, Lela, 246
Findlay, Wm. & Louisa F., 129, 160, 161
Fisher, Charlie, 26, 80
Flake, Thomas, 98, 130, 166
Fleming, Donald, 267, 268
Fletcher, Daniel, 69, 76-9
Fletcher, James, 78
Fletcher, J. A., 27, 139, 145, 147, 148, 161-4
Fletcher, Layman, 110, 175, 246
Fletcher, L. C., 142
Fletcher, Mrs. John, 88
Fletcher, T. L., 110, 123, 127, 139-41, 161, 163, 165, 177
Flinton, Ont., 212
Florence, Ont., 21, 24, 73, 76, 78, 87, 140, 193
F.M.Y., 48, 53, 190, 235, 245, 257, 263
Fonthill, Ont., 84
Foreman, Ada, 146
Foreman, J. E., 100, 146
Foremost, Alta., 173
Forest, Ont., 100, 106
Forrest, A. C., 265
Forrester, D. S., 171, 172
Forrester, G. W., 171, 173
Forrest Road, B. C., 256
Fort Erie, Ont., 95, 106, 147
Fort William, Ont., 54, 128, 143, 144, 152, 237, 251, 253, 271
Fox, C. A., 113, 133
Foy, Elizabeth Allan, 35, 137, 139, 145, 147, 184
Frankford, Ont., 133-5, 204, 236, 248, 249
Franks, Wm., 198, 231
Free, Eliza, 125
Freeman, Adolphus, 29, 46, 68, 69, 72
Freeman, Andrew, 31, 68, 69, 72
Freeman, Barbara, 68
Freeman, Elmira Webb, 8, 128
Freeman, George W., 31, 72
Freeman, James, 72
Freeman, Leslie A., 5, 31, 72, 220, 229
Freeman, Stanley, 72, 146
Freemantle, Harry C., 143, 144, 148
Free Methodist, The, 6, 20, 42, 47, 49-51, 63, 66, 72, 74, 159, 174, 188, 190, 196, 222, 244, 249, 259, 260, 263, 273
Fuller, George, Jr., 59, 119, 200, 204, 219, 220, 259, 260
Fuller, George, Sr., 103, 200, 216
Fuller, N. J., 142

G

Gadsy, Alta., 171
Gaines, A. D., 84, 89, 97
Galt, Ont., 25, 32, 39, 56, 63, 65-8, 70, 74-84, 97, 101, 106, 145, 180, 192, 199, 242, 245, 253
Gananoque, Ont., 25, 39, 55, 59, 66-9, 74, 76, 81, 87, 115, 192, 204, 250
Gare, J. C., 139, 140
Garratt, C. B. & Mrs., 99, 159, 165, 177, 231
Gaudin, E. J., 178
Genesee Conf., 15, 37, 67, 79, 81
Gibbs, Hector, 20
Gillies, Ont., 142, 144
Gilmour Station, Ont., 94
Gilroy, Hiram, 54
Gleddie, Mae Luck, 34
Glen Major, Ont., 90
Glenshea, Ont., 84, 98
Glenvale, Ont., 212, 235
Glover, Thomas, 78
Goderich, Ont., 137
Godfrey, Ont., 119, 120, 135, 211, 212, 215
Goheen, Elmer & Grace, 124, 128, 248
Goheen, Wm., 236
Golden, B. C., 257
Goldlands, Ont., 127, 128, 248, 251
Goodberry, Lorenzo & Hester, 102, 198
Goodberry, Wilhemina, 212
Goodberry, Wm., 42, 87, 117, 119, 198
Goodrich, Charles & Mrs., 59, 129, 133
Goodrich, Roy, 110
Gospel Workers Church, 187, 241, 251, 257-9
Gould, Alton A., 203, 239, 260, 261
Graham, Charles, 94
Grandfield, Charles, 253
Grandfield, Laverna, 259
Grandview, Man., 153, 164, 165, 254
Grant, Mrs. Harvey, 126
Grant, P. K., 126
Gravenhurst, Ont., 124, 125, 248
Green, Annie L. (see A. L. G. Steer)
Green, Robert & Mrs., 153, 165
Green Prairie, Alta., 173
Greenville College, 189, 204, 205, 209, 215, 224, 232, 241, 255, 256
Greenville, Sask., 156, 157
Gregory, Carolyn Brisco, 33, 39, 40, 48, 56, 99, 117, 188
Gregory, James F. & Fredrea, 59, 75, 113, 117, 119, 127, 188, 190, 224, 227, 229, 234, 243, 259
Gregory, Sara, 5, 6, 27, 29, 44, 114, 117,

INDEX

119, 123, 127, 129, 132, 188, 245
Gregory, W. H., 27, 28, 33, 37, 39, 40, 48, 55-7, 59, 87, 98-101, 105-8, 112-5, 117-21, 123, 130, 132-4, 166, 188, 243, 245
Greitrix, Louis & Mrs., 248
Griffith, S. B. & Ethel, 118, 134, 135, 248
Grimsby, Ont., 74, 76, 77, 84
Grindrod, B. C., 178, 237, 257
Guelph, Ont., 145
Gunter, Abe, 93, 94, 103
Gunter, Albert & Alvina, 113, 127
Gunter, D. L., 120, 131
Gunter, Norah, 132
Gunter, Ont., 27, 87, 93-5, 98, 100, 105, 130, 183
Gunter, Sadie, 130
Gunter, Samuel T., 94, 119, 120

H

Hackett, Mr. & Mrs. J. W., 177
Hagle, Maggie Jerusha, 18, 21, 57, 66-8, 70, 73-8, 80, 165, 180, 191
Haight, Arthur L. & Ella, 168, 169, 174
Haight, Florence E., 172
Haight, Merrit S. & Belle, 168
Haight, R. R., 5, 169, 170, 171
Haight, Rickerson R., 167
Haight, Sidney, 168
Haight, Walter, 169
Haight, Wm. H., 169, 170, 171
Haley, Albert E. & Matilda Deyo, 53, 89, 136, 202
Haley, Alma, 254
Haley, Hiram, 70, 103
Haley, J. W. & Esther J. H., 52, 53, 88, 155, 156, 166, 201, 202, 207, 209
Halliday, Aden, 110
Hamilton, Ont., 31, 79, 81, 90, 92, 97, 106, 137, 146, 148, 199, 224, 242, 243, 253
Hamilton, Burton, 187, 220, 231
Hamilton Dist. (W. Ont. Conf.), 84, 89, 106, 144, 152
Hamilton, Eliza, 87
Hamilton, Hazel, 187
Hamilton, Jacob, 88, 152
Hamilton, Jennie Walls, 8, 160, 161, 166, 182, 187, 221
Hamilton, Parkdale, 146, 243, 253
Hamilton, R. H., 5, 50, 88, 92, 124, 137, 144, 158-62, 164-6, 176, 182-7, 194, 197, 211, 217, 220, 221, 244, 258-61, 268, 269
Hamilton, Robert & Mrs., 88, 95, 98, 101, 103, 106, 144, 157, 159, 166

Hamilton, West Ave., 145, 146, 183, 243, 253
Hamilton, Wm., 87
Hammer, H. A., 172
Hanley, Sask., 162
Hannah, Lila, 250
Hannon, Ont., 18, 23, 27-31, 37, 46, 68-70, 74-9, 83, 90, 92, 99, 106, 145, 146, 183, 192, 193, 245, 253
Harland, Alta., 169
Harmer, E. H., 175
Harnden, Alex. 132
Harnden, Angus, 39, 95, 98, 113
Harnden, Emma Snider, 57, 87, 95, 97, 100-6, 122, 125, 127
Harnden's Mills, Ont., 39, 95
Harnden, Wilmott, 104, 127
Harris, Josephus, 88
Harrison, M., 76
Harris, Robin, 40
Harrowsmith, Ont., 31, 59, 118, 119, 211, 212, 235, 249
Hart, Gen. Supt. E. P., 52, 79, 82, 92, 142
Hart, Norman & Mrs., 113
Harvey, George, 132
Harwood, Ont., 41, 81, 92, 95
Havelock, Ont., 92, 101, 129, 135
Hawley, Clarence, 122
Hawley, Earle & Doreen, 239, 260
Hay Bay, Ont., 17, 18, 22
Haywood, A. L., 174
Healey's Falls, Ont., 20, 128, 132
Heath, C. C., 172, 173, 176, 177
Heck, Paul & Barbara, 17
Henderson, Ada, 171, 175
Henderson, Lou & Mrs., 178
Henderson, W. J., 171, 172
Henwood, Albert, 98, 153, 164
Henwood, Margaret (see M. H. Collett)
Hespeler, Ont., 145
Hessler, C. J., 122
Hickling, Charles, 126
Hicks, Louise, 125
Hicks, Olive, 113
Hicks, Ruby, 137, 145, 147
Hicks, Sterling, 251, 254
Hilbourn, John, 66, 73
Hillsdale, Ont., 126, 127
Hoffman, Maggie, 78, 79, 192
Hogle, Almira, 95
Hogue, Bishop W. T., 15, 29, 37, 41, 44, 81, 97, 151, 159, 181
Holdsworth, Della, 232
Holiness Bible College, 234, 239, 255
Holiness Era, 222, 239

291

Holiness Movement Church, 203, 211, 215, 216, 223, 238-41, 249, 254, 257-61, 272
Holiness Movement Merger, 8, 115, 219, 219, 238-41
Holland Landing, Ont., 236
Holleford, Ont., 87, 118, 119, 249
Holmgren, P. B., 160
Holt, Ont., 36, 108, 188, 246
Holton, Reginald, 259
Hong Kong, 53, 203, 239, 260
Hoover, Grant, 126
Hoover, Harold, 248
Hoover, L. S., 127
Hoover, N. P., 122
Hoover, Wm., 126
Hope, B. C., 178
Horner, Ralph C., 92, 215, 238, 239, 241
Horton, Claude A., 253, 254, 259
Houghton, Ont., 58, 150, 151
Housey's Rapids, Ont., 91, 92, 95, 124, 184, 236
Howe, Joseph, 151
Howland, Carl, 53
Huckabee, B. W., 224
Hudmore, Sask., 159
Huff, George, 67
Huff, Peter, 30
Hughes, Amanda (see Amanda H. Norington)
Hughes, Ellis, 176
Hughes, Mabel, 212
Hume, Sask., 162, 165
Humphrey, Annie Knight, 140
Hunt, W E., 170
Huntsville, Ont., 20, 23, 39, 57, 78, 83, 90, 95, 98, 106, 123, 124, 166, 182, 194, 198, 248
Hurlburt, H. A. & Mrs., 156, 157
Hurry, Alta. (see Bruce)
Hutchinson, Bruce, 269
Hutchinson, Jemima, 73
Hutchinson, Mary, 73, 79, 83
Hymers, Ont., 54, 142-4, 152, 237, 253
Hyndman, Howard H., 140, 147-50
Hyndman, John, 149, 150

I

Incorporations, 186, 187, 216, 219, 220, 22-24, 236, 238, 269
India, 38, 53, 207, 259, 260
Ingersol, Ont., 151
Ingleview, Alta., 171, 173
Inkerman, Ont., 212
Iona, Ont. (see Middlemiss)

Ireland, Gertrude Pratt, 123, 131, 132, 135
Ireland, J., 19, 63
Ireland, Wm., 132, 135
Isles, L. H., 142
Ivy Lea, Ont., 66

J

Jamaica, 254, 260
James, Charles Wesley, 177
James, Grace, 178
James, Joseph, 178
James, Kenneth, 178
Japan, 53, 205, 259, 260
Jarnagan, T. P., 19, 65, 69, 74, 75
Jarvis, Charles, 162, 163
Jarvis, Jonah, 88
Jenner, Alta., 173
Jenner, G. S., 220, 255
Jericho, Ont. (see Thedford)
Johnson, Gordon, 251
John Wesley Seminary, 205, 219, 232, 234, 255, 256, 263
Jones, Bishop B. R., 20, 36, 58, 98, 101, 107, 113, 125, 144, 147, 158, 168, 171
Jones, F. J., 225
Jones, F. L., 110
JMS, 48, 53, 263

K

Kahshe Lake, 124
Kakabeka Falls, Ont., 237, 251
Kamloops, B. C., 173, 176, 257
Kay, C. W., 114, 115, 124, 127, 128, 130, 248, 250
Kearns, Aggie, 132
Keith, Ont. (see Charlemont)
Kelly, Mrs. John, 132
Kelowna, B. C., 173, 176-8, 237, 257
Kelt, J., 231
Kelvin, Ont., 27, 31, 46, 55, 58, 73, 75, 77-81, 84-5, 97, 106, 148, 152, 192-3, 236
Kemp, Gerald, 248
Kendall, Wm. C., 37
Kenlis, Sask., 154
Kenney, Roy & Mrs., 239
Kent, Dr. Lois, 53, 137, 207
Kent, H. G. & Mrs., 137, 139, 146, 207
Keswick, Ont., 76, 78
Kettle Point, Ont., 83
Killarney, Man., 241, 254
Killins, Fred, 143, 152
Kimbo, Ont., 106, 144, 145, 193
Kindersley, Sask., 163-6, 223, 254

INDEX

King, John T., 108, 243
King, Oscar L. & Lizzie J., 51, 52, 57, 167-171, 174, 186, 199
King, W. L. Mackenzie, 223
Kingsley, Charles W., 244
Kingston, Ont., 6, 17, 23, 27-31, 54, 59, 89, 90, 99, 100, 113, 114, 120, 133, 190, 204, 205, 210, 212, 235, 240, 249
Kingston Dist. (East Ont. Conf.), 92, 97, 105, 113, 115, 118, 121, 141, 212, 213, 235, 250
Kinney, Wilfred, 232
Kinnondale, Alta., 170, 171
Kinsella, Alta, 172
Kirk, Dalton, 225, 227
Kirk, David & Mrs. 47, 50, 71, 86, 94, 103, 104, 153-5, 158-62, 166
Kirk, John & Sarah, 142, 152
Kirk, Midford, 50, 161
Kirk, Mrs. Lawrence, 161
Kirkland Lake, Ont., 271
Knoll, John, 236, 251
Knox, Lloyd, 104, 259
Kresge, Bessie Reid, 44, 53, 114, 118, 204, 215, 259

L

Labrum, F. J., 121
Lacombe, Alta., 169, 171-4, 237
Lake Geneva, Alta., 171, 172
Lake Huron, 83, 137, 141
Lake, Isaac, 95, 98
Lake Ontario, 89, 91
Lake Simcoe, 78, 79, 91
Lake Superior, 141, 166
Lake Superior Dist. (West Ontario Conf.), 142, 144, 152, 237, 251
Lake Vernon, 124
Lambert, J. R., 151
Lamson, Byron S., 128, 135, 251, 271, 273
Langman, Daisy, 164
Lansdowne, Ont., 44, 55, 66, 90-2, 97, 105, 115, 193, 194, 212
Laurier, Sir Wilfred, 174
Leduc, Alta., 168
Lee, E. J., 119, 135, 212, 243
Lee, Octavius, 142, 152
Lees, Francis & Mrs., 75, 148
Lees, G. A., 5, 148, 217, 218, 224
Leffingwell, Clara, 202
Leise, Pearl, 175
Leonard, A. C., 76, 79
Lewis, F. B., 5, 167, 168, 170-2, 186, 199
Liberty, Sask., 255
Light & Life Hour, 257, 259-61, 274

Light & Life Men's Fellowship, 253, 257, 259, 263
Lincicome, F., 127
Linstead, Eldon, 110, 135, 259
Linstead, Herbert, 135, 227, 234, 259
Linstead, W. H., 109, 118, 135
Lishman, Ella, 144
Lloyd, Ross, 128, 164, 166, 237, 248, 251
Loft, Frank, 117, 127
Logan, J. T., 145
London, Ont., 32, 65-8, 70, 74, 76, 81-4, 137, 149, 196, 251
London Dist. (West Ont. Conf.), 76, 80, 81
Lone Rock, Man., 165
Long Point, Ont., 134
Long, Sarah, 89
Lorne Park College, 8, 35, 50, 79, 108, 113, 126, 137, 150, 164, 178, 183, 185-7, 193, 194, 205, 206, 216, 220, 224-31, 234, 235, 244, 256, 259, 260
Lorne Park College Personnel, 227-9
Losee, Wm., 17, 18, 32.
Loucks, Ira M., 119, 128
Loveless, Elijah E., 93, 103, 107, 136
Loveless, Hannah (see J. M. Eagle)
Loveless, Harold, 227
Loveless, Mary A. (see W. C. Walls)
Loveless, Robert & Jane Thomson, 51, 61-5, 68, 75, 80, 85, 93, 181-3, 222, 243
Loveless, Thomas, 93, 107, 224
Lowetown, Sask., 159
Loyalists, 16, 17
Luck, Clara, 94, 104
Luck, H. B., 36, 83, 108, 109, 134, 172-4, 176, 188, 217
Luck, Thomas, 83, 95, 126
Lynn, Norval, 148
Lyons, W. S., 246, 249

M

Maberly, Ont., 40, 120, 212, 213
MacDonald, John A., 16
MacDonald, Uriah, 28
Macklin, Alex. & Mrs., 71, 103
Macklin, James, 71
Macklin, Jemima, 105
Macklin, John, 71
Macklin, Wm., 71
Mackness, Elizabeth, 193
MacLeod, Alta., 173
Madsen, E. C., 172
Mainprize, Edith, 248, 249
Maitland, J. P., 152

Mallory, Wm. & Violet, 130
Manfred, Alta., 172
Manitoba, 18, 153-6, 160, 238
Manitoba Dist. (W. Ont. Conf.), 52, 165, 255
Manning, Ernest C., 267
Markell, F., 164
Markham, Ont., 18, 74, 76
Marks, G. D., 70
Marlatt, Harold & Martha, 137, 148, 150
Marmora, Ont., 129, 130, 248
Marsh, T. H., 175
Marston, Ont., 81, 192
Marston, Bishop L. R., 15, 66, 234, 243, 245
Marston, D. D., 39, 66-8, 74, 75, 79-81, 91, 243
Martin, John & Annis, 130
Matthewson, A. G., 95
Maxwell, L. E., 274
Mayo, George E., 142, 151
McAuley, Thomas, 71
McCallum, Amy Milton, 80
McCallum, D. H., 151, 157
McCallum, R. C. & Ora E., 113, 137, 183, 253, 259
McCaw, R., 250
McCready, Burton & Dorothy H., 53, 202, 207-9
McCready, W. R. & Harriet C., 38, 141, 144, 203, 207, 253, 260
McEwen, Abe, 212
McGeary, J. S., 83, 90
McGugan, D., 147
McGugan, Neil & Martha, 88, 89, 141, 161-3, 166
McKay, Elmer, 236
McKay, Wm., 68
McKearning, Wm., 68, 76
McKinley, C. S., 175
McLeod, H. A., 248
McNeil, Wm., 55
McNutt, Wm., 132
McQuiggin, Edna, 209
McQuiggin, W. E., 150
Meadow Brook, Alta., 172
Medicine Hat, Alta., 173
Medicine Valley, Alta., 170, 172
Melfort, Sask., 254
Mellor, Henry & Mrs., 55, 56, 82, 92, 94, 95, 97, 190
Mercer, Mrs. J., 178
Meredith, Eldon, 209
Merrill's Mills, Ont., 47, 72, 75, 148
Methodist Church, 18, 40, 61, 149, 151, 164, 210

Methodist Church of Can., 17, 18, 238, 261
Methodist Episcopal Church, 15, 23, 25, 28, 30, 81, 179
Methodist Episcopal Church in Can., 17, 18, 29, 68, 147
Methodist New Connexion, 17
Methodist, Primitive, 17, 18, 23, 29, 30, 45, 61, 67, 78, 92, 139, 181, 182, 191, 193
Methodist, Wesleyan, 17, 132, 163, 189, 210-2, 215, 258, 269, 270
Michigan, 49, 51, 56, 63, 66, 68, 81, 93, 142, 155, 165, 167, 170, 175, 179, 193
Michigan Centre, Alta., 168, 199
Middlemiss, Ont., 18, 44, 58, 68, 76, 80, 82-4, 88, 106, 137, 139, 186, 193, 196, 236
Midland, Ont., 127, 204
Miller, Jacob, 78
Miller, M. C., 5, 165, 224
Miller, P. O., 249
Miller, Wm. A., 106, 163
Millian, J. H., 137
Milliken, Mary (see M. M. Snyder)
Milne, Alice, 61
Milton, Joseph, 80
Miner, Frank, 132
Miner, H. L., 99, 100, 105, 124, 131
Mino, Lloyd & Frances James, 178, 253
Mino, Wm., 127
Missionary Tidings, 51, 184, 196, 204, 259, 263
Mississippi, Ont., 250
Mitchell, George, 224
Mizpah, Sask., 159, 160
Moffatt, A. B., 220, 250
Montague, Ont., 145
Montgomery, John, 94, 104, 111
Montgomery, L. M., 125
Montreal Conf. (Meth. Church), 92, 118, 238
Montreal, Que., 112, 271
Moore, Clarissa, 65
Moore, Doris & Eileen, 259
Moore, George, 142, 143
Moorhouse, Thomas, 74, 75, 80
Moose Jaw, Sask., 46, 52, 153-6, 158-60, 163-5, 168, 187, 223, 237, 254, 255
Moose Jaw Bible College Personnel, 232-33
Morton, M. D., 241
Mountain, Ont., 142
Mountain Grove, Ont., 120
Mount Albert, Ont., 89, 108
Mount Green, Sask., 159, 156

INDEX

Mount Pleasant, Ont., 111
Mudford, Edward, 236
Mullen, Martha, 146
Muskoka Dist., 20, 32, 38, 56, 69, 70, 76, 79, 81, 83, 87, 91, 93, 94, 105, 123, 128, 139, 153, 201, 236, 248, 250
Musselman's Lake, Ont., 68

N

Napanee, Ont., 59, 86, 120, 190, 198, 250
Natal, S. Africa, 202
Nelson, Lena, 173
Newburg, Ont., 117-20, 189, 211, 212
Newmarket, Ont., 108, 109, 188, 189, 224, 226
New Westminster, B.C., 175, 256, 259
New York State, 17, 63, 122, 175, 179, 238
Niagara Falls, Ont., 22, 79, 80, 84, 106, 147, 148, 194, 236, 254
Nixon, W., 162, 163
Nixon, Zella, 8, 166
Norbury, Sask., 164, 165
Norrington, A. H., 19, 20, 41, 58, 85-7, 90, 92, 95, 97, 100, 102, 104, 105, 115, 116, 123, 124, 131-3, 135, 146, 152, 183, 188
Norrington, Amanda Hughes, 123, 131, 132
Norrington, Mary Scott, 20, 85, 86, 97, 104, 194
North Bay, Ont., 236, 271
Northbrook, Ont., 130, 212
North Chili, N.Y., 49, 63, 95
North Dawn, Ont., 140, 141
Northern Dist. (Alta. Conf.), 172, 173
Northern Dist. (Sask. Conf.), 161, 162
Northern Ont. Home Missions Dist., 128, 248, 251, 271
Northfield, Ont., 58, 72, 73, 75, 84, 192, 197
North Marmora, Ont., 27, 129, 130
North Mich. Conf., 64-8, 70, 77, 142, 179, 180, 181, 186
Northwest Dist. (W. Ont. Conf.), 52
North West Territories, 18, 153, 167
Norwich, Ont., 47, 58, 72, 75, 84, 148, 236
Norwood, Ont., 51, 81

O

Oakdale, Ont., 140, 141
Oak Flats, Ont., 27, 54, 87, 92, 115, 117, 204
O'Connor, Ont., 142, 144

Odessa, Ont., 117-20, 198, 212, 235, 249
Okanagan Valley, B. C., 173, 176-8
Olive Branch Mission (Can.), 146, 199
Olmstead, W. B., 134, 139, 141, 144, 155
O'Regan, J., 125
Orillia, Ont., 90, 93, 95, 106, 125-7, 194, 248
Orland, Ont., 235, 236
Ormiston, Sask., 27, 153, 163
Ormston, Bishop M.D., 128, 251
Orser, E. R., 109, 117, 122, 165, 212
Oshawa, Ont., 8, 109, 110, 187, 224, 248, 258, 260
Oswegotchie, Ont., 25, 30
Otonabee River, 92
Ottawa, Ont., 212, 227, 238-41, 250
Ottawa Dist. (E. Ont. Conf.), 250
Otterville, Ont., 89, 90, 106, 150, 192
Oughton, D. D., 153, 168
Oursler, Fulton, 57, 272
Ousley, Ont., 24, 73, 78, 84, 140, 141
Ousley, Gideon, 80
Overpaugh, George W., 97, 98, 105, 113, 120, 134, 144

P

Page, Martha (see M. P. Wilson)
Palmer, Henry, 150
Parham, Ont., 119, 120
Paris, Ont., 63, 66
Pastorius, Dr. Melvin & Betty, 259
Pattison, W. R., 69, 75
Peach, J. W. & Mrs., 144, 207, 224
Peach, Marjorie (see M. P. Rice)
Peachland, Alta., 173, 177
Pearce, Bishop Wm., 34, 114, 134, 161, 171
Pearson, B. H., 48, 112, 114
Peck, Wm., 129
Pekin, N.Y., 15
Pelfrey, Glen & Dorothy, 254, 260
Pentecostal Assemblies of Can., 267, 272
Penticton, B.C., 176, 178, 237
Perkins, Frank, 126
Perry, A. H., 250
Perry, N. F., 108, 118, 128
Perth, Ont., 250
Perth Road, Ont., 100, 105, 121
Peterborough, Ont., 92, 134, 188, 204, 248
Peterborough Dist. (E. Ont. Conf.), 97, 105, 128, 130, 235, 248, 250
Peters, John & Mrs., 126
Petworth, Ont., 20, 27, 41, 57, 86, 87, 92, 95, 97, 100, 105, 118-20, 135, 183, 194, 198

295

Philippines, 259, 260
Philips, Alta., 171, 172, 199
Phoenix, Silas, 71, 75, 192
Phoenix, Wm. John, 75
Pickert, Florence, 231, 232
Picton, Ont., 132, 133, 236, 248
Pilger, Henry, 126
Pilgrim Holiness Church, 258, 259
Pine Lake, Ont., 124, 125, 190
Pine Orchard, Ont., 236, 245
Pink, James & Emma, 65
Pinkham, Sask., 163
Plevna, Ont., 130
Point Edward, Ont. (see Sarnia)
Pointen, W. H., 241
Ponoka, Alta., 172, 237
Port Arthur, Ont., 144, 271
Port Burwell, Ont., 150, 151, 166
Port Credit, Ont., 18, 44, 50, 66, 79, 81, 91-4, 97, 105, 111, 199, 200, 224
Port Rowan, Ont., 151
Port Royal, Ont., 81, 151, 192
Portuguese E. Africa, 53, 201, 202, 204-6, 209
Potter, John W., 93, 94, 134
Pounder, George, 128
Power, Mrs. W. J., 152
Power, W. J., 259
Pratt, Gertrude (see G. P. Ireland)
Presbyterian Church, 23, 30, 61, 119, 120, 129, 137
Prescott, Ont., 17, 241
Prince Albert, Sask., 164, 165
Prior, Charles A., 111, 224
Prior, Fred F. & Mrs., 161, 165, 166, 213
Prior, G. A., 83
Prosser, J. A., 20
Puget Sound Dist. (Wash. Conf.), 176

Q

Qu'Appelle Valley, 154
Quebec, 16, 17, 122, 238, 240, 250, 257, 267, 271

R

Randall, Herbert, 239
Ranfurley, Alta., 168
Rapid City, Man., 165
Ravenshoe, Ont., 101, 108, 236
Reed, C. H., 97, 100, 106
Regina, Sask., 162, 165, 166, 186
Reid, Bessie (see B. R. Kresge)
Reid, Bruce, 114, 220
Reid, Pearl, 53, 114, 205, 259
Renfrew, Ont., 241, 250
Rennie, Wm. & Mrs., 175

Requa, W. F. & Mrs., 67, 78
Reynolds, C. W., 119, 134, 135, 220, 237, 246, 250
Reynolds, W. H., 87, 113, 124, 125
Rhodes, Edward & Mary Ann, 65, 66
Rice, Marjorie Peach, 53, 207
Rice Lake, 41, 92, 98, 130
Richard's Landing, Ont., 142
Richardson, Emma, 29, 65, 132
Richmond Hill, Ont., 246, 250
Ridgeway, Ont., 29, 54, 81, 84, 86, 106, 147, 193, 196, 245, 254
Riverview, Man., 164, 165
Riverview, Sask., 28, 162, 165
Robb, J. A., 54, 136, 137, 144, 151, 220, 254
Roberts, B. H., 144
Roberts, Gen. Supt. B. T., 15, 21, 25, 26, 42, 44, 49, 50, 52, 59, 61, 64, 76, 77, 81-3, 89, 90
Roberts, J. H. & Mary D., 103, 136, 140, 141, 144
Roberts Wesleyan College, 49, 203
Robertson, Annie (see A. R. W. Campbell)
Robertson, Lloyd & Bessie, 254
Robinson, Annie, 88
Robinson, Beatrice, 136
Robinson, B. H., 163
Robinson, Henry & Beulah, 89
Robinson, James, 89, 259
Robinson, Jennie (see J. R. Elsom)
Robinson, Mabel, 124
Robinson, Mrs. M. E., 223
Robinson, Philip & Hannah, 89
Roblin, Man., 163, 165
Robson, Wm., 155
Rochester, N.Y., 49, 63
Rockwood, Ont., 192
Rockyford, Alta., 168
Rogers, Samuel, 81, 105, 113, 123, 125, 130, 133, 144
Roman Catholic Church, 17, 39, 164, 223, 267
Rose, Jim, 97
Roseview, Sask., 157, 158, 187
Round Hill, Alta., 168
Ruanda-Urundi, 199, 201, 202, 206, 260
Rupert, Jane, 129
Rush, Adeline, 34, 83
Rusk, James, 91, 123, 166
Rusk, Josie (see J. R. Wees)
Russell, D. H., 48, 256, 257
Ruttan, J., 81
Ryde, Ont., 83, 124
Ryding, I. S. W., 53, 203, 239

INDEX

Ryerson, Egerton, 17, 25, 40, 50
Ryff, Ethel Davey, 53, 87, 114, 116, 127, 132, 204

S

Sagar, L. A., 89-92, 94, 97, 100, 105
Sage, C. H., 19, 21-26, 32, 33, 37-9, 44, 52, 55-8, 64-70, 72-80, 83, 94, 102, 137-9, 179, 180, 182, 191-3, 265
Sage Publishers, 190, 220
Salvation Army, 15, 258, 274
Sammons, Peter, 144, 148
Sarnia, Ont., 75, 88, 95, 97, 106, 139, 194
Sarnia All-Can. Conv., 5, 182-8, 198, 200, 212, 216-21, 224
Sarnia Dist. (W. Ont. Conf.), 31, 106, 136, 152, 251
Sask. Conf., 5-8, 50, 51, 153-66, 171, 175, 182, 187, 206, 218, 232, 237, 244, 245, 254, 255
Sask. Dist. (W. Can. Conf.), 168
Sask. Dist. (W. Ont. Conf.), 158
Sask. Tidings, 51, 187
Saskatoon, Sask., 162, 163, 166
Sault Ste. Marie, Ont., 141, 152, 192, 196, 236
Sault Ste. Marie Dist. (W. Ont. Conf.), 141, 251
Saunders, George, 128
Saunders, J. E., 141
Scarborough, Ont., 18, 58, 61, 78, 79, 181, 182, 246
Schantz, Christopher, 106
Schantz, Nancy, 20, 67, 73, 77, 80, 92, 97, 105, 115, 145, 193, 194
Schnell, George, 177
Schnell, H. J., 256
Seattle Pacific College, 173, 194, 202, 205, 231, 255
Seattle, Wash., 174, 243
Secret Societies, 15, 59
Sedore, Gerald, 120, 248
Sedore, Roy, 108, 125, 126, 129, 134
Sellers, Lamorah, 173
Sellew, Bishop W. A., 31, 63, 90, 95, 97, 109, 144, 147, 161, 172, 196, 212
Seventh Day Adventists, 65, 224
Severn Bridge, Ont., 20, 32, 44, 78, 79, 91-2, 95, 106, 125, 126, 192, 236
Sexsmith, Jonathan, 100, 106, 121, 123
Sharon, Ont., 139
Sharp, Peter, 79, 146, 199
Shaunavon, Man., 165
Shaver, C. S., 79, 173
Shaver, Eliza, 65

Shaver, T. A., 18, 102
Shawville, Que., 238, 240, 241, 250
Shay, G. F., 221
Shea, Adam J., 163, 210, 211
Shea, George Beverly, 163, 210, 211
Sheffield, Ont., 38, 39, 65, 68, 69, 80, 106
Sheldon, Dr. Harriet, 146, 152
Shelhamer, E. E., 27, 119, 178
Shetland, Ont., 24, 73, 87, 89, 100, 106, 185
Shier, J. D. & Mrs., 98, 104, 123, 154, 194, 244, 274
Shorter, George, 34, 66-8
Shoup, R. H., 5, 169-72, 174
Showers, Albert, 65
Showers, Gilbert, 21, 63, 66, 68
Sifton, Sir Clifford, 174
Sigsworth, Charles & Dexter, 119
Simcoe, Ont., 151, 254
Simcoe, Governor, 17
Simpson, Alice, 176
Sims, Albert & Elizabeth H., 5, 23-7, 41, 47-58, 70-83, 88-105, 111, 115, 120-33, 181-3, 190, 192, 197, 216-24, 274
Sims, Alberta, 127
Sinclair, Sask., 163
Sincock, Maude, 178
Sincock, Rose, 178
Sintaluta, Sask., 153-5, 157
Sipprell, Matilda (see M. S. Taylor)
Skelding, Walker, 127
Slack, Annie (see A. F. Ball)
Slack, R. J., 246, 250
Slate River, Ont., 144, 237
Slingerland, Edward, 93, 98, 106
Slingerland, Leonard, 108, 109, 114, 124, 127, 129, 147
Slingerland, R. E., 110, 198, 237
Smart, Julia, 135
Smith, Aaron, 139
Smith, A. E., 77, 110, 145
Smith, Alma, 58, 150
Smith, Ben, 162, 176
Smith, C. M., 70, 75-7, 80, 81, 145, 150
Smith, D. Eugene, 118, 120, 198, 217, 218
Smith, Dorothy, 248
Smith, Fred, 126, 135
Smith, G. W., & Mrs., 168, 174
Smith, Harry, 127, 168
Smith, John, 173, 176, 177
Smith, L. A., 232, 235
Smith, Mrs. Ashur, 142
Smith, Mrs. Ellen C. (George), 56, 65, 67, 74

297

Smith, Nathaniel, 235
Smith, Oswald J., 271, 274
Smith, P. K. & Mrs., 140, 141, 184, 200, 242, 245
Smith, W. A. & Evangeline, 260
Smith, W. L., 75, 110, 257
Smiths Falls, Ont., 241
Snider, Emma (see E. S. Harnden)
Snider, K. Lavern & Lois, 104, 113, 227, 259, 260
Snider, Lyford, 98, 100, 104
Snowdry, Robert, 157
Snyder, Almiron & Mrs., 87, 159
Snyder, Emerson, 25, 39, 87, 94, 95, 105, 112, 114, 115, 124, 128, 130, 183, 184, 216
Snyder, Mary Milliken, 57, 95, 183, 184, 194
Snyder, Sperry, 87, 109, 111, 114, 118, 129
Sombra, Ont., 24, 39, 78
South Africa, 53, 201, 202, 204, 207, 235, 259
Southern Dist. (W. Can. Conf.), 170
Southern Dist. (Sask. Conf.), 161, 164
Southern Dist. (Alta. Conf.), 173
Southern Rhodesia, 53, 260
Southwold, Ont., 58, 68, 83, 137
Spencer, H., 161
Spinks, Merton, 132
Spiritwood, Sask., 164, 165
Sprattsville, Sask., 163
Spring Arbor Seminary, 49, 112, 160, 181, 184-6, 207
Spring Brook, Ont., 129, 212
St. Armand Centre, Que., 122
St. Catharines, Ont., 80, 84, 147, 254
St. Elmo, Sask., 163
St. Joseph Island, Ont., 33, 54, 141, 142, 236, 251
St. Lawrence River, 39, 66, 270
St. Thomas, Ont., 84, 139
Stambaugh, A. S., 172
Stamp, C. W., 151, 159, 170
Standard Church, 239, 258
Steenburg, George, 135
Steenburg, Grace, 128
Steer, Annie Green, 88, 90, 92, 106, 136, 159, 192, 193
Steer, Edward, 50, 159, 193
Stephenson, Robert, 50
Stevens, G. W., 137, 139, 140, 200, 220, 242, 243, 246, 259, 272
Stevens, Henry, 74
Stevenson, B. E. & Margaret Allan, 35, 108, 112, 115, 120, 136, 148-50, 184

Stewart, Charles, P., 171, 173, 175-7, 233, 256
Stewart, James R., 171, 173
Stewart, John, 171
Stewart, Marion, 71
Stewart, Peter & Mrs., 171
Stewart, Rufus, 197, 198
Stewart, J. Wesley, 233
Stittsville, Ont., 241
Stonehouse, Martha, 71, 81, 86, 192, 193, 224
Stonehouse, Wm., 71, 222
Stonehouse, W. J., 239, 241, 250, 260
Stoness, Neil, 109, 121, 212
Stoney Creek, Ont., 83, 84
Stoney Plain, Alta., 167
Stouffville, Ont., 20, 63, 65-7, 74, 76, 193, 197
Stoughton, Sask., 159
Stuart, J. W., 72, 197
Sudbury, Ont., 267, 271
Sullivan Lake, Alta., 171
Sully, Sidney, 212
Sunday School, 47, 48, 107, 108, 112, 146, 246-57
Sunderland, Ont., 80
Sunny Plains, Alta. (see Armada)
Susquehanna Conf., 66, 78, 97, 175
Sutch, Mrs. Fred, 82
Sutton, Ont., 79
Sutton, B. A., 127
Sutton, Harold, 263
Swart, J. C., 112
Sweigard, Wm. E. & Mrs., 255
Swift Current, Sask., 165
Swindon, Ont., 124
Syndenham, Ont., 92, 181, 211

T

Taite, Joe, 109
Tanner, J. A., 166, 251
Taylor, A. L., 173
Taylor, Bishop J. Paul, 244
Taylor, George & Mary, 82, 144, 192
Taylor, H. B., 175
Taylor, Keith & Jane, 255
Taylor, Matilda Sipprell, 20, 23, 58, 71, 72, 75, 79, 83, 97, 106, 141, 146, 150, 192, 199
Teal, Flossie, 192
Teal, George & Annie, 29, 54, 81, 84, 147, 254
Teal, Robert, 81
Teal, Wilbur N. & Sylvia B., 147, 151, 249, 253

Teeterville, Ont., 31
Terminus, Ont., 139
Thamesford, Ont., 236, 254
Thaxter, Austin J., 110, 246, 248
Thedford, Ont., 19, 27, 34, 65-8, 70, 73-9, 82-4, 97, 106, 139, 153, 191, 193, 199, 245, 251
Thomas, Martha, 18, 21, 46, 73, 76, 78, 80, 191
Thornbury, Ont., 251
Thorncliffe, Ont., 34, 44, 58, 58, 89, 92, 140, 201
Thornyhurst, Ont., 139, 140
Thousand Islands, 39, 78, 91
Tichborne, Ont., 119
Tidball, John, 108
Tillsonburg, Ont., 34, 78, 81, 83, 84, 151, 152, 254
Tillsonburg Dist. (W. Ont. Conf.), 143, 148, 254
Timbers, John, 103, 136, 139
Timmins, Ont., 127, 128, 248, 251
Tisdale, Sask., 200
Tittemore, Lucy, 53, 203
Tofield, Alta., 170
Tonawanda, N.Y., 23, 63, 65, 70, 181
Toole, Daniel & Hattie, 147
Toole, John, 66, 67
Toronto, Ont., 15-8, 34, 38, 51, 55, 58-61, 78, 83, 85, 86, 91-4, 97, 100, 103, 105, 111, 134, 153, 154, 181, 212, 224, 248, 258, 266
Toronto All-Can. Conv., 219
Toronto, Broadview, 111, 112, 200, 204, 205, 212
Toronto Dist. (E. Ont. Conf.), 20, 23, 81, 87, 95, 97, 107, 135, 236, 246, 250
Toronto, Eglington, 112, 185, 212, 246
Toronto, Wesley Chapel, 248
Toronto, West, 112, 113, 246
Toth, Kelly, 260
Transvaal, 53, 201, 204, 206, 260
Travers, Alta., 173
Trent Bridge, Ont., 51, 81, 92, 97, 105, 113, 128, 129, 132, 135
Trenton, Ont., 134, 135
Tristram, Alta., 172
Trumble, Dexter, 94
Tupperville, Ont., 89, 99
Turner, George A., 45
Twiddy, Walter, 250

U

Underwood, Francis, 71
Unionville, Ont., 141
United Brethren Church, 68, 75

United Church of Can., 18, 164, 198, 222, 259, 265, 267, 268
United Missionary Church, 258
Upper Canada, 9, 16, 17, 30
Urundi, Africa (see Ruanda-Urundi)
Uxbridge, Ont., 20, 28, 35, 59, 71, 72, 77, 79, 81, 84, 85, 87, 89-92, 95, 103, 105, 110, 111, 135, 183, 186, 192, 197, 236, 246, 250

V

Vail, Olive, 137, 144
Vallier, Alec & Lurena, 141
Vancouver, B.C., 175, 176, 178, 257
Vancouver Island, 175, 257
Vancouver, Rupert Chapel, 175, 257
Vanguard, Sask., 161, 165
VanLuven, Myles & Mrs., 127
Vennacher, Ont., 27, 59, 98, 100, 101, 104, 105, 129, 130, 188
Vermilion Valley, Alta., 167, 170
Vernon, B.C., 237
Verona, Ont., 20, 23, 27, 35, 38, 42, 57, 86-9, 91-7, 100, 101, 105, 115-20, 133, 135, 183, 184, 188, 194, 198, 204, 210, 211, 235, 238, 249
Victoria, B.C., 176, 257
Victoria, Ont., 97, 128, 129
Victoria Corners, Ont., 79
Vines, J. M., 176
Violet, Ont., 97, 105, 117, 118
Voteary, Arthur, 239, 253, 272

W

Wabash, Ont., 140
Wagerville, Ont., 87, 117, 119, 120, 135, 212
Wainfleet, Ont., 148
Waldie, Thomas & Lucy, 168
Walker, Robt., 18, 29, 45
Walker, Stewart, 87, 92, 106, 108
Walker, W. S., 172
Wallaceburg, Ont., 87, 136
Walls, Alice E., 5-8, 44, 137, 139, 182, 192-6, 224, 227, 242, 259
Walls, Annie Robertson (see A. R. W. Campbell)
Walls, C.E.L., 147, 182
Walls, Wesley C. & Mary Loveless, 20, 23, 78-85, 91, 92, 103-6, 148, 152, 182, 194
Walrath, J. L., 255
Walrath, Marion, 231

Walsh, H. H., 17, 30, 263, 268, 273, 274
Walsingham (Centre), Ont., 32, 44, 81-4, 89, 90, 95, 98, 106, 142, 151, 185, 194, 236
Ward, S. E., 130
Waring, Bessie Grass, 151
Warkworth, Ont., 29, 81, 118, 123, 130-2, 212, 236, 248
Warner, Bishop D. S., 135
Warren, A. T., 239
Warren, Laura J. (see Coleman)
Warren, L. F., 220
Warren, R. B., 6, 126, 127, 222, 227, 235, 241, 246, 249, 258
Wartman, D. S. & Margaret, 118, 119, 164, 165, 215, 231, 232, 237, 244, 250, 253
Wartman, Mrs. George, 118
Warwick, Ont. (see Thedford)
Washington Conf., 173-6, 186, 256, 257
Waterloo, Ont., 80, 192, 193
Watson, C. A., 137, 219, 221, 240, 249, 250
Wattam, Alfred, 86, 91-4, 97, 103, 183
Wattam, Henry & Maggie, 57, 100, 119
Wayne, Alta., 173
Webb, Elmira (see Freeman)
Wedge, Andrew & Mrs., 69
Wees, F. M., 50, 52, 97, 156-9, 162, 165, 166, 175, 185, 186, 194, 199, 217, 244
Wees, Josie Rusk, 52, 57, 95, 104, 106, 147, 156, 159, 160, 186, 194, 200, 244
Wees, Eliza, 95
Wees, Wm., 97
Welland, Ont., 145-8, 187, 202, 207, 254
Wells, Fred, 129
Wells Island, 39, 78
Wells, Charles & Mrs., 129
Wesley, Charles, 13, 22, 23, 42
Wesley, John, 13, 19, 22-6, 29, 35, 36, 40, 42, 45, 46, 49, 50, 188, 270
Wesley, Susanna, 42
Wesleyan University, 25
Western Can. Conf., 153, 158, 159, 168, 170, 171, 185, 193
Western Dist. (Sask. Conf.), 161
Western Tidings, 51, 170, 171, 174, 186, 199
West Ont. Conf., 5, 8, 19, 44, 47, 48, 52, 87, 93, 106, 139, 141-4, 154, 164, 167, 172, 182-6, 192, 196, 202, 203, 206, 236, 243, 245, 248, 249, 251-4, 259, 260
Westport, Ont., 39, 40, 56, 58, 105, 120, 121, 212
West Summerland, B.C., 177, 237, 257

Westview, Sask., 27, 52, 155-60, 165, 166, 170, 176, 187, 194, 198
Wetaskiwin, Alta., 167
Weyburn, Sask., 27, 50, 160-3, 165, 170, 171, 187, 254
Weyburn Dist. (Sask. Conf.), 161
Widder Station, Ont. (see Thedford)
Wildmere, Alta., 172
Wilkins, Harry, 35, 117
Wilkins, Georgia, 35
Williamsford, Ont., 251
Willoughby, Senator W. B., 223
Wilmur, Ont., 93, 211
Wilson, F. C., 217
Wilson, George, 119
Wilson, Henry & Eliza, 89
Wilson, Miranda Coatsworth, 140
Wilson, Mrs. James, 97
Wilson, T. M., 220
Wilson, W. H. & Martha P., 20, 52, 88, 89, 92, 93, 103-7, 111, 154-7, 159, 166, 185, 243, 244
Wilton, Ont., 97, 98, 105, 117, 118, 211, 235
Winans, J. W., 53, 203
Windsor, Ont., 137, 140, 251
Winfield, B.C., 178, 257
Winget, B., 20, 90, 123
Winnifred, Alta., 170, 171
Winnipeg, Man., 165, 166, 169, 234, 238-40
Winnipeg, Wesley Chapel, 254
Winona Lake, Ind., 196, 240, 244, 245, 259, 263
Winslow, J. Leon, 227
Winslow, Norman, 144
Winter, James H., 68, 73, 76, 105
Wiseman, Peter, 211
Withenshaw, Byron, 227, 253
Withenshaw, J., 137
Wittenberg, Alta., 170
Whaley, R. J., 121, 212
Wheat Centre, Alta., 171
Wheelock, Paul, 119
Whiffen, Thos., 66, 74, 101
White, Donald, 250
Whiting, H., 231
Whitney, Lily, 135
Whittaker, Nellie, 174, 217
Whittaker, Wm., 153
W.M.S., 52, 53, 95, 106, 128, 129, 148, 159, 181, 184, 193, 196, 204, 235, 250, 254, 263
Woodstock, Ont., 27, 34, 66, 67, 70-2, 76, 77, 181, 193
Wright, Clarence, 95

INDEX

Wright, Edna, 120
Wright, J., 76
Wyevale, Ont., 126, 127

Y
Yarker, Ont., 120, 183
Yorkton Dist. (Sask. Conf.), 164
Youmans, David, 142
Y.P.M.S. (see F.M.Y.)

Z
Zahniser, Bishop A. D., 15, 117, 134
Zahniser, C. H., 227, 234
Zahniser, R. A., 114
Zion, Ont. (Sarnia Dist.), 140, 141, 236
Zion, Ont. (Peterboro Dist.), (see Burnley)
Zion, Ont. Kingston Dist.), 120
Zurbrigg, Daniel, 113
Zurbrigg, Wm. & Minnie Rusk, 110, 115, 124, 127, 186, 220, 224, 225

www.ingramcontent.com/pod-product-compliance
Lightning Source LLC
Chambersburg PA
CBHW051748040426
42446CB00007B/273